WITHDRAWN

Family Psychology

Family Psychology

SCIENCE-BASED INTERVENTIONS

EDITED BY

Howard A. Liddle
Daniel A. Santisteban
Ronald F. Levant
James H. Bray

AMERICAN PSYCHOLOGICAL ASSOCIATION

WASHINGTON, DC

Published by
American Psychological Association
750 First Street, NE
Washington, DC 20002
www.apa.org

To order
APA Order Department
P.O. Box 92984
Washington, DC 20090-2984

Tel: (800) 374-2721, Direct: (202) 336-5510
Fax: (202) 336-5502, TDD/TTY: (202) 336-6123
Online: www.apa.org/books/
Email: order@apa.org

In the U.K., Europe, Africa, and the Middle East, copies may be ordered from
American Psychological Association
3 Henrietta Street
Covent Garden, London
WC2E 8LU England

Typeset in Berkeley Book by EPS Group Inc., Easton, MD

Printer: Edwards Brothers, Inc., Ann Arbor, MI
Cover designer: Ed Atkeson, Berg Design, Albany, NY
Production Editor: Catherine Hudson
Project Manager: Debbie K. Hardin, Charlottesville, VA

The opinions and statements published are the responsibility of the authors, and such opinions and statements do not necessarily represent the policies of the American Psychological Association.

Library of Congress Cataloging-in-Publication Data
Family psychology : science-based interventions / edited by Howard A. Liddle . . . [et al.].
    p. cm.
    Includes bibliographical references and index.
    ISBN 1-55798-786-6
      1. Family psychotherapy.   2. Marital psychotherapy.
    3. Family—Psychological aspects.   4. Operant behavior.   I. Liddle, Howard A.

    RC488.5 .F3325 2001
    616.89'156—dc21

                                                              2001022300

British Library Cataloguing-in-Publication Data
A CIP record is available from the British Library.

Printed in the United States of America
First Edition

APA Science Volumes

Attribution and Social Interaction: The Legacy of Edward E. Jones

Best Methods for the Analysis of Change: Recent Advances, Unanswered Questions, Future Directions

Cardiovascular Reactivity to Psychological Stress and Disease

The Challenge in Mathematics and Science Education: Psychology's Response

Changing Employment Relations: Behavioral and Social Perspectives

Children Exposed to Marital Violence: Theory, Research, and Applied Issues

Cognition: Conceptual and Methodological Issues

Cognitive Bases of Musical Communication

Cognitive Dissonance: Progress on a Pivotal Theory in Social Psychology

Conceptualization and Measurement of Organism–Environment Interaction

Converging Operations in the Study of Visual Selective Attention

Creative Thought: An Investigation of Conceptual Structures and Processes

Developmental Psychoacoustics

Diversity in Work Teams: Research Paradigms for a Changing Workplace

Emotion and Culture: Empirical Studies of Mutual Influence

Emotion, Disclosure, and Health

Evolving Explanations of Development: Ecological Approaches to Organism–Environment Systems

Examining Lives in Context: Perspectives on the Ecology of Human Development

Global Prospects for Education: Development, Culture, and Schooling

Hostility, Coping, and Health

Measuring Patient Changes in Mood, Anxiety, and Personality Disorders: Toward a Core Battery

Occasion Setting: Associative Learning and Cognition in Animals

Organ Donation and Transplantation: Psychological and Behavioral Factors

Origins and Development of Schizophrenia: Advances in Experimental Psychopathology

The Perception of Structure

Perspectives on Socially Shared Cognition

Psychological Testing of Hispanics

Psychology of Women's Health: Progress and Challenges in Research and Application

Researching Community Psychology: Issues of Theory and Methods

The Rising Curve: Long-Term Gains in IQ and Related Measures

Sexism and Stereotypes in Modern Society: The Gender Science of Janet Taylor Spence

Sleep and Cognition

Sleep Onset: Normal and Abnormal Processes

Stereotype Accuracy: Toward Appreciating Group Differences

Stereotyped Movements: Brain and Behavior Relationships

Studying Lives Through Time: Personality and Development

The Suggestibility of Children's Recollections: Implications for Eyewitness Testimony

Taste, Experience, and Feeding: Development and Learning

Temperament: Individual Differences at the Interface of Biology and Behavior

Through the Looking Glass: Issues of Psychological Well-Being in Captive Nonhuman Primates

Uniting Psychology and Biology: Integrative Perspectives on Human Development

Viewing Psychology as a Whole: The Integrative Science of William N. Dember

APA Decade of Behavior Volumes

Computational Modeling of Behavior in Organizations: The Third Scientific Discipline

The Nature of Remembering: Essays in Honor of Robert G. Crowder

New Methods for the Analysis of Change

Personality Psychology in the Workplace

Psychosocial Interventions for Cancer

Unraveling the Complexities of Social Life: A Festschrift in Honor of Robert B. Zajonc

Memory Consolidation: Essays in Honor of James L. McGaugh

Animal Research and Human Health: Advancing Human Welfare Through Behavioral Science

Family Psychology: Science-Based Interventions

Contents

Contributors   xiii

Foreword   xv

Acknowledgments   xvii

Introduction   xix

PART 1: SCIENCE OF FAMILY PSYCHOLOGY: OVERVIEW OF THE FIELD   1

CHAPTER 1   Family Psychology Intervention Science: An Emerging Area   3
             of Science and Practice
             Howard A. Liddle, James H. Bray, Ronald F. Levant, and
             Daniel A. Santisteban

CHAPTER 2   The Developmental Status of Family Therapy in Family   17
             Psychology Intervention Science
             James F. Alexander, Thomas L. Sexton, and
             Michael S. Robbins

CHAPTER 3   Studying a Matrix of Change Mechanisms: An Agenda for   41
             Family-Based Process Research
             Guy S. Diamond and Gary M. Diamond

PART 2: ADVANCES IN ASSESSMENT AND METHODS   67

CHAPTER 4   Conceptual Issues in Assessing Couples and Families   69
             Douglas K. Snyder, Jebber J. Cozzi, and Laurel F. Mangrum

CHAPTER 5   Methodological Issues and Innovations in Family   89
             Psychology Intervention Research
             James H. Bray

PART 3: ADVANCES IN MARITAL INTERVENTION RESEARCH   103

CHAPTER 6   Developments in Couple Therapy Research   105
             Jackie K. Gollan and Neil S. Jacobson

CHAPTER 7   Preventive Interventions for Couples   123
             Benjamin Silliman, Scott M. Stanley, William Coffin,
                 Howard J. Markman, and Pamela L. Jordan

CHAPTER 8   Toward a Scientifically Based Marital Therapy   147
             John M. Gottman, Kimberly D. Ryan, Sybil Carrère, and
                 Annette M. Erley

PART 4: ADVANCES IN FAMILY INTERVENTION RESEARCH   175

CHAPTER 9   Toward Prevention and Clinical Relevance: A Preventive   177
                 Intervention Model for Family Therapy Research
                 and Practice
             William M. Pinsof and Alexandra B. Hambright

CHAPTER 10   Family-Focused Prevention Research: "Tough but Tender"   197
             Patrick H. Tolan

CHAPTER 11   Toward Family-Level Attribute x Treatment Interaction   215
                 Research
             Michael J. Rohrbaugh, Varda Shoham, and
                 Melissa W. Racioppo

CHAPTER 12   Linking Basic and Applied Research in a Prevention   239
                 Science Process
             Marion S. Forgatch and Nancy M. Knutson

CHAPTER 13   Mental Health Services Research and Family-Based   259
                 Treatment: Bridging the Gap
             Sonja K. Schoenwald and Scott W. Henggeler

CHAPTER 14   Challenges in a 30-Year Program of Research: Conduct   283
                 Disorders and Attention Deficit Hyperactivity Disorder,
                 the Marital Discord and Depression Link, and
                 Partner Abuse
             K. Daniel O'Leary

PART 5: CONTEXTUAL CONSIDERATIONS IN FAMILY INTERVENTION RESEARCH

PART 5: CONTEXTUAL CONSIDERATIONS IN FAMILY
INTERVENTION RESEARCH   299

CHAPTER 15   Conceptualizing Gender in Marital and Family Therapy   301
              Research: The Gender Role Strain Paradigm
              Ronald F. Levant and Carol L. Philpot

CHAPTER 16   Integrating the Study of Ethnic Culture and Family   331
              Psychology Intervention Science
              Daniel A. Santisteban, Joan A. Muir-Malcolm,
              Victoria B. Mitrani, and José Szapocznik

Author Index   353

Subject Index   369

About the Editors   383

Contributors

James F. Alexander, University of Utah, Salt Lake City

James H. Bray, Baylor College Medical School, Houston, TX

Sybil Carrère, University of Washington, Seattle

William Coffin, Silver Springs, MD

Jebber J. Cozzi, Texas A&M University, College Station

Gary M. Diamond, Ben-Gurion University of the Negev, Beer-Sheva, Israel

Guy S. Diamond, Children's Hospital of Philadelphia, University of Pennsylvania

Annette M. Erley, University of Washington, Seattle

Marion S. Forgatch, Oregon Social Learning Center, Eugene

Jackie K. Gollan, Massachusetts General Hospital and Harvard Medical School, Boston, MA

John M. Gottman, University of Washington, Seattle

Alexandra B. Hambright, University of Illinois at Chicago

Scott W. Henggeler, Family Services Research Center, Medical University of South Carolina, Charleston

Neil S. Jacobson, deceased

Pamela L. Jordan, University of Wyoming, Laramie

Nancy M. Knutson, Oregon Social Learning Center, Eugene

Ronald F. Levant, Center for Psychological Studies, NOVA Southeastern University, Fort Lauderdale, FL

Howard A. Liddle, Center for Treatment Research on Adolescent Drug Abuse, University of Miami School of Medicine

Laurel F. Mangrum, Texas A&M University, College Station

Howard J. Markman, University of Denver

Victoria B. Mitrani, Center for Family Studies, University of Miami School of Medicine

Joan A. Muir-Malcolm, Center for Family Studies, University of Miami School of Medicine

K. Daniel O'Leary, SUNY at Stony Brook, Stony Brook, NY

Carol L. Philpot, Florida Institute of Technology, Melbourne

William M. Pinsof, The Family Institute, Northwestern University, Evanston, IL

Melissa W. Racioppo, National Institute on Drug Abuse, Rockville, MD

Michael S. Robbins, Center for Family Studies, University of Miami School of Medicine

Michael J. Rohrbaugh, University of Arizona, Tucson

Kimberly D. Ryan, New College of South Florida, Sarasota

Daniel A. Santisteban, Center for Family Studies, University of Miami School of Medicine

Sonja K. Schoenwald, Family Services Research Center, Medical University of South Carolina, Charleston

Thomas L. Sexton, Indiana University, Bloomington

Varda Shoham, University of Arizona, Tucson

Benjamin Silliman, North Carolina State University, Raleigh

Douglas K. Snyder, Texas A&M University, College Station

Scott M. Stanley, University of Denver

José Szapocznik, Center for Family Studies, University of Miami School of Medicine

Patrick H. Tolan, Institute for Juvenile Research, University of Illinois—Chicago

Foreword

In early 1988, the American Psychological Association (APA) Science Directorate began its sponsorship of what has become an exceptionally successful activity in support of psychological science: the APA Scientific Conferences program. This program has showcased some of the most important topics in psychological science, and the conference participants have included many leading figures in the field.

As we enter a new century, it seems fitting that we begin with a new face on this book series, that of the Decade of Behavior (DoB). The DoB is a major interdisciplinary initiative designed to promote the contributions of the behavioral and social sciences to address some of our most important societal challenges and will occur from 2000 to 2010. Although a major effort of the initiative will be related to informing the public about the contributions of these fields, other activities will be put into place to reach fellow scientists. Hence, the series that was the "APA Science Series" will be continued as the "Decade of Behavior Series." This represents one element in APA's efforts to promote the DoB initiative as one of its partner organizations.

Please note the DoB logo on the inside jacket flap and the full title page. We expect this logo will become a familiar sight over the next few years. For additional information about DoB, please visit http://www.decadeofbehavior.org.

As part of the sponsorship agreement with APA, conference organizers commit themselves not only to the conference itself but also to editing a scholarly volume that results from the meeting. This book is such a volume. Over the course of the past 12 years, we have partnered with 44 universities to sponsor 60 conferences on a variety of topics of interest to psychological scientists. The APA Science Directorate looks forward to continuing this program and to sponsoring other conferences in the years ahead.

We are pleased that this important contribution to the literature was supported in part by the Scientific Conferences program. Congratulations to the editors and contributors on their sterling effort.

Richard McCarty, PhD
Executive Director for Science

Virginia E. Holt
Assistant Executive Director for Science

Acknowledgments

The foundation of this book was the national conference, "Marital and Family Therapy and Process and Outcome Research: The State of the Science," sponsored by the Division of Family Psychology of the American Psychological Association (APA) and Temple University in Philadelphia, PA. Guy Diamond served as conference coordinator. We wish to thank him for his hard work in putting this event together. We also acknowledge the financial support provided by a grant from the Science Directorate of the APA and contributions from the Division of Independent Practice of the APA and the Philadelphia Child Guidance Center.

We wish to thank our many colleagues who participated in the conference and contributed to the ideas that made development of this book possible. They include David Miklowitz, Michael Goldstein, Anna Marie Cauce, Frank Fincham, Mike Stoolmiller, David Kenney, Mavis Heatherington, James Coyne, Myrna Friedlander, and Lyman Wynne. In addition, we thank the staff at the APA, including Anne Woodworth and Gary VandenBos, for their editorial contributions.

Introduction

Interest in family relationships, dynamics, and processes and the impact they have on individual and family health and well-being has grown dramatically over the last 25 years. Despite, or perhaps in response to, the multiple changes in modern families, news surveys report that family relationships are a top priority and concern for the vast majority of people. The interest in family and intimate relationships and the problems that arise from them have also become a focal point for many psychologists and other health professionals (social workers, family therapists, and physicians). The increased focus on family relationships and the changing social contexts of families contributed to the development of the field of family psychology.

Family psychology is a specialty within contemporary psychology. It has basic and applied aspects, covers treatment and prevention interventions, and is taught in graduate training programs, generally under clinical child or counseling psychology programs. Although the field of family psychology is relatively new, the roots of this emerging specialty lie deep within psychology (L'Abate, 1983; Liddle, 1992); it now stands among the new specialties, such as health and forensic psychology.

Although its name may indicate otherwise, family psychology covers a broad territory. Family psychology researchers consider biological, intrapsychic, interpersonal, and social context factors to understand marital and family functioning, health, distress, and treatment. Family psychology is not limited to mental health, but is part of the broader health care field—topics involving family and marital issues, process research and interventions, as well as the core theoretical ideas of family psychology (e.g., contextualism and systems perspective) appear under the headings of many psychology content areas, including developmental, social, research design and methodology, environmental and community, gender psychology, industrial and organizational, health, forensic, and of course clinical, counseling, and school psychology (Liddle, 1987).

One of the first tasks in family psychology's early history concerned its definition, in particular its definition in relationship to the more widely known movement of family therapy. The inaugural issue of family psychology's first journal, the *Journal of Family Psychology*, included the following definition:

> Family psychology, using a systemic perspective, broadens psychology's traditional emphasis on the individual, and, while it retains a primary emphasis on marriage and the family, it uses the systemic view to focus on the nature and role of individuals in primary relationship structures, as well as, more

broadly, the social ecology of the family—those networks in which the family interacts and resides. (Liddle, 1987, p. 9)

Definitions of the family psychology specialty have emphasized several themes: the systems perspective and contextual tradition of family therapy (representing the clinical wing of family psychology), the theoretical perspectives of contextualism, reciprocal causality and influence, and an ongoing attempt to define the processes or mechanisms that mediate the relationship between different systems and levels of functioning. Family psychology embraced the newly forming traditions of conceptual complexity, movements that took form in many sectors of psychology and related sciences (Kazdin, 1998). One of the most important ways in which family psychology exemplified this complexity is how it transcended the literal meaning of its own name. Family psychology, like family therapy, invokes images of a particular conceptual or intervention unit—the family. By embracing systems philosophy and contextualism at its core, it surely includes family and marital processes in its theoretical, research, and clinical purviews, but it has moved beyond family as well. The emphasis is on the behavioral, cognitive, and emotional transactions and interactions that occur not only in the family but also between the family and other developmentally and situationally influential social systems (Bronfenbrenner, 1979). This broadened emphasis, consistent with Kazdin's (1998) recommendations for new kinds of conceptual frameworks and interventions, has been the hallmark of contemporary family psychology interventions.

This edited volume focuses on family psychology's applied branch, which we call *family psychology intervention science*. The contributors to this book are among the foremost clinical investigators in the field. The work presented in this volume provides both an overview of their many years of clinical investigation and their cutting-edge developments for treating the wide array of marriage and family problems.

This book grows out of a national conference, "Marital and Family Therapy and Process and Outcome Research: The State of the Science," which was sponsored by the Division of Family Psychology of the American Psychological Association and Temple University in May 1995. Three of the editors—Liddle, Levant, and Bray—developed the conference to bring together experts to assess the current state of knowledge in family psychology intervention science. Some of the chapters are based on presentations from the conference, and others were invited from experts who were unable to attend. Authors were asked to review the state of the science in their area and focus on the clinical implications of their work.

Part 1 begins with chapter 1 (by Liddle, Bray, Levant, and Santisteban), which is an overview of the field and the applied area we term *family psychology intervention science*. It provides a general assessment of the current state of the science and areas that are addressed in the rest of the book. Chapters 2 and 3 provide overviews of the field from two perspectives. These chapters give the reader an assessment of the history of family therapy within family psychology intervention science, its current challenges, and some of its possibilities (chapter 2, by Alexander, Sexton, and Robbins), and an overview and evaluation of family therapy process research (chapter 3, by Diamond and Diamond). The Diamonds propose a comprehensive framework for process research that builds on the innovative conceptual and methodological contributions of discovery-oriented research. The authors argue that process research would advance more rapidly if it focused on a few generic, common processes that transcend model-specific theories

Part 2 focuses on advances in assessment and evaluation methods. In chapter 4, Snyder, Cozzi, and Mangrum identify what they believe to be core deficits in marital and family therapy assessment strategies and present a conceptual model for assessment across diverse domains that operate at multiple levels of the family system. The model is then used to examine recent research findings and to suggest future research. In chapter 5, Bray presents critical issues in understanding context and systemic relationships in marital and family research. The author presents innovations in methodologies and statistical analyses that are central to the work of family psychology intervention science.

Part 3 presents advances in marital intervention research. In chapter 6, Gollan and Jacobson profile research that demonstrates key clinical, methodological, and conceptual issues in couple therapy. The authors also introduce *integrative couple therapy* as an example of the evolution of previous intervention research and practice models as well as a product that has diminished the divide between research and practice. Chapter 7, by Silliman, Stanley, Coffin, Markman, and Jordan, reviews different conceptual frameworks and treatments aimed at preventing marital distress and divorce and promoting marital adjustment. The authors identify key issues that are likely to determine the field's next stage of development. In chapter 8, Gottman, Ryan, Carrère, and Erley review recent research in the field of marital therapy and present their own longitudinal research on divorce prediction. The authors describe their *sound marital house theory*, with its emphasis on experimental intervention studies as the basis for theory building.

The chapters in Part 4 focus on advances in family intervention research. In chapter 9, Pinsof and Hambright present an integrative model for family therapy process and outcome research that can help to increase the prevention and clinical relevance of family therapy research. Their relevance model integrates family interaction research, new traditions in psychotherapy process and outcome research, and core concepts and methods from epidemiological research. In chapter 10, Tolan argues that there has not been adequate critical discussion about the specific value of prevention efforts and, within family circles, of the role of the family in these efforts. Tolan presents an approach to family-focused prevention that can organize and advance knowledge and practice. In chapter 11, Rohrbaugh, Shoham, and Racioppo argue that the pessimism about attribute x treatment interaction (ATI) research and client–treatment matching is premature given the complexity of these treatments. The authors present evidence for relational moderators of treatment response and show that meaningful ATIs can be obtained when treatments differ clearly on dimensions theoretically relevant to the hypothesized moderator variables. Chapter 12, by Forgatch and Knutson, describes the work of the Oregon Social Learning Center in Eugene and the manner in which it has linked basic research and practical application within prevention science. The authors present promising areas and challenges in moving prevention science into broader community settings. In chapter 13, Schoenwald and Henggeler articulate the place of mental health services research within family psychology intervention science and present critical challenges in conducting this type of work. The authors also present *multisystemic therapy* as an example of the interface between treatment and services research. In chapter 14, O'Leary describes the rich history of his 30-year program of research and reflects on the major factors that helped to shape that work.

Part 5 focuses on contextual considerations in family intervention research. In chapter 15, Levant and Philpot present an updated framework for conceptualizing gender within family psychology intervention science. They present the *gender role strain paradigm* and demonstrate its application to women. In chapter 16, Santisteban, Muir-Malcolm, Mitrani, and Szapocznik present a framework for integrating ethnicity-related cultural factors into marital and family research. The authors highlight the many ways in which cultural factors influence constructs and processes that are core to family psychology intervention science.

The editors hope that this book will provide readers with an in-depth understanding of science-based family interventions and an appreciation of the innovative developments in this field. We also hope that this volume will provide the field with a "state of the science" resource regarding family psychology intervention and that it will stimulate further work in this important and emerging area.

References

Bronfenbrenner, U. (1979). *The ecology of human development: Experiments by nature and design.* Cambridge, MA: Harvard University Press.

Kazdin, A. E. (Ed.). (1998). *Methodological issues and strategies in clinical research* (2nd ed.). Washington DC: American Psychological Association.

L'Abate, L. (1983). *Family psychology: Theory, therapy, and training.* Washington, DC: University Press of America.

Liddle, H. A. (1987). Editor's introduction 1: Family psychology: The journal, the field. *Journal of Family Psychology, 1,* 5–22.

Liddle, H. A. (1992). Family psychology: Progress and prospects of a maturing discipline. *Journal of Family Psychology, 5,* 249–263.

PART 1

Science of Family Psychology: Overview of the Field

Family Psychology Intervention Science: An Emerging Area of Science and Practice

Howard A. Liddle

James H. Bray

Ronald F. Levant

Daniel A. Santisteban

The last two decades have witnessed a dramatic increase in psychological studies of couples and families and the development of interventions for treating marital and family problems. The increase in this area of interest led to the development of family psychology as a identified specialty within the field of psychology. This applied branch has also developed rapidly over the last decade. Evidence on several fronts suggests that we have a subspecialty within family psychology—*family psychology intervention science*. This chapter provides an overview of this subspecialty and proposes areas of future study and expansion.

Today's family psychology interventions include assessment and intervention attention to multiple systems and levels of social influence, including peer, school, and community and neighborhood influences (Alexander, Holtzworth-Monroe, & Jameson, 1994; Forgatch, Patterson, & Ray, 1995; Henggeler, Schoenwald, Borduin, Rowland, & Cunningham, 1998; Liddle, 1995). These interventions draw on family systems ideas, particularly those of family therapy, but are not tied exclusively to them. Developmental and social psychology, developmental psychopathology, as well as the intersection of psychophysiological processes and cognitive and affective processes (Gottman & Levensan, 1992; Parke, 1998) are among other content foci that can now be included in the specialty. These basic research areas inform intervention development considerably (Bray, 1995b; Liddle, Rowe, Diamond, Sesra, Schmidt, & Ettinger, 2000; Tolan, Guerra, & Kendall, 1995).

There continue to be significant unmet mental health needs of children and adolescents. These unmet needs and the documented decline within some sectors of our nation's youth require intervention. Family psychology interventions, which emphasize evaluating and intervening in the multiple ecologies of children's and adolescents' lives, can strengthen psychology's societal contribution.

Family psychology can also contribute to treatment and prevention science in general. By design, its interventions attempt to assess and intervene in the settings in which children and adolescents develop and in which dysfunction develops and is exacerbated. Attempts to change the processes of development and dysfunction in these important settings have yielded knowledge about the development of dysfunction in general as well as the processes of normative adaptation.

The broad field of intervention science has made significant advances in the last two decades. Prevention and treatment research is now conducted according to a more rigorous, well-developed set of standards than in earlier historical periods (Bryant, Windle, & West, 1997; Coie et al., 1993). Experience with and learning from large-scale clinical trials have yielded research guidelines (Carroll & Rounsaville, 1990; Elkin, Parloff, Hadley, & Autry, 1985)— agreed-on standards for the conduct of clinical trial studies. New methodological developments, including more and varied designs, statistical analyses (including meta-analyses), and types of research questions have transformed the type and quality of current studies.

Clinical research is now more varied than ever before. Complementing large-scale outcome trials, process research studies attempt to illuminate the processes or mechanisms by which change occurs (Greenberg & Pinsof, 1986). Contemporary clinical research addresses the irrelevance of clinical research to real-world clinical practice. An organized, standard-seeking set of activities oriented toward establishing and disseminating empirically supported therapies has taken hold (Chambless, 1996). The empirically supported therapy movement has influenced public discourse about therapy and has involved funders of research, third-party payers, and consumers of services, as well as providers and trainers of providers. Considerable professional attention has been devoted to development of practice guidelines for a variety of clinical problems and disorders (American Academy of Child and Adolescent Psychiatry [AACAP], 1997), and family interventions figure prominently in the treatment of child and adolescent disorders such as attention deficit hyperactivity disorder (ADHD), conduct disorder, and substance abuse (Center for Substance Abuse Treatment [CSAT], 1998; AACAP, 1997). Treatment manuals for a similar range of problems are more available than ever before (e.g., the National Institute on Drug Abuse [NIDA] home page [www.nih.nida.gov], the Cannabis Youth Treatment [CYT] Multisite Study, and CSAT [www.chestnut.org]). These advances can be thought of as a broad-based, not entirely organized or coherent, and still evolving treatment development movement. Interestingly, this movement is so far-reaching that scientific, academic, and managed care constituencies are aligning, perhaps out of necessity.

Within existing standards and guidelines for treatment development (Kazdin, 1994), family psychology intervention science compares well to other specialties. The past decade has demonstrated that family-based treatment and family prevention studies can be done, and they can be done in a way that conforms to the rigorous standards of contemporary intervention science (Alexander et al., 1994; Stanton & Shadish, 1997). The challenges to conducting these studies can be surmounted, and advances in family psychology intervention science are numerous (Liddle, 1995).

Research Infrastructure

Contemporary family-oriented research has significantly contributed to our understanding of functional and dysfunctional relationships and processes within marriages and families, as well as to how these processes affect child, adolescent, and adult adjustment (Bray & Hetherington, 1993; Gottman, 1994; Jacob, 1987; Pinsof & Wynne, 1995). Furthermore, some of this research, such as Gottman's marital studies (Gottman, 1994; Gottman, Ryan, Carrère, & Erley, chapter 8, this volume), have integrated multiple systems, from the biological to the interactional, into an understanding of marital relationships and an ability to predict relationship outcomes. This type of research has resulted in development of many types of interventions. Communication skills training, one of the new kind of interventions, is commonly used in marital and family therapies (Gottman, Notarius, Gonso, & Markman, 1976; Markman & Hahlweg, 1993). In addition, studies of family transitions provide much-needed information about the typical and atypical changes that occur across the family life cycle and the impact that these transitions have on children and adults (Bray & Hetherington, 1993; Hetherington, 1989).

Family psychologists have also been instrumental in studying how marital and family therapies can be used to treat other psychological and health problems. For example, several researchers have demonstrated that marital therapy is effective for treating depression (e.g., Jacobson, Dobson, Fruzzetti, Schmaling, & Salusky, 1991; O'Leary & Beach, 1990); that family interventions are useful for treating child and adolescent behavior problems (e.g., Alexander & Parsons, 1982; Diamond, Serrano, Dickey, & Sonis, 1996; Liddle & Dakof, 1995); and that marital and family therapy is beneficial for recovery from cardiac problems (e.g., Coyne & Smith, 1994), adjustment to diabetes (e.g., Drotar, 1992), and cancer coping (e.g., Kazak & Nachman, 1991).

A combination of factors, including an expanded cohort of trained researchers, developments and advances in the fields that address marital and family issues, and advances in application of these knowledge bases to a broad range of clinical problems have interacted to yield an increase in funding opportunities for family-focused intervention research (e.g., the National Institute of Mental Health, the National Institute of Drug Abuse, the Center for Substance Abuse Treatment, and the Center for Substance Abuse Prevention). Federal agencies and foundations have shown strong interest in funding family-oriented intervention research. The increased funding support has continued and expanded many research programs in family psychology intervention science. Research training in this subspecialty prepares early career scholars with specialized research backgrounds for careers in family-oriented intervention research (e.g., the NIMH Postdoctoral Family Consortium; Liddle, 1994).

The number and variety of family-oriented intervention studies continues to grow (Ozechowski & Liddle, 2000; Shadish et al., 1993). A monograph reviews some of the many areas in which considerable intervention research exists (Pinsof & Wynne, 1995). These reviews summarized family intervention research findings across a variety of content areas, including alcohol and drug abuse, conduct disorder, marital problems, physical health problems, and major mental illnesses. The conclusion of these reviews was that family-oriented interventions are useful and effective in the treatment of a broad range of individual and family problems.

Research Nature and Quality

Studies in family-based treatment intervention and prevention conform to contemporary standards of intervention science. The studies are theory-based (e.g., a theory of dysfunction and normative behavior guides intervention design and assessment). Basic psychological research on particular aspects of development (e.g., social cognition, affect regulation, or the influence of peers on acquiring antisocial beliefs) inform intervention development. These studies evaluate the impact of interventions on clinical populations of diverse ethnicity and race, thus addressing some of the limits of previous treatment and basic research about sample restrictiveness (Henggeler et al., 1998; Szapocznik et al., 1988).

Family psychology intervention science is exemplary in its attempt to connect and use basic and applied science at every stage of its intervention development and evaluation. The risk and protective factor framework, developmental psychopathology, and developmental and social psychology are primary areas that are used for contemporary intervention design as well as to provide research leads (Liddle, Rowe, Dakof, & Lyke, 1998).

Family psychology research requires many types of quantitative and qualitative methodologies (Bray, 1995a). Basic science investigations into family and marital processes include both experimental and nonexperimental methods and a variety of measurement techniques, including surveys of individuals about their families, self-reports from multiple family members, observations and ratings of family interactions, and physiological measurements during family interactions (Bray, 1995b). A limiting factor is the lack of a unified theory of family functioning (Bray, 1995b). There is no consensus about defining what healthy or dysfunctional family relationships are or even the key processes that need to be assessed. Further, there is no established diagnostic system, such as the *DSM-IV* or ICD systems, to use for marital and family problems. Each of these research approaches needs statistical methods to analyze data from multiple sources (e.g., family members, trained raters) and methods (self-report, behavioral observations) and to combine the data in meaningful ways to understand family relationships (Cole & McPherson, 1993).

Research on family psychology interventions has the same problems as other clinical psychology outcome research, with the ultimate goal of determining which treatments are most effective (Bray, 1995a). It is also complicated by the fact that psychopathology is not viewed as within one individual, and the focus of treatment is usually on multiple individuals, their interactions, and at times the social context of the interactions (i.e., school, hospital). Thus, the outcome of a successful treatment is not only change in the behavior of an identified patient but also change in the interactions that are related to the problem behavior or to social institutions that have an impact on the problem behavior (e.g., schools, juvenile justice systems).

This is a central yet complex issue. For example, research on marriage and divorce indicates that spouses often relate such varied perceptions of marital relations that they are described as "his and her" marriages or divorces (Hetherington, 1989). Therefore, determining if a treatment is effective requires integrating and resolving such differences in perceptions with behavioral interactions predictive of marital satisfaction. Furthermore, the focus of family psychology intervention research has moved away from studying only comparisons between different treatments to understanding which processes are critical for engendering therapeutic change (Friedlander, 1998; Jacobson & Addis, 1993; Pinsof, 1992).

It is also critical in both basic family process and outcome research to consider the dynamic and reciprocal nature of family relationships (Bray, 1995a). Understanding how families change and what role change plays in family functioning further complicates research in this area. Most traditional statistical methods are based on linear, mathematical approaches that describe family relations at discrete time points. In contrast, systems theories are inherently nonlinear and circular and emphasize the continuous nature of relationships and the mutual influence on various aspects of the system. Methodologies that address change processes, and particularly the reciprocal nature of change within families, are critical for future study in family psychology. These methodologies include nonlinear mathematical modeling (Cook et al., 1995; Gottman et al., chapter 8, this volume) and hierarchical, structural, and multilevel linear modeling (Bryk & Raudenbush, 1992) and its application to studying change over time and how various trajectories of change may be related to various outcomes (Raudenbush, Brennan, & Barnett, 1995). Use of these innovative methodologies allows us to address previously unasked questions.

Efficacy, effectiveness, and process of therapy questions are now asked within single, large-scale clinical trials (Clarke, 1995). Common exemplary design features also include attention to multiperson, multilevel, and multicontext assessments over multiple time points, including extended follow-up periods (Borkovec, 1993). Study instrumentation assesses symptom reduction as well as increases or change in prosocial or adaptive functioning, such as school attendance or grades (Kazdin, 1994; Liddle & Hogue, 2000). Interventions can now be specified in great detail. This should be considered impressive, considering how interventions have changed over the last decade. Complex intervention models have been developed, and many of them could be considered combination interventions. These new models are comprehensive in scope and are intended to address the range of functional and developmental impairments in the affected youth, family, and environment. Although dissemination and use of treatment manuals must be considered at an early stage, the manuals are increasingly available through many sources (e.g., commercial publishers [Henggeler et al., 1998; Liddle, in press] and funding agencies such as the Center for Substance Abuse Treatment's Cannabis Youth Treatment Initiative and the National Institute on Drug Abuse).

These contemporary treatments are theoretically based, are tailored according to important contextual factors such as culture (Santisteban, Muir-Malcolm, Mitrani, & Szapocznik, chapter 16, this volume), use basic research (Liddle et al., 1998), are principle-driven (Henggeler et al., 1998; Liddle, 2001), and are organized according to a preferred intervention sequence/stages of therapy notion (Alexander & Barton, 1980). The intervention approaches target characteristics and processes that are related to dysfunction. The engagement studies of Szapocznik and colleagues and Liddle and colleagues, for example, blended a knowledge of cultural processes with family therapy engagement methods to successfully create and test specialized, culture- and clinical method-informed engagement strategies (Diamond, Liddle, Hogue, & Dakof, 1999; Jackson-Gilfort, Liddle, Dakof, & Tejeda, in press; Santisteban, Szapocznik, Kurtines, Murray, & LaPerriere, 1996; Szapocznik et al., 1988).

Therapists can be taught to adhere to and to implement these complex, comprehensive interventions (Hogue et al., 1998), and family psychology training and supervision models have been developed to accomplish this (Green, 1985; Liddle, Becker, & Diamond, 1997). Furthermore, studies have begun to appear that confirm the importance of adherence to well-developed, previously established, and efficacious interventions (Henggeler, 1994; Liddle, 2000). Family psychology interventions can not only be developed into manuals, they can be successfully subjected to the same kind of conformity to adherence standards (adherence studies and instrumentation) as individual psychotherapy models (Hogue, Liddle, & Rowe, 1996).

Challenges and Future Directions

Although the field of family psychology has made an excellent start in contributing to our understanding of marital and family process and outcomes from interventions, there is still much to be learned about both basic family process and interventions to resolve marital, family, and individual problems. For further advancement the field needs to develop standards of measurement and reach agreement on the central concepts for study. The field of psychophysiology made major gains in its research efforts after it developed standards for measuring basic physiological processes. There are consistent and critical family processes (e.g., conflict and communication) that have been identified by research, and standardized measurements that can be used in family psychology research are needed (Bray, 1995b). National panels of researchers in various areas should be brought together to identify these critical processes and to develop measurement standards.

Basic research in all areas that identifies patterns of marital and family relationships related to problem development is still needed. In particular, more research is necessary on families with adolescents and elderly individuals. More basic research is required on family responses to acute and chronic illness, such as HIV/AIDS, cancer, cardiac problems, and trauma, in addition to more traditional mental health areas such as adolescent conduct problems, ADHD, alcohol and other drug abuse, and childhood depression.

Future research that recognizes the diversity of modern families is essential. Diversity includes differences as a result of family structure variations (e.g., single-parent families, stepfamilies), ethnic minorities and cultural differences, and gay and lesbian families. Much of the research on marital and family process and outcomes is based on White, middle-class families, yet the largest growing segments of our population are ethnic minorities, such as Hispanics, and these families frequently experience high rates of psychosocial problems. There has been only limited research on whether our family assessment tools and instruments can be applied to these ethnic groups, and even less research on whether our interventions work with these families (Bray, 1995b; Bray & Jouriles, 1995).

The American family is also diversifying in terms of structure and function (Bray & Hetherington, 1993). The high rates of divorce, remarriage, and children born to unmarried mothers and the documented differences in family process in these types of families when compared to two-parent nuclear families give rise to special needs for interventions with these types of families. Again, there is only meager research on interventions designed to decrease divorce or to prevent problems caused by these family transitions.

Although findings thus far have revealed that family psychology interventions can be effective, even when compared to non–family-oriented interventions, many puzzles and gaps related to these research-based clinical outcomes remain (Pinsof & Wynne, 1995; Shadish et al., 1993). As many constituencies and forces act on the consumption of research outcome data, the matter of how satisfied we should be with the levels of outcomes achieved is yet to be determined. Basically, this point pertains to the evolution of questions such as, Are these interventions effective? What are the circumstances under which they are effective? Are they effective enough? As studies add more prosocial measures to their batteries while continuing to measure symptom reduction, will the improvements in functioning and the remediations of impairment justify what are, in some cases, expensive and not very generalizable interventions? The topic of a model's transportability is one of the major research issues that family psychology interventionists face. This matter intersects considerably with policy issues, policy makers, and program planners.

Economic realities in the mental health care marketplace may influence programmers' willingness to adopt treatments, even treatments with proven efficacy. Process research, and particularly studies that can unlock the mysteries of why and how change occurs (Friedlander, 1998), has been and will continue to be an important area of development to family psychology. This is particularly so as the new kinds of studies, partly because of funding-related reasons (clinical trial studies are being asked to justify their large budgets), continue to develop along integrative lines. In other words, today's studies, like the therapy models many of them are attempting to evaluate, are becoming more integrative —combining different kinds of research designs, methodologies, and different genres of research questions into a single proposal or project. Just as integrative forces helped to break down ideological barriers in the therapy development sphere, the same is happening in therapy and intervention research studies. The treatment development movement, with its first few guidelines now being articulated (Kazdin, 1994), will likely be the major organizing force for intervention science generally and thus for family psychology as well. The degree to which a framework such as Kazdin's might require adaptation to fit the kind of research done by family psychology researchers remains to be determined.

There have been a number of important studies during the last decade that point to the importance of prevention of marital and family problems (Coie et al., 1993). Markman's research (Markman & Hahlweg, 1993; Renick, Blumberg, & Markman, 1992) using the Prevention and Relationship Enhancement Program (PREP) has provided very promising data on the prevention of marital conflict and divorce. As we identify early markers of family problems, the challenge will be to develop programs that can impede further development of these types of problems. This often requires longitudinal research on normative and clinical samples to determine processes and risk factors that lead to problems and normal adjustment (Baer & Bray, 1999).

Conclusion

It is clear that more attention is needed to develop sophisticated methodologies that can capture the rich and varied phenomena of family relationships (Bray, 1995a). There are many new and promising methodologies in progress, but more funding is needed to continue and expand this work. Specifically, further work is required to develop reliable and valid measures that can be applied to the diversity of families as well as methodologies that can consider the variety of family structures and relationship patterns. We also need to develop ways to successfully recruit and retain participants in longitudinal studies, particularly those from diverse ethnic and socioeconomic backgrounds, and procedures for dealing with the varied methods and data from multiple family members. Finally, as family-based interventions have become more broad-based and comprehensive, questions about the limitations of this complexity and comprehensiveness remain.

References

Alexander, J. F., & Barton, C. (1980). Intervention with delinquents and their families: Clinical, methodological, and conceptual issues. In J. Vincent (Ed.), *Advances in family intervention, assessment and theory*. Greenwich, CT: JAI Press.

Alexander, J. F., Holtzworth-Munroe, A., & Jameson, P. B. (1994). Research on the process and outcome of marriage and family therapy. In A. E. Bergin & S. L. Garfield (Eds.), *Handbook of psychotherapy and behavior change* (4th ed., pp. 595–630). New York: Wiley.

Alexander, J. F., & Parsons, B. V. (1982). *Functional family therapy*. Belmont, CA: Brooks/ Cole.

American Academy of Child and Adolescent Psychiatry. (1997). Practice parameters for the assessment and treatment of children and adolescents with substance use disorders. *Journal of American Child and Adolescent Psychiatry, 36*(Suppl.), 140–156.

Baer, P. E., & Bray, J. H. (1999). Adolescent individuation and alcohol usage. *Journal of Studies on Alcohol, 13,* 52–62.

Borkovec, T. D. (1993). Between-group therapy outcome research: Design and methodology. In L. S. Onken, J. D. Blaine, & J. J. Boren (Eds.), *Behavioral treatments for drug abuse and dependence* (pp. 249–289). Rockville, MD: National Institute on Drug Abuse.

Bray, J. H. (1995a). Methodological advances in family psychology. *Journal of Family Psychology, 9,* 107–109.

Bray, J. H. (1995b). Family assessment: Current issues in evaluating families. *Family Relations, 44,* 469–477.

Bray, J. H., & Hetherington, E. M. (1993). Families in transition: Introduction and overview. *Journal of Family Psychology, 7,* 3–8.

Bray, J. H., & Jouriles, E. (1995). Treatment of marital conflict and prevention of divorce. *Journal of Marital and Family Therapy, 21,* 461–473.

Bronfenbrenner, U. (1979). *The ecology of human development: Experiments by nature and design.* Cambridge, MA: Harvard University Press.

Bryant, K. J., Windle, M., & West, S. G. (Eds.). (1997). *The science of prevention: Methodological advances from alcohol and substance abuse research.* Washington, DC: American Psychological Association.

Bryk, A. S., & Raudenbush, S. W. (1992). *Hierarchical linear models: Applications and data analysis techniques.* Newbury Park, CA: Sage.

Carroll, K. M., & Rounsaville, B. J. (1990). Can a technology model of psychotherapy be applied to cocaine abuse treatment? In L. Onken & J. Blaine (Eds.), *Psychotherapy and counseling in the treatment of drug abuse* (pp. 79–94; NIDA Research Monograph 104). Washington, DC: U.S. Government Printing Office.

Center for Substance Abuse Treatment. (1998). *Guidelines for adolescent drug abuse treatment* (Treatment improvement series). Rockville, MD: Author.

Chambless, D. L. (1996). In defense of dissemination of empirically supported psychological interventions. *Clinical Psychology: Science and Practice, 3,* 230–235.

Clarke, G. N. (1995). Improving the transition from basic efficacy research to effectiveness studies: Methodological issues and procedures. *Journal of Consulting and Clinical Psychology, 63,* 718–725.

Coie, J. D., Watt, N. R., West, S. G., Hawkins, J. D., Asarnow, J. R., Markman, J. J., Ramey, S. L., Shure, M. B., & Long, B. (1993). The science of prevention: A conceptual framework and some directions for a national research program. *American Psychologist, 48,* 1013–1022.

Cole, D. A., & McPherson, A. E. (1993). Relation of family subsystems to adolescent depression: Implementing a new family assessment strategy. *Journal of Family Psychology, 7,* 119–133.

Cook, J., Tyson, R., White, J., Rushe, R., Gottman, J., & Murray, J. (1995). The mathematics of marital conflict: Qualitative dynamic mathematical modeling of marital interaction. *Journal of Family Psychology, 9,* 110–130.

Coyne, J. C., & Smith, S. A. F. (1994). Couples coping with a myocardial infarction: Contextual perspective on patient self-efficacy. *Journal of Family Psychology, 8,* 43–54.

Diamond, G. M., Liddle, H. A., Hogue, A., & Dakof, G. A. (1999). Alliance building interventions with adolescents in family therapy: A process study. *Psychotherapy: Theory, Research, Practice, & Training, 36,* 355–368.

Diamond, G. S., Serrano, A. C., Dickey, M., & Sonis, W. A. (1996). Current status of family-based outcome and process research. *Journal of American Academy on Child and Adolescent Psychiatry, 35,* 6–16.

Drotar, D. (1992). Integrating theory and practice in psychological intervention with families of children with chronic illness. In T. J. Akamatsu, M. A. P. Stephens, S. E. Hobfoll, & J. H. Crowther (Eds.), *Family health psychology* (pp. 175–192). Washington, DC: Hemisphere.

Elkin, I., Parloff, M. B., Hadley, W. W., & Autry, J. H. (1985). NIMH Treatment of Depression Collaborative Research Program: Background and research plan. *Archives of General Psychiatry, 42,* 305–316.

Forgatch, M. S., Patterson, G. R., & Ray, J. A. (1995). Divorce and boys' adjustment problems: Two paths with a single model. In E. M. Hetherington & E. A. Blechman (Eds.), *Stress, coping, and resiliency in children and families* (pp. 67–105). Hillsdale, NJ: Erlbaum.

Friedlander, M. (1998). Family therapy process research. In M. Nichols & R. Schwartz (Eds.), *Family therapy* (4th ed., pp. 503–534). Needham Heights, MA: Allyn & Bacon.

Gottman, J. M. (1994). *Why marriages succeed or fail.* New York: Simon & Schuster.

Gottman, J. M., Notarius, C., Gonso, J., & Markman, H. (1976). *A couple's guide to communication.* Champaign, IL: Research Press.

Gottman, J. M., & Levenson, R. W. (1992). Marital processes predictive of later dissolution: Behavior, physiology, and health. *Journal of Personality & Social Psychology, 63,* 221–234.

Gottman, J. M., Swanson, C., & Murray, J. (1999). The mathematics of marital conflict: Dynamic mathematical nonlinear modeling of newlywed marital interaction. *Journal of Family Psychology, 13,* 3–19.

Green, B. J. (1985). System intervention in the schools. In M. P. Mirkin & S. L. Korman (Eds.), *Handbook of adolescent and family therapy* (pp. 193–206). New York: Gardner.

Greenberg, L. S., & Pinsof, W. M. (1986). Process research: Current trends and future perspectives. In L. S. Greenberg & W. M. Pinsof (Eds.), *The psychotherapeutic process: A research handbook* (pp. 3–20). New York: Guilford Press.

Haynes, S. (1992). *Models of causality in psychopathology: Toward dynamic, synthetic, and nonlinear models of behavior disorders.* Needham Heights, MA: Allyn & Bacon.

Henggeler, S. W. (1994). A consensus: Conclusions on the APA task force report on innovative models of mental health services for children, adolescents, and their families. *Journal of Clinical Child Psychology, 23,* 3–6.

Henggeler, S. W., Schoenwald, S. K., Borduin, C. M., Rowland, M. D., & Cunningham, P. B. (1998). *Multisystemic treatment of antisocial behavior in children and adolescents.* New York: Guilford Press.

Hetherington, E. M. (1989). Coping with family transitions: Winners, losers, and survivors. *Child Development, 60,* 1–14.

Hogue, A., Liddle, H. A., & Rowe, C. (1996). Treatment adherence process research in family therapy: A rationale and some practical guidelines. *Psychotherapy, 33,* 332–345.

Hogue, A., Liddle, H. A., Rowe, C., Turner, R. M., Dakof, G. A., & Lapann, K. (1998). Treatment adherence and differentiation in individual versus family therapy. *Journal of Counseling Psychology, 45,* 104–114.

Jackson-Gilfort, A., Liddle, H. A., Dakof, G., & Tejeda, M. (in press). The relationship of cultural theme discussion to engagement with a clinical sample of substance abusing, African American male adolescents in family therapy. *Journal of Black Psychology.*

Jacob, T. (Ed.). (1987). *Family interaction and psychopathology: Theories, methods, and findings.* New York: Plenum Press.

Jacobson, N. S., & Addis, M. E. (1993). Research on couples and couple therapy: What do we know? Where are we going? *Journal of Consulting and Clinical Psychology, 61,* 85–93.

Jacobson, N. S., Dobson, K., Fruzzetti, A., Schmaling, K. B., & Salusky, S. (1991). Marital therapy as a treatment for depression. *Journal of Consulting and Clinical Psychology, 59,* 547–557.

Kazak, A., & Nachman, G. (1991). Family research on childhood chronic illness: Pediatric oncology as an example. *Journal of Family Psychology, 4,* 462–483.

Kazdin, A. E. (1994). Psychotherapy for children and adolescents. In A. E. Bergin & S. L. Garfield (Eds.), *Handbook of psychotherapy and behavior change* (4th ed., pp. 543–594). New York: Wiley.

Liddle, H. A. (1994). Research training in adolescent drug abuse intervention. Rockville, MD: National Institute on Drug Abuse (Grant No. 2 T32 DA07297-06).

Liddle, H. A. (1995). Conceptual and clinical dimensions of a multidimensional, multisystems engagement strategy in family-based adolescent treatment. *Psychotherapy: Theory, Research, Practice, and Training, 32,* 39–58.

Liddle, H. A. (2001). *Multidimensional family therapy treatment (MDFT) for adolescent cannabis users. (Volume 5 of the Cannabis Youth Treatment (CYT) manual series).* Rockville, MD: Center for Substance Abuse Treatment, Substance Abuse and Mental Health Services Administration.

Liddle, H. A. (in press). Theory development in a family-based therapy for adolescent drug abuse. *Journal of Clinical Child Psychology.*

Liddle, H. A., Becker, D., & Diamond, G. M. (1997). Family therapy supervision. In C. Watkins (Ed.), *Psychotherapy supervision* (pp. 400–418). New York: Wiley.

Liddle, H. A., & Dakof, G. A. (1995). Family-based treatments for adolescent drug abuse: State of the science. In E. Rahdert & D. Czechowicz (Eds.), *Adolescent drug abuse: Clinical assessment and therapeutic interventions* (NIDA Research Monograph No. 156, pp. 218–254). Rockville, MD: National Institute on Drug Abuse.

Liddle, H. A., & Hogue, A. (2000). A developmental, family-based, ecological preventive intervention for antisocial behavior in high-risk adolescents. *Journal of Marital and Family Therapy, 26*(3), 265–280.

Liddle, H. A., Rowe, C. L., Dakof, G., & Lyke, J. (1998). Translating parenting research into clinical interventions for families of adolescents. *Clinical Child Psychology and Psychiatry, 3,* 419–443.

Liddle, H. A., Rowe, C., Diamond, G. M., Sessa, F., Schmidt, S., & Ettinger, D. (2000). Towards a developmental family therapy: The clinical utility of adolescent development research. *Journal of Marital and Family Therapy, 26*(4), 491–505.

Markman, H. J., & Hahlweg, K. (1993). The prediction and prevention of marital distress: An international perspective. *Clinical Psychology Review, 13,* 29–43.

O'Leary, K. D., & Beach, S. R. H. (1990). Marital therapy: A viable treatment for depression and marital discord. *American Journal of Psychiatry, 147,* 183–186.

Ozechowski, T., & Liddle, H. A. (2000). Family-based therapy for adolescent drug abuse: Knowns and unknowns. *Clinical Child and Family Psychology Review, 3*(4), 269–298.

Parke, R. D. (1998). Editorial. *Journal of Family Psychology, 12,* 3–6.

Pinsof, W. M. (1992). Toward a scientific paradigm for family psychology: The integrative process systems perspective. *Journal of Family Psychology, 5,* 432–447.

Pinsof, W. M., & Wynne, L. (1995). The effectiveness and efficacy of marital and family therapy. *Journal of Marital and Family Therapy, 21,* 339–623.

Raudenbush, S. W., Brennan, R. T., and Barnett, R. C. (1995). A multivariate hierarchical model for studying psychological change within married couples. *Journal of Family Psychology, 9,* 161–174.

Renick, M. J., Blumberg, S. L., & Markman, H. J. (1992). The Prevention and Relationship Enhancement Program (PREP): An empirically based preventive intervention program for couples. *Family Relations, 41,* 141–147.

Santisteban, D., Szapocznik, J., Kurtines, W. M., Murray, E. J., & LaPerriere, A. (1996). Efficacy of intervention for engaging youth and families into treatment and some variables that may contribute to differential effectiveness. *Journal of Family Psychology, 10,* 35–44.

Shadish, W. R., Montgomery, L. M., Wilson, P., Wilson, M. R., Bright, I., & Okwumabua, T. (1993). Effects of family and marital psychotherapies: A meta-analysis. *Journal of Consulting and Clinical Psychology, 61,* 992–1002.

Stanton, M. D., & Shadish, W. R. (1997). Outcome, attrition, and family–couples treatment for drug abuse: A meta-analysis and review of the controlled, comparative studies. *Psychological Bulletin, 122,* 170–191.

Szapocznik, J., Perez-Vidal, A., Brickman, A. L., Foote, F. H., Santisteban, D., Hervis, O., & Kurtines, W. (1988). Engaging adolescent drug abusers and their families in treatment: A strategic structural systems approach. *Journal of Consulting and Clinical Psychology, 56,* 552–557.

Tolan, P. H., Guerra, N. G., & Kendall, P. C. (1995). A developmental–ecological perspective on antisocial behavior in children and adolescents: Toward a unified risk and intervention framework. *Journal of Consulting and Clinical Psychology, 63,* 579–584.

CHAPTER 2

The Developmental Status of Family Therapy in Family Psychology Intervention Science

James F. Alexander
Thomas L. Sexton
Michael S. Robbins

"Not everything that can be counted counts, and not everything that counts can be counted"—Albert Einstein

Family therapy as a body of theory, practice, and professional identifications was developed primarily outside the mainstream of psychology. Many of the foundational constructs and early theoretical concepts emanated from thinking by major figures in such diverse fields as anthropology, information theory, cybernetics, and mathematics (Hoffman, 1981). Initial theoretical developments in family intervention and family intervention science were spurred by the recognition that traditional methods of psychological research were inadequate to deal with the overly complex issues of measuring, explaining, and intervening on family process. It became clear to many that a "new" perspective was needed (Fisher, 1982; Fisher, Terry, & Ransom, 1990).

Our goal in this chapter is to map the developmental trajectory of family therapy in family psychology intervention science (FT-FPIS) from its early roots to its current status. We also hope to provide a perspective on its developmental process with an eye toward future challenges.

What Is Implied by "Developmental Status"?

With respect to human behavior, most lay persons (and probably most professionals) without reflection often consider development as a positively valenced process or movement over time to a "fuller" or "greater" state; not all developmental trajectories are necessarily positive, however. For example, *entropy,* a fundamental principle of family systems, is seen as anything but a positive developmental process when used to describe the boundary violations and role diffusions that evolve in closed or incestuous families. Thus, we do not automatically place the developmental level of FT-FPIS at some point on a trajectory that implies a positively valenced change. It is clear that we are not in the same place we were 30, 20, or 10 years ago; whether we are developmentally "more mature" in any positive sense remains to be seen. We believe that we are, but to examine such an issue we must first examine our past, and in particular the roots of FT-FPIS.

It is important to note that the developmental processes (see Figure 2-1) that emerge in each generation of FT-FPIS are capable of reciprocal influence on the contextual influences from which they have emerged, just as children can and do influence their parents and even their parents' relationship. As family theorists we respect the differences between mapping a linear influence from one generation to the next as opposed to capturing the dynamic flow of reciprocally influencing relational processes.

Because FT-FPIS has a rich and complex history influenced by many different forces, to accomplish our task we will have to take apart something that by its very nature exists only as a whole. As a result, much of what we will do is punctuate the factors and identify relevant threads in the developmental complexity to highlight some ideas about our current status and future possibilities. In doing so we suggest that the current developmental status of family therapy is not another small step in some linear path, but a major "shift in frame" that calls into question many of the assumptions as well as content of our roots, both distal and proximal.

Roots

From our perspective, there are four key elements in the developmental evolution of FT-FPIS:

1. science (the scientific method and modernist thought);

2. theory and techniques of family therapy (systems theory, multicultural perspectives, postmodern thought);

3. core principles in basic psychology (e.g., information processing, attribution theory); and

4. the broader cultural and sociopolitical contexts (such as managed care, multicultural movement) in which FT-FPIS has evolved and currently exists.

Figure 2-1 is an illustration of the impact of these factors in the evolutionary and dynamic path that FT-FPIS has taken to date.

FIGURE 2-1

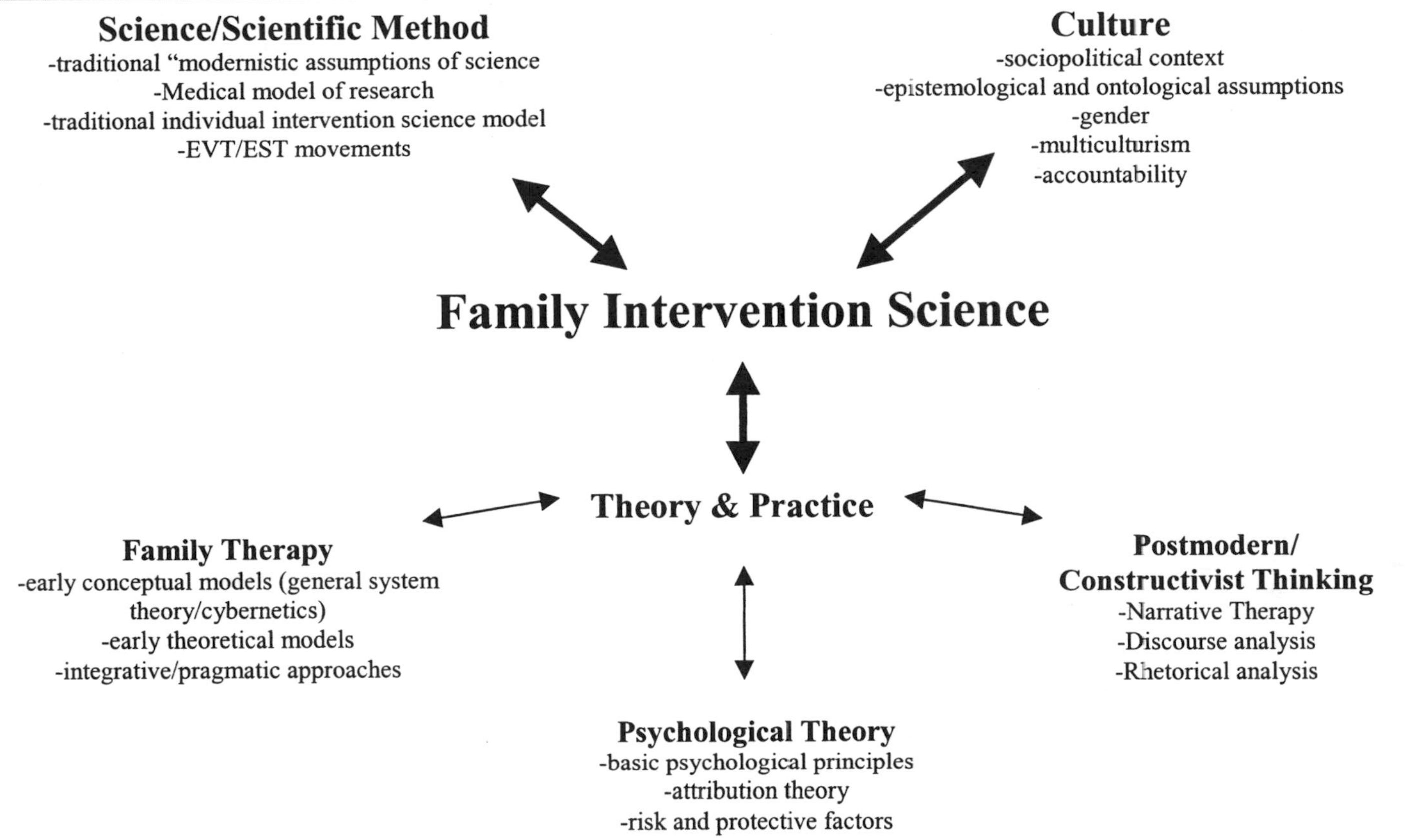

Science/Scientific Method
-traditional "modernistic assumptions of science
 -Medical model of research
-traditional individual intervention science model
 -EVT/EST movements

Culture
-sociopolitical context
-epistemological and ontological assumptions
 -gender
 -multiculturism
 -accountability

**Postmodern/
Constructivist Thinking**
-Narrative Therapy
-Discourse analysis
-Rhetorical analysis

Family Intervention Science

Theory & Practice

Family Therapy
-early conceptual models (general system
 theory/cybernetics)
 -early theoretical models
 -integrative/pragmatic approaches

Psychological Theory
-basic psychological principles
 -attribution theory
 -risk and protective factors

Scientific, cultural, and theoretical contexts that shaped the dynamic, developmental evolution of family therapy intervention science.

Theory and Practice

Theory and practice from both psychology and marriage and family therapy have had an impact on the emergence of FT-FPIS. For example, the principles of basic psychology, such as attribution theory and theories of developmental processes, have had an indirect impact by establishing a foundational knowledge set from which the ideas of family therapy models have emerged (Jameson & Alexander, 1993).

However, the systems theory that grounded family therapy was presented as an alternative to the existing linear, individualistic, and contextual "medical models" of behavioral therapies. Systems-based family therapy was asserted to be a more appropriate, effective, and perhaps even moral and humane way to deal with a number of problems. The early developers of family therapy models championed a holistic, bidirectional (or even multidirectional) view of dysfunctional behavior and its treatment, with the emphasis on relational as opposed to intrapsychic processes (Bateson, Jackson, Haley, & Weakland, 1956; Bowen, 1978; Lidz, Cornelison, Fleck, & Terry, 1957; Minuchin, 1974; Wynne, Ryckoff, Day, & Hirsch, 1958).

It didn't take long, however, for opposition to these founding principles to emerge from within as well as outside the field. The early articulated family therapy models were questioned (some would say "attacked") with respect to issues of gender, culture, class, and race. Family therapy also was questioned with respect to epistemology, rigor of research foundations, and the sociopolitics of professional organizations purporting to represent family therapy. This era was characterized by zealous allegiance to "schools" of therapeutic practice that seemed to spend as much time discounting each other's perspectives as they did providing strong conceptual, empirical, and practical foundations for family therapy as a whole.

More recently, family therapy practice has again been "pushed" by two emerging theoretical forces. The first is a move toward pragmatic and integrative models of practice (LeBow, 1997; Pinsof, 1983). Functional family therapy (FFT) is one of the "mature" clinical models that has integrated practice, training, and research protocols around a comprehensive and systematic set of core theoretical principles (Alexander, 1999). Both the integrative and mature models represent a movement away from theoretical dogma toward systematic approaches to practice.

The second, and quite conceptually distinct, influence has been the constructivist perspective. This perspective includes an array of specific dialogues that share a common core and long philosophical tradition and that recently have found their way into family therapy (Anderson & Goolishan, 1988; Foucault, 1980; Mahoney, 1991; Maturana & Varela, 1979). This movement maintains a central epistemological position of knowing as socially based in constructed meaning and reality as constructed, relative, and variable (Gergen, 1985; Hayes & Oppenheim, 1997; Wittgenstein, 1969). From this perspective, knowledge is based less on the discovery of principles of truth than on the viability of ideas within the professional and cultural context. The constructivist challenge to the assumptions of the "modern" period has spawned a growing number of new theoretical models (Efran, Lukens, & Lukens, 1990; White & Epston, 1990) and research methodologies (Hoshmand & Martin, 1995; Howard, 1985; Nelson & Poulin, 1997) where the focus is on description rather than cause, discussion rather than findings, and meaning rather than truth. The constructivist theory is an important challenge to the other theoretical roots of family intervention science.

Science and Scientific Method

Beginning with the effectiveness challenge issued by Eysenck (1952) and the early meta-analysis of Smith, Glass, and Miller (1980), we have steadily improved our ability to measure the outcome and process of psychological interventions. In many ways, the profession has answered questions of general effectiveness and now is focusing on more "prescriptive treatment" that might answer the early challenge from Paul (1969) to find what treatment delivered by whom is most effective with a specific problem under which set of circumstances. The philosophy and guidelines embedded in the empirically validated and supported treatment movement have come to define the practical application of current psychological intervention science (see Chambless et al., 1996). The evolution of this movement is at the hub of several social, professional, and historic forces that are converging (Waehler, 1998). The broader cultural factors in this movement center on the increased interest in accountability in response to the rapid rise in behavioral health care costs (Rice, 1996) as manifested in managed health care. Within psychology, empirically validated and supported treatments are a logical development in the progression of outcome research.

As currently practiced, intervention science is deeply rooted in the logical positivist assumptions of traditional scientific method. From this perspective, the primary orientation is one where knowledge is believed to be objective fact, independent of the person or the observer. "Truth" is seen as a set of stable and objective laws and universal principles that are discoverable through objective observation, formal logic, and rational thought. As suggested by Mahoney (1991), the logical positivist assumptions of the "modern era" have become synonymous with the methods of "good science."

The unitary philosophical foundation of current intervention science poses an interesting set of dialectic developmental tensions. On the one hand, a number of positive outcomes are associated with the empirical movement, including improved dissemination of knowledge, the potential improvement in client care, influence on policy makers, fostering better training, encouraging psychother-apy research, and promoting discussion (R. Elliott, 1998). On the other hand, the empirical movement has fueled the race for the most effective interventions based on the rules of traditional scientific method. The search for this inter-vention "holy grail" now leads one to argue effect sizes, to insist on treatment adherence, and to use linear, directed treatment protocols and overly narrow approaches (Henry, 1998). In this context, many have argued that this process has the potential for actually harming intervention science. For example, Henry (1998) asserted that the empirical movement's dictate that "a certain type of research (diagnosis-based clinical trials), based on certain assumptions (the im-portant elements of therapy can be more or less standardized), with specific criteria for success (empirical validation) which . . . entrench an outdated re-search paradigm that mitigates the discovery of new knowledge" (p. 127).

Curiously, with all the emphasis in intervention science on identifying "best practices" in individual psychotherapy, the family-based approaches are not in-cluded in any of the lists generated by the empirical movement in psychology, despite impressive efficacy and effectiveness evidence, which will be discussed in more detail later. Thus, FT-FPIS remains an "outsider," yet this outsider status may actually have created a positive context. In particular, FT-FPIS has accu-mulated its impressive outcome evidence in numerous efficacy studies—hallmark strengths of the empirical focus—but seems to have done so through avoiding many of the earlier noted criticisms that have been levied against randomized controlled trials.

The Context of Culture

Culture mediates our conceptions of reality and causality and thus sets the stage for ways in which we view issues that are at the very center of the discipline (e.g., who is normal, what is considered a problem, in what way should we approach problems, and what are the goals of research and practice). Family therapy has always been attuned to social issues, the social structure, and power hierarchies within culture. Gender, race, and class have been major organizing themes within the context of culture, and the family systems models often have struggled with issues relating to the treatment of women as well as issues of power regarding gender, class, and race. These cultural values became part of the fabric of the "internal dialogue" of family therapy and characterize much of the published literature and the agendas of professional meetings.

The recently emerging cultural values of accountability and pragmatism are another genre of increasingly powerful contextual forces. In 1996, the cost of health care topped $1 trillion for the first time, an increase that focused considerable attention on the efficiency of our system. Managed health care is both a social and business entity that has come about in the climate of dramatically increasing health care costs. Managed care groups have a significant investment in promoting a movement that defines accountability, cost–benefit analysis, and the identification of effective treatment as the most important goals of psychology intervention science. These cultural factors are now being demonstrated in the decision of various federal and state agencies to mandate empirically validated treatments for social problems of delinquency (e.g., the Washington State Community Juvenile Accountability Act Conference; Sexton, Alexander, & Harrison, 1998).

The Emergence of Coherence

It is not intuitively obvious how and why the inherent contradictions of the roots of FT-FPIS (theory, science, and culture) could emerge as an organized and growing body of thought, research, and practice. With perhaps rare exception, it is doubtful that the Hegelian dialectic process was consciously undertaken by participants in the formative years of FT-FPIS. It is more likely that those trajectories intersected (often in dia*tribe* rather than dia*logue*) in a dynamic systemic process, and a "new frame" emerged that was different from the aggregated content of the individual contributors. Such a process is not foreign to family therapy scholars, who from the conceptual beginnings of their field often asserted the principle that "the whole is greater than the sum of the parts" and that emergent properties could not be described in terms of their component contributors.

By arguing the emergence of a coherent FT-FPIS, we are not suggesting that dynamic tension did not and does not continue to exist among the forces of theory, culture, and science. For example, Minuchin (1998) recently questioned the absence of a family focus in narrative approaches to family therapy. The earlier review of family therapy undertaken by Gurman and Kniskern (1978), which is considered by some to be a punctuation of the formal emergence of FT-FPIS, seemed to reflect a strong "science" emphasis and a downplaying of family therapy "practice" that existed outside the domain of methodologically sound research. Thereafter, however, Gurman, Kniskern, and Pinsof (1986) criticized intervention programs that were not replicated on different populations, thereby reflecting at least an openness to a major emphasis of multicultural thought as a distal root of FT-FPIS. We suggest that such examples illustrate a natural state of tension that is both the result of and source of the developmental process of family intervention science.

Current Status: The Emergence of Family-Based, Empirically Supported Treatments

Despite the ongoing natural tensions, the emerging domain of FT-FPIS is epitomized by programs that have accomplished what Szapocznik, Kurtines, Santisteban, and Rio (1990) referred to as "the dynamic interplay between theory, research, and practice" (p. 701). In fact, we suggest that FT-FPIS is epitomized by family-based, empirically supported treatments (FBESTs; Alexander, 1998), which evolved out of the early pragmatic approaches to family therapy (Hazelrigg, Cooper, & Borduin, 1987). Each of these approaches is built on the meta-analytic studies that find family therapy as a general intervention approach to be successful with a variety of clients in many different settings (Hazelrigg et al., 1987; Shadish et al., 1993). Approaches used in FBESTs, although different from each other in several ways, share much in common in that they each combine specific treatment protocols (manuals) that are conducted with realistic populations, in actual clinical settings, and within ongoing, systematic programs of research and evaluation. As such, FBEST approaches focus on (a) core therapeutic processes as well as outcome; (b) the principles of "good science"; (c) the importance of applying theory in a manner responsive to the co-created (therapist and family) reality of the clinical session; and (d) doing so in a way that incorporates sensitivity to cultural and other factors relating to diversity. Currently, four clinical intervention programs seem to meet these FBEST criteria: functional family therapy (Alexander & Parsons, 1973), multidimensional family therapy (Liddle, 1995, 2001), multisystemic therapy (Borduin, Henggeler, Blaske, & Stein, 1990; Henggeler et al., 1991), and brief strategic structural family therapy (as developed by Szapocznik & Kurtines, 1989). To date, these FBEST intervention programs have focused primarily on areas of adolescent disruptive disorders and the accompanying problems of delinquency, drug abuse, and family conflict. We think these programs are an important developmental milestone in that they capture the frame shift of FT-FPIS and enjoy the positive effect of developing outside the mainstream of psychology while holding fast to the principles of intervention science.

Do Family-Based, Empirically Supported Treatments Work in a Variety of Settings?

In a series of randomized clinical trials spanning 30 years (e.g., Alexander & Parsons, 1973; Borduin et al., 1990; Hansson et al., 1998; Henggeler et al., 1991; Liddle et al., in press; Szapocznik, et al., 1988), plus additional controlled outcome studies (Barton, Alexander, Waldron, Turner, & Warburton, 1985; Gordon, 1995; Gordon et al., 1988, Gordon, Graves, & Arbuthnot, 1995), FBEST researchers and program developers have demonstrated dramatic decreases in adolescent disruptive behavior disorders. The positive effects of FBEST interventions have been evident as long as 4 and 5 years posttreatment (Gordon et al., 1995), and positive preventive effects of functional family therapy have been shown to extend to at least 3 years with siblings of treated youth (Klein, Alexander, & Parsons, 1977). In addition, Szapocznik and colleagues (Santisteban et al., 1996; Szapocznik et al., 1988) have demonstrated that a family-based, structural strategic systems engagement intervention before formal intervention was successful in doubling (to more than 90%) the engagement and retention rate of Hispanic youths and their families in treatment. Table 2-1 presents a sample of representative FBEST studies of adolescents with behavior problems and the degree of improvement in FBEST versus alternatively treated youths.

A key development of the clinical research teams of Liddle and Szapocznik is the expansion of family-based interventions into clinical work that incorporates interactions among the youth, family, school, peer, justice, and neighborhood systems (Liddle, 1995; Liddle, Dakof, & Diamond, 1991; Szapocznik et al., 1997). In large part these ecosystemic developments have been influenced by Henggeler and colleagues' development of multisystemic therapy (Henggeler, Melton, & Smith, 1992) to work with youths with severe behavior problems.

Do Family-Based, Empirically Supported Treatments Work With Naturally Occurring Disorders, Diverse Populations, and in "Real" Community Settings?

One of the unique aspects of family-based intervention research is that it has been replicated in community settings with local therapists and actual varied client problems. For example, multisystemic therapy (Henggeler et al., 1992, 1993) produced significant reductions in recidivism with African American and Caucasian youths and families, and strategic structural family therapy (Szapocznik & Kurtines, 1989) has been successfully implemented with Hispanic and African American youths and families.

The extent to which FBEST programs have been locally implemented is impressive. For example, in the recently published *Blueprints for Effective Violence Prevention* series (D. Elliott, 1998; Alexander, Pugh, & Parsons, 1998; see also Alexander, Pugh, Parsons, & Sexton, 2000), many independent replications were listed with various populations and conditions:

- African American and mixed ethnicity urban families, many headed by single mothers, treated with in-home functional family therapy provided by already practicing community professionals (Schulman, 1998);

TABLE 2-1

Review of findings from selected family-based, empirically supported treatment studies

STUDY	MODEL	OUTCOME	COMPARISON CONDITION	FOLLOW-UP PERIOD
Alexander & Parsons (1973)	FFT	- 23% reduction in recidivism/rearrest compared to - 47% - 25%	- Juvenile court-group therapy - Eclectic/dynamic therapy - No treatment	6–18 months
Barton et al. (1985)	FFT	- 33% reduction in recidivism/rearrest compared to - 29%	- Group home therapy - Average institutional base rate	16 months
Borduin et al. (1990)	MST	- 45% reduction in recidivism/rearrest compared to	- Juvenile court-regular services	48 months
Gordon et al. (1988)	FFT	- 56% reduction in recidivism/rearrest compared to	- Juvenile court-regular services	30 months
Gordon et al. (1995)	FFT	- 32% reduction in arrests as adults compared to	- Juvenile court-regular services	60 months
Gordon (1995)	FFT	- 31% reduction in recidivism/rearrest compared to	- Juvenile court-regular services	16 months
Hansson (1998)	FFT	- 30% reduction in recidivism/rearrest compared to	- Social services therapy/ case management	24 months
Henggeler et al. (1992)	MST	- 23% reduction in recidivism/rearrest compared to	- Juvenile court-regular services	12 months

Henggeler et al. (1993)	MST	- 19% reduction in recidivism/rearrest compared to	- Juvenile court-regular services	29 months
Klein et al. (1977)	FFT	- 20% reduction in recidivism/rearrest compared to - 39% - 43%	- No treatment - Juvenile court-group therapy - Eclectic/dynamic therapy	30–42 months
Liddle et al. (in press)	MDFT	- 31% reduction in drug use compared to - 3%	- Multifamily therapy - Group therapy	12 months
Santisteban et al. (1996)	SFT	- 44% clinically reliable improvement in conduct disorder compared to	- Group therapy	- Termination
Szapocznik et al. (1988)	SFT	- 51% improvement in engagement compared to - 52% improvement in retention	- Group therapy - Engagement-as-usual condition	- Engagement - Retention

Note. FFT = functional family therapy; MST = multisystemic therapy; MDFT = multidimensional family therapy; SFT = structural family therapy.

- White and Hispanic youths treated with functional family therapy provided by university personnel as well as community professionals (Waldron, 1998),

- White, African American, and mixed ethnic families treated with functional family therapy in a community mental health study by already practicing professionals (Barton, 1998);

- poor, rural, Appalachian families treated with functional family therapy provided in the home by supervised graduate students (Gordon, 1995); and

- Hispanic, African American, White, and a few Native American and Asian American families, many headed by a single parent, treated with functional family therapy in the home by a mixture of university-based graduate students and already practicing community professionals (Sexton, 1998).

Why Do Family-Based, Empirically Supported Treatments Work?

One of the unique features of the family-based interventions is the long-term and systematic research effort aimed at identifying the mechanisms and processes of therapeutic change. This research links specific within-session processes with the outcome of family-based interventions in such a way that therapists can be informed about which constructs and processes appear across many, if not all, interventions, and which ones are unique to specific populations. Family-based intervention programs have a particularly impressive record of process research primarily focused on four areas: (a) the therapeutic alliance, (b) within-family negativity, (c) family interaction, and (d) family communication patterns. In addition, there is a growing interest in issues of program adherence and treatment fidelity and their effects on therapeutic outcome. Given the substantial research evidence, these areas represent systematic therapeutic mechanisms to which we can attribute client change.

Family-Based, Empirically Supported Treatment as an Intervention Science

These diverse, controlled studies reveal a picture of outcome evaluations, which render the traditional criticisms regarding empirical shortcomings inappropriate with respect to FBESTs. Rather than being an exception, these therapies in fact have been characterized by intervention with "real" youths (e.g., comorbid, ethnically diverse, and representing a wide range of socioeconomic status) in "real" settings (e.g., home, community) by "real" therapists (practicing professionals with diverse training backgrounds). Follow-up periods have often been of long duration, with outcome criteria reflecting clinical significance (e.g., back in school, rearrest) as well as statistical superiority.

In addition to having already obviated many of these traditional criticisms, FBESTs have undertaken, often as a matter of course, the activities recommended by Henry (1998), principles that are necessary to avoid long-term negative consequences of psychotherapy research:

- using "aptitude x treatment" interaction designs that are broadly defined and emphasize central therapeutic processes and core pathologies;
- redefining research problems as formulations that take into account problem processes and maintaining conditions;
- identifying phase-specific therapy goals; and
- combining basic science and services research.

For example, rather than inhibiting further process research, in the case of functional family therapy, as noted earlier, the long history of outcome research has been paralleled by ongoing careful investigations of in-session change mechanisms (e.g., Robbins, Alexander, et al., 1996) and the impact of therapist characteristics and family member roles on interactive behaviors (Alexander, Barton, Schiavo, & Parsons, 1976; Mas, Turner, & Alexander, 1991; Newberry, Alexander, & Turner, 1991; Warburton & Alexander, 1985).

Probably one of the most important developments in this regard is the cross-site (University of Utah Department of Psychology and University of Miami School of Medicine) collaboration to identify "core change mechanisms" in family therapy with drug-abusing youths and their families. As part of the National Institute on Drug Abuse (NIDA)-funded Center for Treatment Research with Adolescent Drug Abuse (P50 DA 11328; Howard Liddle, Principal Investigator), this study examines the in-session behaviors of therapists and family members in three intervention models (functional family therapy, multidimensional family therapy, and structural family therapy) to identify core family processes and therapist interventions in family therapy with drug-abusing youths. The data thus are based on a multisite, multimodel, and multiethnic (African American, White, Hispanic) focus on core- and site-specific processes that involve FBESTs with adolescent disruptive behavior disorders involving both male and female adolescents.

FBESTs are also noteworthy in that they have, as suggested by Henry (1998), articulated and studied phase-specific goals (see Figure 2-2), therapist characteristics, and interventions (Alexander, Barton, Waldron, & Mas, 1983) as reflected in the current functional family therapy training manual (Alexander et al., in press).

FIGURE 2-2

	Engagement/ Motivation	Behavior Change	Generalization
Phase Goal	• develop therapeutic alliance • reduce negativity communication • minimize hopelessness • refocus solution attempts • reduce dropout • increase motivation for change	• develop and implement individualized change plans • change presenting delinquency behavior • build relational skills (communication, parenting, problem solving)	• maintain/generalize change • relapse prevention • community support/resources necessary to maintain change
Risk & Protective factors addressed	• negativity & blaming (risk) • hopelessness (risk) • credibility (protective) • alliance (protective) • •treatment availability (protective) • lack of motivation (risk)	• poor parenting (risk) • negative/blaming communication (risk) • positive parenting (protective) • supportive communication (protective) • temperament (context) • interpersonal needs (context) • parental pathology (context) • developmental level (context)	• poor relationship-school/community (risk) • low social support (risk) • •positive relationship-school/ community (protective)
Assessment focus	• behavioral (presenting problem, risk and protective factors) • relational • contextual (risk and protective factors)	• quality of relational skills (communication, problem solving, parenting) • compliance with behavior change plan • relational problem sequence	• community resources needed • maintenance of change

Functional Family Therapy

The dynamic, overlapping phases of functional family therapy are presented in the top portion. In the bottom portion, specific activities of each phase of therapy are addressed, including treatment goals, risk and protective factors addressed, focus of assessment, and interventions. From Sexton and Alexander (1999). Reprinted with permission.

At the same time, FBEST manuals are anything but linear and unresponsive at a level that would threaten sensitive and competent therapist functioning. For example, the functional family therapy manual is articulated as a clinical map (Sexton et al., 1998) that facilitates therapists' clinical decision making and guides their contingent responding behavior during the engagement and motivation phases of intervention (Alexander et al., 1983). Similarly, multisystemic therapy principles (Henggeler et al., 1996) emphasize the "fit between the identified problems and their broader systemic context" (p. 18) and the importance of interventions that "fit the developmental needs of the youth" (p. 20).

Conclusion

The emergence of FBESTs has been characterized by an integration of the trajectories of science, practice, and culture. The successful emergence of this "impossible" integration occurred only because of a frame shift in the development of family psychology that ushered in a new set of epistemological rules with which to think about research and practice. This frame shift is not so much based on the content of FT-FPIS but on the assumptions out of which it emerged and from which it continues to evolve. This process parallels in many ways the evolution of systems theory into dynamic systems theory (Fogel & Lyra, 1997).

The dynamic systems perspective suggests that new structures sometimes emerge out of the mutually constraining effect that two or more trajectories have on each other in a dynamic, dialogical manner (Fogel & Lyra, 1997). Naturally occurring examples of emergent structures include the parent–child bond, a peer relationship, an adult friendship, and a couple relationship. These structures are dynamic, self-organizing systems that over time may remain the same in name but change dramatically in process. Further, such change can be very positive, as in the case of children who mature and emancipate from parents (move from complementarity to symmetry in relational hierarchy) but retain a warm and loving relationship throughout. Unfortunately, we also know that some parent–child bonds can turn into destructive, enmeshed, and stifling processes, that friendships can deteriorate, and that some couples experience such terrible relational processes as domestic abuse.

Metaphorically we see family psychology intervention science and the family therapy that has evolved in that context as a dynamically self-organized emergent system that is conceptually akin to the relationships mentioned earlier. Although the evolutionary outcome of organizational development is not determinable (Colarelli, 1998), what is certain is that FT-FPIS continues to evolve and mature. Instead of seeing it as someday finding a finite, static answer to complex questions, we would suggest that there should and hopefully will be a constant evolution with a never-ending stream of new perspectives. From this perspective, the current tension that exists among the forces of science, practice, and culture is natural and desirable rather than a problem that needs to be solved. One could expect that the developmental trajectory will, as it should, be characterized by debate, dialogue, and discussion in which we retain the perspective of each of these factors and thus retain the uniqueness of FT-FPIS.

Colarelli (1998) suggested that at any point in time multiple choices exist in the evolution of a system, but those early in its history are likely to have the most lasting impact. At any point the particular path chosen has the effect of constraining the course of some future events while promoting others. Thus, despite all the impressive accomplishments chronicled earlier, family psychology quite naturally will continue to have important choice points. For FT-FPIS, choice points reflect the converging factors of theory, science, and culture, each of which pulls in seemingly contradictory ways.

Now that FT-FPIS occupies a "position" in intervention science, we face the challenge of considering how the assumptions inherent in mainstream intervention science will influence its future. The origins of the modernistic perspective grew out of the assumptions of mechanism rooted in Newtonian mechanics and Descartian rationalism (Prigogine & Stengers, 1984) and positivism (Colarelli, 1998). Positivism assumes that scientifically verifiable knowledge is the primary and most appropriate view of reality (Cronbach, 1986) and that any other knowledge is less valid. Family researchers have long suggested that such narrowly focused research should not continue to be carried out in narrowly reductionistic ways in which only improvement rates are reported without attention to contextual conditions (Wynne, 1988). This challenge is as significant today as ever, given what appears to be the increased press of intervention science to reify only positivist research strategies. If we are to remain true to our current developmental trajectory, we will resist this modernistic temptation to make complex processes overly simple and thereby lose their meaning.

To accomplish this, researchers in family psychology will need to continue to investigate the complex factors that promote and maintain problems as well as the therapeutic methods to change them. Of most importance is that we retain the complexity of the behavior change process. Clinical studies that focus on the efficiency of programs and measuring the multiple outcomes of a phasically based change model by a wide range of interventionists will further our understanding of the ecological validity of our therapy models. Studies will need to address the concerns of treatment manuals and model adherence. Process research, exemplified by the FBEST approaches, contributes to our understanding of various change mechanisms that contribute to successful outcome. To further improve the effectiveness of our interventions we must continue to be attuned to our own experience of the clinical environment to identify critical in-session processes that influence relevant outcomes (e.g., Diamond & Liddle, 1996; Robbins, Mitrani, et al., 1996).

This attention to the clinical environment has also influenced the research questions we have asked and has shaped the designs and analytic strategies we have used to answer these questions. New approaches to those efforts regarding redefining client problem definitions (Friedlander & Hetherington, 1998) and the narrative nature of relational systems (Sexton & Griffin, 1997) are among many research programs from the constructivist epistemology that have added to this tradition. This perspective has the potential to help FT-FPIS further unravel the complexity of relational systems through emphasizing the central importance of language and meaning (Efran & Fauber, 1995; Gergen, 1985; Gordon & Efran, 1997), reformulating research questions, and expanding research methods. For example, although functional family therapy is strongly rooted in intervention science through its rigorous process and outcome research, it is also clear that the principles of constructivist thinking offer an intriguing perspective on the core notions of reframing and cultural sensitivity. In this regard, the role of language and meaning in the construction of problems both within families and therapy is a rich area for bridging the gap between traditional intervention science and constructivist thinking within this therapy.

The future also holds the challenge of combining basic science and services research (see Schoenwald & Henggeler, chapter 13, this volume). The family therapies described earlier have always integrated the principles of intervention science into real-world settings. Such integration helps to bridge the research–practice gap and to better integrate science from one side and relevance from the other (Sexton, Whiston, Bleuer, & Walz, 1997). It also focuses attention on questions that are rarely addressed in traditional research settings, such as: What degree of training of interventionists is optimal? To what extent do interventionists need to adhere to the original model? How can a treatment manual be developed so that it provides a guiding map of therapy while accounting for the unique occurrences in treatment? Studies are just now beginning to investigate these questions.

In the same way that dynamic systems theory challenged our traditional views of human behavior (Masterpasqua & Perna, 1997), we have tried to simultaneously chronicle and challenge the implicit assumptions of development in family psychology. Such a challenge is important because the assumptions one holds about the purpose and outcome of development shape the future course of the developmental trajectory.

In light of this, we argue that the traditional intervention science philosophy can tend to promote a hierarchical, oppositional, and "better than" mentality, using already existing frameworks to evaluate ourselves. Such a path would simply be a continuation along a developmental trajectory that might appear to represent change but in reality is "more of the same."

Instead, we put our faith in the same dialectic that has been so beneficial to the present emergence of FT-FPIS. We suggest viewing debate, dialogue, and change as the desired products of development rather than merely the mechanism to a final state, and we hope that the inclusiveness of inputs to FT-FPIS that we have described encourage more debate and dialogue.

References

Alexander, J. F. (1998, October). *Effective family therapies with indicated youth*. Invited presentation at the CSAP Science Symposia Series: Bridging the Gap Between Research and Practice in Substance Abuse Prevention, Rockville, MD.

Alexander, J. F. (1999, April). *Helping troubled families change: Providing hope and direction*. Keynote speaker, Plenary, Fourth Annual Parenting Conference, LaTrobe University, Melbourne.

Alexander, J. F., Barton, C., Schiavo, R. S., & Parsons, B. V. (1976). Behavioral intervention with families of delinquents: Therapist characteristics and outcome. *Journal of Consulting and Clinical Psychology, 44*, 656–664.

Alexander, J. F., Barton, C., Waldron, H., & Mas, C. H. (1983). Beyond the technology of family therapy: The anatomy of intervention model. In K. D. Craig & R. J. McMahon (Eds.), *Advances in Clinical Behavior Therapy*. New York: Brunner/Mazel.

Alexander, J. F., & Parsons, B. V. (1973). Short term behavioral intervention with delinquent families: Impact on family process and recidivism. *Journal of Abnormal Psychology, 81*, 219–225.

Alexander, J. F., Pugh, C., & Parsons, B. (Eds.). (1998). Book three: Functional family therapy. In D. Elliott (Series Ed.), *Blueprints for violence prevention*. Golden, CO: Venture.

Alexander, J. F., Pugh, C., Parsons, B., & Sexton, T. L. (Eds.). (2000). Book three: Functional family therapy. In D. Elliott (Series Ed.), *Blueprints for violence prevention* (2nd ed.). Golden, CO: Venture.

Anderson, H., & Goolishian, H. (1988). Human systems as linguistic systems: Preliminary and evolving ideas about the implications for clinical theory. *Family Process, 27*, 371–394.

Barton, C. (1998). Fayetteville, North Carolina: Community Mental Health Center: Treatment of aggressive/conduct disordered youth. In J. F. Alexander, C. Pugh, &

B. Parsons (Vol. Eds.), *Blueprints for violence prevention, book three: Functional family therapy* (pp. 64–66). Golden, CO: Venture.

Barton, C., Alexander, J. F., Waldron, H., Turner, C. W., & Warburton, J. (1985). Generalizing treatment effects of Functional Family Therapy: Three replications. *American Journal of Family Therapy, 13,* 16–26.

Bateson, G., Jackson, D., Haley, J., & Weakland, J. (1956). Toward a theory of schizophrenia. *Behavioral Science, 1,* 251–254.

Borduin, C. M., Cone L. T., Mann, B. J., Henggeler, S. W., Fucci, B. R., Blaske, D. M., & Williams, R. A. (1995). Multisystemic treatment of serious juvenile offenders: Long-term prevention of criminality and violence. *Journal of Consulting and Clinical Psychology, 63,* 569–578.

Bowen, M. (1978). *Family therapy in clinical practice.* New York: Jason Aronson.

Chambless, D. L., Sanderson, W. C., Shoham, V., Bennett Johnson, S., Pope, K. S., Crits-Christoph, P., Baker, M., Johnson, B., Woody, S. R., Sue, S., Beutler, L., Williams, D. A., & McCurry, S. (1996). An update on empirically validated therapies. *Clinical Psychologist, 49,* 5–18.

Colarelli, S. M. (1998). Psychological interventions in organizations: An evolutionary perspective. *American Psychologist, 53,* 1044–1056.

Cronbach, L. J. (1986). Social inquiry by and for earthlings. In D. W. Fiske & R. A. Shweder (Eds.), *Metatheory in social science: Pluralism and subjectives* (pp. 83–107). Chicago: University of Chicago Press.

Diamond, G. S., & Liddle, H. A. (1996). Resolving therapeutic impasses between parents and adolescents in multidimensional family therapy. *Journal of Consulting and Clinical Psychology, 64*(3), 481–488.

Efran, J. S., & Fauber, R. L. (1995). Radical constructivism: Questions and answers. In R. A. Neimeyer & M. J. Mahoney (Eds.), *Constructivism in psychotherapy* (pp. 275–304). Washington, DC: American Psychological Association.

Efran, J. S., Lukens, M. D., & Lukens, R. J. (1990). *Language, structure, and change: Frameworks of meaning in psychotherapy.* New York: Norton.

Elliott, D. (Series Ed.). (1998). *Blueprints for effective violence prevention.* Golden, CO: Venture.

Elliott, R. (1998). Editor's introduction: A guide to the empirically supported treatments controversy. *Psychotherapy Research, 8,* 115–125.

Eysenck, H. J. (1952). The effects of psychotherapy: An evaluation. *Journal of Consulting Psychology, 16,* 319–324.

Fisher, L. (1982). Transactional theories but individual assessment: A frequent discrepancy in family research. *Family Process, 21,* 313–320.

Fisher, L., Terry, H. E., & Ransom, D. (1990). Advancing a family perspective in health research: Models and methods. *Family Process, 29,* 177–189.

Fogel, A., & Lyra, M. (1997). Dynamics of development in relationships. In F. Masterpasqua & P. Perna (Eds.), *The psychological meaning of chaos: Self-organization in human development and psychotherapy* (pp. 75–94). Washington, DC: American Psychological Association.

Foucault, M. (1980). *Power/Knowledge: Selected interviews and other writings*. New York: Pantheon Books.

Friedlander, M. L., & Heatherington, L. (1998). Assessing clients' constructions of their problems in family therapy discourse. *Journal of Marital and Family Therapy, 24*(3), 289–304.

Gergen, K. (1985). The social constructionist movement in modern psychology. *American Psychologist, 40,* 266–273

Gordon, D. A. (1995). Functional family therapy for delinquents. In R. P. Ross, D. H. Antonowicz, & G. K. Dhaliwal (Eds.), *Going straight: Effective delinquency prevention and offender rehabilitation* (pp. 163–178). Ottawa, Canada: Air Training & Publications.

Gordon, D. A., Arbuthnot, J., Gustafson, K. E., & McGreen, P. (1988). Home-based behavioral–systems family therapy with disadvantaged juvenile delinquents. *American Journal of Family, 16,* 243–255.

Gordon, D. A., Graves, K., & Arbuthnot, J. (1995). The effect of functional family therapy for delinquents on adult criminal behavior. *Criminal Justice and Behavior, 22,* 60–73.

Gordon, D. E., & Efran, J. S. (1997). Therapy and the dance of language. In T. L. Sexton & B. L. Griffin (Eds.), *Constructivist thinking in counseling practice, research, and training*. New York: Teachers College Press.

Gurman, A. S., & Kniskern, D. P. (1978). Research on marital and family therapy; Progress, perspective, and prospect. In S. L. Garfield & A. E. Bergin (Eds.), *Handbook of psychotherapy and behavior change: An empirical analysis* (2nd ed., pp. 817–901). New York: Wiley.

Gurman, A. S., Kniskern, D. P., & Pinsof, W. M. (1986). Research on the process and outcome of marital and family therapy. In S. L. Garfield & A. E. Bergin (Eds.), *Handbook of psychotherapy and behavior change* (3rd ed., pp. 565–624). New York: Wiley.

Hansson, K. (1998, February). *Functional family therapy replication in Sweden: Treatment outcomes with juvenile delinquents*. Paper presented to the Eighth International Conference on Treating Addictive Behaviors, Santa Fe, NM.

Hayes, R. L., & Oppenheim, R. (1997). Constructivism: Reality is what you make it. In T. L. Sexton & B. L. Griffin (Eds.), *Constructivist thinking in counseling practice, research, and training*. New York: Teachers College Press.

Hazelrigg, M. D., Cooper, H. M., & Borduin, C. M. (1987). Evaluating the effectiveness of family therapies: An integrative review and analysis. *Psychological Bulletin, 101,* 428–442.

Henggeler, S. W., Borduin, C. M., Melton, G. B., Mann, B. J., Smith, L. A., Hall, J. A., Cone, L., & Fucci, B. R. (1991). Effects of multisystemic therapy on drug use and abuse in serious juvenile offenders: A progress report from two outcome studies. *Family Dynamics Addiction Quarterly, 1,* 40–51.

Henggeler, S. W., Melton, G. M., & Smith, L. A. (1992). Family preservation using multisystemic therapy: An effective alternative to incarcerating serious juvenile offenders. *Journal of Consulting and Clinical Psychology, 60,* 953–961.

Henggeler, S. W., Melton, G. M., Smith, L. A., Schoenwald, S. K., & Hanley, J. H. (1993). Family preservation using multisystemic treatment: Long-term follow-up to a clinical trial with serious juvenile offenders. *Journal of Child and Family Studies, 2,* 283–293.

Henggeler, S. W., Rodick, J. D., Borduin, C. M., Hanson, C. L., Watson, S. M., & Urey, J. R. (1996). Multisystemic treatment of juvenile offenders: Effects on adolescent behavior and family interaction. *Developmental Psychology, 22,* 132–141.

Henry, W. P. (1998). Science, politics, and the politics of science: The use and misuse of empirically validated treatment research. *Psychotherapy Research, 8*(2), 126–140.

Hoffman, L. (1981). *Foundations of family therapy.* New York: Basic Books.

Hoshmand, L. T., & Martin, J. (1995). Concluding comments on therapeutic psychology and the science of practice. In L. T. Hoshmand & J. Martin (Eds.), *Research as praxis* (pp. 235–241). New York: Teachers College Press.

Howard, G. S. (1985). Can research in the human sciences become more relevant to practice? *Journal of Counseling and Development, 63,* 539–544.

Jameson, P. B., & Alexander, J. F. (1993). Implications of a developmental family systems model for clinical practice. In L. L'Abate (Ed.), *Handbook of developmental family psychology and psychopathology.* New York: Wiley.

Klein, N. C., Alexander, J. F., & Parsons, B. V. (1977). Impact of family systems intervention on recidivism and sibling delinquency: A model of primary prevention and program evaluation. *Journal of Consulting and Clinical Psychology, 45,* 469–474.

Lebow, J. (1997). The integrative revolution in couple and family therapy. *Family Process, 36*(1), 1–17.

Liddle, H. A. (1995). Conceptual and clinical dimensions of a multidimensional, multisystems engagement strategy in family-based adolescent treatment [Special issue]. *Psychotherapy: Theory, Research and Practice, 32,* 39–58.

Liddle, H. A. (2001). *Multidimensional family therapy treatment (MDFT) for adolescent cannabis users. (Volume 5 of the Cannabis Youth Treatment (CYT) manual series).* Rockville, MD: Center for Substance Abuse Treatment, Substance Abuse and Mental Health Services Administration.

Liddle, H. A., Dakof, G. A., & Diamond, G. (1991). Multidimensional family therapy with adolescent substance abuse. In E. Kaufman & P. Kaufman (Eds.), *Family therapy with drug and alcohol abuse* (pp. 120–178). Boston: Allyn & Bacon.

Liddle, H. A., Dakof, G. A., Parker, K., Diamond, G. S., Barrett, K., & Tejeda, M. (in press). Multidimensional family therapy for adolescent substance abuse: Results of a randomized clinical trial. *American Journal of Drug and Alcohol Abuse.*

Lidz, T., Cornelison, A., Fleck, S., & Terry, D. (1957). Intrafamilial environment of the schizophrenic patient. I: The father. *Psychiatry, 20,* 329–342.

Mahoney, M. J. (1991). *Human change processes: The scientific foundations of psychotherapy.* New York: Basic Books.

Mas, C. H., Turner, C. W., & Alexander, J. F. (1991). Dispositional attributions and defensive behavior in high and low conflict delinquent families. *Journal of Family Psychology, 5,* 176–191.

Masterpasqua, F., & Perna, P. (1997). *The psychological meaning of chaos: Self-organization in human development and psychotherapy.* Washington, DC: American Psychological Association.

Maturana, H. R., & Varela, F. J. (1979). *The tree of knowledge: The biological roots of human understanding.* Boston: New Science Library.

Minuchin, S. (1974). *Families and family therapy.* Cambridge, MA: Harvard University Press.

Minuchin, S. (1998). Where is the family in narrative family therapy? *Journal of Marital and Family Therapy 24*(4), 397–403.

Nelson, M. L., & Poulin, K. (1997). Methods of constructivist inquiry. In T. L. Sexton & B. L. Griffin (Eds.), *Constructivist thinking in counseling practice, research, and training.* New York: Teachers College Press.

Newberry, A. M., Alexander, J. F., & Turner, C. W. (1991). Gender as a process variable in family therapy. *Journal of Family Psychology, 5*(2), 158–175.

Paul, G. (1969). Outcome research in psychotherapy. *Journal of Consulting and Clinical Psychology, 31,* 109–118.

Pinsof, W. M. (1983). Integrative Problem-Centered Therapy: Toward a synthesis of family and individual therapies. *Journal of Marital and Family Therapy, 9*(1), 19–35.

Prigogine, I., & Stengers, I. (1984). *Order out of chaos: Man's new dialogue with nature.* New York: Bantam Books.

Rice, T. (1996). Measuring health care costs and trends. In Anderson, R. T., & Kominski, G. (Eds.), *Changing the U.S. health care system: Key issues in health services, policy, and management.* San Francisco: Jossey-Bass.

Robbins, M. S., Alexander, J. F., Newell, R. M., & Turner, C. W. (1996). The immediate effect of reframing on client attitude in family therapy. *Journal of Family Psychology, 10,* 28–34.

Robbins, M. S., Mitrani, V., Zarate, M., Coatsworth, D., & Szapocznik, J. (1996, June). *Linking process to outcome in structural family therapy with drug using youth: An examination of the process of family therapy in successful and unsuccessful outcome cases.* Paper presented at the 27th annual meeting of the Society for Psychotherapy Research, Amelia Island, FL.

Santisteban, D. A., Szapocznik, J., Perez-Vidal, A., Kurtines, W., Murray, E. J., & La Perriere, A. (1996). Efficacy of interventions for engaging youth/families into treatment and some variables that may contribute to differential effectiveness. *Journal of Family Psychology, 10*(1), 35–44.

Schulman, S. (1998). Urban Ann Arbor, Michigan: COPE/O'BRIEN center: Delinquency prevention in a high-crime urban area. In D. Elliott (Series Ed.) & J. F. Alexander, C. Pugh, & B. Parsons (Vol. Eds.), *Blueprints for violence prevention, book three: Functional family therapy.* Golden, CO: Venture.

Sexton, T. (1998). Las Vegas: University of Nevada at Las Vegas, Harmony Health Care Agency and Boyd Gaming Co.: Treatment of conduct disorders through a collaborative, community-base approach. In D. Elliott (Series Ed.) & J. F. Alexander, C. Pugh, & B. Parsons (Vol. Eds.), *Blueprints for violence prevention, book three: Functional family therapy.* Golden, CO: Venture.

Sexton, T. L., & Alexander, J. F. (1999). *Functional family therapy: Principles of clinical intervention, assessment, and implementation.* Henderson, NV: FFT.

Sexton, T. L., Alexander, J. F., & Harrison, R. (1998, August). *Functional family therapy: Overview & state-wide initial training.* Paper presented at the Washington State Department of Social and Health Services, Juvenile Rehabilitation Administration, Washington State Community Juvenile Accountability Act Conference, Seattle, WA.

Sexton, T. L., & Griffin, B. L. (1997). *Constructivist thinking in counseling practice research and training.* New York: College Press, Columbia University.

Sexton, T. L., Whiston, S. C., Bleuer, J. C., & Walz, G. R. (1997). *Integrating outcome research into counseling practice and training.* Alexandria, VA: American Counseling Association.

Shadish, W. R., Montgomery, L. M., Wilson, P., Wilson, M. R., Bright, I., & Okwumabua, T. (1993). Effects of family and marital psychotherapies: A meta-analysis. *Journal of Consulting and Clinical Psychology, 61,* 992–1002.

Smith, M. L., Glass, G. V., & Miller, T. I. (1980). *The benefits of psychotherapy.* Baltimore: Johns Hopkins University Press.

Szapocznik, J., & Kurtines, W. M. (1989). *Breakthroughs in family therapy with drug abusing and problem youth.* New York: Springer.

Szapocznik, J., Kurtines, W., Santisteban, D. A., Pantin, H., Scopetta, M., Mancilla, Y., Aisenberg, S., McIntosh, S., Perez-Vidal, A., & Coatsworth, J. D. (1997). The evolution of structural ecosystemic theory for working with Latino families. In J. Garcia & M. C. Zea (Eds.), *Psychological interventions and research with Latino populations.* Boston: Allyn & Bacon.

Szapocznik, J., Kurtines, W. M., Santisteban, D. A., & Rio, A. T. (1990). Interplay of advances between theory, research, and application in treatment interventions aimed at behavior problem children and adolescents. *Journal of Consulting and Clinical Psychology, 58*(6), 696–703.

Szapocznik, J., Perez-Vidal, A., Brickman, A. L., Foote, F., Santisteban, D., Hervis, O., & Kurtines, W. (1988). Engaging adolescent drug abusers and their families into treatment. A strategic structural systems approach. *Journal of Consulting and Clinical Psychology, 56,* 552–557.

Waehler, C. A. (1998, August). *The EVT movement in professional psychology: A short history.* Paper presented at the Annual Convention of the American Psychological Association, San Francisco.

Waldron, H. (1998). Albuquerque, New Mexico: University of New Mexico: NIDA research, substance abusing youth. In D. Elliott (Series Ed.) & J. F. Alexander, C. Pugh, & B. Parsons (Vol. Eds.), *Blueprints for violence prevention, book three: Functional family therapy.* Golden, CO: Venture.

Warburton, J. R., & Alexander, J. F. (1985). The family therapist: What does one do? In L. L'Abate (Ed.), *Handbook of family psychology and therapy.* Homewood, IL: Dorsey Press.

White, M., & Epston, D. (1990). *Narrative means to therapeutic ends.* New York: Norton.

Wittgenstein, L. (1969). *Philosophical investigations* (3rd ed., G. Anscombe, Trans.). New York: Macmillan.

Wynne, J. C., Ryckoff, I., Day, J., & Hirsch, S. I. (1958). Pseudo-mutuality in the family relationships of schizophrenics. *Psychiatry, 21,* 205–220.

Wynne L. C. (1988). *The state of the art in family therapy and research: Controversies and recommendations.* New York: Family Process Press.

CHAPTER 3

Studying a Matrix of Change Mechanisms: An Agenda for Family-Based Process Research

Guy S. Diamond

Gary M. Diamond

Increasing evidence supports the efficacy of family-based psychotherapies for a variety of psychological disorders (G. S. Diamond, Serrano, Dickey, & Sonis, 1996; Pinsof & Wynne, 1995; Shadish, Montgomery, Wilson, Bright, & Okwimabua, 1993). To further improve the potency of these treatments, some family researchers have turned their attention to understanding the processes by which family therapy works. This research tradition, known as *process research,* strives to identify the active ingredients within the "black box" of therapy that lead to change. Researchers have begun to develop a body of empirical knowledge about the processes or mechanisms of change in family treatments. Excellent reviews of the literature are provided by Friedlander, Wildman, Heatherton, and Skowron (1994), Pinsof (1989), and Shoham-Salomon (1990). Unfortunately, only a few investigators have used process research to systematically identify, study, and enhance essential change mechanisms (for examples, see Liddle, 1999; Patterson & Chamberlain, 1988). A programmatic investigation of these mechanisms should promote treatment development and facilitate training of therapists, thereby enhancing treatment potency, cost effectiveness, and transportability.

In this chapter we present a framework for conceptualizing and conducting a programmatic process research agenda. This framework builds on the innovative epistemological and methodological contributions of discovery-oriented research, particularly task analysis (Rice & Greenberg, 1984). Although researchers usually use task analysis to study single, isolated change events, we propose extending this method to look at a matrix of change processes and how they evolve and interact over time. We then offer a three-stage investigative agenda to examine such a matrix. Finally, we suggest that process research would advance more rapidly if researchers focused on a few transtheoretical change processes that are common to many family interventions. Selection and study of these processes should be informed by psychological science. Based on our model of attachment-based family therapy (ABFT; G. S. Diamond, 1998; G. S. Diamond & Siqueland, 1995), we suggest four specific mechanisms for this agenda: *reattribution, alliance, parenting,* and *reattachment*. Finally, we review selected process studies that represent innovative work being done on each of these mechanisms.

Historical Context of the Discovery-Oriented Paradigm

Process research began more than 50 years ago. Until recently, process studies traditionally relied on naturalistic designs where frequency counts of variables across sessions were correlated with other processes or outcomes. These studies generally focused on variables such as client and therapist characteristics, the therapeutic bond, therapeutic interventions, and patient psychological functioning (Beutler, Cargo, & Arizmendi, 1986; Kiesler, 1973; Orlinsky & Howard, 1986). Over the last two decades, this approach has been criticized for its narrow focus on individual processes, lack of attention to context, small sample sizes, diverse and investigator-specific instruments, different definitions of similar constructs, correlational designs, minimal use of control groups, and reliance on frequency counts (see Elkin, 1985; Garfield, 1990). For example, knowing that 10 interpretations per session is more strongly correlated with outcome than 20 interpretations does not really help the therapist to know when to use interpretations. Further, Rice and Greenberg (1984) argued that past studies too often assumed a static delivery of therapeutic interventions and a fixed range of client responses. This uniformity myth prevented researchers from investigating specific processes that are critical mechanisms believed to contribute to change. Consequently, these studies have failed to inform clinical practice (VandenBos, 1989).

Discovery-Oriented Process Research

Many process researchers have responded to these criticisms by shifting focus from hypothesis testing or predictive methodologies to a discovery-oriented research paradigm (Elliott, 1984; Greenberg & Pinsof, 1986; Horowitz, 1979; Luborsky, 1984; Mahrer, 1988; Rice & Greenberg, 1984). Several principles characterize this new research approach. First, early stage investigations emphasize hypothesis generating and model building. Studies focus on describing moment-by-moment client and therapists patterns of change. Second, investigations are theory driven. Researchers use their theoretical and clinical assumptions about change to guide the selection and examination of clinical processes. Third, investigations focus on therapeutic events in the context of other therapeutic processes. For example, researchers might examine client behaviors before and after a particular intervention, taking into consideration the strength of the alliance and stage of therapy. Although traditional process research has failed to have an effect on the day-to-day practice of psychotherapy (Morrow-Bradley & Elliot, 1986), discovery-oriented, model-building studies yield clinically relevant information that can improve therapists' ability to identify and facilitate critical change opportunities. The discovery-oriented paradigm has freed investigators from the confines of a positivistic, hypothesis-testing tradition by offering creative yet rigorous scientific methods for studying the complex and elusive phenomena of therapy.

Task analysis (Rice & Greenberg, 1984) is the most developed and commonly used discovery-oriented paradigm. It uses qualitative and quantitative techniques to identify and describe the client's essential patterns of performance (e.g., behaviors, attributions, and emotions) during a critical change event in therapy. Change events often consist of four components: (a) a problem state (e.g., parent's negative attribution about the child's symptoms), (b) a specific intervention to resolve the problem state (e.g., reframing), (c) the client's response pattern to the interventions (e.g., parent's resistance followed by an emotional softening leading to a shift in attributions), and (d) the desired outcome or resolution (e.g., parent's acceptance of a systemic view of the problem). Change events, or tasks, usually represent core mechanisms in a given model of therapy believed to bring about change (e.g., enactment, reframing, two-chair technique). Examples of task analytic studies include resolving a therapeutic impasse (Coulehan, Friedlander, & Heatherington, 1998; G. S. Diamond & Liddle, 1996), resolving unfinished business (Greenberg & Foerster, 1996), and repairing ruptures in the alliance (Safran & Muran, 1996).

We applaud the current applications of the task analytic paradigm for understanding within-session processes. Still, these studies usually examine one task at a time, independent of the treatment context, when in fact therapy consists of several distinct, interdependent treatment tasks that evolve and interact over time. The sequencing of and relationship between these tasks may be as important as any single tasks itself. Based on these assumptions, we propose expanding the change event paradigm to include a focus on the evolution of single tasks over multiple sessions and the interaction of these multiple tasks over time.

Evolution of a Single Task

Change occurs in increments over time. Yet most task analysis studies are cross-sectional (i.e., one task occurring in several different cases) rather than longitudinal (i.e., the evolution of a single task over time within one or more cases). Analysis of single, isolated therapy events assume that therapy consists of discrete, one-time learning experiences. In contrast, therapists often work and rework therapeutic material (Liddle, 1999), taking several sessions to create the foundation for a task, working through it, and assimilating its outcome. Similarly, the nature, processes, and subgoals of a task may evolve each time the therapist revisits it.

For example, in ABFT, the first task is to shift the nature or explanation of the problem from a linear perspective (e.g., "My daughter is just selfish") to a more relational perspective on the problem (e.g., "We are no longer close"; G. S. Diamond & Siqueland, 1998). Although this shift can occur in session one, parents often revert back to blaming and criticizing during a later family crisis. Consequently, the therapist has to reintroduce the reframe (e.g., "It sounds like you both feel disrespected") in order to reestablish the treatment momentum. This second reframing process may unfold differently from the first because of new factors in the parent–child dyad, including the gains and failures of previous sessions. Studies of this evolution over time would shed light on the subtle decision rules that guide therapists in the moment-by-moment action of therapy.

Treatments as Multiple Tasks

Once a task-based approach is adopted for understanding change processes, a treatment model can be conceptualized as consisting of multiple, distinct, yet interrelated tasks. Family-based treatments in particular focus on multiple domains, each with its own treatment goals and processes to accomplish (e.g., improving parenting, building multiple alliance, reestablishing attachment, or promoting autonomy; G. S. Diamond, 1998; Liddle, 1999). Treatment is then viewed as a flow of several distinct therapeutic processes that interact, overlap, and intermingle with each other.

A task-based treatment framework can be conceptualized at varying levels of specification. Structural family therapy (Minuchin, 1974), for example, proposes several general principles and treatment goals that can be applied to any disorder at any time (e.g., improving boundaries, strengthening hierarchy, and engendering more developmentally appropriate interactions). Multidimensional family therapy (Liddle, 1999) targets a specific disorder and population (adolescent substance abusers), focuses on several specific treatment domains (e.g., adolescent, parent, family, and extrafamilial), and outlines several possible treatment goals and strategies within each domain. Attachment-based family therapy (G. S. Diamond, 1998) goes one step farther by defining specific tasks, articulating the procedures to accomplish them, and recommending the most effective sequence by which these tasks should be delivered.

For example, ABFT posits five primary change mechanisms and, when possible, suggests delivering them in a predetermined, clinically logical order (G. S. Diamond & Siqueland, 1995; G. S. Diamond, 1998). These mechanisms include (a) a reattribution task, (b) an alliance-building task alone with the adolescent and then (c) with the parent, (d) a reattachment task, and (e) a competency-promoting task. In the ideal treatment course, the success of one task sets the foundation for the next. For example, the reattribution task shifts the treatment goal from fixing the adolescent's problem behaviors to improving family relationships. This intervention reduces parental blame and criticism of the adolescent and establishes relationship repair as the primary initial treatment goal. In addition, this intervention establishes therapist credibility with the adolescent (foundation of the alliance task) and engages the parent with the adolescent (preparation for the reattachment task). Then the alliance-building task focuses on (a) identifying problems that have damaged trust between family members and (b) getting an agreement from the adolescent and parent to openly and nondefensively discuss these issues (G. S. Diamond & Liddle, 1996). In this regard, all the previous tasks culminate in the reattachment task: an open, honest, nondefensive, often emotion-laden parent–adolescent conversation about past attachment failures and the hope for future connectedness. Ideally during this task, parents become more emotionally available and attentive, while adolescents begin to confide more in their parents. As trust emerges, the adolescent increasingly uses the parents as a secure base from which to explore his or her own emerging autonomy (competency task). Therapists can accomplish tasks in one session, but often several sessions are needed before moving to the next task. However, awareness of the tasks and the logic of their ideal progression guide therapists' decision making during the treatment course.

Conceptualizing treatment as a multitask, multimechanism process allows investigators to ask interesting questions about psychotherapy processes. First, does each task have its own unique set of implementation procedures as well as desired and undesired client processes? In other words, how truly distinct are these tasks from one another? Second, is each task the primary focus of treatment at a specific point in time or a secondary or tertiary focus at other times as well? For example, when a parent accepts a reframe in the first session, does this cognitive change need continuous monitoring and reworking? If so, how much and how often? Third, what is "good enough" outcome for a task? Is a parent's partial acceptance of a reframe enough of a "sign on" for the therapist to begin the next task? If so, by what criteria does the therapist weigh this judgment? If not, how is the reworking of the task different the second time (e.g., intensity, content, duration)? Fourth, are the different tasks interrelated? Are processes in one task actually setting the foundation for processes in another task? Does a good reframe, for example, set the foundation for alliance building and eventually the reattachment task? Does the order of the tasks matter? What variations might be needed for which kind of patient or family? Answers to these questions could help us to understand the treatment process as a matrix of distinct yet interlocking change events that ebb and flow in and out of prominence across the course of treatment. The degree of success of each task, the sequence of tasks, and the cumulative effect of several tasks may all equally contribute to outcome.

Investigating Multiple Mechanisms

To study a matrix of change events, we propose a three-stage research agenda. Stage I consists of using traditional change event, discovery-oriented research methods (e.g., task analysis) to identify and study several independent yet essential change mechanisms within a model. This requires reconceptualizing therapy as a series of treatment tasks. Stage II consists of identifying (or developing) and applying measurement tools to assess the success and evolution of each task. Stage III consists of examining how multiple distinct change mechanisms overlap and interact with each other over the course of treatment to produce the intended therapeutic outcomes.

Stage I: Task Analysis

The systematic thinking and innovative model-building methods of task analysis serve as an excellent starting point for studying a matrix of change mechanisms. In this paradigm, investigators begin with the identification of the essential change mechanisms of the given model. Theoretical, empirical, and clinical knowledge inform the building of an initial ideal model of the change processes. Investigators operationalize these mechanisms as specific therapeutic tasks or events and then identify examples in actual therapy sessions (typically on videotape). Comparing the ideal model against the actual therapy segments, investigators arrive at a new performance model. Researchers then use objective coders to assess processes associated with the change event. This information is used to further elaborate the model. For example, in a study examining therapeutic impasses in family therapy (G. S. Diamond & Liddle, 1996), we used scales from the Beavers Timberlawn interactional instrument (Beavers, Hampson, & Hulgus, 1985) to code eight family functioning variables before, during, and after the change event. Integrating this objective information into the model, investigators arrive at a final descriptive "performance" map describing both patient and family processes and therapist procedures. Methods for validating these models have been proposed but rarely performed. We suggest that this process be performed on each core task or treatment mechanism.

Stage II: Measuring Task Outcome and Components

Once each treatment task has been identified and developed, assessment tools are needed to track the evolution of these processes over time. Unfortunately, measuring therapy process is a complicated and underdeveloped aspect of family research (Pinsof, 1989). Few psychometrically sound family measures exist that assess essential treatment processes and their relationship to outcome (Tolan, Hanish, McKay, & Dickey, 1997). For the purpose of assessing processes over time, however, two types of measurement tools are needed: observational or self-report instruments that would measure the outcome of tasks themselves, and ones that would measure the subtasks of a task. Task outcome measures would assess the extent to which a task has been resolved (e.g., whether a parent's attributions have shifted from a linear, blaming perspective to a more systemic view of shared responsibility). This has typically been referred to as small "o" outcome. Toward this goal, many studies have operationalized successful and unsuccessful tasks in order to identify actual change events to serve as the database for a study (e.g., five successful and five unsuccessful episodes). Investigators then typically measure other associated processes that characterize the change event (e.g., changes in voice quality) rather than define the extent of task success over time. For example, one might measure parent attributions about a problem (i.e., linear or systemic) for each session. Dichotomous (success or not) or continuous (to what degree) ratings could be used to assess change in this core construct. Evaluation of each family individually would also help capture the true complexity of clinical practice.

Several measurement tools could be adapted for this purpose. For example, Friedlander and Heatherington (1998) developed a rating scale that assesses each family member's attribution about the presenting problem (e.g., internal versus external, linear versus circular). Using this categorical instrument across several sessions, one could track whether family members accept a new systemic perspective after a reframing task and whether they regress back to their original attritional stance if this is not reinforced. As another example, Schmidt, Liddle, and Dakoff (1996) developed a coding system for assessing positive and negative parenting practices along several germane dimensions (e.g., discipline, monitoring, positive affect). This instrument could assess the development of effective parenting practices over time. Similarly, investigators could measure alliance across sessions, thereby assessing whether and when alliance is established and maintained.

An alternative method for assessing outcome would be to operationalize the change events into subtasks. For example, G. S. Diamond and Liddle (1996) conceptualized the resolution of an impasse as consisting of four subtasks: (a) parent shifts from feeling hostile to feeling sad, (b) adolescent shifts from indirectly to directly expressing anger, (c) parent acknowledges adolescent's hurt, and (d) adolescent forgives parent. In many episodes, not all subtasks are accomplished, but sessions may be "good enough" to move the therapy process along. An instrument that assesses subtasks could address which subtasks are necessary and sufficient for change as well as the possible impact of different sequencing of these subtasks.

Prochaska, DiClemente, and Norcross (1992) offered an interesting pantheoretical model for conceptualizing and measuring the subtasks or stages of change for drug treatment. They operationalized five generic stages of change: (a) precontemplation, (b) contemplation, (c) preparation, (d) action, and (e) maintenance. These categories could be used to assess family members' response patterns during a treatment task. For instance, parents may initially resist a systemic reframe (precontemplation). If the therapist skillfully persists, the parents may begin to consider this new perspective (contemplation). Once parents accept the systemic perspective, they may consider new ways of behaving (preparation), and then try new behaviors (action). The therapist can then help them to maintain these new interactional skills (maintenance). Recognizing that change does not follow a linear progression, Prochaska and colleagues characterize change as a spiral process that moves up and down these stages, not unlike many therapeutic processes.

Systems for measuring therapist behaviors would also enhance the investigations of tasks over time. For example, the Therapist Behavior Coding System (Pinsof, 1986) is a transtheoretical, categorical measurement tool that assesses an exhaustive list of family therapist procedures representative of a variety of treatment approaches. Unfortunately, the instrument has received minimal use. Adherence and competency measures could also be used as a process-coding tool (Hogue, Liddle, & Rowe, 1996). Outcome investigators usually measure adherence globally to assess how extensively therapists implement each procedure across a single session. However, these tools could be used microanalytically to rate each therapist statement (Sosna, Diamond, & Diamond, 1999). In contrast to the Pinsof tool, adherence tools measure model-specific therapist procedures that should be closely tied to the proposed patient change mechanisms. Unfortunately, with only a few exceptions (e.g., Joyce & Piper, 1996; Safran & Muran, 1996), discovery-oriented researchers assume that treatment is delivered as intended and therefore they often neglect to assess therapist interventions (Greenberg, 1984). Unfortunately, this approach ignores the complex mix of therapist factors, client behaviors, stage of therapy, and quality of the alliance that influences therapists' decision making.

Stage III: Linking Process to Outcome

Several studies provide interesting models for linking process variables to outcome. Mann, Borduin, Henggeler, and Blaske (1990) explored how improvement in parental functioning was linked to reductions in delinquent behavior. They correlated pre- and postresidual change scores on both patient symptomatology and six dimensions of family interaction. They found that decreases in adolescent symptomatology were significantly linked with increases in supportiveness and verbal activity within the father–mother dyad. DeRubeis et al. (1990) explored whether changes in cognitive functioning as a result of cognitive behavior therapy preceded changes in depression. Using a framework set out by Baron and Kenny (1986), they collected pre-, mid-, and posttreatment data and then used regression analyses to demonstrate how improvement in cognitions mediates change in depression. Patterson and colleagues (see Patterson and Chamberlain, 1988) developed an observational coding system to assess core family constructs. They collected data across several time points and then used structural equation modeling to understand the interaction of the measured domains over time and their relation to outcome. These design methods and statistical procedures are a few of the strategies available to examine how processes change over time (see also Gottman & Rushe [1993] for a special section on analysis of change; and Hahlweg [1988] for a discussion of time series analysis).

The study that most closely approximates the investigative model we are proposing was conducted by Tolan et al. (1997). Based on empirical and clinical literature, they developed a set of self-report, postsession measures that were given to parents, children, and providers at least five times over the course of a 22-week treatment. Dimensions measured included alliance, program satisfaction, parenting practices, and child cooperation with treatment, as well as some behavioral measures on the child. Path analysis showed that controlling for initial parenting skills, child cooperation, child's prosocial and aggressive behavior, and mother's report of alliance predicted mother's increased use of skills emphasized by the program. Improvement in parenting skills predicted increased child cooperation in treatment, both of which predicted decreases in antisocial behavior and increase in prosocial behavior.

Selecting Core Tasks

The three research stages suggested earlier could help guide the systematic dismantling, refining, and repackaging of a multitask treatment approach. Central to this process is the selection of the essential change mechanisms of a given model. Rather than promote a plethora of idiosyncratic processes, however, we encourage the investigation of transtheoretical, generic mechanisms that are relevant across treatment models (e.g., improving parenting practices). Like the call for a common set of outcome measures (Elkin, 1985), identification of a core set of family treatment processes could accelerate the development of transtheoretical measures (Tolan et al., 1997) and the accumulation of clinically relevant knowledge.

One set of core family treatment tasks is represented in our ABFT model. We have designed this model to focus on four essential treatment tasks that we believe are fundamental to any good family therapy approach: (a) alliance building (adolescent and parent), (b) reattribution, (c) effective parenting, and (d) reattachment. Psychological science informs our understanding of the psychological and interpersonal processes involved in the ABFT tasks (see Hennggeler & Borduin, 1990; Liddle, 1999; and Shirk & Russell, 1996, for examples of other empirically informed treatment models). For example, we understand reframing within the context of attributional theory (Fincham & Bradbury, 1990). Interventions that reinforce parental hierarchy and nurturance are informed by research in developmental psychopathology (Baumrind, 1967; Steinberg, Lamborn, Dornbusch, & Darling, 1992). Family systems concepts of cohesion and communication are informed by attachment theory (Ainsworth, 1989; Allen, Hauser, & Borman-Spurrell, 1996; Kobak & Sceery, 1988; Marvin, 1992). These well-developed domains of psychological knowledge deepen our understanding of these therapeutic processes, focus us on important targets of change, and in general give family interventions a firmer scientific basis (Dadds, 1995). The remainder of this chapter focuses on these four ABFT tasks. First we argue that these tasks are central to many family treatment models, and then we present some of the psychological research that supports their importance. We then present selected process studies that have explored some aspect of these mechanisms. Finally, we suggest some direction for future research on each mechanism.

Alliance-Building Task

Establishing a strong therapeutic alliance is a primary task in almost all treatment modalities. In the adult, individual, and couples and family treatment literature, alliance, particularly early alliance, repeatedly predicts retention, client satisfaction, and outcome (Eltz, Shirk, & Sarlin, 1995; Holtzworth-Munroe, Jacobson, DeKlyen, & Whisman, 1989; Horvath & Symonds, 1991; Pinsof & Catherall, 1986; Quinn, Dotson, & Jordan, 1997). Interestingly, we know little about how alliance contributes to change. Rogers (1957) proposed that the therapeutic relationship provides support and validation for the client. This buffers clients from becoming overwhelmed, increases their sense of self worth, helps them to regulate distressing feelings, and potentiates their innate drive for growth. Henry and Strupp (1994) proposed that alliance is a more active ingredient, providing a corrective emotional experience that counters the client's expected maladaptive relational patterns. Alternatively, alliance may function as a form of social support that buffers against stress (Compas, 1987) or helps to build self-esteem (Harter, 1985).

Understanding alliance in family treatment is more complicated than in individual treatment. The therapeutic action is presumed to be primarily between family members, not between therapist and client. Alliance with the therapist may be best understood as a transitional relationship that helps individual family members to uncover or learn about new parts of themselves (e.g., authoritative parenting, unacknowledged hurts). As individuals acquire new skills and knowledge through their relationship with their therapist, treatment then focuses on helping family members to develop trust and new interactions with each other. Assessing the evolution of alliance over time could reveal if it is an active ingredient in and of itself or if it primarily serves as a mediator of other essential processes.

In addition to studying how alliance works, understanding how to establish it with difficult clients would make a strong contribution to the field. Toward this goal, G. M. Diamond, Liddle, Hogue, and Dakof (1999) used a discovery-oriented methodology to identify and describe eight therapist behaviors associated with improving initially poor therapist–adolescent alliance during the treatment of substance-abusing patients. They then compared the extent to which therapists used these behaviors in five improved versus five unimproved alliance cases. Results suggested that early alliance initially involves orienting adolescents to the collaborative nature of therapy and helping them to define tangible, personally meaningful goals while generating hope that these goals can be achieved. This study illustrates the manner in which descriptive, discovery-oriented methodologies can facilitate our understanding of therapist techniques associated with changes in alliance.

A number of studies have used the self-report Couple and Family Therapy Alliance Scale (Pinsof, 1986) in order to assess the complexity of alliance in family treatment. This instrument assesses each family member's view of tasks, goals, and bonds between the therapist and themselves, the therapist and other family subsystems, and the therapist and the entire family. Quinn, Dotson, and Jordan (1997) found that alliance measured at Session 3 predicted posttreatment outcome. More important, they found that the association between alliance and outcome was stronger for wives and mothers than for husbands and fathers. In another study, Heatherington and Friedlander (1990) looked at the relationship between therapist–client process in family therapy and the development of the therapeutic alliance. They found that neither complementary nor symmetrical therapist–client interactions was predictive of alliance. Instead, clients rated a higher alliance when the therapist was more in charge of the session. The authors suggest that therapists' directives may be interpreted as competency and authority. In a study examining the immediate impact of various categories of therapist interventions on families with delinquent adolescents, Robbins, Alexander, Newell, and Turner (1996) found that mothers responded most positively to organizing and structuring interventions, and adolescents responded most positively to the use of positive connotation and reframing. Although this study did not measure the therapeutic alliance per se, studies linking therapists' behavior to positive client outcomes will further develop our understanding of this process.

Given the scarcity of studies on alliance in family-based treatments, many basic questions still need to be addressed. Does early alliance predict outcome? What characteristics of the client, therapist, and treatment predict the development of alliance? Can therapists improve a poor alliance, and how? Do constructs such as tasks, goals, and bonds cluster together, or do they differentially predict distinct outcomes? Is alliance an active ingredient in and of itself or does it merely provide a necessary foundation for model-specific interventions?

In addition to these questions, the unique nature of alliance in family treatments should be explored. Family treatments involve multiple participants who may each have different motivations for coming to treatment. For example, whereas the child or adolescent is usually the patient, the parents pay for treatment and bring kids to sessions (Weisz, Stanley, & Weersing, 1998). In treatment of young children, alliance with the parents may initially be more important, whereas engaging adolescents may be the first order of business in family treatment with this older population (G. S. Diamond & Reis, 2000; Liddle & Diamond, 1991). Research exploring the importance of the therapist alliance with each family member at different stages of therapy and with diverse populations would help therapists learn to manage the complex task of building and maintaining multiple alliances in family treatments.

Reattribution Task

This task refers to shifting, redefining, or expanding family members' definition of the presenting problem. Most commonly referred to as *reframing*, this concept is at the core of structural family therapy, narrative or constructivist approaches, and even psychoeducational approaches (Boscolo, Cecchin, Hoffman, & Penn, 1987; Goolishian & Anderson, 1987; Minuchin, 1974; Sluzki, 1992; White & Epstein, 1990). For example, Goldstein's (1991) approach to treating schizophrenia focuses on reeducating parents about the cause of the patient's behavior: "This behavior is not willful or malicious; it is caused by a mental illness" (p. 120). This change in problem definition elicits from parents' more constructive attributions, motivations, emotions, and behaviors. Research on attributions in marital relationships suggests that distressed couples are more likely to see the causes of problems as stable, global, and located in the partner and to see the partner's behavior as intentional, selfishly motivated, and blameworthy (Fincham & Bradbury, 1988). Therefore, interventions aimed as reducing negative attributions (e.g., reframing) can not only improve family functioning but facilitate therapeutic engagement.

Not surprisingly, several process studies have focused on reattribution tasks. For example, Alexander and colleagues have investigated the impact of positive connotation, or relabeling, on families with a delinquent teen (e.g., Mas, Alexander, & Turner, 1991). In this study, families were divided into two groups. In one group, parents were asked to identify positive events related to their teen and explain why these events happened. In the second group, parents were asked to identify negative events and to explain why these events happened. Families in both groups then completed a family interaction task. Results suggested that the induction of positive attributions did not improve the negative attributions or interactional style of high-conflict families, but it did improve the attributional set and interactional style of low-conflict families. Although the intervention in this study is weak, the idea of studying attributions before and after the delivery of a specific attribution-focused intervention seems promising.

Toward this goal, our team studied self-reports of change in parents' and adolescents' attributions before and after a first family session for treating depressed adolescents. Relational reframing techniques (G. S. Diamond & Siqueland, 1998) were used to shift the treatment goal from fixing the patient to improving the quality of family relations (Siqueland, Diamond, Diamond, & Brown, 1997). Within a week of the first session, parents were interviewed (involving reviewing tape excerpts from the first session, as in Elliot [1984]). Contrary to our expectation, both before and after the sessions, parents and adolescents rated themselves high as contributing to the problem and as willing, capable, and responsible for changing it. Postsession, parents reported feeling criticized by the therapist yet understood the therapist's need to join with the adolescent. This self-blaming attributional set and compliance may be indicative of families with a depressed adolescent, suggesting that the reattributional mechanism may differ depending on the population. This study also highlights the complexity of managing temporary imbalances in the alliance.

The most systematic investigation of reattribution, or cognitive restructuring, comes from Friedlander and Heatherington. They conducted three studies that explored this essential mechanism from different vantage points. First, using task analysis, Coulehan, Friedlander, and Heatherington (1998) discovered a seven-stage sequence leading to changes in attributions: (a) eliciting individuals' views and attributions about the problem, (b) identifying interpersonal contributions, (c) acknowledging differences of opinion, (d) acknowledging positive attributes in the child, (e) linking problem behaviors with family stressors, (f) identifying strengths, and (g) generating hope for change. In a second study, Heatherington et al. (1998) developed a self-report measure that asked 27 questions about causal attributions of an identified problem. Finally, Friedlander and Heatherington (1998) developed an observational rating system to assess family members' attributions about the presenting problem. This instrument rates patients' causal explanations as internal versus external, intrapersonal versus interpersonal, responsible versus not responsible, and linear versus circular. The measure initially demonstrated good reliability and construct validity and has since been improved by other investigators (G. M. Diamond & Moran, 2000).

Given the importance of reframing in family-based therapies, more process research is warranted to help understand and teach this process. As a starting point, attributional constructs and dimensions studied in marital research could be modified and used for family-level research (see Fincham & Bradbury, 1988). These include locus, stability, globality, responsibility, blame, and intentionality, to name a few. In addition, there is a plethora of creative methodologies and self-report and observer rating systems that could be adapted from marital research (Weiss & Heyman, 1990). Using these studies as a guide could accelerate our learning about construction and change of attributional sets and how to measure them over time (see Bugental, New, Johnston, & Silvester [1998] as an example). For clinical purposes, basic task analytic descriptive studies are needed to develop better clinical models of the reframing process. Cognitive behavioral techniques that directly target this domain would be one place to start (Baucom & Lester, 1986). As discovered by Siqueland et al. (1997) and Coulehan et al. (1998), however, affective shifts are an important component of attributional change. A detailed clinical model that incorporates both therapist intervention strategies and client cognitive and emotional responses might improve the potency of the reframing process.

Parenting Practices

Improving parenting practices has long been a primary focus of family-based interventions. Whether approaches are systemic, behavioral, or psychoeducational, improving parental cooperation, strengthening hierarchy, or teaching parenting skills constitutes at least half of the work with any given family. Developmental research certainly supports this treatment focus. For example, an authoritative parenting style (i.e., supportive and challenging) has repeatedly been associated with positive developmental outcomes (e.g., school performance, self-esteem, social adjustment; Baumrind, 1967; Maccoby & Martin, 1983; Steinberg et al., 1992). Similarly, positive parenting practices such as setting clear standards, consistently enforcing rules, and monitoring children's behaviors have been highly predictive of fewer emotional and behavioral problems such as depression, aggression, and substance abuse (Block, Block, & Keyes, 1988; Loeber & Stouthamer-Loeber, 1986; Patterson, 1982). In contrast, authoritarian, permissive, and inconsistent parenting practices have frequently been associated with negative developmental outcomes for adolescents (see Liddle, Rowe, Dakof, & Lyke, 1998, for a comprehensive review). Improving parenting practices may be the single most common and potent mechanism of change in family-based treatments.

Although no discovery-oriented, model-building studies have focused on parenting, several well-designed studies have explored this mechanism. For example, Schmidt, Liddle, and Dakof (1996) investigated whether improvement in parenting practices was associated with a reduction in adolescent drug use and delinquent behaviors. Based on empirical studies, theoretical writings, and clinical observations, they developed an observational coding system of eight positive and eight negative parenting behaviors. They coded the first three and last three sessions of 29 completed cases treated with multidimensional family therapy (Liddle, 1999). Results indicated a significant relationship between improvement in parenting practices and decreases in adolescent target behaviors. Although the findings are important in and of themselves, this coding instrument could serve as the foundation for a pantheoretical tool to code parenting behaviors across the course of treatment.

In a groundbreaking study on parenting, Mann et al. (1990) examined two central tenets of family therapy: (a) that child behavioral problems are associated with cross-generational coalitions, and (b) that the realignment of these coalitions can reduce child target behaviors. To test the first tenet, 45 families with a delinquent teen and 16 nonclinical families were assessed. Self-report and observational data suggested that families with a delinquent teen had higher rates of verbal activity between mother and adolescent, lower support between mother and father, and higher rates of conflict and hostility between mother and father and between father and son. The second tenet was tested by randomizing this cohort to multisystemic family therapy (Henggeler & Borduin, 1990) or to individual supportive therapy. In families treated with multisystemic family therapy, fathers and sons became more supportive, and mothers and fathers became more verbal and less hostile with each other. In addition, reduction in adolescent problems and improvement in parent coalition were highly correlated. Although correlation is a weak test of mediation, this creative study was the first to test these core family therapy principles.

The 25 years of work at the Oregon Social Learning Center (OSLC) epitomizes the use of process research to inform treatment development (see Patterson & Chamberlain, 1988). After demonstrating the effectiveness of parent management training in several clinical trials, researchers at OSLC turned their attention to two questions: (a) What are the essential treatment components? and (b) Why do some families improve while others do not? The researchers became interested in parental noncompliance and developed an observational coding system to assess resistance. As anticipated, parental resistance predicted attrition and poor outcome. Following up on the parent–therapist interaction, they found that resistance increased in response to therapists' efforts to teach skills and confront noncompliance. Further, as parental noncompliance increased, so did therapist efforts to teach and confront (Patterson & Forgatch, 1995).

Whereas improving parenting practices is essential when working with patients with externalizing problems, investigations of this task with other disorders would broaden our understanding of this mechanism. For example, in our work with parents of depressed adolescents, parent skills training focuses more on affective attunement and engagement than on the monitoring and discipline skills typically taught to parents of externalizing youth (G. M. Diamond, Diamond, & Liddle, 2000). Similarly, in our family work with anxious adolescents (Siqueland & Diamond, 1998) parent skills training focuses on encouraging autonomy. In addition to examining other disorders, we also advocate for more investigations that study the interaction of parenting practices with other core mechanisms. For example, in our work with depressed adolescents, a relational reframe makes parents more agreeable to learning new parenting skills, while a successful reattachment task makes an adolescent more receptive to parental authority. Given the importance of this process in family treatment, it certainly warrants more investigation.

Reattachment Task

Many family intervention models view improving the quality of the emotional bond in families as an essential treatment target. Concepts such as cohesion (Olsen, Sprenkel, & Russell, 1979), mutual reciprocity (Boszormenyi-Nagy & Krasner, 1986), and connectedness (Reiss, 1989) reflect a shared concern with improving the basic emotional fabric of family life. Attachment theory provides an overarching construct to understand this interpersonal domain. Unlike the radical constructivist assumptions of general systems theory or cybernetics, attachment theory posits the need for enduring connectedness and bonding to significant others as a basic human motivation (Bowlby, 1969, 1988). Unlike many psychodynamic models, attachment theory offers a framework for understanding the lifelong reciprocity between one's individual needs and one's interpersonal experience. In this regard, many investigators have started to look to attachment theory as an organizational framework for understanding family development and intervention science (Anderson, Beach, & Kaslow, 1999; Cummings & Davies, 1996; Hazan & Shaver, 1994; Johnson, 1996; Kobak, Duemmler, Burland, & Youngstrom, 1998; Wynne, 1984).

Several studies have now associated disturbed patterns of attachment with a number of psychiatric problems in infants, children, adolescents, and adults (Ainsworth, 1989). For example, studies have focused on the role of attachment in depression (Kobak & Sceery, 1988), schizophrenic disorders (Parker, Fairley, Greenwood, & Splove, 1982), conduct disorder (Rosenstein & Horowitz, 1993), and borderline personality disorder (Doane & Diamond, 1994). Attachment theory has influenced many treatment models as well. Many therapy models promote the establishment or reestablishment of a secure relationship base as the foundation for all other interpersonal processes (Boszormenyi-Nagy & Krasner, 1986; Byng-Hall, 1990; G. S. Diamond & Siqueland, 1995; Doane & Diamond, 1994; Johnson, 1996; Liddle, Rowe, Dakof, & Lyke, 1998). As both Wynne (1984) and Boszormenyi-Nagy and Krasner (1986) have argued, trust and attachment form the necessary foundation on which other interpersonal problem-solving skills must rest.

Only two discovery-oriented process studies have addressed the reattachment process (G. S. Diamond & Liddle, 1996; Heatherington & Friedlander, 1990). Both studies explored how interpersonal family conflict fuels arguing about day-to-day management of behavior (usually daily routines such as chores and curfews) In the G. S. Diamond and Liddle study (1996, 1999), 10 therapy sessions were identified that contained an intervention that targeted repairing attachment failures. Objective raters identified three phases of the episode: the problem state, intervention, and success or failure of the intervention (five of each). More than 100 hours of tape review yielded a highly detailed map of client performances and therapist behaviors that lead to a successful or unsuccessful resolution. The tapes were then edited into each phase, randomized, and coded with eight subscales from the Beavers Timberlawn scale. These rating were used to support and further embellish the clinical performance map. Findings suggested that the therapist needed to temporarily provide support to the adolescent's perspective and shift the parent's affective tone from blame and accusation to disappointment and loss. As parents became less defensive and more empathic, adolescents became less hostile and guarded, often resulting in the adolescent disclosing core conflictual themes that fueled day-to-day hostility (e.g., abandonment, neglect, and abuse). Processes identified in this model development study have served as the foundation for attachment-based family therapy with depressed adolescents (G. S. Diamond, 1998).

In the Heatherington and Friedlander study (1990), a very similar impasse was studied, conceptualized as a parent pursuing–child distancing process. Using the family relational control coding system (Freidlander & Heatherington, 1989), they demonstrated a shift in interpersonal patterns of control, from parental domination (impasse) to a more give-and-take process between parent and child (resolution). Interestingly, they found that as the child became more vocal about core conflicts, conflict between parents increased. In a follow-up paper (Friedlander, Heatherington, Johnson, & Skowron, 1994) they identified four stages for resolving this impasse: accepting individual responsibility for the impasse, disclosing more vulnerable thoughts and feelings, acknowledging these disclosures, and developing new attributions about the problems. Both the Diamond and Liddle and Friedlander et al. studies suggest that helping family members to identify and disclose core conflictual themes in the context of softer or more authentic affective states (Greenberg & Johnson, 1988) can facilitate productive family dialogue.

Attachment theory is an untapped resource for guiding family-based interventions. This theoretical framework can contribute to family systems clinical theory and intervention strategies (Kobak et al., 1998; Marvin, 1992). More descriptive studies of reattachment episodes and processes are needed to better understand the profound nature of this therapeutic process. We also need assessment tools that can operationalize attachment-related behaviors in the context of therapy. Doane and Diamond (1994) have made important steps in this direction using the expressed emotion and affective styles constructs. Other self-report and observer rating systems have also been developed that could be adapted as potential process research tools (e.g., Allen, Hauser, & Borman-Spurrell, 1996; Florsheim, Henry, & Benjamin, 1996). The important question is, of course, whether psychotherapy can fundamentally and substantially improve attachment styles and internal representations. Given that in family therapy therapists and clients have access to both actual relationships and internalized object relations, the potential to rework memories or create new relational experiences give family therapists powerful leverage for change.

Conclusion

Clearly the future of family treatment still rests in the demonstration of its efficacy through randomized clinical trials. However, the outcome of these studies will be enhanced if we can identify, refine, and thereby potentiate the most active treatment ingredients. This goal can be reached through systematically applying process research methods, beginning with discovery-oriented models and progressing to more sophisticated assessment and analytic strategies. To accomplish this goal, we first encourage the reconceptualization of treatment as consisting of several specific treatment tasks, where each task represents the facilitation of an essential mechanism of change. Although each treatment may have its own idiosyncratic mechanisms, we encourage examining treatment elements that transcend model-specific boundaries and instead represent transtheoretical processes that are indicative of many family-based interventions (e.g., reframing). This will facilitate research collaboration, the accumulation of clinically relevant knowledge, and the examination of subtle variations across treatment models. Once core mechanisms are identified, each task should be studied and refined in order to increase its potency and teachability. Discovery-oriented, task analytic methods are well suited for this purpose. These studies should also yield outcome measures that judge the degree to which these processes are resolved, completed, or obtained. These measures could be used to assess the maintenance or evolution of these mechanisms over time. With session-by-session outcome data on multiple mechanisms, investigators could examine the sequencing and interaction of different change processes. Such a data set could rigorously ask questions regarding which processes with which person can mediate, moderate, or cause outcome and at which point in treatment those processes should be used. This research agenda would give new meaning to the study of patterns of change.

References

Ainsworth, M. D. S. (1989). Attachment beyond infancy. *American Psychologist, 44,* 709–716.

Allen, J. P., Hauser, S. T., & Borman-Spurrell, E. (1996). Attachment as a framework for understanding sequelae of severe adolescent psychopathology: An 11-year follow-up study. *Journal of Consulting and Clinical Psychology, 64,* 254–263.

Anderson, P., Beach, S. R. H., & Kaslow, N. J. (1999). Marital discord and depression. The potential of attachment theory to guide integrative clinical intervention. In. T. Joiner & J. C. Coyne (Eds.), *The interactional nature of depression* (pp. 271–298). Washington, DC: American Psychological Association.

Baron, R. M., & Kenny, D. A. (1986). The moderator–mediator variable distinction in social psychological research: Conceptual, strategic, and statistical considerations. *Journal of Personality and Social Psychology, 51,* 1173–1182.

Baucom, D. H., & Lester, G. W. (1986). The usefulness of cognitive restructuring as an adjunct to behavioral marital therapy. *Behavior Therapy, 17,* 385–403.

Baumrind, D. (1967). Child care practices anteceding three patterns of preschool behavior. *Genetic Psychology Monographs, 75,* 327–333.

Beavers, W. R., Hampson, R. B., & Hulgus, Y. F. (1985). The Beavers systems approach to family assessment. *Family Process, 24,* 398–405.

Beutler, L. E., Cargo, M., & Arizmendi, T. G. (1986). Research on therapist variables in psychotherapy. In S. Garfield & L. A. Bergin (Eds.), *Handbook of psychotherapy and behavior change* (pp. 257–310). New York: Wiley.

Block, J., Block, J. H., & Keyes, S. (1988). Longitudinally foretelling drug usage in adolescence; Early childhood personality and environmental precursors. *Child Development, 59,* 336–355.

Boscolo, L., Cecchin, G., Hoffman, L., & Penn, P. (1987). *Milan systemic family therapy: Conversations in theory and practice.* New York: Basic Books.

Boszormenyi-Nagy, I., & Krasner, B. R. (1986). *Between give and take: A clinical guide to contextual therapy.* New York: Brunner/Mazel.

Bowlby, J. (1969). *Attachment and loss: Vol. 1 attachment.* New York: Basic Books.

Bowlby, J. (1988). *A secure base.* New York: Basic Books.

Bugental, D. B., New, M., Johnston, C., & Silvester, J. (1998). Measuring parental attributions: Conceptual and methodological issues. *Journal of Family Psychology, 15*(4), 459–480.

Byng-Hall, J. (1990). Attachment theory and family therapy: A clinical view. *Infant Mental Health Journal, 11,* 228–236.

Compas, B. (1987). Coping with stress during childhood and adolescence. *Psychological Bulletin, 101,* 393–403.

Coulehan, R., Friedlander, M. L., & Heatherington, L. (1998). Transforming narratives: A change event in constructivist family therapy. *Family Process, 37,* 17–33.

Cummings, E. M., & Davies, P. T. (1996). Emotional security as a regulatory process in normal development and the development of psychopathology. *Development and Psychopathology, 8,* 123–129.

Dadds, M. N. (1995). *Families, children and the development of dysfunction.* Thousand Oaks, CA: Sage.

DeRubeis, R. J., Evans, M. D., Hollon, S. D., Garvey, M. J., Grove, W. M., & Tuason, V. B. (1990). How does cognitive therapy work? Cognitive change and symptom change in cognitive therapy and pharmacotherapy for depression. *Journal of Consulting and Clinical Psychology, 58,* 862–869.

Diamond, G. M., Diamond, G. S., & Liddle, H. A. (2000). The therapist–parent alliance in family-based therapy for adolescents. *Journal of Clinical Psychology, 56*(8), 1037–1050.

Diamond, G. M., Liddle, H. A., Hogue, A., & Dakof, G. A. (1999). Alliance-building interventions with adolescents in family therapy: A process study. *Psychotherapy, 36,* 355–367.

Diamond, G. M., & Moran, G. (2000). *Revised coding manual for the cognitive constructions coding system.* Beer-Sheva, Israel: Ben-Gurion University.

Diamond, G. S. (1998, August). *Anatomy of a family based model for treating adolescent depression.* Paper presented at the American Psychological Association Convention, San Francisco.

Diamond, G. S., & Liddle, H. A. (1996). Resolving a therapeutic impasse between parents and adolescents in multidimensional family therapy. *Journal of Consulting and Clinical Psychology, 64*(3), 481–488.

Diamond, G. S., & Liddle. H. A. (1999). Transforming negative parent–adolescent interaction: From impasse to dialogue. *Family Process, 38*(1), 5–26.

Diamond, G. S., & Reis, B. (2000, August). *Engaging depressed adolescents in Attachment Based Family Therapy.* Paper presented at the American Psychological Association Convention, Washington, DC.

Diamond, G. S., Serrano, A., Dickey, M., & Sonis, W. (1996). Current status of family-based outcome and process research. *Journal of the Academy of Child and Adolescent Psychiatry, 35*(1), 6–16.

Diamond, G. S., & Siqueland, L. (1995). Family therapy for the treatment of depressed adolescents [Special issue]. *Psychotherapy, 32*(1), 77–90.

Diamond, G. S., & Siqueland, L. (1998). Emotion, attachment and the relational reframe: The first session. *Journal of Strategic and Systemic Therapies, 17*(2), 37–49.

Doane, J. A., & Diamond, L. (1994). *Affect and attachment with disturbed families.* New York: Basic Books.

Elkin, I. E. (1985). *Psychotherapy process research: Current status and future directions. Report of the 1983 NIMH workshop.* Unpublished manuscript, National Institute of Mental Health.

Elliot, R. (1984). A discovery-oriented approach to significant change events in psychotherapy: Interpersonal recall and comprehensive process analysis. In L. Rice & L. S. Greenberg (Eds.), *Patterns of change: Intensive analysis of psychotherapy process* (pp. 249–286). New York: Guilford Press.

Eltz, M. J., Shirk, S. R., & Sarlin, N. (1995). Alliance formation and treatment outcome among maltreated adolescents. *Child Abuse and Neglect, 19,* 419–431.

Fincham, F. D., & Bradbury, T. N. (1988). The impact of attributions in marriage: Empirical and conceptional foundations. *British Journal of Clinical Psychology, 27,* 77–90.

Fincham, F. D., & Bradbury, T. N. (1990). *The psychology of marriage.* New York: Guilford Press.

Florsheim, P., Henry, W. P., & Benjamin, L. S. (1996). Integrating individual and interpersonal approaches to diagnosis: The structural analysis of social behavior and attachment theory. In F. W. Kaslow (Ed.), *Handbook of relational diagnosis and dysfunctional family patterns* (pp. 81–101). New York: Wiley.

Friedlander, M. L., & Heatherington, L. (1989). Analyzing relational control in family therapy interviews. *Journal of Counseling Psychology.* 36, 139–148.

Friedlander, M. L., & Heatherington, L. (1998). Assessing clients' constructions of their problems in family therapy discourse. *Journal of Marriage & Family Counseling, 24,* 289–303.

Friedlander, M. L., Heatherington, L., Johnson, B., & Skowron, E. A. (1994). Sustaining engagement: A change event in family therapy. *Journal of Consulting Psychology, 41*(4), 438–448.

Friedlander, M. L., Wildman, J., Heatherington, L., & Skowron, E. A. (1994). What we do and don't know about the process of family therapy. *Journal of Family Psychology, 8*(4), 390–416.

Garfield, S. L. (1990). Issues and methods in psychotherapy process research. *Journal of Consulting and Clinical Psychology, 58,* 273–280.

Goldstein, M. J. (1991). Psychosocial (non-pharmacological) treatments for schizophrenia. In A. Taxman & S. M. Goldfinger (Eds.), *Review of psychiatry* (pp. 116–135). Washington, DC: American Psychiatric Association.

Goolishian, H. A., & Anderson, H. (1987). Language systems and therapy: An evolving idea. *Psychotherapy, 24,* 529–538.

Gottman, J. M., & Rushe, R. H. (1993). Analysis of change [Special section]. *Journal of Consulting and Clinical Psychology, 61*(6), 907–911.

Greenberg, L. S. (1984). A task analysis of conflict resolution. In L. Rice & L. S. Greenberg (Eds.), *Patterns of change: Intensive analysis of psychotherapy process* (pp. 67– 123). New York: Guilford Press.

Greenberg, L. S., & Foerster, F. S. (1996). Task analysis exemplified: The process of resolving unfinished business. *Journal of Consulting and Clinical Psychology, 64*(3), 439–446.

Greenberg, L. S., & Johnson, S. M. (1988). *Emotionally focused therapy for couples.* New York: Guilford Press.

Greenberg, L. S., & Pinsof, W. M. (1986). Process research: Current trends and future perspectives. In L. Greenberg & W. M. Pinsof (Eds.), *The psychotherapeutic process: A research handbook* (pp. 3–20). New York: Guilford Press.

Hahlweg, K. (1988) Statistical methods for studying family therapy process. In L. C. Wynne (Ed.), *The state of the art in family therapy research: Controversies and recommendations* (pp. 189–226). New York: Family Process Press.

Harter, S. (1985). *The self perception profile for children.* Denver, CO: University of Denver.

Hazan C., & Shaver, P. R. (1994). Attachment as an organizational framework for research on close relationships. *Psychological Inquiry, 5,* 1–22.

Heatherington, L., & Friedlander, M. L. (1990). Applying task analysis to structural family therapy. *Journal of Family Psychology, 4,* 36–48.

Heatherington, L., Johnson, B., Burke, L. E., Friedlander, M. L., Buchanan, R. M., & Shaw, D. M. (1998). Assessing individual family members' constructions of family problems. *Family Process, 37,* 167–184.

Henggeler, S. W., & Borduin, C. M. (1990). *Family therapy and beyond: A multisystemic approach to treating the behavior problems of children and adolescents.* Pacific Grove, CA: Brooks/Cole.

Henry, W. P., & Strupp, H. H. (1994). The therapeutic alliance as interpersonal process. In A. O. Horvath & L. S. Greenberg (Eds.), *The working alliance: Theory, research and practice* (pp. 51–84). New York: Wiley.

Hogue, A., Liddle, H. A., & Rowe, C. (1996). Treatment adherence process research in family therapy: A rationale and some practical guidelines. *Psychotherapy, 33*(2), 332–345.

Holtzworth-Munroe, A., Jacobson, N. S., DeKlyen, M., & Whisman, M. A. (1989). Relationship between behavioral marital therapy outcome and process variables. *Journal of Consulting and Clinical Psychology, 57*(5), 658–662.

Horowitz, M. J. (1979). *States of mind.* New York: Plenum Press.

Horvath, A. O., & Symonds, B. D. (1991). Relation between working alliance and outcome in psychotherapy: A meta-analysis. *Journal of Counseling Psychology, 39,* 32–38.

Johnson, S. M. (1996). *The practice of emotionally focused marital therapy: Creating connections.* New York: Brunner/Mazel.

Joyce, A. S., & Piper, W. E. (1996). Interpretive work in short-term individual psychotherapy: An analysis using hierarchical linear modeling. *Journal of Consulting and Clinical Psychology, 64*(3), 505–512.

Kiesler, D. J. (1973). *The process of psychotherapy: Empirical foundations and systems of analysis.* Chicago: Aldine.

Kobak, R., Duemmler, S., Burland, A., & Youngstrom, E. (1998). Attachment and negative absorption states: Implications for treating distressed families. *Journal of Systemic Therapies. 2,* 93–107.

Kobak, R., & Sceery, A. (1988). Attachment in late adolescence: Working models, affect regulations, and representations of self and others. *Child Development, 59,* 135–146.

Liddle, H. A. (1999). Theory development in a family-based therapy for adolescent drug abuse. *Journal of Clinical Child Psychology, 28*(4), 521–532.

Liddle, H. A., Rowe, C., Dakof, G., & Lyke, J. (1998). Translating parenting research into clinical interventions for families of adolescents. *Clinical Child Psychology and Psychiatry, 3*(3), 419–443.

Liddle, H. L., & Diamond, G. S. (1991). Adolescent substance abusers in family therapy: The critical initial phase of treatment. *Family Dynamics of Addictions Quarterly, 1,* 63–75.

Loeber, R., & Stouthamer-Loeber, M. (1986). Family factors as correlates and predictors of juvenile conduct problems and delinquency. In M. Tonry & N. Morris (Eds.), *Crime and justice: An annual review of research* (Vol. 7, pp. 29–149). Chicago: University of Chicago Press.

Luborsky, L. (1984). *Principles of psychoanalytic psychotherapy.* New York: Basic Books.

Maccoby, E. E., & Martin, J. A. (1983). Socialization in the context of the family: Parent–child interaction. In E. M. Heatherington (Ed.), *Mussen manual of child psychology, 4*(4), 1–102.

Mahrer, A. R. (1988). Discovery oriented psychotherapy research: Rationale, aims and methods. *American Psychologist, 43,* 694–702.

Mann, B. J., Borduin, C. M., Henggeler, S. W., & Blaske, D. M. (1990). An investigation of systemic conceptualizations of parent–child coalitions and symptom change. *Journal of Consulting and Clinical Psychology, 58,* 336–344.

Mas, C. H., Alexander, J. F., & Turner, C. W. (1991). Dispositional attributions and defensive behaviors in high- and low-conflict delinquent families. *Journal of Family Psychology, 5,* 176–191.

Marvin, R. S. (1992). Attachment- and family systems-based intervention in developmental psychopathology. *Development and Psychopathology 4,* 697–711.

Minuchin, S. (1974). *Families and family therapy.* Cambridge, MA: Harvard University Press.

Morrow-Bradley, C., & Elliot, R. (1986). Utilization of psychotherapy research by practicing psychotherapist. *Journal of Consulting and Clinical Psychology, 41,* 179–188.

Olsen, D. H., Sprenkle, D. H., & Russell, C. (1979). *Circumplex model of marital and family systems. I. Cohesion and adaptability dimensions, family types and clinical applications.* New York: Family Process Press.

Orlinsky, D. E., & Howard, K. I. (1986). Process and outcome in psychotherapy. In S. Garfield & L. A. Bergin (Eds.), *Handbook of psychotherapy and behavior change.* New York: Wiley.

Parker, G., Fairley, M., Greenwood, J., Jurd, A., & Splove, D. (1982). Parental representations of schizophrenics and their associations with onset and course of schizophrenia. *British Journal of Psychiatry, 141,* 575–581.

Patterson, G. R. (1998). *Coercive family process.* Eugene, OR: Castalia.

Patterson, G. R., & Chamberlain, P. (1988). Treatment process: A problem at three levels. In L. C. Wynne (Ed.), *The state of the art in family therapy research: Controversies and recommendations* (pp.189–226). New York: Family Process Press.

Patterson, G. R., & Forgatch, M. S. (1995). Predicting future clinical adjustment from treatment outcome and process variables. *Psychological Assessment, 7*(3), 275–285.

Pinsof, W. M. (1986). The process of family therapy: The development of the family therapist coding system. In L. S. Greenberg & W. M. Pinsof (Eds.), *The psychotherapeutic process: A research handbook* (pp. 201–284). New York: Guilford Press.

Pinsof, W. M. (1989). A conceptual framework and methodological criteria for family therapy process research. *Journal of Consulting and Clinical Psychology, 57*(1), 53–59.

Pinsof, W. M., & Catherall, D. R. (1986). The integrative psychotherapy alliance: Family, couple and individual therapy scales. *Journal of Marital and Family Therapy, 12*(2), 137–151.

Pinsof, W. M., & Wynne, L. C. (1995). The effectiveness and efficacy of marital and family therapy: Introduction to the special issue. *Journal of Marital and Family Therapy, 21*(4), 341–343.

Prochaska, J. O., DiClemente, C. C., & Norcross, J. C. (1992). In search of how people change: Applications to addictive behaviors. *American Psychologist, 47*(9), 1107–1114.

Quinn, W. H., Dotson, D., & Jordan, K. (1997). Dimensions of therapeutic alliance and their associations with outcome in family therapy. *Psychotherapy Research, 7*(4), 429–438.

Reiss, D. (1989). The represented and practicing family: Contrasting visions of family continuity. In A. Sameroff & R. Emde (Eds.), *Relationship disturbances in early childhood: A developmental approach* (pp. 191–220). New York: Basic Books.

Rice, L. N., & Greenberg, L. S. (1984). *Patterns of change: Intensive analysis of psychotherapy process.* New York: Guilford Press.

Robbins, M. S., Alexander, J. F., Newell, R. N., & Turner, C. W. (1996). The immediate effect of reframing on client attitude in family therapy. *Journal of Consulting and Clinical Psychology, 10*(1), 28–34.

Rogers, C. (1957). The necessary and sufficient conditions of personality change. *Journal of Consulting and Clinical Psychology, 21,* 95–103.

Rosenstein, D. S., & Horowitz, H. A. (1993, March). *Working models of attachment in psychiatrically hospitalized adolescents: Relation to psychopathology and personality.* Paper presented at the biennial meeting of the Society for Research in Child Development, New Orleans, LA.

Safran, J. D., & Muran, J. C. (1996). The resolution of ruptures in the therapeutic alliance. *Journal of Consulting and Clinical Psychology, 64*(3), 447–458.

Schmidt, S. E., Liddle, H. A., & Dakof, G. A. (1996). Changes in parenting practices and adolescent drug abuse during multidimensional family therapy. *Journal of Family Psychology, 10,* 12–27.

Siqueland, L., & Diamond, G. S. (1998). Engaging parents in cognitive behavioral treatment for children with anxiety disorders. *Cognitive and Behavioral Practice, 5,* 81–102.

Siqueland, L., Diamond, G. S., Diamond, G. M., & Brown, P. (1997, June). *Relational reframing in the first session of therapy with depressed adolescents.* Paper presented at meeting of the Society of Psychotherapy Research, Santa Fe, NM.

Shadish, W. J., Montgomery, L. M., Wilson, P., Bright, I., & Okwimabua, T. (1993). Effects of family and marital psychotherapies: A meta-analysis. *Journal of Consulting and Clinical Psychology, 61,* 992–1002.

Shirk, S. R., & Russell, R. L. (1996). *Change processes in child psychotherapy: Revitalizing treatment and research.* New York: Guilford Press.

Shoham-Salomon, V. (1990). Interrelating research processes of process research. *Journal of Consulting and Clinical Psychology, 58*(3), 295–303.

Sluzki, C. E. (1992). Transformations: A blueprint for narrative changes in therapy. *Family Process, 31*(3), 217–230.

Sosna, B. A., Diamond, G. M. & Diamond, G. S. (1999, June). *Therapists' decision making strategies in family therapy for depressed adolescents.* Paper presented at meeting of the Society for Psychotherapy Research, Chicago.

Steinberg, L. D., Lamborn, S. D., Dornbusch, S. M. N., & Darling, N. (1992). Impact of parenting practices on adolescent achievement: Authoritative parenting, school involvement, and encouragement to succeed. *Child Development, 63,* 1266–1281.

Tolan, P. H., Hanish, L. D., McKay, M. M., & Dickey, M. H. (1997). *Measuring process in child and family interventions: An example in prevention of aggression.* Manuscript submitted for publication.

VandenBos, G. R. (1989, September). Practice publications focus on applications. *APA Monitor, 20,* 13.

Weiss, R. L., & Hayman, R. E. (1990). Observation of marital interaction. In F. D. Findham & T. N. Bradlary (Eds.), *The psychology of marriage* (pp. 87–117). New York: Guilford Press.

Weisz, J. R., Stanley, J. H., & Weersing, V. R. (1998). Psychotherapy outcome research with children and adolescents: The state of the art. *Advances in Clinical Child Psychology, 20*(2), 49–91.

White, M., & Epstein, D. (1990). *Narrative means to therapeutic ends.* New York: Norton.

Wynne, L. C. (1984). *The epigenesis of relational systems: A model for understanding family development* (pp. 297–318). New York: Family Process Press.

PART 2

Advances in Assessment and Methods

CHAPTER 4

Conceptual Issues in Assessing Couples and Families

Douglas K. Snyder

Jebber J. Cozzi

Laurel F. Mangrum

The ability to accurately measure relevant phenomena lies at the heart of any scientific discipline. Whether engaged in the process of theory development and evaluation or clinical assessment and intervention, critical decisions must be reached regarding which constructs to examine, phenotypic markers of those constructs, and optimal measurement strategies and techniques. Although measurement tools for use with couples and families number well over 1,000 (Snyder & Rice, 1996), the discipline of marital and family therapy suffers from three core deficits in its assessment strategies: (a) an emphasis on individual and dyadic measures to the neglect of measurement strategies that target broader systemic constructs, (b) an excessive reliance on self-report measures to the neglect of other-report and formal observational techniques, and (c) the proliferation of measures without adequate attention to issues of reliability and validity.

Two molar consequences of these deficits have stunted the development of family psychology as an intervention science. First, many constructs assessed informally in clinical intervention with couples and families fail to be incorporated in empirical investigations of treatment outcome because of a shortage of appropriate formal measurement techniques; theory development, clinical application, and treatment studies often suffer from a failure to measure those constructs that appear to be most clinically relevant. Second, the absence of a common conceptual model and consensual measurement strategy frustrates efforts to integrate findings across independent studies; there is little consensus on relevant constructs for couple and family intervention, let alone common techniques for assessing those constructs.

Numerous conceptual and methodological issues in assessment confront those who work in the discipline of family psychology. Our primary purpose in this chapter is to encourage both practitioners and researchers to expand their conceptual models across diverse construct domains operating at multiple levels of the family system in a manner that may enhance both the understanding of families as well as the development and implementation of effective interventions. Although issues related to the development of specific measurement techniques, self-report and observational methods, and analysis of dyadic and family data all bear on selection of assessment strategies, their treatment lies outside the scope of this discussion. We have addressed several of these issues elsewhere (Kashy & Snyder, 1995; Snyder, Cavell, Heffer, & Mangrum, 1995; Snyder & Rice, 1996).

In this chapter we expand on a conceptual model we have advanced previously (Snyder et al., 1995), identifying specific construct domains that warrant consideration in both clinical and research applications and articulating their relevance across levels of the family and social system within those domains. We then apply this model as a context for examining research findings within a specific application—predicting marital therapy outcome—and discuss implications of the model for future research regarding both the methods and substance of couples and family assessment.

A Conceptual Model for Assessing Couples and Families

The model we propose for directing couples and family assessment is depicted in Figure 4-1. Our model proposes five construct domains similar to those identified in previous family assessment models: (a) cognitive; (b) affective; (c) communication and interpersonal; (d) structural and developmental; and (e) control, sanctions, and related behavioral domains. Constructs relevant to each of these domains can be assessed at each of the multiple levels comprising the psychosocial system in which the couple or family functions. The model posits five distinct levels of this system: (a) individuals, (b) dyads, (c) the nuclear family, (d) the extended family and related social systems, and (e) the community and cultural systems. Each of the five target domains may be assessed with varying degrees of relevance and specificity across each of the five system levels using both formal and informal assessment approaches to self-report and observational techniques.

Several aspects of this model merit elaboration. With respect to construct domains, the model emphasizes the fluid nature of individual as well as system structure by linking structural with developmental processes. Assessment findings at any system level are best understood within a broader temporal context. Second, our model presumes that individual members of a couple or family recursively influence, and are influenced by, the broader social system. Whereas early psychodynamic approaches to couples and family therapy emphasized

FIGURE 4-1

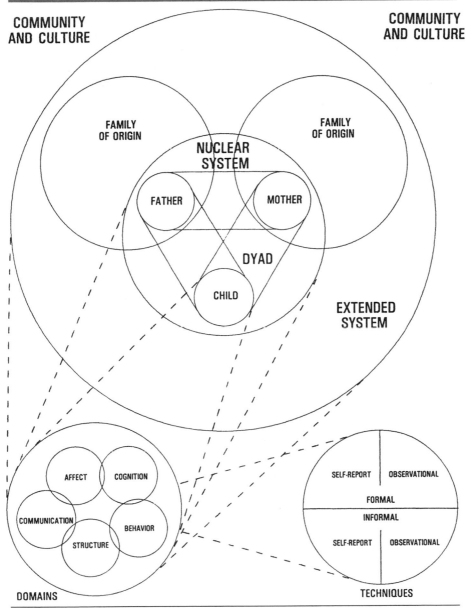

COMMUNITY
AND CULTURE

COMMUNITY
AND CULTURE

FAMILY
OF ORIGIN

FAMILY
OF ORIGIN

NUCLEAR
SYSTEM

FATHER

MOTHER

DYAD

CHILD

EXTENDED
SYSTEM

AFFECT

COGNITION

COMMUNICATION

BEHAVIOR

STRUCTURE

SELF-REPORT | OBSERVATIONAL

FORMAL

INFORMAL

SELF-REPORT | OBSERVATIONAL

DOMAINS

TECHNIQUES

Conceptual model for assessing families from a systems perspective. The model
presents five system levels, including (a) individuals, (b) dyads, (c) the nuclear
family, (d) the extended family system, and (e) the community and cultural systems.
Each system level may be assessed across five overlapping domains, including (a)
cognitive; (b) affective; (c) communication and interpersonal; (d) structural and
developmental; and (e) control, sanctions, and related behavioral domains.
Information across domains may be gathered using multiple assessment strategies,
including both formal and informal self-report and observational techniques. From
Snyder, Cavell, Heffer, and Mangrum (1995). Copyright 1995 by the American
Psychological Association. Reprinted with permission.

individual psychopathology to the neglect of dyadic and family processes, subsequent systemic approaches initially emphasized broader social influences to the neglect of individual factors. Such elements as capacity for self-observation, emotional empathy, and inhibition of aggressive impulses are critical components that contribute to the well-being of the couple or family system.

Most if not all of the constructs identified as relevant to dyads also apply to assessing nuclear systems. Differences at the family level include the following: (a) the number and complexity of dyadic relationships increase in nonlinear fashion as a function of the number of individuals comprising the family system; (b) each individual directly affects (and is affected by) two or more others in the system, so that the likelihood of competing forces and potential for conflict increases commensurately; (c) the range in developmental stages of individual members expands dramatically, increasing interpersonal differences in values, expectations, and ability to engage in system-enhancing behaviors; and (d) the structure of relationships within the family requires analysis beyond dyads involving simultaneous observation of all members comprising the nuclear system. The model distinguishes between extended systems in which family members interact on an affective basis with individuals outside the nuclear family versus broader social systems at the community or cultural levels.

In the discussion that follows, we articulate representative constructs from each of the target domains across the five system levels specified by the model. Our selection of constructs is not exhaustive but instead emphasizes those dimensions receiving greater attention in the research literature or, from our experience, having special relevance to clinical interventions.

Assessing the Cognitive Domain

Important constructs within the cognitive domain at the individual level include general cognitive resources underlying the ability to understand and apply concepts and the capacity for self-reflection and insight. Related to issues of cognitive ability are considerations of cognitive style, attitudes, and distortions ranging from irrational beliefs to more serious thought disorder. A second cognitive dimension involves each individual's self-view, including self-efficacy and the extent to which individuals regard themselves as contributing to their own distress and ability to effect change. Both level and style of defensiveness may direct the content, pacing, and impact of interventions. For example, a global affective response style requires integration with more specific and cognitive analysis; a hypervigilant response style requires attention to issues of interpersonal trust and a willingness to suspend critical judgment for the sake of collaborative efforts toward relationship change.

Cognitive constructs at the dyadic level emphasize views toward the relationship. Baucom, Epstein, Sayers, and Sher (1989) proposed five categories of cognitions that moderate intimate relationships: (a) assumptions the individual makes about how this relationship or relationships in general function, (b) standards the person holds for how a relationship or members of a relationship *ought to* function, (c) selective attention to relationship events congruent with existing belief systems, (d) expectancies regarding the course and impact of their own and others' behaviors in a relationship, and (e) attributions regarding the causes for relationship events. Additional cognitive facets at a dyadic level include the degree of tolerance for differences in members' assumptions and standards for their relationship, as well as the degree of similarity or incongruence in these domains.

Similar to "standards" at the dyadic level are "values" at the family level. Families differ in the extent to which they espouse intellectual and aesthetic endeavors, recreational activity, religious or moral pursuits, personal achievement, and independence. Important assessment dimensions include the manner in which such values are communicated and pursued by different members. For example, Moos and Moos (1986) have constructed a self-report approach for assessing family differences in these personal growth dimensions within the family environment.

The most salient cognitive component of extended systems involves standards and assumptions regarding the nuclear system. Friends and extended family offer an outsider's perspective that may bring a more rational or objective view to processes within the nuclear system or, conversely, may promote a more biased view based on limited or prejudiced information. For example, assumptions within the family of origin regarding appropriate child-rearing practices may conflict with emerging values or practices within the family of procreation, thereby generating anxiety, guilt, resentment, or conflict between spouses or sets of in-laws.

Cultural expectations contribute to patterns of interaction within the family regarding expression of feelings, distribution of authority, gender roles, child rearing practices, values placed on achievement and independence, and related constructs (Falicov, 1995). Family members' assumptions and attributions regarding the community system also require careful assessment. Relevant constructs include the knowledge that family members possess regarding community resources and their expectations regarding the availability and potential helpfulness of these resources.

Assessing the Affective Domain

The content, intensity, and mutability of emotions influence an individual's response to others. Anxiety constricts and immobilizes; depression often suppresses level of responsiveness more generally. Similarly, anger and hostility may exert a suppressive effect on other members' willingness to engage in collaborative exchange. Persons vary in their general range of affective intensity and the extent to which affect persists across time and situations despite other persons' initiatives; the more intense, narrow, and persistent the affect, the more likely that clinical interventions may be limited in their impact.

Affective dimensions of cohesion, expressiveness, satisfaction, commitment, and acceptance have all been identified in the dyadic relationship literature. *Cohesion* refers to the level and quality of emotional bonding between two individuals, similar to the concept of attachment in the developmental literature. The clinical literature suggests that extremes in cohesion—either enmeshment or disengagement—are associated with a variety of relationship dysfunctions. Related to cohesion are the nature and degree of emotional expressiveness. Affective content may range from support and empathy to intrusive concern to hostile rejection. For example, the effects of families' emotional expressiveness on patients' relapse have a long history of research in the areas of schizophrenia and affective disorders (Miklowitz, Goldstein, & Nuechterlein, 1995).

Relationship satisfaction is the most widely investigated dimension of intimate dyads. As a construct of comfort or contentment, it is distinct from both closeness (cohesion) or emotional expressiveness. Unlike other dyadic dimensions of affect, relationship satisfaction is almost entirely a subjective phenomenon. A variety of measures attempt to assess relationship satisfaction along specific dimensions of interaction (e.g., leisure time together, sexual interaction, or child rearing; Snyder, 1997). Commitment is an additional component of relationship affect. Although commitment may be inferred on a behavioral level (failure of a spouse to pursue divorce, willingness of an adolescent to engage with a parent in relationship dialogue), our impression is that commitment is both perceived and experienced on an affective level.

Although issues of how to treat assessment data across family members for interpretation or statistical analysis apply to constructs across domains, these have been discussed most frequently with respect to integrating self-report measures of relationship satisfaction or accord. Kashy and Snyder (1995) emphasized issues of nonindependence in couples data and discussed data analytic techniques that are applicable when the relevant construct varies between couples, within couples, or both. From the perspective of statistical analysis, issues of nonindependence become increasingly complex when applied to systems of three or more members.

Recent literature has started to address the construct of *acceptance* in relationships—a recognition of relationship conflicts and an ability to suspend the hurt or anger associated with them (Jacobson & Christensen, 1996). We perceive the construct of acceptance, or letting go of anger, as similar to the construct of forgiveness—a construct only recently gaining closer theoretical and empirical scrutiny (Gordon, Baucom, & Snyder, 2000; Hargrave, 1994).

These same affective dimensions relevant to couples have all received attention in the family literature. Families often convey a collective mood or tone that may vary along dimensions of optimism, contentment, anger, worry, guilt, or despair. Olson et al. (1982) have conceptualized affective components of family functioning under the rubric of family "pride" (including elements of loyalty, trust, and respect) and regard this dimension as one of two central axes of family strength (the other being accord or sense of competency). The strength of affective bonds within the family and their intensity relative to individuals' relationships outside the family contribute to the identity of the family as a distinct, vital system by its members.

Extended family systems provide vital sources of emotional support that may buffer relationship distress and enrich the quality of interactions within the nuclear family. From a systemic perspective, closed systems gradually deteriorate from an inability to draw on external resources. Social support is a vital resource for family as well as individual functioning. However, while drawing on extended systems for assistance or emotional support, failure to place priority on affective attachments within the nuclear family places that family system at risk. An important focus of assessment involves the extent to which family members have balanced developmental tasks of differentiating from extended systems while retaining the ability to draw on the support functions of those systems.

Family members' affective attachments at the community and cultural level involve two important considerations. The first concerns family members' community involvement and their respective experiences of isolation, withdrawal, rejection, or acceptance. To what extent do they feel a member of the broader community? The second consideration involves family members' degree of acculturation or identification with any specific ethnic heritage. For example, within a nuclear family of Asian descent, the parents may embrace values and behavioral codes consistent with their Asian heritage, while their children may actively resist these expectations and pursue identification with American western culture.

Assessing Communication and the Interpersonal Domain

Two dominant themes emerge in discussions of communication style: the individual's capacity to (a) relate warmly and agreeably with others, and (b) resolve conflict and engage in goal-directed negotiation (Grotevant & Carlson, 1989). Although communication typically is viewed as involving two or more persons, consistency in a person's relational style across diverse topics and situations with others points to an important individual source of communication behaviors.

Communication difficulties rank first among reasons couples give for entering marital therapy and rank high among families entering therapy as well (Geiss & O'Leary, 1981). A variety of self-report and observational techniques have been developed for evaluating communication at the dyadic level (cf. Heyman, 2001; Sayers & Sarwer, 1998). Many of these evaluate both verbal and nonverbal communication processes, such as affect of speaker or listener inferred from facial or other nonverbal cues. Most frequently studied among dyads is the ability to resolve conflicts and negotiate mutually acceptable solutions. Elements of problem-solving communication include problem identification; problem clarification; and solution generation, implementation, and evaluation. Separate from problem-solving communication is the expression and experience of each individual's affect. Some research data suggest that, among couples, emotional disengagement predicts poor treatment response (Jacobson & Addis, 1993).

Similar to individuals and dyads, two major components of communication emerge at the nuclear system level: (a) conflict resolution behaviors and (b) expression of both positive and negative feelings. The process of both affective and problem-solving communication among any subset of members within the family is likely to change with the entry of an additional member, particularly when communication at a horizontal level (between spouses or among siblings) incorporates a vertical element (between parent and child).

In order for extended systems to function as a source of support, two elements must be communicated: (a) one or more members of the nuclear system must convey both their need for and receptiveness to external support; and (b) one or more individuals in the extended system must convey both their ability and willingness to offer support. In contrast to constituting a base of social support, extended systems may also function as a source of conflict and stress. Critical to family functioning are the means by which members of the nuclear family attempt to negotiate conflict resolution with elements of the extended system, the extent to which these efforts are shared by family members, and their level of success.

Communication and interpersonal considerations at the community or cultural systems level emphasize coping strategies used by the family to acquire social support and mobilize community resources. Similar to communication at the extended system level, the family must convey their receptiveness to community involvement, and the social system must indicate opportunities for assistance or other social exchange. At this level, issues of racial and ethnic prejudice should be considered because they influence family members' expectations regarding assistance from social institutions and their ability to communicate openly with the broader community.

Assessing Structural and Developmental Components

Both intrapersonal structure and structural connections of the individual to his or her environment are important assessment domains. Intrapersonal considerations include consistency across cognitive, affective, and behavioral dimensions (i.e., whether the individual behaves in a manner congruent with his or her values, beliefs, or feelings). Relevant extrapersonal components include sources of individual stress (e.g., educational, occupational, or interpersonal).

Developmental considerations are also of central importance. For example, from a psychosocial perspective, the successful resolution of identity issues necessarily precedes attainment of intimacy. Evaluating the developmental context looms prominently in family therapy with children and adolescents; however, developmental context is no less important for adults (Levinson, 1986).

Among structural considerations at the dyadic level, the one most frequently cited involves *adaptability,* roughly akin to flexibility and effectiveness in responding to demands both internal and external to the relationship. Related constructs from systems theory include *entropy* (i.e., disorder and chaos) and *negentropy* (i.e., organization and structure). Adaptive relationships require an optimal balance of organization and flexibility; excesses toward either extreme (chaos or rigidity) impair the relationship's capacity to grow and respond effectively to change.

Another structural component at the dyadic level involves *affective and behavioral independence.* Conceptually, this refers to the degree to which one member's functioning is determined by the other and the degree of patterning across time; operationally, the degree of independence can be evaluated by time–series analyses (Kashy & Snyder, 1995). For example, sequential analyses of couples' interactions have demonstrated greater negative reciprocity among distressed couples than nondistressed couples (Heyman, 2001).

Developmental context applies to dyads as well as to individuals. Both the likelihood of specific conflicts as well as their interpretation and impact may vary not only as a function of a partner's age but also as a function of the stage or duration of the relationship.

Functional family systems must possess both flexibility and hierarchy. Family routines provide an organization and predictability to family life that enhance security and efficiency. Most families develop both implicit and explicit conventions regarding such tasks as household chores, management of meals, bedtime preparations, transportation, and facilitation of schoolwork.

Family hierarchy reflects the differential allocation of authority, responsibilities, and privileges across family members. In dysfunctional families parents sometimes seek emotional ties with their children in exaggerated and inappropriate ways; other parents fail to set limits or implement consequences for fear of eliciting their children's anger. It is important to assess the structure of influence both vertically and horizontally within the family system. Related to hierarchy is the structure of affective relationships within the family system. Relationships may be characterized by companionship or competition and by affection or antagonism. Patterns of attachment may be organized along generational dimensions, gender, or personality style. Which members assume primary responsibility for the functions of leadership versus nurturance? Seriousness versus play? Conflict engagement versus compromise? How rigid or predictable are these roles across situations and across time?

Consideration of developmental context is critical in evaluating family structure. Changes in family development are marked by the emergence and alteration over time of norms, roles, and other family characteristics necessary for the persistence of the family as a social system. The interrelatedness of members within a family requires that changes in roles for one person lead to changes in roles for all family members. Moreover, developmental changes in patterns of interaction commonly associated with progression across the family life cycle may differ markedly among stepfamilies, depending on what developmental stage each child was in when the parent and stepparent married (Bray, 1995); however, empirical studies of couples and family functioning often neglect critical distinctions among traditional and nontraditional family structures.

The most common approach to assessing family life cycle has been to demarcate stages based on age of the oldest child and status of the couple as pre- or post-child rearing years. Not only does this approach ignore complex structures of nontraditional families but also developmental variation within these broad stages. For example, one could expect marital satisfaction in older, retired adults to be influenced differently from younger "empty nest" adults by such factors as changes in social roles, financial status, organization of leisure time, and disability or declining health (Norris, Snyder, & Rice, 1997).

Extended systems exhibit the same potential for coalitions with members of the nuclear family and with each other as do elements within the nuclear system. Common coalitions occur in family members' relationships with in-laws and in friendships sought by one family member but rejected by another. The structural relationships between the nuclear family and elements of the extended system may either strengthen or undermine the priority that members assign to preserving the nuclear system. The structure of extended systems also changes over time. Indeed, the very definition of the nuclear system exhibits a developmental progression, with parents assuming the role of extended family as their children marry and establish nuclear families of their own.

At a more general level, structural considerations include both formal and implicit rules that govern family members' interactions with broader social institutions within the community. For example, administrative or managerial hierarchies at work may either contribute to stress that affects the family or provide a means for reducing sources of stress. Similarly, the structure of relationships among various social agencies may facilitate or impede coordination of services to a family in need. McCubbin and Patterson (1983) have proposed a model for viewing family stress that includes precipitating events, individuals' interpretations of these events, mobilization of resources, and ensuing distress at both initial and subsequent stages of response to stressors.

Assessing Control, Sanctions, and Related Behavioral Domains

Capacity for behavioral self-control determines the extent to which individuals can defer immediate impulses toward self-gratification either for the sake of other persons' benefit or for preferred delayed rewards for themselves. Whereas relational style concerns individuals' efforts to affiliate with others and to develop emotional ties, issues of control and power involve individuals' efforts to act independently on their own behalf and their efforts to influence others. As L'Abate and Colondier (1987) noted, virtually every theory that attempts to explain how couples and families function is based on individuals' conflicting needs for autonomy and emotional security. Therefore, it seems critical to assess clients' capacity to perform the dual tasks of negotiating power and forming positive emotional bonds.

An equitable distribution of power is central to dyadic relationship satisfaction, if not stability (Huston, 1983). The means by which two persons each struggle to exert influence on the other (positive versus negative, verbal versus nonverbal) and the models adopted for decision making (unilateral versus collaborative) are key dimensions in a dyadic relationship.

The process by which families allocate and execute authority may be evaluated across two dimensions: (a) models of family decision making, and (b) parents' approaches to discipline. Families may use different decision-making models across different domains of family life or across different subsystems within the family; thus, assessment should differentiate between typical decision-making strategies and their variability across situations. For example, parents might adopt a consultative or advisory stance with regard to an adolescent's decisions about career planning but take an authoritative stance regarding the same adolescent's decisions concerning drug use or a younger sibling's decisions about homework completion. In addition to differences in decision-making models, families differ in the means they adopt to enforce these decisions. Differences in parenting style have received considerable attention, particularly in the developmental literature. Extending across patterns of discipline are issues of (a) degree of parental concurrence on standards and methods of discipline, (b) degree of consistency by one or both parents across situations and time, and (c) the affective tone of discipline (e.g., control by anxiety, guilt, positive affect, or punishment).

Extended systems exert influence or control to the degree that they make the availability of desired resources contingent on one or more family members' behavior. Common control dynamics involving extended systems include the influence of families of origin on parents and the influence of peers on children. An important consideration involves the extent to which family members concur in their perceptions of these external influences and collaborate to challenge or maintain these influences.

Finally, control at the community level occurs on both formal and informal levels. An example of the latter involves the degree of influence and acceptance afforded to family members on the basis of their conformance with social norms. Similarly, some families may be disadvantaged in terms of balance of power when dealing with broader social or governmental institutions because of their economic, political, or ethnic status. Control at a formal level involves explicit negative or positive consequences implemented by elements of one system contingent on the behaviors of another. For example, repeated failure of a child to comply with school policies regarding conduct may require parental response to formal actions to suspend the youngster from school. Similarly, an adolescent's drug involvement might lead to a family's removal from public housing.

The Model as Applied to Marital Therapy Prediction Research

To what extent does the conceptual model described here facilitate integration of existing research findings and direct future investigations? In this section, we apply the multifaceted, multilevel model to the research literature regarding predictors of couples' response to marital therapy. In general, research in this area has emphasized dyadic constructs with secondary attention to individual factors but has largely neglected higher system levels of nuclear or extended family, friendships and other sources of social support, and community or cultural influences. With the exception of studies examining couples' communication, the extant research relies almost exclusively on self-report measures. Examination of structure—the patterning of affect, behavior, or cognition either within spouses or across members of the extended family and community systems—remains virtually nonexistent.

At the individual level, studies of demographic characteristics as predictors of response to marital therapy have produced largely nonsignificant or inconsistent results. Within this category, age has emerged as the only variable to receive moderate support as a predictor. Although some studies suggest a poorer response rate for older couples when compared to younger couples (Baucom, 1984; Bennun, 1985; Hahlweg, Schindler, Revenstorf, & Brengelmann, 1984;

O'Leary & Turkewitz, 1981), other studies have not replicated the predictive utility of age (Jacobson, Follette, & Pagel, 1986; Snyder, Mangrum, & Wills, 1993). Results to date suggest that demographic variables have at best only weak predictive value in isolation but may be important as possible moderators when examining differential outcome in comparative treatment studies.

Demographic predictors of treatment response have often relied on measures of convenience affording only rough approximation of constructs having greater theoretical relevance. For example, educational level seems less likely to influence response to therapy than cognitive flexibility, capacity for conceptualization and generalization of constructs, or reflectiveness and capacity for introspection—all more appropriately viewed as cognitive factors at the individual level. Occupational level would seem less critical than direct measures of job-related or financial stressors, a structural variable at an extramarital system level. Even ages and number of children may covary more reliably with marital distress or treatment response if converted to measures of spacing or density of childbearing within a given time period.

Studies that relate dimensions of psychopathology to either marital distress or treatment response have emphasized Axis I disorders to the exclusion of personality disorders, which potentially bear greater relevance to modal relationship functioning. For example, depression in one or both spouses appears to be a negative prognostic indicator in the majority of studies examining this variable (Sher, Baucom, & Larus, 1990; Snyder et al., 1993). Studies that examine the effects of nondepressive symptomatology on couples' response to marital therapy are limited, primarily because of the use of exclusionary criteria that eliminate individuals who are experiencing major psychopathology or substance abuse problems from marital outcome studies. Little consideration has been given to such affective domains as anxiety or hostility. Only recently has some discussion been afforded to the mutability of negative affect and the role of acceptance in moderating treatment response. Behavioral dimensions of individual functioning—including substance abuse and more general deficits in self-control or ability to defer gratification of needs for another's benefit—would also seem likely predictors of response to marital therapy but have received scant attention.

Gender role orientation has been identified as a predictor of both marital satisfaction and treatment response (Baucom & Aiken, 1984; Snyder et al., 1993). This finding may occur because measures of femininity often emphasize emotional expressiveness, a characteristic linked to relationship intimacy. Other personality traits have received modest support as predictors of treatment outcome, with some evidence indicating that measures of husbands' personality functioning afford higher prediction in comparison to measures of wives' functioning (Jacobson et al., 1986; Kelly & Conley, 1987; Kurdek, 1993; Snyder et al., 1993).

Finally, cognitive variables that reflect spouses' relationship beliefs and attributions hold promise as potential predictors of treatment response. Maritally satisfied and distressed couples appear to make different types of attributions for marital events that may contribute to or maintain distress levels (Bradbury & Fincham, 1990; Eidelson & Epstein, 1982; Halford, Sanders, & Behrens, 1993). For example, maritally distressed spouses tend to make external, unstable, and specific causal attributions for their partners' positive behavior and the opposite causal attributions (i.e., internal, stable, and global) for their partners' negative behavior. Moreover, similarity in spouses' marital assumptions reflected in marital paradigms (e.g., traditional versus individualistic) were found to predict outcome of systems-oriented marital therapy (Nugent & Constantine, 1988). Further research is needed to clarify the predictive utility of cognitive variables across different treatment modalities.

Overall, research that examines the relationship functioning domain suggests that pre- and posttreatment marital satisfaction levels (Baucom & Mehlman, 1984; Beach & O'Leary, 1992; Snyder et al., 1993), direct and indirect measures of commitment to the marital relationship (Beach & Broderick, 1983; Crane, Newfield, & Armstrong, 1984; Hahlweg et al., 1984; Kurdek, 1993), and the quality of affection and intimacy within the relationship (Bennun, 1985; Hahlweg et al., 1984; Snyder et al., 1993) all predict couples' response to marital therapy.

Studies have revealed a complex relationship between the nature of couples' communication and both marital satisfaction and treatment response and suggest a possible temporal interaction among these variables (Gottman, 1993; Hahlweg et al., 1984; Halford et al., 1993; Markman, 1991; Smith, Vivian, & O'Leary, 1991; Snyder et al., 1993). Specifically, particular forms of conflict engagement have predicted improved marital accord longitudinally, despite a concurrent association with relationship distress. In addition, research indicates that communication skill acquisition during the course of therapy is not necessarily associated with increased marital satisfaction (Baucom & Mehlman, 1984; Iverson & Baucom, 1990; Jacobson, Schmaling, & Holtzworth-Munroe, 1987; Sayers, Baucom, Sher, Weiss, & Heyman, 1991).

Other structural components of the marital relationship, such as differential allocation of authority, responsibility, and privileges have largely been ignored. Perhaps because behavioral approaches to treatment advocate collaborative approaches to decision making and most investigations of treatment response have been conducted within this theoretical framework, the consequences of alternative decisional models (e.g., unilateral or consultative) have not been systematically investigated. Surprisingly, the effects of verbal and physical aggression on couples' treatment response have also gone largely unexamined.

As noted earlier, potential components of marital distress and predictors of couples' response to therapy at the extended family, social network, or community system levels have been virtually ignored. Family and community values regarding the viability of marital dissolution likely exert strong influence on spouses' own commitment and tolerance for relationship distress. Assumptions and standards at broader system levels regarding marital and parental roles and their congruence across spouses' respective families and cultures also likely influence the compatibility of spouses' own expectations in this regard. Extramarital systems may provide either buffering effects or additional stressors for individuals experiencing marital distress, and these could be expected to moderate couples' response to therapy. Similarly, the effects of extramarital sexual relationships on couples' marital satisfaction, commitment, or treatment response have rarely been examined in controlled studies, perhaps because data on these relationships often do not emerge until some time following initial assessment.

One could anticipate that factors exerting direct effects on marital accord and response to treatment are more likely to be identified at the dyadic level of functioning, particularly within the affective domain. For example, Snyder et al. (1993) found that measures of global marital distress at intake consistently predicted termination status better than measures of specific dimensions of relationship dissatisfaction, behavioral measures of communication or spousal exchange, or measures of individual functioning—typically accounting for two to four times as much variance in treatment outcome. By contrast, factors outside the affective domain or system levels other than dyadic (i.e., individual, family, or community) are likely to exert weaker or indirect effects. For example, cognitive flexibility or openness to introspection at the individual level may wield little direct influence on marital affect but may determine the potential for change in spousal attributions or behavioral interaction once relationship distress has developed. Similarly, the influence of assumptions and standards for marital roles at the extended family level may hinge on the level of emotional dependence spouses experience toward their families of origin and the salience of alternative models available in their community.

Conclusion

The conceptual model articulated here provides a comprehensive framework for organizing research findings and directing future investigations with couples and families. The model posits that the construct domains of affect, cognition, and behavior—along with related interpersonal, structural, and developmental components—can each be mapped onto multiple system levels, ranging from the individual to the broader social and community context.

It seems unlikely, and even unwise, that any one study would attempt to address each of the facet X level domains proposed here. Our explication of the model has been deliberately inclusive. Assessment strategies in research, as in clinical practice, will likely yield the most utility when these are sampled according to constructs having the greatest theoretical relevance. However, our review of research findings in one area—prediction of couples therapy outcome —suggests that some levels and domains of couples and family functioning have received only scant attention. One would be hard pressed to argue that constructs of social support or cultural relationship standards have little relevance to couples' response to therapy; rather, the noncorrespondence of constructs routinely considered in clinical contexts to those characterizing treatment outcome research likely stems both from an absence of adequate measures that address higher system levels and from an overly narrow conceptualization of treatment factors and moderators at a theoretical level when designing these studies.

If family psychology is to advance as an intervention science, new assessment strategies must be developed to measure relevant constructs at these higher system levels. Research that examines specific constructs will benefit from assessment at multiple system levels, participation of multiple respondents, and use of multiple perspectives, including observational and other-report strategies in addition to self-report techniques. The measures that contribute to the development of family psychology as a scientific discipline will be those that afford not only descriptive accuracy but predictive and prescriptive utility as well. In other words, the assessment strategies and techniques that will have the greatest impact will be those that identify specific clinical interventions likely to be most efficacious for a given couple or family. Ultimately, adopting a broad conceptual model similar to the one proposed here should facilitate a theoretical organization in the field that can identify important phenomena that warrant careful study and that will contribute to more effective intervention strategies.

References

Baucom, D. H. (1984). The active ingredients of behavioral marital therapy: The effectiveness of problem-solving/communication training, contingency contracting, and their combination. In K. Hahlweg & N. S. Jacobson (Eds.), *Marital interaction: Analysis and modification* (pp. 73–88). New York: Guilford Press.

Baucom, D. H., & Aiken, P. A. (1984). Sex role identity, marital satisfaction, and response to behavioral marital therapy. *Journal of Consulting and Clinical Psychology, 52,* 438–444.

Baucom, D. H., Epstein, N., Sayers, S., & Sher, T. G. (1989). The role of cognitions in marital relationships: Definitional, methodological, and conceptual issues. *Journal of Consulting and Clinical Psychology, 57,* 31–38.

Baucom, D. H., & Mehlman, S. K. (1984). Predicting marital status following behavioral marital therapy: A comparison of models of marital relationships. In K. Hahlweg & N. S. Jacobson (Eds.), *Marital interaction: Analysis and modification* (pp. 89–104). New York: Guilford Press.

Beach, S. R. H., & Broderick, J. E. (1983). Commitment: A variable in women's response to marital therapy. *American Journal of Family Therapy, 11*(4), 16–24.

Beach, S. R. H., & O'Leary, K. D. (1992). Treating depression in the context of marital discord: Outcome and predictors of response of marital therapy vs. cognitive therapy. *Behavior Therapy, 23,* 507–528.

Bennun, I. (1985). Prediction and responsiveness in behavioural marital therapy. *Behavioural Psychotherapy, 13,* 186–201.

Bradbury, T. N., & Fincham, F. D. (1990). Attributions in marriage: Review and critique. *Psychological Bulletin, 107,* 3–33.

Bray, J. H. (1995). Family assessment: Current issues in evaluating families. *Family Relations, 44,* 469–477.

Crane, D. R., Newfield, N., & Armstrong, D. (1984). Predicting divorce at marital therapy intake: Wives' distress and the marital status inventory. *Journal of Marital and Family Therapy, 10,* 305–312.

Eidelson, R. J., & Epstein, N. (1982). Cognition and relationship maladjustment: Development of a measure of dysfunctional relationship beliefs. *Journal of Consulting and Clinical Psychology, 50,* 715–720.

Falicov, C. J. (1995). Cross-cultural marriages. In N. S. Jacobson & A. S. Gurman (Eds.), *Clinical handbook of couple therapy* (pp. 231–246). New York: Guilford Press.

Geiss, S. K., & O'Leary, D. (1981). Therapist ratings of frequency and severity of marital problems: Implications for research. *Journal of Marital and Family Therapy, 7,* 515–520.

Gordon, K. C., Baucom, D. H., & Snyder, D. K. (2000). The use of forgiveness in marital therapy. In M. E. McCullough, K. I. Pargament, & C. E. Thoresen (Eds.), *Forgiveness: Theory, research, and practice* (pp. 203–227). New York: Guilford Press.

Gottman, J. M. (1993). The roles of conflict engagement, escalation, and avoidance in marital interaction: A longitudinal view of five types of couples. *Journal of Consulting and Clinical Psychology, 61,* 6–15.

Grotevant, H. D., & Carlson, C. I. (1989). *Family assessment: A guide to methods and measures.* New York: Guilford Press.

Hahlweg, K., Schindler, L., Revenstorf, D., & Brengelmann, J. C. (1984). The Munich marital therapy study. In K. Hahlweg & N. S. Jacobson (Eds.), *Marital interaction: Analysis and modification* (pp. 3–26). New York: Guilford Press.

Halford, W. K., Sanders, M. R., & Behrens, B. C. (1993). A comparison of the generalization of behavioral marital therapy and enhanced behavioral marital therapy. *Journal of Consulting and Clinical Psychology, 61,* 51–60.

Hargrave, T. D. (1994). *Families and forgiveness: Healing intergenerational wounds.* New York: Brunner/Mazel.

Heyman, R. E. (2002). Observation of couple conflicts: Clinical assessment applications, stubborn truths, and shaky foundations. *Psychological Assessment, 13,* 5–35.

Huston, T. L. (1983). Power. In H. H. Kelley, E. Berscheid, A. Christensen, J. H. Harvey, T. L. Huston, G. Levinger, E. McClintock, L. A. Peplau, & D. R. Peterson (Eds.), *Close relationships* (pp. 169–219). New York: Freeman.

Iverson, A., & Baucom, D. H. (1990). Behavioral marital therapy outcomes: Alternate interpretations of the data. *Behavior Therapy, 21,* 129–138.

Jacobson, N. S., & Addis, M. E. (1993). Research on couples and couple therapy: What do we know? Where are we going? *Journal of Consulting and Clinical Psychology, 61,* 85–93.

Jacobson, N. S., & Christensen, A. (1996). *Integrative couple therapy: Promoting acceptance and change.* New York: Norton.

Jacobson, N. S., Follette, W. C., & Pagel, M. (1986). Predicting who will benefit from behavioral marital therapy. *Journal of Consulting and Clinical Psychology, 54,* 518–522.

Jacobson, N. S., Schmaling, K. B., & Holtzworth-Munroe, A. (1987). Component analysis of behavioral marital therapy: 2-year follow-up and prediction of relapse. *Journal of Marital and Family Therapy, 13,* 187–195.

Kashy, D. A., & Snyder, D. K. (1995). Measurement and data analytic issues in couples research. *Psychological Assessment, 7,* 338–348.

Kelly, E. L., & Conley, J. J. (1987). Personality and compatibility: A prospective analysis of marital stability and marital satisfaction. *Journal of Personality and Social Psychology, 52,* 27–40.

Kurdek, L. A. (1993). Predicting marital dissolution: A 5-year prospective longitudinal study of newlywed couples. *Journal of Personality and Social Psychology, 64,* 221–242.

L'Abate, L., & Colondier, G. (1987). The emperor has no clothes! Long live the emperor: A critique of family systems thinking and a reductionistic proposal. *American Journal of Family Therapy, 15,* 19–33.

Levinson, D. J. (1986). A conception of adult development. *American Psychologist, 41,* 3–13.

Markman, H. J. (1991). Constructive marital conflict is not an oxymoron. *Behavioral Assessment, 13,* 83–96.

McCubbin, H. I., & Patterson, J. M. (1983). Family transitions: Adaptation to stress. In H. I. McCubbin & C. R. Figley (Eds.), *Stress and the family: Vol. 1: Coping with normative transitions* (pp. 5–25). New York: Brunner/Mazel.

Miklowitz, D. J., Goldstein, M. J., & Nuechterlein, K. H. (1995). Verbal interactions in the families of schizophrenic and bipolar affective patients. *Journal of Abnormal Psychology, 104,* 268–276.

Moos, R. H., & Moos, B. S. (1986). *Family Environment Scale manual* (rev. ed.). Palo Alto, CA: Consulting Psychologists Press.

Norris, M. P., Snyder, D. K., & Rice, J. L. (1997). Marital satisfaction in older adults: A comparison of community and clinic couples. *Journal of Clinical Geropsychology, 3,* 111–122.

Nugent, M. D., & Constantine, L. L. (1988). Marital paradigms: Compatibility, treatment, and outcome in marital therapy. *Journal of Marital and Family Therapy, 14,* 351–369.

O'Leary, K. D., & Turkewitz, H. (1981). A comparative outcome study of behavioral marital therapy and communication therapy. *Journal of Marital and Family Therapy, 7,* 159–169.

Olson, D. H., McCubbin, H. I., Barnes, H., Larsen, A. S., Muxen, M., & Wilson, M. (1982). *Family inventories.* St. Paul, MN: Department of Family Social Science, University of Minnesota.

Sayers, S. L., Baucom, D. H., Sher, T. G., Weiss, R. L., & Heyman, R. E. (1991). Constructive engagement, behavioral marital therapy, and changes in marital satisfaction. *Behavioral Assessment, 13,* 25–49.

Sayers, S. L., & Sarwer, D. B. (1998). Assessment of marital dysfunction. In A. S. Bellack & M. Hersen (Eds.), *Behavioral assessment: A practical approach* (4th ed., pp. 293–314). Boston: Allyn & Bacon.

Sher, T. G., Baucom, D. H., & Larus, J. M. (1990). Communication patterns and response to treatment among depressed and nondepressed maritally distressed couples. *Journal of Family Psychology, 4,* 63–79.

Smith, D. A., Vivian, D., & O'Leary, K. D. (1991). The misnomer proposition: A critical reappraisal of the longitudinal status of "negativity" in marital communication. *Behavioral Assessment, 13,* 7–24.

Snyder, D. K. (1997). *Manual for the Marital Satisfaction Inventory—Revised.* Los Angeles: Western Psychological Services.

Snyder, D. K., Cavell, T. A., Heffer, R. W., & Mangrum, L. F. (1995). Marital and family assessment: A multifaceted, multilevel approach. In R. H. Mikesell, D. D. Lusterman, & S. H. McDaniel (Eds.), *Integrating family therapy: Handbook of family psychology and systems theory* (pp. 163–182). Washington, DC: American Psychological Association.

Snyder, D. K., Mangrum, L. F., & Wills, R. M. (1993). Predicting couples' response to marital therapy: A comparison of short- and long-term predictors. *Journal of Consulting and Clinical Psychology, 61,* 61–69.

Snyder, D. K., & Rice, J. L. (1996). Methodological issues and strategies in scale development. In D. H. Sprenkle & S. M. Moon (Eds.), *Research methods in family therapy* (pp. 216–237). New York: Guilford Press.

CHAPTER 5

Methodological Issues and Innovations in Family Psychology Intervention Research

James H. Bray

The last 20 years have seen a dramatic increase in psychological studies of couples and families and the development of interventions for treating marital and family problems. The development of theory and therapeutic interventions have outpaced the scientific basis of family psychology. Family psychology intervention research has been slowed by a lack of methodologies that can be used to study the complexity of families. This chapter discusses issues and innovations in methodologies and statistical methods that are applicable to the study of marital and family interventions.

Although traditional psychological methodologies may be useful in family psychology research, methods from related disciplines may not always be applicable for family psychology intervention research because of the interactional and systemic view of problem development and psychopathology. Describing and understanding the context and systemic relationships of families often require more sophisticated theory and methods (Bray, 1995a). Research on family psychology interventions face problems common in other clinical psychology outcome research. However, family psychology interventions are complicated by the fact that psychopathology is not viewed as solely within one individual. Current family systems theories are usually biopsychosocial in nature and consider the biological and social context of individuals and the interactions between individuals and between other social and biological systems. Thus, the outcome of a successful treatment is both change in the behavior of an identified patient and change in the pattern of family or system interactions that are related to the problem behavior. For example, research on marital therapy indicates that spouses often have divergent perceptions of the relationship and that after treatment one spouse may report good marital satisfaction and the

Preparation of this chapter was partially supported by National Institute of Alcohol Abuse and Alcoholism grant RO1 AA/DA 08864.

89

other reports marital dissatisfaction (Bray & Jouriles, 1995). Consequently, resolving such differences is necessary to determine if therapy is effective.

As our knowledge about marital and family therapy interventions has increased, family psychology intervention research has expanded its focus to understanding which processes are critical for engendering therapeutic change (Jacobson & Addis, 1993; Pinsof, 1992). Most reviews indicate that there are relatively few differences in the outcomes of different schools of marital and family therapy (Bray & Jouriles, 1995; Dunn & Schwebel, 1995; Pinsof & Wynne, 1995). Further research is needed to determine the exact nature of the effective change ingredients that contribute most to successful therapy outcomes.

It is also central in both basic family process and outcome research to consider the dynamic and reciprocal nature of family relationships. Most traditional statistical methods are based on linear, mathematical approaches that describe family relations at discrete time points. Although these cross-sectional views are useful, systems theories are nonlinear and circular and emphasize the changing nature of relationships and the mutual influence of various aspects of the system on individual behavior. Methodologies that address change processes, and particularly the reciprocal nature of change within families, are critical for future study in family psychology interventions (Gottman & Rushe, 1993).

Multiple types of quantitative and qualitative methodologies are needed in family psychology intervention research. Assessing family and marital process and outcomes include both experimental and nonexperimental methods. A variety of measurement techniques are also necessary These methods include self-reports from multiple family members, observations and ratings of family interactions, and physiological measurements during family interactions (Bray, 1995c). Each of these approaches needs statistical methods to handle data from multiple sources (e.g., family members, trained raters) and methods (self-report, behavioral observations), and to combine them in meaningful ways to investigate family relationships.

Measurement Issues

At the heart of evaluating the effectiveness of family psychology interventions is whether the critical aspects of individual and family processes and outcomes are measured in reliable and valid ways. Unlike individual psychotherapy and assessment, there are no "gold standard" measurement tools in our field (Bray, 1995b). Thus, family psychology researchers usually rely on multiple methods for assessing process and outcomes. There are benefits and limitations to each of these methods that need to be considered when selecting the appropriate measurement strategies. The three most common measurement methods in family assessment are self-report, paper-and-pencil instruments; behavioral observations of family interactions; and clinician or expert ratings (Bray, 1995c). Although there is modest overlap between self-perceptions and observer ratings, the correlations between the ratings are moderate, at best, between scores from these different methods (Cole & McPherson, 1993; Cook & Goldstein, 1993; Kolevzon, Green, Fortune, & Vosler, 1988; Lashley & Kenny, 1998; Markman & Notarius, 1987).

Self-Report Methods

Self-reports of marital and family functioning are the most widely used method for assessing family relations and processes. Self-reports include self ratings and perceptions of the family by individual family members, reports of affect and emotions while engaging in certain behaviors, and ratings of other family members' behavior or relationships. There are many advantages to self-reports. First, they are relatively easy to gather and inexpensive to use. They can also be administered in recurrent sessions as a gauge for treatment effectiveness and to investigate changes within the family. Thus, they can be used as both process and outcomes measures; however, in this context it is important to select measures that will reflect changes over time rather than only stable family or individual characteristics. Furthermore, it is important to select both global and specific measures of family functioning. It should be noted that self-reports of family functioning are only individual perceptions of family relations or represent attitudes of the reporter and thus do not represent relational data (Bray, 1995b, 1995c; Fisher, Kokes, Ransom, Phillips, & Rudd, 1985). Fredman and Sherman (1987), Grotevant and Carlson (1989), and Touliatos, Perlmutter, and Straus (1990) provide excellent reviews of various family self-report measures.

Observational Methods

Observation of families includes a variety of methods, such as narrative descriptions of family relations or microanalytic coded interactional sequences (Bakeman, & Casey, 1995; Carlson & Grotevant, 1987; Ransom, Fisher, Phillips, Kokes, & Weiss, 1990). The three components of standardized observations are (a) what is observed, such as what task family members are asked to perform; (b) where the task is observed, such as in the home or laboratory; and (c) how the interaction is observed, such as which coding or rating system is used (Bray, 1995c). A common type of task in standardized observations is a problem-solving interaction (Markman & Notarius, 1987) in which family members are asked to identify a common problem, discuss it, and attempt to develop a solution to the problem. This type of interaction task tends to elicit family discord, conflict, and negative emotions. There are also standardized games that are used for problem-solving tasks. Other types of tasks include naturalistic observations, such as observing dinner time or play; planning something together, such as a family trip or vacation; describing qualities of the family; and putting together puzzles or games that require negotiation or problem solving (Grotevant & Carlson, 1989). These varied tasks tend to elicit different types of family interactions. For example, the planning tasks tend to draw out positive interactions and role relationships, while the games tend to elicit problem-solving and conflict resolution behaviors.

The setting for observation can be the home, laboratory, school, or clinic and usually depends on the purpose of the evaluation (Bray, 1995c). For example, parent–child problems are typically observed in the home, while observations of pathology may benefit from a clinic or laboratory setting. Jacob, Tennenbaum, Seilhamer, Bargiel, and Sharon (1994) reported that families show little reactivity to observation, although, as previously noted, different types of behavior may be exhibited in different settings. There may need to be more naturalistic and longer term observations for low base rate behavior than for more frequently occurring behaviors.

How families are observed also varies depending on the purpose and outcome. Observational methods are usually costly and labor-intensive (Bakeman, & Casey, 1995; Markman & Notarius, 1987). However, the advantage for understanding family interaction, emotions, and their relationships to individual and family functioning and outcome is invaluable. Most observational methods range from global or macroanalytic coding systems to microanalytic coding systems.

Global coding systems use trained observers to make ratings or appraisals about a standardized family interaction after viewing all or some large part of a session. In contrast, micro-level coding systems are used to analyze family interactions to provide a rating of interaction process and affect on an interaction-by-interaction basis. This type of coding system provides a sequential accounting of the intercourse and can be useful for identifying patterns of interactions (Bakeman & Casey, 1995; Gottman, 1993; Markman & Notarius, 1987). Other methods of rating families include Q-sorts, in which raters sort a standard set of cards that describe the interactions from *most like* to *least like* (Reiss, 1981; Wampler, Halverson, Moore, & Walters, 1989). Grotevant and Carlson (1989) and Markman and Notarius (1987) provided excellent reviews of various behavioral observation systems.

Clinician Rating Methods

Clinician or expert ratings are a specialized form of observational method. Clinician ratings of family interactions have been developed to provide clinicians with systematic methods for coding and observing family interactions (Bray,

1995c). This type of data draws on the training and experience of the clinician. Some concepts in family psychology, such as differentiation of self or triangulation, may require the extensive training and development of clinicians to make valid ratings. Clinician rating systems can be used in clinical interviews (standardized or unstandardized) and provide valuable information about family interactions and outcomes (Carlson & Grotevant, 1987).

Establishing Comparability in Measurements: Item Response Theory Methods

A fundamental issue in studying families is whether measures are reliable, valid, and applicable to the diversity of families that are found in contemporary society. A central question in comparing groups of individuals from different ethnic, cultural, and demographic backgrounds is whether the measures are comparable across groups. In addition, it is important to know that the measures provide sufficient reliable information across the full range of the construct of interest. In making such comparisons, one assumes that the scores have measurement invariance across groups (Reise, Widaman, & Pugh, 1993).

Although the reliability and validity indices of most family measures are acceptable for research purposes, the measures have typically been developed with White and middle-class samples and have not been psychometrically evaluated with other ethnic groups or examined across the broad developmental family life cycle (Bray, 1995b, 1995c; Embretson, 1996; Hampson, Beavers, & Hulgus, 1990; Morris, 1990; Okazaki & Sue, 1995). Nevertheless, the measures tend to be applied to ethnic and family groups other than those with which they were developed. The meaning of the items it measures in the psychosocial domains could be subject to cultural, developmental, and ethnic differences. It is therefore not clear that group differences reflect "true differences" or simply "measurement differences." In addition, is an item or scale's ceiling too limited to allow for developmental growth and change? The methods used to establish reliability and validity are usually based on classical test theory (Lord, 1980; Nunnally, 1978). Classical test theory tends to focus on the development of scales that represent unmeasured constructs of interest rather than items and their information value.

Two approaches have been developed to examine measurement invariance: confirmatory factor analysis (CFA) and item response theory (IRT) methods (Hulin, Drasgow, & Parsons, 1983; Reckase, Acermean, & Carlson, 1988; Reise et al., 1993; Thissen, 1991; Thissen, Steinberg, & Gerrard, 1986). Confirmatory factor analysis models account for the covariance between test items, while IRT models account for individual item responses (Reise et al., 1993). Item response theory models use a nonlinear function to describe the relation between an individual's level on a latent variable and the probability of a particular item response (Lord, 1980). Equivalence among items is established by examining item discrimination and item difficulty parameters. If these are established as invariant, individuals' scores can be placed on a common metric by using item response functions, even across different groups of people. This enables researchers to examine substantive differences across groups.

Bray and colleagues (Baer & Bray, 1999; Bray, Baer, & Getz, 2000) used IRT methods to establish comparability among three ethnic groups of adolescents (White, Mexican American, and Black adolescents) in a study of family and social influences on adolescent alcohol use. After a first round of data collection, items were evaluated across ethnic groups with the Multilog computer program for IRT analysis (Thissen, 1991). Each scale yielded usable data from adolescent boys and girls ranging from 6th to 12th grade. However, for a few items distributed over several scales it was clear that the information value provided and intergroup comparability were poor. In those instances we modified items by simplifying their language, improving their focus, or making them more culturally and ethnically sensitive and appropriate. We also increased the number of response categories per item to five in those instances where scale items were dichotomous or trichotomous. Increasing response categories adds information value to most items. A second round of data collection was conducted using the modified instruments. Item response theory analyses and factor analyses across samples and ethnic groups revealed substantial improvement for most items that had been problematic in the first round of data. The second-round analyses revealed the nonutility of only a few items.

Although there were a few individual items revealing differential ability to convey meaningfully useful information across groups, a composite of the item information values for each scale did not differ across groups. We considered these results very encouraging, particularly because they allowed us to use second-round data for assessing aspects of our model. Certain adjustments, such as those that clarify and simplify items or expand the response range, should be made routinely. By establishing measurement invariance, we can evaluate ethnic differences on our models and be confident that any differences among groups are not because of measurement invariance.

Evaluating Therapy Outcomes With Clinical Significance

There are multiple experimental and quasi-experimental designs to evaluate the effects of interventions (see Cook & Campbell [1979] and Maxwell & Delaney [1990] for discussions of design issues). Beyond the traditional methods for determining whether an intervention has been successful in changing outcomes of interest is the notion of clinical significance or relevance of outcomes (Hahlweg & Markman, 1988; Jacobson, Follette, & Revenstorf, 1984; Shadish et al., 1993). Clinical significance is measured by comparing posttreatment outcomes to normative data. For example, the clinical cutoff on the Dyadic Adjustment Scale (Spanier, 1976) is 100, with scores below this number considered to reflect distressed couples. In this case the clinical effectiveness of a treatment is assessed by the percentage of couples who are in the nondistressed range (i.e., >100) following marital therapy. This type of bottom-line indication of effectiveness is central to evaluating family psychology interventions.

Although reviewers agree that marital therapy is effective in reducing marital conflict, there is less support for the clinical significance of these outcomes (Bray & Jouriles, 1995). Jacobson and Addis (1993) concluded that "most tested treatments report no better than 50% success" (p. 86). Likewise, Hahlweg and Markman (1988) reported that the clinical significance of change in marital satisfaction and adjustment from participation in behavioral marital therapy had an average effect size of .15. This effect size indicates that a substantial number of couples still report unsatisfying and distressed marriages after treatment. Further, Shadish et al. (1993) found that 41% of couples in marital therapy moved from distressed to nondistressed status following treatment, using a broader sample of marital therapy studies. The use of a clinical significance outcome indicates that existing treatments for marital discord and distress need substantial improvement.

Innovative Modeling and Statistical Methods

Methodologies that address change processes, and particularly the reciprocal nature of change within families, is critical for future study in family psychology (Gottman & Rushe, 1993). For years, family systems theorists have argued that family relationships are not linear, cause-and-effect processes, but rather are circular, nonlinear, and reciprocal. However, until recently there have been no or limited statistical methods that can actually address these types of interdependent relationships.

Hierarchical Linear Modeling

The development of hierarchical linear modeling and growth curve analysis (HLM; Bryk & Raudenbush, 1987, 1992) is an important innovation for studying family psychology interventions. It provides a useful method for considering the effects of context and other nested factors (e.g., family atmosphere or school context) and interdependence of data (i.e., correlations between couple reports) within research designs. In this case the effects of different context factors on individual or family outcomes can be examined.

The application of HLM for growth curve analysis and studying change over time is a major development that facilitates understanding of how various trajectories of change in explanatory variables or interventions may be related to changes in outcomes (Bryk & Raudenbush, 1987; Francis, Fletcher, Stuebing, Davidson, & Thompson, 1991; Raudenbush, Brennan, & Barnett, 1995). The use of HLM is particularly well-suited to the analysis of individual, couple, or family growth curves (Bryk & Raudenbush, 1987; Francis et al., 1991; Raudenbush et al., 1995). Conceptually, HLM application to the study of change consists of two stages. In the first stage, within-subjects analysis (Level 1) estimates the parameters of the individual growth curve for each participant, couple, or family. For example, these parameters might include the rate of change in adolescent alcohol use as measured at each assessment period (the slope with respect to time) and the intercept, which could be scaled to reflect the average level of use for the person. The second stage of HLM examines the degree to which differences between participants (Level 2) predict differences in growth parameters (i.e., individual differences in slopes and intercepts). For example, the rate of change in adolescents' use may be a function of ethnicity, treatment intervention, or gender. Although both phases of the analysis take place simultaneously, it is helpful to conceptualize the process as a within-subjects multiple regression analysis used to obtain estimates of slope and intercept parameters for each participant (Level 1 analysis) where the parameter estimates then become the dependent measures in a between-subjects (Level 2) analysis. In addition, HLM models can include time-varying covariates to answer critically important questions. For example, individuation or family conflict are time-varying covariates that can be incorporated to answer a number of important questions related to alcohol use (Bray, Adams, Getz, & Baer, in press). Examples of questions might be: How are individuation and alcohol use related over time? How does alcohol use change as individuation changes? This type of analysis helps to examine interdependent data from couples or families and how observations for an individual are related to those of another individual or family.

Raudenbush et al. (1995) demonstrated the use of the HLM approach for studying couple relationships. The HLM approach can address issues in a baseline model into which no explanatory variables are incorporated other than time, and it can address explanatory variables on changes in outcomes over time. In the first case, an HLM approach can address questions such as testing for differences in correlated trajectories of husbands and wives that include their initial status, rate of change, and acceleration of change in marital satisfaction. This approach can also enable correlations between husband's and wive's reports of marital satisfaction and correct for measurement errors. Explanatory, time-invariant variables can then be incorporated to explain their influence on changes in outcomes over time. The relative impact of these explanatory variables on husband's and wive's marital satisfaction can then be tested. Further, HLM can model how change in a predictor relates to change in outcomes for each member of the couple, and strength of these relationships for each partner can be compared.

There are several advantages to the HLM approach to the study of change over traditional methodologies such as change score analysis and repeated analysis of variance measures (Francis et al., 1991). Specifically, the latter approaches look only at mean change, while HLM allows examination of the form of individual growth, its correlates, and mean growth. In addition, HLM offers greater power to detect effects of between-subjects characteristics on growth parameters because of its greater precision in estimating within-subjects parameters. HLM also allows separate estimation of variance in slopes caused by sampling error and variance because of participant differences in true slopes. This methodology is flexible and handles common problems of longitudinal family research such as missing data points, unbalanced designs, and variations in time of data collection. It also makes use of whatever within-subjects data are available for a given participant—in other words, it is not necessary to eliminate participants from the analysis because they failed to be present or did not complete all of the measures (Bryk & Raudenbush, 1992). Linear and nonlinear growth patterns, interactions between independent variables, and tests for deviation from linearity in each of the outcome domains are all possible with HLM analyses.

Mathematical Modeling of Marital Relations

Gottman and colleagues (Cook et al., 1995; Gottman, 1993) developed a nonstatistical, mathematical approach to model marital interactions through the use of nonlinear differential equations. This approach is based on Murray's (1989) mathematical models of change in the biological sciences. Gottman's approach provides an empirical method for examining nonlinear and qualitative mathematical modeling of marital relations and provides a new procedure for using existing data to model marital relations. These models can later be validated by experiments. Gottman, Ryan, Carrere, and Erley (chapter 8, this volume) further explain this approach.

Conclusion

There is still much to be learned about both basic family process and interventions to treat marital and family problems. The field needs to develop standards of measurement and agree on the central concepts for study. The field of psychophysiology made major gains in its research efforts after it developed standards for measuring basic physiological processes (Gottman, personal communication, 1995). There are consistent and critical family processes that have been identified by research, such as conflict and communication, that need standardized measurements that can be used in family psychology research

(Bray, 1995b). National panels of researchers in various areas should be brought together to identify these critical processes and develop measurement standards.

Future interventions that include the diversity of modern families is essential (Bray & Hetherington, 1993). Diversity includes differences because of family structure variations (e.g., single-parent families, stepfamilies), ethnic minorities and cultural differences, and gay and lesbian families. Much, if not most, of the research on marital and family process and outcomes is based on White, middle-class families, but the largest growing segments of our population are ethnic minorities, such as Hispanics, and these families frequently experience high rates of psychosocial problems. There has been only limited research on whether our family assessment tools and interventions are applicable to diverse ethnic groups, and even less research on whether our interventions work with these families.

It is clear that more attention is needed to develop sophisticated methodologies that can capture the rich and varied phenomena of family relationships (Bray, 1995a). There are many new and promising methodologies in progress. We need new methods of successfully recruiting and retaining participants in longitudinal studies, particularly from diverse ethnic and socioeconomic backgrounds. Future work is important to develop procedures for dealing with the varied methods and data from multiple family members. These types of innovations will support further development of effective family psychology interventions into the next century.

References

Baer, P. E., & Bray, J. H. (1999). Adolescent individuation and alcohol usage. *Journal of Studies on Alcohol, 13,* 52–62.

Bakeman, R., & Casey, R. L. (1995). Analyzing family interaction using SDIS and GSEQ. *Journal of Family Psychology, 9,* 131–143.

Bray, J. H. (1995a). Methodological advances in family psychology. *Journal of Family Psychology, 9,* 107–109.

Bray, J. H. (1995b). Assessment of family health and distress: An intergenerational–systems perspective. In J. C. Conoley & E. Werth (Eds.), *Family assessment* (pp. 67–102). Lincoln, NE: Buros Institute of Mental Measurement.

Bray, J. H. (1995c). Family assessment: Current issues in evaluating families. *Family Relations, 44,* 469–477.

Bray, J. H., Adams, G., Getz, J. G., & Baer, P. E. (in press). Developmental, family, and ethnic influences on adolescent alcohol usage: A growth curve approach. *Journal of Family Psychology.*

Bray, J. H., Baer, P. E., & Getz, J. G. (2000). Adolescent individuation and alcohol use in multi-ethnic youth. *Journal of Studies on Alcohol, 61,* 588–597.

Bray, J. H., & Hetherington, E. M. (1993). Families in transition: Introduction and overview. *Journal of Family Psychology, 7,* 3–8.

Bray, J. H., & Jouriles, E. (1995). Treatment of marital conflict and prevention of divorce. *Journal of Marital and Family Therapy, 21,* 461–473.

Bryk, A. S., & Raudenbush, S. W. (1987). Application of hierarchical linear models to assessing change. *Psychological Bulletin, 101,* 147–158.

Bryk, A. S., & Raudenbush, S. W. (1992). *Hierarchical linear models: Applications and data analysis techniques.* Newbury Park, CA: Sage.

Carlson, C. I., & Grotevant, H. D. (1987). A comparative review of family rating scales: Guidelines for clinicians and researchers. *Journal of Family Psychology, 1,* 23–47.

Cole, D. A., & McPherson, A. E. (1993). Relation of family subsystems to adolescent depression: Implementing a new family assessment strategy. *Journal of Family Psychology, 7,* 119–133.

Cook, J., Tyson, R., White, J., Rushe, R., Gottman, J., & Murray, J. (1995). The mathematics of marital conflict: Qualitative dynamic mathematical modeling of marital interaction. *Journal of Family Psychology, 9,* 110–130.

Cook, T. D., & Campbell, D. T. (1979). *Quasi-experimentation: Design and analysis issues for field settings.* Chicago: Rand McNally.

Cook, W. L., & Goldstein, M. J. (1993). Multiple perspectives on family relationships: A latent variables model. *Child Development, 64,* 1377–1388.

Dunn, R. L., & Schwebel, A. I. (1995). Meta-analytic review of marital therapy outcome research. *Journal of Family Psychology, 9,* 58–68.

Embretson, S. E. (1996). The new rules of measurement. *Psychological Assessment, 8,* 341–349.

Fisher, L., Kokes, R. F., Ransom, D. C., Phillips, S. L., & Rudd, P. (1985). Alternative strategies for creating "relational" family data. *Family Process, 24,* 213–224.

Francis, D. J., Fletcher, J. M., Stuebing, K. K., Davidson, K. C., & Thompson, K. C. (1991). Analysis of change: Modeling individual growth. *Journal of Consulting and Clinical Psychology, 59,* 27–37.

Fredman, N., & Sherman, R. (1987). *Handbook of measurements for marriage and family therapy.* New York: Brunner/Mazel.

Gottman, J. M. (1993). A theory of marital dissolution and stability. *Journal of Family Psychology, 7,* 57–75.

Gottman, J. M., & Rushe, R. H. (1993). The analysis of change: Issues, fallacies, and new ideas. *Journal of Consulting and Clinical Psychology, 61,* 907–910.

Grotevant, H. D., & Carlson, C. I. (1989). *Family assessment: A guide to methods and measures.* New York: Guilford Press.

Hahlweg, K., & Markman, H. J. (1988). Effectiveness of behavioral marital therapy: Empirical status of behavioral techniques in preventing and alleviating marital distress. *Journal of Consulting and Clinical Psychology, 56,* 440–447.

Hampson, R. B., Beavers, W. R., & Hulgus, Y. (1990). Cross-ethnic family differences: Interactional assessment of White, Black, and Mexican-American families. *Journal of Marital and Family Therapy, 16*, 307–319.

Hulin, C. L., Drasgow, F., & Parsons, C. K. (1983). *Item response theory applied to psychological measurement.* Homewood, IL: Dow Jones-Irwin.

Jacob, T., Tennenbaum, D., Seilhamer, R. A., Bargiel, K., & Sharon, T. (1994). Reactivity effects during naturalistic observation of distressed and nondistressed families. *Journal of Family Psychology, 8*, 354–363.

Jacobson, N. S., & Addis, M. E. (1993). Research on couples and couple therapy: What do we know? Where are we going? *Journal of Consulting and Clinical Psychology, 61*, 85–93.

Jacobson, N. S., Follette, W. C., & Revenstorf, D. (1984). Psychotherapy outcome research: Methods for reporting variability and evaluating clinical significance. *Behavior Therapy, 15*, 336–352.

Kolevzon, M. S., Green, R. G., Fortune, A. E., & Vosler, N. R. (1988). Evaluating family therapy: Divergent methods, divergent findings. *Journal of Marital and Family Therapy, 11*, 277–286.

Lashley, B. R., & Kenny, D. A. (1998). Power estimation in social relations analyses. *Psychological Methods, 3*, 328–338.

Lord, F. M. (1980). *Applications of item response theory to practical testing problems.* Hillsdale, NJ: Erlbaum.

Markman, H. J., & Notarius, C. I. (1987). Coding marital and family interaction: Current status. In T. Jacob (Ed.), *Family interaction and psychopathology: Theories, methods, and findings* (pp. 329–390). New York: Plenum Press.

Maxwell, S. E., & Delaney, H. D. (1990). *Designing experiments and analyzing data: A model comparison perspective.* Belmont, CA: Wadsworth.

Morris, T. M. (1990). Culturally sensitive family assessment: An evaluation of the Family Assessment Device used with Hawaiian-American and Japanese-American families. *Family Process, 29*, 105–116.

Murray, J. D. (1989). *Mathematical biology.* Berlin: Springer-Verlag.

Nunnally, J. C. (1978). *Psychometric theory.* New York: McGraw-Hill.

Okazaki, S., & Sue, S. (1995). Methodological issues in assessment research with ethnic minorities. *Psychological Assessment, 7*, 367–375.

Pinsof, W. M. (1992). Toward a scientific paradigm for family psychology: The integrative process systems perspective. *Journal of Family Psychology, 5*, 432–447.

Pinsof, W. M., & Wynne, L. C. (1995). The effectiveness and efficacy of marital and family therapy: Introduction to the special issue. *Journal of Marital and Family Therapy, 21*, 341–344.

Ransom, D. C., Fisher, L., Phillips, S., Kokes, R. F., & Weiss, R. (1990). The logic of measurement in family research. In T. W. Draper & A. C. Marcus (Eds.), *Family variables: Conceptualization, measurement, and use* (pp. 48–66). Newbury Park: CA: Sage.

Raudenbush, S. W., Brennan, R. T., and Barnett, R. C. (1995). A multivariate hierarchical model for studying psychological change within married couples. *Journal of Family Psychology, 9,* 161–174.

Reckase, M. D., Acermean, T. A., & Carlson, J. E. (1988). Building a unidimensional test using multidimensional items. *Journal of Educational Measurement, 25,* 193–203.

Reise, S. P., Widaman, K. F., & Pugh, R. H. (1993). Confirmatory factor analysis and item response theory: Two approaches for exploring measurement invariance. *Psychological Bulletin, 114,* 552–566.

Reiss, D. (1981). *The family's construction of reality.* Cambridge. MA: Harvard University Press.

Shadish, W. R., Montgomery, L. M., Wilson, P., Wilson, M. R., Bright, I., & Okwumabua, T. (1993). Effects of family and marital psychotherapies: A meta-analysis. *Journal of Consulting and Clinical Psychology, 61,* 992–1002.

Spanier, G. B. (1976). Measuring dyadic adjustment: New scales for assessing the quality of marriage and similar dyads. *Journal of Marriage and the Family, 38,* 15–28.

Thissen, D. (1991). Multilog TM user's guide (Version 6) [Computer software]. Chicago: Scientific Software.

Thissen, D., Steinberg, L., & Gerrard, M. (1986). Beyond group–mean differences: The concept of item bias. *Psychological Bulletin, 99,* 118–128.

Touliatos, J., Perlmutter, B. F., & Straus, M. A. (Eds.). (1990). *Handbook of family measurement techniques.* Newbury Park, CA: Sage.

Wampler, K. S., Halverson, C. F., Moore, J. J., & Walters, L. H. (1989). The Georgia family q-sort: An observational measure of family functioning. *Family Process, 28,* 223–238.

PART 3

Advances in Marital Intervention Research

CHAPTER 6

Developments in Couple Therapy Research

Jackie K. Gollan
Neil S. Jacobson

Intriguing research developments in the past decade regarding the treatment of distressed couple relationships are the supportive pillars for current couple intervention theory and research. In the past 10 years, marital researchers have produced effective treatments for couple distress, and further refined relationship education programs (Halford, 1999). Couple intervention research has also extended its purview to investigate the course of relationship satisfaction and stability over time (sometimes lasting years) to investigate how couple distress develops and fluctuates before and during marriage (Bradbury, 1998; Gottman, 1998). Current research also uses more reliable technologies for assessment and measures of treatment outcome (Berscheid, 1999; Johnson & Lebow, 2000), in addition to relying on methods for monitoring the integrity of couple intervention research (e.g., measuring adherence and competence of research therapists in clinical trials). These findings along with other innumerable developments suggest that the field of couple therapy research has begun a more complicated phase of research investigation. As the foundation of couple therapy has been developed satisfactorily, we now need to address structural questions about adopting new research approaches that will result in improved patient response to treatment.

More empirical investigations of couple interventions are necessary, particularly given the high prevalence and significant public health impact of couple distress. Conflict and dissatisfaction in marriage are common clinical problems among outpatients presenting for psychological treatment. In addition to being highly prevalent, distress in relationships increases the risk of substantial individual maladjustment (e.g., occupational and social disruptions). Moreover, distressed couples also face increased risk for acquiring psychiatric conditions, including major depression (Beach, 2001) and substance use (O'Farrell, Choquette, & Cutter, 1998), in addition to immunological suppression that increases the risk of health problems (Kiecolt-Glaser, Malarkey, Chee, & Newton, 1993; Schmaling & Sher, 2000). Moreover, couple distress increases the risk of divorce. Though the divorce rate has stabilized over the past 8 years, about 50% of first marriages end in divorce (Centers for Disease Control and Prevention, 1995). In addition, compared to never-married and divorced individuals, people in satisfying marriages are significantly more likely to have healthier lifestyles, greater resiliency to the effects of negative life stress, and greater work productivity (Burman & Margolin, 1992). In addition, they also use more health services, detect physical problems earlier, and have a lower chance of developing medical illness (Schmaling & Sher, 2000). Given the public health relevance of couple distress for individuals and their communities, in combination with the significant health advantages of being in a satisfying relationship, new research on improving couple interventions is vital for reducing the impact of this clinical problem.

Significant evidence that supports the utility of couple therapy for distressed individuals has been described in the literature, but there is little systematic research on the long-term effects of couple interventions. Few available controlled trials have evaluated the longevity of treatment effects, and even fewer have included diverse ethnic patient samples. We believe that the emerging paradigm of family psychology intervention science (FPIS) is a promising research program to guide future research on couple interventions. This paradigm is promising because it upholds the ideals of enhancing scientific credibility and interpretive value of couple-based research. For example, the FPIS agenda espouses using research strategies that investigate the process and outcome of psychological treatments for couple distress. It also encourages us to examine factors that protect and create vulnerability to couple distress. Both of these initiatives are consistent with the efforts of relationship researchers to produce scientifically adequate research that supports the viability of couple interventions. In addition to these strategies, the FPIS approach encourages research that reflects the spirit of theoretical integration, relying on cognitive, personality, social, and biological approaches to explain couple processes and response to treatment. Finally, this paradigm encourages efforts to increase the interpretive value of couple therapy research by attending to ecological issues in clinical trials (e.g., sociocultural context, gender issues, etc). This kind of work is important because it increases the flexibility of clinical approaches to diverse populations as well as the generalizability of couple therapy research to managed health care settings.

In this chapter, we begin with a brief review of clinical research on couple interventions to illustrate the research strategies espoused in the model of FPIS. Specifically, we comment on the status of treatment research that investigates the efficacy of couple therapy for relationship distress. Although couple therapies vary widely in terms of explaining the treatment of distress, we examine the ways in which future research may promote the use of empirically supported approaches to treat distressed married and cohabiting couples. We also briefly outline specific couple factors that influence response to treatment in an effort to target couples who do not respond to treatment. Consistent with the emphasis in the FPIS model of synthesizing existing research from different sources, we describe an integrative couple treatment that constitutes a progression from past intervention research (Jacobson & Christensen, 1996). Finally, we review important methodological research strategies that increase the focus on understudied patient populations and the generalizability of couple therapy to managed care.

Current Research

The field of couple therapy is lacking a monolithic theory of change pertaining to adult relationships. It is not particularly worrisome, however, that such a theory has not emerged, in fact, it is unlikely that it ever will. Although most current treatments appear to work equally well, research also indicates that there are many types of good marriages (Gottman, 1993). We suspect, despite the equal efficacy of current treatments, that they all create different types of happy couples when they work. Just as there is more than one way to peel an orange, there is more than one way to facilitate a better relationship—and more than one kind of satisfying relationship can result from our clinical efforts.

Efficacy of Couple Treatments

Six couple treatments have currently been found to be more effective than no therapy (Johnson & Lebow, 2000; Gortner, Gollan, & Jacobson, 1996). These include behavioral marital therapy (BMT; Baucom, Shoham, Mueser, Daiuto, & Stickle, 1998); emotionally focused therapy (EFT; Greenberg & Johnson, 1988; Johnson, Hunsley, Greenberg, & Schindler, 1999); integrative couple therapy (ICT; Cordova, Jacobson, & Christensen, 1998; Jacobson & Christensen, 1996); cognitive–behavioral marital therapy (CBMT; Baucom & Epstein, 1990; Baucom, Epstein, & Rankin, 1995); strategic therapy (Goldman & Greenberg, 1992); and insight-oriented marital therapy (IOMT; Snyder & Wills, 1989; Snyder, Wills, & Grady-Fletcher, 1991). Although limited by small sample sizes, these studies provide useful data for developing subsequent research in confirmatory studies.

Of the six, two treatments are considered to be empirically validated for the treatment of couple distress: BMT (Jacobson & Margolin, 1979) and EFT (Johnson et al., 1999). Behavioral marital therapy is one of the more successful forms of couple treatment and certainly one of the most researched. This approach proposes that couple distress is generated from ineffectual efforts to obtain positive reinforcement from the relationship (Baucom et al., 1998). Partners influence each other's sense of relationship satisfaction through a reciprocal series of punishing and reinforcing responses. Therapy includes behavioral exchange contracts to increase positive interactions, as well as training in problem solving and communication. A meta-analysis indicates that couples receiving BMT had higher scores on outcome measures than 83% of untreated couples (Shadish et al., 1993). There remain, however, unanswered questions about which of these specific behavioral interventions are necessary for therapeutic change (Jacobson & Addis, 1993; Lebow & Gurman, 1995).

Emotionally focused therapy is the second empirically validated couple treatment. Treatment aims to broaden each partner's emotional responses using principles that integrate systemic and gestalt theories. The EFT therapist works with the couple to help each partner soften emotional responses, restructure negative interactional cycles, and develop a more secure attachment. This therapy has demonstrated short-term efficacy with distressed couples in numerous controlled trials (Baucom et al., 1998; Johnson et al., 1999), with approximately 70% of couples reporting no distress at the follow-up assessment (Johnson & Greenberg, 1994).

In general, couples who participate in treatment are typically better off than couples assigned to either no treatment, wait-list control, or attention–placebo conditions. Approximately two thirds of distressed couples report clinical improvement following treatment. Summary statistics from a meta-analysis of 27 studies examining the efficacy of couple therapy in reducing global relationship dissatisfaction (16 studies) and other specific presenting problems (11 studies) indicate that, on average, 65% of couples who participated in active treatment responded favorably, as compared to 36% of couples in the no-treatment comparison groups (Shadish et al., 1993). Notably, the treatment effects reported among these studies vary, depending on the type of control group and the method of analyses. For example, stronger treatment effects that were found in clinical trials that compared BMT to no-treatment conditions versus placebo conditions (Dunn & Schwebel, 1995). The difference may be explained by higher dropout rates often associated with inactive treatment conditions and its contribution to potential bias in experimental group versus control group comparisons. The difference may also be explained by the method of analysis, in which researchers often compare the results of the active treatment to the inactive treatment. We prefer that researchers use this strategy only to show that the experimental condition works and rely on a more sophisticated alternative, using the criteria of clinical significance, to determine couple change and treatment activity (Jacobson & Truax, 1991). In addition, placebo conditions may not be as therapeutically neutral as they are presented to be in clinical trials. Given that 20 to 40% of couples in placebo conditions responded, placebo conditions may offer important nonspecific therapeutic benefits. Finally, placebo control groups constitute a more stringent test of an active treatment, where smaller effect sizes for such comparisons are the norm in psychotherapy research. A preferable strategy for future efficacy studies is to include some form of "treatment as usual" or an established treatment as the control group. This is particularly important considering the methodological difficulties in designing adequate psychotherapy placebo conditions.

It is typical in psychotherapy research to find that different active treatments produce equivalent outcomes for a particular disorder. Closer analysis, however, reveals that in couples intervention research couples report changes in the target areas that are consistent with the theory of clinical change (Baucom & Lester, 1986; Baucom, Sayers, & Sher, 1990; Behrens, Sanders, & Halford, 1990; Dunn & Schwebel, 1995). Couples who participated in CBMT experienced more changes in relationship-related beliefs than couples who participated in IOMT (Baucom et al., 1998). Likewise, EFT couples changed more on measures of marital adjustment, intimacy, and target complaints than couples who received problem-solving training (Johnson & Greenberg, 1985a, 1985b). Because few studies have compared the "specific-target" hypotheses directly, this area is still in the preliminary stages of study. There is evidence, however, that clinical techniques from different couple therapies may complement each other, thereby improving overall outcome. For example, Jacobson and colleagues found that behavior exchange, a component of BMT, showed greater short-term effects than the more process-oriented component of BMT, specifically, communication and problem-solving training (CPT; Jacobson, 1984; Jacobson & Follette, 1985; Jacobson et al., 1985). On the other hand, CPT was associated with more enduring change and less relapse than behavior exchange. Short-term change from behavior exchange, combined with more enduring change from CPT, produced the best outcomes in a complete BMT package that combined both components.

Long-Term Outcome

Many couples who respond to treatment report the recurrence of distress shortly after treatment has ended. Jacobson, Schmaling, and Holtzworth-Munroe (1987) reported that approximately 30% of their initially recovered couples relapsed within 2 years of the end of BMT. Snyder et al. (1991) reported that 38% of their BMT couples divorced within 4 years of exiting therapy. Further, Jacobson's (1989) review indicated that about one fourth of BMT couples relapsed within the first 6 months. Although other investigators have found better results (Bray & Jouriles, 1995), they define recovery as marital stability and divorce prevention rather than the more typical definition of improved relationship satisfaction. Although this underscores the importance of generating a consensus about the definition of treatment outcome, the fact remains that few longitudinal studies have examined the longevity of treatment effects after treatment ends.

Predicting Response to Treatment

Three factors are associated with improved responses to treatment: demographic characteristics, relationship factors and processes, and therapy process characteristics. Younger couples and couples without children respond more readily to therapy than older couples (Baucom, 1984; Hampson, Prince, & Beavers, 1999). In addition, relationship dissatisfaction, emotional disengagement (infrequent sex, low emotional responsiveness), and low relationship commitment (filing for divorce) are associated with a poorer treatment prognosis (Beach & Broderick, 1983; Crowe, 1978; Jacobson, Follette, & Pagel, 1986; Snyder, Mangrum, & Wills, 1993). Treatment efficacy is also reduced among heterosexual couples who follow traditional gender roles (e.g., males as "distancers" and females as "pursuers"; Jacobson, Follette, & Pagel, 1986), when the wife expresses high levels of femininity (Baucom & Aiken, 1984), or when severe psychopathology exists (Snyder et al., 1993). Finally, the therapy process itself predicts future response. Better outcome in BMT is related to the therapist's induction of collaborative behavior between partners and the couple's success in behaving collaboratively outside the session (Holtzworth-Munroe, Jacobson, DeKlyen, & Whisman, 1989). Further, the match between the treatment approach and clients' perception about the goodness of fit with treatment predicts outcome (Crane, Newfield, & Armstrong, 1986). In one study, however, consumer dissatisfaction with the therapist's performance, therapy content, and overall experience were not associated with poor outcome (Jacobson, 1989). Finally, Cookerly (1980) found that participation of both spouses produced better results than the attendance of just one partner. Although these predictor studies provide many intriguing clues, a replication of findings is the missing component.

So why do treated couples reexperience relationship distress? Several hypotheses exist, including the possibilities that (a) the reemergence of negative life stress after therapy may undo the benefits of treatment (Jacobson et al., 1987); (b) couples have difficulty generalizing their learning to situations outside the therapy context; (c) standardized manuals do not address unique problems that couples experience; (d) fewer naturally reinforcing contingencies in the couple's environment encourage the maintenance of adaptive skills (Behrens et al., 1990); and (e) BMT is not potent enough to produce sustainable changes. Although each of these hypotheses are deserving of independent study, we suggest that extending therapy may indeed produce sustainable change and, moreover, help couples to apply what they have learned using naturally reinforcing contingencies.

Integrative Couple Therapy

We are testing these ideas with our new integrative couple therapy (ICT). Whereas typical couple interventions vary between 8 and 16 weeks, our most recent work on ICT allows therapists up to 25 sessions. These are no longer considered short-term treatments in an era of managed care. Our challenge is to produce effects that are large and durable without lengthening treatment. We have high hopes for ICT, although one comparative study is hardly sufficient to prove its worth. As we finish a more definitive comparison between ICT and BMT with 180 couples and two sites (University of Washington and UCLA), we are testing some of the new ideas involved in the integration of change with acceptance as treatment goals. ICT attempts to capitalize on adapting therapy to the individual and to put couples in touch with natural reinforcers. Our manual (Jacobson & Christensen, 1996) is flexible enough to address individual differences in presenting couples. Only time will tell if these innovations truly enhance treatment outcome.

Integrative couple therapy, developed by couple therapy researchers Jacobson and Christensen (Christensen, Jacobson, & Babcock, 1995; Jacobson & Christensen, 1996), returns to the philosophical roots of behaviorism, or contextualism. The therapy emphasizes using functional analyses to determine the problems and treatment formulation for distressed couples. The therapy relies more on the use of natural contingencies to improve relationships than on the rule-governed procedures that characterize BMT. For example, ICT attempts to make use of natural reinforcers rather than the contrived ones used in traditional contingency contracts. ICT relies on two generic goals to promote emotional acceptance between partners: (a) to promote empathic joining or unified detachment with the goal of turning problem areas into sources of renewed intimacy; and (b) to build tolerance for negative behavior, with the goal of reducing the toxicity of problems so that even if they do not go away, they do less damage to the relationship. This therapy continues to include the traditional change strategies that characterize BMT but integrates those strategies with others that are necessary to promote acceptance.

The efficacy of these acceptance strategies is being tested in a recent study (Jacobson, Christensen, Prince, Cordova, & Eldridge, 2000). Integrative couple therapy produced improvement rates that were higher than any that we have seen in a marital therapy outcome study, and despite a very small sample ($N = 20$), significantly outperformed BMT: 89% of ICT couples improved or recovered after 13 to 25 sessions of therapy, compared to 64% of traditional BMT couples. If future studies replicate and extend this finding, ICT may emerge as a particularly effective intervention with distressed couples (Cordova et al., 1998).

Couple Treatments for Other Psychiatric Disorders

Couple therapy has become a viable treatment modality for other psychiatric conditions, including depressive disorders (Beach, 2001), substance abuse disorders (Maisto, McKay, & O'Farrell, 1998), and trauma-related conditions (Johnson & Williams-Keeler, 1998). In treatment, couple therapy for depression or for substance abuse relies on altering the couple's relationship as a means of promoting therapeutic change for the individual. Because the treatment focuses on modifying couple dynamics, couple therapy is most useful in cases where the psychopathology is related to the relationship distress and when both partners agree to participate. In the area of depression, which has received the most research attention, findings indicate that couple therapies for depression offer effective treatment for depression and relationship distress, particularly in cases where the mood disorder is related to the relationship problems (Beach, Fincham, & Katz, 1998).

Evidence for the viability for couple therapy for psychiatric disorders, particularly depression, derives from research showing that couple-based therapies for depression generate better treatment response compared to individual treatments among distressed–depression couples (Beach, 2001). Because couple therapy improves the quality of relationships more than individual therapies for depression, it may be that couple therapy is more appropriate for couples experiencing concurrent distress and depression. This suggests that couple therapies may be able to modify important relational factors that individual therapies cannot reach, thereby having greater therapeutic value over and above what individual psychotherapies offer.

Research Considerations

This section describes a set of conceptual issues and methodological strategies that we believe should be addressed to guide future scientific investigations of couple treatments. Specifically, we highlight the use of contextual definitions to describe successful treatment outcome and the need for using the criterion of clinical significance instead of statistical significance. Following this, we review the limitations of existing research and make suggestions for remedying these problems to produce scientifically adequate research.

Defining Treatment Response

A shift in our understanding about what defines successful response to treatment is under way. The most common criterion for defining response is evidence of continued relationship stability as well as an increase in relationship satisfaction. Likewise, ending a relationship through divorce has commonly been thought of as a treatment failure, yet there are cases where one or both partners end their relationship as a result of therapy and then report satisfaction with the therapy process and outcome. Indeed, we would consider such an outcome to be a success in our clinical practices. Couple therapy is not just about promoting long relationships despite continued misery on the part of one or both partners. In our view, the success of couple therapy depends on the emotional health of both individuals and their children. We recommend that measures of individual well-being, psychopathology, and child outcomes be included in a standard battery of outcome measures. If comprehensive assessments of both adults and children were included as a standard battery and the follow-ups were long enough, we would be able to determine empirically whether divorce was a positive or a negative outcome for a particular couple. In the meantime, we suggest that divorce not be considered a treatment failure but rather a third potential outcome of couple therapy (the first two being either the relationship improves or it does not). Until we are informed about who benefited and who was harmed by divorce, we should reserve judgment that divorce is a poor outcome of couple therapy. In other words, we should not automatically assume that divorce is a bad outcome, or for that matter that staying together is a good outcome.

Clinical Significance

One significant advance in couple therapy methodology is the emphasis on ascertaining clinically significant change. Before 1984, the conventional approach was to describe therapeutic change by using inferential statistics, comparing the differences between groups based on mean scores from pre- to post-treatment. These analyses adequately identified whether group differences were statistically significant but did not address the practical importance of the effects, that is, their clinical significance. Jacobson and Truax (1991) popularized a method developed earlier for determining the clinical significance of treatment effects (Jacobson, Follette, & Revenstorf, 1984, 1986; Jacobson & Revenstorf, 1988). We hope that such methods help investigators present more informative results, including both variability in outcome across the sample and the extent to which couples return to relationship satisfaction as a result of therapy. By focusing on both clinical and statistical significance, intervention research is more relevant to clinical practice.

If we apply the more stringent criteria of clinical significance to our review of the effectiveness of couple therapy, we find that the success rates are less impressive than either meta-analyses or significance tests would have led us to believe. Research studies that used clinical significance statistics have reported thus far that only a small proportion of couples are truly happily married by the end of the therapy (Hahlweg & Markman, 1988). One reanalysis of four

BMT studies reported that, on average, 35% of the couples recovered (joined the ranks of the nondistressed) and approximately 65% remained at least somewhat distressed at the end of therapy (Jacobson, Follette, Revenstorf, et al., 1984). These rates are comparable to Shadish and colleagues (1993), who reported that 41% of the active treatment couples experienced clinically significant improvement. Although the results are disappointing, clinical significance criteria generate more meaningful and realistic standards for measuring the efficacy of couple therapy.

Clinical Trials

The merits of previous efficacy findings have been compromised by three limitations (Pinsof & Wynne, 2000). First, large-scale studies that compare theoretically different treatments are rarely informative about change, particularly given their expense. They usually produce null findings, and they are typically difficult to manage. Second, large sample sizes are often used to detect effects that are so small as to be clinically trivial, and yet null findings are still the norm. Third, multiple-site studies often fail to control for the omnipresent allegiance effect within each site. With large-scale studies it is often impossible to keep both the investigators' communication of biases from the research therapists and maintain the necessary blindness to the experimental conditions. It is also difficult to ensure adherence to treatment protocols without supervising the therapists so intensively as to make the results totally devoid of clinical relevance. If multiple-site studies are to be conducted where different treatments are compared, allegiance must be controlled for within each site or, if possible, we should attempt to remove the competing biases and use neutral experts as primary investigators.

There may be a reason why studies that compare theoretically distinct models fail to show differential treatment effects: Such effects may not exist. It is more likely that outcome is related to interactions among treatment, therapist, and client characteristics that are difficult to detect and predict in current underpowered studies. Studies that examine whether certain types of clients will benefit from certain targeted treatments, so-called matching studies, may be able to disentangle some of these interactions. We've already identified characteristics that promote therapy success in BMT, but it may be that different factors are crucial with other therapies to promote their optimal potency. For example, emotion-focused, strategic, and insight-oriented couple therapies all might require different clinical skills.

The development of more sophisticated methodologies for aggregating and interpreting findings from individual studies has clearly advanced the field. One obvious example is meta-analysis, where, through simultaneous analyses of multiple studies, we can now discern general trends and recommend where to direct future research. Conceptually and statistically, this type of analysis is conducted by using the study, rather than the individual, as the unit of analysis. The primary advantage of meta-analysis is that it provides a method for summarizing the findings from many studies and often leads to conclusions that were not visible based simply on a narrative, integrative review. Furthermore, investigators can generate and evaluate hypotheses based on the results from a number of studies, including hypotheses that cannot be tested in just one study. Meta-analyses advance the field through their decision rules for selecting studies. They identify deficiencies in current studies that actually matter, such as the incomplete presentation of results or inadequate aspects of the design (e.g., small sample sizes leading to insufficient statistical power).

Critics have questioned the utility of meta-analyses, noting that human error may influence the selection of exclusion and inclusion criteria. Meta-analytic reviews can create erroneous and misleading conclusions that are not necessarily superior to traditional narrative reviews of the literature. Wilson (1985) reviewed some of the controversies regarding the correct equation for computing effect sizes, including weighing studies with different sample sizes and outcome measures, treating poorly conceived and well-designed studies equally, and collapsing data based on homogeneous samples across diverse patient populations.

Treatment Integrity

There are several things that research investigators should do to ensure that they have set up a strong test of any particular treatment. The first step involves using a version of the treatment that fairly represents an optimal test of its efficacy. Then, once efficacy has been established, it is important to make sure that future studies concern themselves with a fair representation of how the treatment is actually carried out in a typical clinical practice. When we are at this stage of research, the concern is with effectiveness rather than efficacy. In the couple therapy arena, however, we are typically still operating at the basic level of efficacy, asking questions such as, Does the treatment work? A recent example of problematic efficacy research can be found in the study by Snyder and colleagues (Snyder & Wills, 1989; Snyder et al., 1991). Jacobson (1991) concluded, after reviewing Snyder's manuals, that insight-oriented couple therapy (IOCT) was more representative of contemporary behavioral therapy than Snyder's BMT manual. Therefore, BMT may not have been given a fair test in this study. In fact, neither treatment condition was adequately or realistically represented. To establish comparative efficacy, it is important that future studies ensure that the two or more treatments are both "state of the art."

Researchers have developed treatment manuals in an effort to standardize theory-driven treatments. These manuals offer detailed descriptions of procedures and techniques that operationalize therapy practices. The methodological advantages these manuals present include a standardization of therapist training and therefore increased accuracy in replication at other sites. Manuals facilitate use of state-of-the-art treatment protocols in clinical practice, which narrows the gulf between research and practice. Although manuals represent a methodological advance, adherence to a manual may reduce a therapist's clinical flexibility. Further, manuals may not adequately describe how to treat complex therapeutic processes.

A third methodological advance is the development of technology to measure the integrity of the psychotherapy protocol. This includes the analysis of treatment adherence and therapist competence during and after the study (see Waltz, Addis, Koerner, & Jacobson, 1993). *Therapist adherence* refers to the therapist's ability to perform the interventions reviewed in the treatment manual and avoid the implementation of intervention strategies that are incompatible with the manual. *Treatment competence* refers to the therapist's ability to use the desired treatment strategies effectively. One basis for the plethora of null findings in comparative trials may be the incompetent administration of one or more treatments. Treatment integrity may have been compromised by adherence failures such as unwanted overlap between treatments intended to be distinct. We recommend the following: (a) define competence for any given study using the manual in that study as the basis for operationalizing the construct; (b) assess adherence using a manual-based measure that is behaviorally specific and includes ratings of therapist behaviors that are specific and nonspecific relative to the treatment modality; and (c) refine rating systems that rate the extent to which therapists are doing what was prescribed (Waltz et al., 1993). Future studies should regularly include documentation of treatment integrity to establish that therapists adhered competently to treatment protocols.

Effectiveness of Treatment

Another way to advance the field is to better understand the clinical utility of each therapy approach. Most of our knowledge in couple therapy is based on efficacy studies where the aim is to determine whether a treatment effect exists and to err on the side of experimental precision at the expense of generalizability. Efficacy studies are most precise when they recruit large homogeneous samples, randomize participants to treatment conditions, and train therapists to confine themselves to the techniques of interest. Efficacy studies, however, bear little resemblance to what goes on in clinical practice. For example, trials concerned with generalizability (often called effectiveness studies) use self-referred, heterogeneous samples; focus on complicated problems, including patients with multiple disorders; and use therapists who use multiple techniques and rarely confine themselves to a treatment manual. In summary, efficacy studies do not say much about the generalizability, feasibility, and cost-effectiveness of the therapy in normal clinical practice.

Investigators have suggested methodological innovations as a way to combine experimental precision with generalizability. Kendall and Lipman (1991) have pointed out that studies may construct a research design where the level of experimental control over the therapy protocol is manipulated, ranging from rigid adherence to clinician freedom. One example of this strategy is a study completed by Jacobson et al. (1989) where a "research structured" version was compared to "clinically flexible" versions of BMT. This type of study simultaneously measured and compared an approach emphasizing efficacy with one emphasizing clinical utility, bringing clinical trial conditions into a more naturalistic setting. This strategy provides useful information about how clinicians deviate from protocols when left to their own devices and the relative degree of success when they are allowed to deviate. Other researchers suggest a strategy that looks at the interaction of treatment and problem complexity and stratifies clients on the basis of problem complexity (based on level of severity or co-morbidity) and then randomly assigns clients within these stratified conditions (Clarke, 1995). Investigators need to refocus some of their efforts toward understanding clinical effectiveness issues by balancing their need for rigor and accountability with clinicians' needs for informed and pragmatic decision making.

We note that studies could increase generalizability by including more representative samples. Most studies use very strict participant inclusion criteria, creating a sample that limits the applicability of treatment to practicing clinicians. Virtually no program of research has systematically analyzed the effectiveness of couple therapy for couples with varying ethnic, cultural, or religious backgrounds (Falicov, 1995) or same-sex couples (Bepko & Johnson, 2000; Brown, 1995). Investigators need to address cross-cultural issues by including participants with varied ethnic backgrounds and same-sex as well as heterosexual couples (Jones & Chao, 1997).

Finally, anticipating the challenges that couple therapy will face with the changing health delivery system, there needs to be substantial effort in learning more about the cost-effectiveness of couple therapy. We currently have little data about the direct costs of treatment and the benefits of deciding whether to divorce or stay married. Costs of treatment include therapeutic services (covering rent, record keeping, therapist's costs, and interface with managed care), and costs to the patient include wages lost, fees paid, and transportation costs. The couple's insurers and employers may also incur costs from marital distress and ineffective therapy. Information of this kind will pressure the field to justify and modify its expenses, demonstrate its financial benefits to insurers and the health care system, and play a larger role in social policy development.

Conclusion

Despite the growth in this field, there are limits to our understanding of how couples do and do not respond to treatment. Further research goals include tailoring couple treatments to diverse clinical and ethnic populations, attention to treatment integrity protocols, and integration with effectiveness research. There is significant evidence supporting the continued clinical development and empirical study of couple therapy. Although there has been considerable work so far, couple therapy can be considered to be in its adolescence, particularly when compared to research on individual psychological treatments. We believe that the emerging area of family psychology intervention science represents a promising new paradigm in the study of distressed couples that may significantly improve the clinical care of this population.

References

Baucom, D. H. (1984). The active ingredients of behavioral marital therapy: The effectiveness of problem-solving/communication training, contingency contracting, and their communication. In K. Hahlweg & N. S. Jacobson (Eds.), *Marital interaction: Analysis and modification* (pp. 73–88). New York: Guilford Press.

Baucom, D. H., & Aiken, P. (1984). Sex role identity, marital satisfaction, and response to behavioral marital therapy. *Journal of Consulting and Clinical Psychology, 52,* 438–444.

Baucom, D. H., & Epstein, N. (1990). *Cognitive–behavioral marital therapy.* New York: Brunner/Mazel.

Baucom, D. H., Epstein, N., & Rankin, L. A. (1995). Cognitive aspects of cognitive–behavioral marital therapy. In N. S. Jacobson & A. S. Gurman (Eds.), *Clinical handbook of couple therapy* (pp. 65–90). New York: Guilford Press.

Baucom, D. H., & Lester, G. W. (1986). The usefulness of cognitive restructuring as an adjunct to behavioral marital therapy. *Behavior Therapy, 17,* 385–403.

Baucom, D. H., Sayers, S. L., & Sher, T. G. (1990). Supplementing behavioral marital therapy with cognitive restructuring and emotional expressiveness training: An outcome investigation. *Journal of Consulting and Clinical Psychology, 58,* 636–645.

Baucom, D. H., Shoham, V., Mueser, K., Daiuto, A., & Stickle, T. (1998). Empirically supported couple and family interventions for marital distress and adult mental health problems. *Journal of Consulting and Clinical Psychology, 66,* 53–88.

Beach, S., & Broderick, J. E. (1983). Commitment: A variable in women's response to marital therapy. *American Journal of Family Therapy, 11,* 16–24.

Beach, S. R. H. (2001). *Marital and family processes in depression: A scientific foundation for clinical practice.* Washington, DC: American Psychological Association.

Beach, S. R. H., Finehow, F. B., & Katz, J. (1998). Marital therapy in the treatment of depression: Toward a third generation of therapy and research. *Clinical Psychology Review, 18*(6), 635–661.

Behrens, B. C., Sanders, M. R., & Halford, K. (1990). Behavioral marital therapy: An evaluation of treatment effect across high and low risk settings. *Behavior Therapy, 21,* 423–433.

Bepko, C., & Johnson, T. (2000). Gay and lesbian couples in therapy: Perspectives for the contemporary family therapist. *Journal of Marriage and Family Therapy, 26,* 409–419.

Berscheid, E. (1999). The greening of relationship science. *American Psychologist, 54,* 260–266.

Bradbury, T. N. (Ed.). (1998). *The developmental course of marital dysfunction.* New York: Cambridge University Press.

Bray, J. H., & Jouriles, E. N. (1995). Treatment of marital conflict and prevention of divorce. *Journal of Marital and Family Therapy, 21,* 461–473.

Brown, L. S. (1995). Therapy with same-sex couples: An introduction. In N. S. Jacobson & A. S. Gurman (Eds.), *Clinical handbook of couple therapy* (pp. 274–294). New York: Guilford Press.

Burman, B., & Margolin, G. (1992). Analysis of the association between marital relationships and health problems: An interactional perspective. *Psychological Bulletin, 112,* 39–63.

Centers for Disease Control and Prevention. (1995). *Monthly Vital Statistics* (Report 43, No. 13). Washington, DC: U.S. Public Health Service.

Christensen, A., Jacobson, N. S., & Babcock, J. C. (1995). Integrative behavioral couple therapy. In N. S. Jacobson, & A. S. Gurman (Eds.), *Clinical handbook of couple therapy* (pp. 31–62). New York: Guilford Press.

Clarke, G. N. (1995). Improving the transition from basic efficacy research to effectiveness studies: Methodological issues and procedures. *Journal of Consulting and Clinical Psychology, 63,* 718–725.

Cookerly, J. R. (1980). Does marital therapy do any lasting good? *Journal of Marital and Family Therapy, 6,* 393–397.

Cordova, J. V., Jacobson, N. S., & Christensen, A. (1998). Acceptance versus change interventions in behavioral couple therapy: Impact on couples' in-session communication. *Journal of Marital and Family Therapy, 24,* 437–455.

Crane, D. R., Newfield, N., & Armstrong, D. (1986). Predicting divorce at marital therapy intake: Wives' distress and the marital status inventory. *Journal of Marital and Family Therapy, 10,* 305–312.

Crowe, M. J. (1978). Conjoint marital therapy: A controlled outcome study. *Psychological Medicine, 8,* 623–636.

Dunn, R. L., & Schwebel, A. I. (1995). Meta-analytic review of marital therapy outcome research. *Journal of Family Psychology, 9,* 58–68.

Falicov, C. J. (1995). Cross-cultural marriages. In N. S. Jacobson & A. S. Gurman (Eds.), *Clinical handbook of couple therapy* (pp. 231–246). New York: Guilford Press.

Goldman, A., & Greenberg, L. (1992). Comparison of integrated systemic and emotionally focused approaches to couple therapy. *Journal of Consulting and Clinical Psychology, 60,* 962–969.

Gortner, E., Gollan, J. K., & Jacobson, N. S. (1996). Couples therapy. In A.Tasman, J. Kay, & J. A. Lieberman (Eds.), *Psychiatry* (pp. 1452–1474). Philadelphia: Saunders.

Gottman, J. M. (1993). The roles of conflict engagement, escalation, and avoidance in marital interaction: A longitudinal view of five types of couples. *Journal of Consulting and Clinical Psychology, 61,* 6–15.

Gottman, J. M. (1998). Psychology and the study of marital processes. *Annual Review of Psychology, 49,* 169–197.

Greenberg, L. S., & Johnson, S. M. (1988). *Emotionally focused couples therapy.* New York: Guilford Press.

Hahlweg, K., & Markman, H. J. (1988). Effectiveness of behavioral marital therapy: Empirical status of behavioral techniques in preventing and alleviating marital distress. *Journal of Consulting and Clinical Psychology, 56,* 440–447.

Halford, W. K. (1999). *Australian couples in millennium three: A research and development agenda for marriage and relationship education.* Report to the National Family Strategy Task Force, Australian Department and Community Services. Brisbane: Australian Academic Press.

Hampson, R. B., Prince, C. C., & Beavers, W. R. (1999). Marital therapy: Qualities of couples who fare better or worse in treatment. *Journal of Marital and Family Therapy, 25,* 411–424.

Holtzworth-Munroe, A., Jacobson, N. S., DeKlyen, M., & Whisman, M. A. (1989). Relationship between behavioral marital therapy outcome and process variables. *Journal of Consulting and Clinical Psychology, 57,* 658–662.

Jacobson, N. S. (1984). A component analysis of behavioral marital therapy: The relative effectiveness of behavioral exchange and communication/problem-solving training. *Journal of Consulting and Clinical Psychology, 52,* 295–305.

Jacobson, N. S. (1989). The maintenance of treatment gains following social learning-based marital therapy. *Behavior Therapy, 20,* 325–326.

Jacobson, N. S. (1991). Behavioral versus insight-oriented marital therapy: Labels can be misleading. *Journal of Consulting and Clinical Psychology, 59*(1), 142–145.

Jacobson, N. S., & Addis, M. (1993). Research on couples and couple therapy: What do we know? Where are we going? *Journal of Consulting and Clinical Psychology, 61,* 85–93.

Jacobson, N. S., & Christensen, A. (1996). *Integrative couple therapy: Promoting acceptance and change.* New York: Norton.

Jacobson, N. S., Christensen, A., Prince, S., Cordova, J., & Eldridge, K. (2000). Integrative behavioral couple therapy: An acceptance-based, ICT versus TBCT treatment outcome study promising new treatment for couple discord. *Journal of Consulting and Clinical Psychology 68,* 351–355.

Jacobson, N. S., & Follette, W. C. (1985). Clinical significance of improvement resulting from two behavioral marital therapy components. *Behavior Therapy, 16,* 249–262.

Jacobson, N. S., Follette, V. M., Follette, W. C., Holtzworth-Munroe, A., Katt, J. L., & Schmaling, K. B. (1985). A component analysis of behavioral marital therapy: 1-year follow-up. *Behavior Research and Therapy, 23,* 549–555.

Jacobson, N. S., Follette, W. C., & Pagel, M. (1986). Predicting who will benefit from behavioral marital therapy. *Journal of Consulting and Clinical Psychology, 54,* 518–522.

Jacobson, N. S., Follette, W. C., & Revenstorf, D. (1984). Psychotherapy outcome research: Methods for reporting variability and evaluating clinical significance. *Behavior Therapy, 15,* 336–352.

Jacobson, N. S., Follette, W. C., & Revenstorf, D. (1986). Toward a standard definition of clinical significant change. *Behavior Therapy, 17,* 308–311.

Jacobson, N. S., Follette, W. C., Revenstorf, D., Baucom, D. H., Hahlweg, K., & Margolin, G. (1984). Variability in outcome and clinical significance of behavioral marital data: A reanalysis of outcome data. *Journal of Consulting and Clinical Psychology, 52,* 497–504.

Jacobson, N. S., & Margolin, G. (1979). *Marital therapy: Strategies based on social learning and behavior exchange principles.* New York: Brunner/Mazel.

Jacobson, N. S., & Revenstorf, D. (1988). Statistics for assessing the clinical significance of psychotherapy techniques: Issues, problems, and new developments. *Behavioral Assessment, 10,* 133–145.

Jacobson, N. S., Schmaling, K. B., & Holtzworth-Munroe, A. (1987). Component analysis of behavioral marital therapy: 2-year follow-up and prediction of relapse. *Journal of Marital and Family Therapy, 13,* 187–195.

Jacobson, N. S., Schmaling, K. B., Katt, J. L., Wood, L. F., Holtzworth-Munroe, A., & Follette, V. M. (1989). Research structured versus clinically flexible versions of social learning-based marital therapy. *Behavior Research Therapy, 27,* 173–180.

Jacobson, N. S., & Truax, P. (1991). Clinical significance: A statistical approach to defining meaningful change in psychotherapy research. *Journal of Consulting and Clinical Psychology, 59,* 12–19.

Johnson, S., & Lebow, J. (2000). The "coming of age" of couple therapy: A decade review. *Journal of Marital and Family Therapy, 26,* 23–28.

Johnson, S. M., & Greenberg, L. S. (1985a). Differential effects of experiential and problem solving interventions in resolving marital conflict. *Journal of Consulting and Clinical Psychology, 53,* 175–184.

Johnson, S. M., & Greenberg, L. S. (1985b). Emotionally focused couple therapy: An outcome study. *Journal of Marital and Family Therapy, 11,* 313–317.

Johnson, S. M., & Greenberg, L. S. (Eds.). (1994). *The heart of the matter: Perspectives on emotion in marital therapy.* New York: Brunner/Mazel.

Johnson, S. M., Hunsley, J., Greenberg, L., & Schindler, D. (1999). Emotionally focused couples therapy: Status and challenges. *Clinical Psychology: Science and Practice, 6,* 67–79.

Johnson, S. M., & Williams-Keeler, L. (1998). Creating healing relationships for couples dealing with trauma: The use of emotionally focused marital therapy. *Journal of Marital and Family Therapy, 24,* 25–40.

Jones, A. C., & Chao, C. M. (1997). Racial, ethnic and cultural issues in couple therapy. In W. K. Halford & H. Markman (Eds.), *Clinical handbook of marriage and couples interventions* (pp. 157–176). New York: Wiley.

Kendall, P. C., & Lipman, A. J. (1991). Psychological and pharmacological therapy: Methods and modes for comparative outcome research. *Journal of Consulting and Clinical Psychology, 59,* 78–87.

Kiecolt-Glaser, J., Malarkey, W., Chee, M., & Newton, T. (1993). Negative behavior during marital conflict is associated with immunological breakdown. *Psychosomatic Medicine, 55,* 395–409.

Lebow, J. L., & Gurman, A. S. (1995). Research assessing couple and family therapy. *Annual Review of Psychology, 46,* 27–57.

Maisto, S., McKay, J. R., & O'Farrell, T. J. (1998). Twelve-month abstinence from alcohol and long-term drinking and marital outcomes in men with severe alcohol problems. *Journal of Studies on Alcohol, 59,* 591–598.

O'Farrell, T. J., Choquette, K. A., & Cutter, H. S. G. (1998). Couples relapse prevention sessions after behavioral marital therapy for male alcoholics: Outcomes during three years after starting treatment. *Journal of Studies on Alcohol, 59,* 357–370.

Pinsof, W. M., & Wynne, L. C. (2000). Towards progress research: Closing the gap between family therapy practice and research. *Journal of Family and Marital Therapy, 26,* 1–8.

Schmaling, K. D., & Sher, T. G. (Eds.). (2000). *The psychology of couples and illness.* Washington, DC: American Psychological Association.

Shadish, W. R., Montgomery, L. M., Wilson, P., Wilson, M. R., Bright, I., & Okwumabua, T. (1993). Effects of family and marital psychotherapies: A meta-analyses. *Journal of Consulting and Clinical Psychology, 61,* 992–1002.

Snyder, D. K., Mangrum, L. F., & Wills, R. M. (1993). Predicting couples' response to marital therapy: A comparison of short- and long-term predictors. *Journal of Consulting and Clinical Psychology, 61,* 61–69.

Snyder, D. K., & Wills, R. M. (1989). Behavioral versus insight-oriented marital therapy: Effect on individual and interspousal functioning. *Journal of Consulting and Clinical Psychology, 57,* 39–46.

Snyder, D. K., Wills, R. M., & Grady-Fletcher, A. (1991). Long-term effectiveness of behavioral versus insight-oriented marital therapy: A 4-year follow-up study. *Journal of Consulting and Clinical Psychology, 59,* 138–141.

Waltz, J., Addis, M., Koerner, K., & Jacobson, N. S. (1993). Testing the integrity of a psychotherapy protocol: Assessment of adherence and competence. *Journal of Consulting and Clinical Psychology, 61,* 620–630.

Wilson, G. T. (1985). Limitations of meta-analyses in the evaluation of the effect of psychological therapy. *Clinical Psychology Review, 5,* 35–47.

CHAPTER 7

Preventive Interventions for Couples

Benjamin Silliman
Scott M. Stanley
William Coffin
Howard J. Markman
Pamela L. Jordan

Couple bonds create significant developmental and social niches for adults. The emotional and financial consequences of these relationships have a major impact on the well-being of adults (Cowan & Cowan, 1995; Kitson & Morgan, 1990), children (Grych & Fincham, 1990), and communities (Larson, Sawyers, & Larson, 1995; Popenoe, 1993). Additionally, marital conflict and distress negatively affects worker productivity (Forthofer, Markman, Cox, Stanley, & Kessler, 1996). Increased marital distress is correlated with a pattern of rising expectations for egalitarian partnerships in conjunction with declining social support, living standards, and requisite interpersonal skills (Olson & DeFrain, 1994). Nevertheless, many couples, including some at risk for distress, violence, or breakup, show remarkable resiliency in the face of these challenges (Karney & Bradbury, 1995) as a result of personal effort and help seeking. Understanding the dynamics of resilient marriages and enhancing couple competence through prevention programs is viewed as critical to effective couple and parental role performance (Coie et al., 1993; Markman, Floyd, Stanley, & Lewis, 1986).

The objectives of this chapter are to (a) review conceptual frameworks for approaches to preventing distress and divorce and promoting marital adjustment; (b) review current approaches for preventing marital distress and divorce; and (c) outline key issues in the development of the field.

Preparation of this chapter was supported in part by a National Institute of Mental Health, Prevention Research Grant, Grant 5-RO1-MH35525-12, Long Term Effects Of Premarital Intervention.

A Framework for Preventive Intervention With Couples

Interest in prevention of distress and divorce is relatively recent (Hahlweg & Markman, 1988), and professional intervention with couples generally has followed a medical model (Stahmann & Hiebert, 1987). In addition to averting or moderating human dysfunctional processes or consequences, prevention advocates and emphasizes building couple competence in the face of increasing expectations and demands (Guerney & Maxson, 1990; L'Abate & Lantz, 1990). Preventive approaches can be the most effective and economical way to address couple issues over the long term (Price, Cowen, Lorion, & Ramos-McKay, 1989). Prevention or health promotion programs developed for couples fit the public health classification (Commission on Chronic Illness, 1957) of (a) *primary prevention,* or proactive efforts to reduce emotional and behavioral deficits or disorders or maintain healthy functioning; and (b) *secondary prevention,* or early identification, diagnosis, and treatment of deficits to avert more serious breakdown or to establish healthy functioning. Primary and secondary interventions can be used with non- or mildly symptomatic couples to facilitate (a) developmental transitions (e.g., first or remarriage, empty nest), (b) resolution of conflict over differences (e.g., financial decisions, parenting styles), (c) relationship deterioration caused by life crises (e.g., strains related to child hospitalization), and (d) social support (e.g., esteem and practical aid). As discussed later, primary and secondary programs for couples have typically focused on assessment, self and other awareness, enhancing knowledge for decision making, and interpersonal skills development.

Risk and Protective Factors

Effective intervention in prevention science relies on systematic study of risk and protective factors that predispose dysfunction and health (Coie et al., 1993). *Risk factors* include individual and environmental hazards that predispose negative developmental outcomes. *Protective factors* are safeguards against risks or conditions that foster adaptation and competence. Specific outcomes emanate from complex interactions of risks and protective factors, which vary across individuals, developmental stages, and contexts (Coie et al., 1993).

The etiology of marital distress and divorce is increasingly well understood, providing a research base that can inform preventionists with regard to the optimal targets for raising protective factors and lowering risk factors for couples (Clements, Stanley, & Markman, 1997; Gottman, 1993, 1994; Karney & Bradbury, 1995; Kurdek, 1993; Larson & Holman, 1994; Matthews, Wickrama, & Conger, 1996). Nevertheless, in a review of marital research, Glenn (1990) noted the preponderance of atheoretical and methodologically flawed investigations. He urged greater scrutiny of the processes underlying patterns of satisfaction across the life cycle such as marital duration, attrition of research participants, and differences among age cohorts.

Although more and better research is needed, preventionists have much to act on from the current knowledge base. A survey of longitudinal investigations of marital quality and stability led Karney and Bradbury (1995) to propose a model that integrates (a) environmental and dispositional influences identified by attachment theory with (b) interactive dimensions featured in behavioral theory and (c) life events critical to crisis theory into a path model describing the elements and mechanisms that shape marital outcomes. This broader theoretical and methodological context incorporates the strengths of various theories while focusing attention on interacting and mediating effects not often examined by most research. Demographic, historical, personality, and experiential factors that precede or evolve during marriage constitute enduring vulnerabilities to discord and dissolution and are reciprocally related to developmental transitions and stage demands or unexpected stressors external to the couple. Adaptive processes such as positive communication and conflict resolution buffer the effects of vulnerabilities and stressful events and are in turn affected by them. Couple strengths and processes vary by interactive (e.g., validating, avoidant, volatile; Gottman, 1994) or ideological (e.g., traditional, separate, independent; Fitzpatrick, 1987) style. Adapting teaching strategies to couple styles and strengths is a major goal of many relationship enhancement programs (Guerney, 1977; Markman, Floyd, Stanley, & Storaasi, 1988; Olson, Fournier, & Druckman, 1989).

One approach to prevention is to focus on the pragmatic distinction between factors that are dynamic versus those that are static when it comes to understanding risks in marriage (Stanley, 1997a; Stanley, Blumberg, & Markman, 1999). Many factors that turn out to be highly predictive of future marital failure also are among the dimensions with the most potential for change (e.g., communication, conflict management, and beliefs and attitudes; Stanley, Blumberg, & Markman, 1999). For example, a review of research on communication (Noller & Fitzpatrick, 1990) identified many of the processes that distinguish distressed from nondistressed marriages: destructive communication behavior or conflict avoidance, and discrepancies in perception, attribution, and affect. Distressed partners tend to be less aware of and accurate in hearing each other (Noller, 1984), more highly reactive (Jacobson, Follette, & McDonald, 1982), and higher in negative reciprocity (Hahlweg, Revensdorf, & Schindler, 1984). Such couples tend to attribute negative partner behavior to more intransigent dispositional factors (Fincham & Bradbury, 1993), and see problem-related behavior as global and stable (Holtzworth-Munroe & Jacobson, 1985).

In addition to these more process-oriented, dynamic factors, many other factors affect a couple's chances of success (Clements et al., 1997). Among these factors are financial management styles (Kurdek, 1993), religious dissimilarity (e.g., Maneker & Rankin, 1993), meeting a short time before marriage (e.g., Kurdek, 1993), age at time of marriage (e.g., Martin & Bumpass, 1989), and low conscientiousness (e.g., Kurdek, 1993), just to name a few. However, many of these latter factors represent relatively static dimensions that make poor targets for prevention because they are not amenable to change. Preventive interventions can only be effective if they make changes that can either raise protection or lower risks (Coie et al., 1993).

Strategies for Prevention

Programs for couple growth using a prevention rather than treatment modality emerged from the shadow of therapy over the last 30 years. Guerney and Maxson (1990) described the more systematic, research-evaluated enrichment efforts as "psycho-educational programs designed to strengthen couples . . . promote high present and future harmony and strength . . . characterized by programmatic, replicable, economical methods" (p. 1127). Traditionally, programs were distinguished by relationship stage, for example, premarital counseling (Schumm & Denton, 1979; Stahmann & Hiebert, 1987) or marriage enrichment (Denton, 1986; Mace, 1983). More recently, relationship enhancement models (Guerney & Maxson, 1990; Stanley, Markman, St. Peters, & Leber, 1995) offer social skills training without stage segregation. Prevention programs for couples are most prevalent in community settings (schools, churches, synagogues, mental health centers), yet even these serve few couples, often lack quality or continuity, and rarely practice systematic, long-term evaluation of effects (Stahmann & Salts, 1993).

Worthington, Buston, and Hammonds (1989) noted three strategies typical of enrichment programs: (a) structured enrichment (e.g., L'Abate & Weinstein, 1987), in which a leader systematically reviews issues with couples with little interaction; (b) semistructured discussion groups, such as those spawned by the Association for Couples in Marriage Enrichment (Doherty, Lester, & Leigh, 1986; Mace & Mace, 1976); and (c) insight- and skills-focused programs such as Couple Communication (Miller, Wackman, & Nunnally, 1976), Relationship Enhancement (Guerney, 1977), and the Prevention and Relationship Enhancement Program (PREP; Markman, Stanley, & Blumberg, 1994), which feature some lecture, partner interaction, and skills practice.

For purposes of this review, inventories of couple experiences, values, and perceptions are classed with structured enrichment to describe assessment approaches. Description of information and awareness approaches combines premarital enrichment discussion approaches with classroom instruction and discussion models. Skills training is reviewed as a third strategy typical of prevention programs. In practice, most program designs use elements of all three approaches.

Assessment Approaches

Assessment approaches seek to gather data on partner attitudes and behaviors that can be used to set growth goals and attitude or behavior change. The underlying belief is that insights about one's attitudes, behaviors, and expectations can lead to changes in thinking or behaving that give marriages a better chance. Bradbury (1995) reported that the minority of counselors who engage in formal assessment with couples use relatively few instruments, including some with poor psychometric qualities—a point equally true for both therapeutic and preventive interventions. Larson et al. (1995) reviewed five comprehensive premarital instruments, finding Premarital Personal and Relationship Evaluation (PREPARE; Olson, Fournier, & Druckman, 1989), Facilitating Open Couple Communication, Understanding and Study (FOCCUS; Markey, Micheletto, & Becker, 1985), and Preparation for Marriage (PREP-M; Holman, Larson, & Harmer, 1994) the most psychometrically sound, although noting the need for expanded validity and reliability testing across time and target populations. The first two instruments were rated best for couple counseling, while PREP-M was considered best for classroom use. The PREPARE instrument (Olson, Fournier, & Druckman, 1989) is the most extensively tested and marketed assessment for prevention use that is available. Grounded in research, systems theory, and clinical experience, premarital scores have predicted divorce and dissatisfaction with 80 to 85% accuracy in two 3-year longitudinal studies of premarital couples (Fowers & Olson, 1986; Larson & Olson, 1989). The approach taken in PREPARE involves comprehensive assessment of a number of areas, including communication, conflict resolution, parenting, religion, closeness, flexibility, self-confidence, and assertiveness. The instrument is most often used by prevention practitioners who want to help couples zero in on areas of potential strength and weakness. Training seminars and resource materials are offered by PREPARE/ENRICH, Inc. to help over 20,000 users administer the survey, interpret results, and facilitate attitude and behavior change. Although the research on the predictive validity of the instrument is very strong, a lack of sustained contact with couples has precluded specific assessment of preventive effects.

Assessment approaches are most likely to be a useful prevention component when variables measured are relevant to the circumstances of the couple (i.e., age, stage, culture, growth issues, risk status) and can be used to guide awareness, knowledge, or skills training in order to reduce risks. Identification of partner differences or prediction of marital success may be counterproductive without interventions that help partners deal with differences that are identified. Feedback on compatibility (e.g., personality, attitudes) can lead to profitable talking about differences, but couples who lack problem-solving or conflict resolution skills may be unable to cope well with the differences uncovered by the assessment. To this end, the developers of PREPARE have been adding to and expanding the skills training segments to go along with the assessment tools (PREPARE/ENRICH, Inc., 1997).

Informational and Awareness Approaches

Informational approaches to prevention seek to supply partners with facts about relationships or their component parts. School-based classes are typically informational in nature. College courses in marriage and family began in the 1920s (Stahmann & Hiebert, 1987) and high school classes became widespread during the 1960s (Sheek, 1984). Structured texts such as Cox (1990), Rice (1990), or Olson and DeFrain (1994) have been staples of college courses. Higher-quality texts are generally lacking at the high school level (Mack, 2000). Research on college courses shows improvement in knowledge (Avery, Ridley, Leslie, & Mulholland, 1980), mate selection, sexuality, and conflict resolution attitudes (Olson & Gravatt, 1968), realistic expectations, and egalitarian attitudes (Laner & Russell, 1994), and communication and conflict resolution skills (Ridley, Avery, Harrell, Haynes-Clements, & McCunney, 1981). High school programs continue to experience an upsurge in popularity that began in the 1970s, although budget cuts diminished their availability to some degree.

Information and awareness are also prominent goals in marriage enrichment programs (Stahmann & Salts, 1993). Marital enrichment provides primarily nondistressed couples with instruction, experience, and dialogue to attain competencies associated with marital success. Exchange of ideas and feelings in the context of nonjudgmental feedback from partners, workshop facilitators, or other couples can also establish a behavioral regimen and network of support that strengthens the effects of information and awareness exercises.

Information-focused programs are often implicitly or explicitly linked to self- and other-awareness goals. Information regarding general expectations or specific issues in marriage provides the means to augment or alter attitudes that govern relationship behavior. Couples do better when they hold more realistic expectations and beliefs (Eidelson & Epstein, 1981) that can be facilitated by the informational approach.

Skills Training Approaches

Skills training approaches focus on teaching couples to manage their lives better by actively teaching specific strategies for improved relationship functioning. Three approaches that stand out for their empirical basis are (a) Relationship Enhancement (RE), Couple Communication (CC), and the Prevention and Relationship Enhancement Program (PREP).

Relationship Enhancement

Relationship Enhancement (Guerney, 1977), an empathy-building, social learning program of 16 to 24 hours, is one of the most extensively tested skills-building programs in existence. This program is based on a Rogerian communication model and shows impressive results for a variety of types of couples. Relationship enhancement focuses strongly on the development and enhancement of empathic communication ability. It also emphasizes attention to communication cues in self and other, self-changing skills, problem-solving and conflict resolution skills, and attention to the need for generalization by participants beyond the training setting (Guerney, 1987). Although the program has been used for treating an array of problems, its use with premarital and marital couples is the focus here. Related to this use, several treatment groups of college-age, dating couples gained significantly in empathy (e.g., Ridley, Jorgenson, Morgan, & Avery, 1982) and problem-solving skills (Ridley, Avery, Harrell, Leslie, & Dent, 1981) from pre- to posttest and relative to control groups.

One 6-month follow-up found disclosure and empathy gains for RE participants relative to a lecture–discussion control group (Avery et al., 1980), while another found communication but not problem-solving skills retention for experiential versus discussion group couples (Ridley, Jorgenson, et al., 1981). Sustained gains in self-disclosure were not evident at follow-up in comparisons of participants and nonparticipants in another study (Ridley & Bain, 1983). Heitland (1986) observed significant pre- to posttest differences on listening, expression, and problem solving for college and high-school participants in an 8-hour RE workshop, relative to control group couples. Meta-analytic research on many major marital programs (RE, CC, Engaged Encounter; Giblin, Sprenkle, & Sheehan, 1985) found that RE had the strongest effect sizes of those tested (ES = .96; other program ES no higher than .58).

Couple Communication

Like RE, CC is one of the older and best researched skills-based programs for couples. Topics covered include self-awareness and disclosure, effective listening, conflict resolution, and information on styles of communication. Each of these areas is broken down further into specific skills that participants can learn. For example, the listening skills that are taught include attending, acknowledging, inviting, summarizing, and question-asking. Although the program can be used in a variety of formats and settings, most of the outcome research on CC has studied the effects of the 12-hour structured skills training program, with most samples being married couples from middle-class backgrounds (Wampler, 1990). The most recent fliers on the program suggest four 2-hour sessions for the format.

There is evidence suggesting the relevance of the material for couples at various stages and with various backgrounds (Wampler, 1990). Miller et al. (1976) originally developed CC (earlier called the Minnesota Couple Communication Program) to improve communication quality for couples. Miller, Wackman, and Nunnally (1983) reported that small-group participants valued self- and other-awareness exercises and the climate of support emerging from the exercises. Studies also show clear gains in communication behavior posttraining (e.g., Russell, Bagarozzi, Atilanao, & Morris, 1984).

Wampler (1990) reviewed studies on CC, noting strong gains in communication quality following training but also that these effects diminish over time. Gains in individual functioning and relationship quality are more durable, although the longest term follow-up assessments are significantly less than 1 year in duration (Wampler, 1990). Couple communication is used by clergy, lay leaders, therapists, business personnel, and chaplains in all branches of the U.S. armed forces. As redesigned and updated in 1991, CC can be used with individuals or in group settings.

Prevention and Relationship Enhancement Program

The Prevention and Relationship Enhancement Program targets changes in attitudes and behavior that are specifically related to risk and protective factors in an array of marital research (Markman, Stanley, & Blumberg, 1994; Stanley, Blumberg, & Markman, 1999; Stanley, Trathen, McCain, & Bryan, 1998). The program primarily targets those dimensions that are both highly predictive of marital success or failure and that are amenable to change (dynamic versus static factors; Clements et al., 1997; Stanley, 1997a; Stanley et al., 1995).

A 12-hour sequence of mini-lectures, discussion, and interpersonal skills practice is offered in weeknight, weekend, or 1-day formats (Markman et al., 1986; Stanley et al., 1995). Topics of focus include communication, conflict management, forgiveness, religious beliefs and practices, expectations, fun, and friendship (Markman et al., 1994). Strategies for enhancing and maintaining commitment have also come to play an increasingly larger role in the kinds of cognitive changes attempted in PREP (e.g., Stanley, Lobitz, & Dickson, 2001). Both secular (or nonsectarian) and Christian versions of PREP are available (Stanley & Trathen, 1994).

The program has been more extensively researched regarding long-term effects than have other programs; most of the research has been with premarital couples. In the long-term study in Denver, program effects have been tracked using both self-report and observational coding of couple interaction (Markman et al., 1988; Markman, Renick, Floyd, Stanley, & Clements, 1993). Three years following intervention, the PREP couples maintained higher levels of relationship satisfaction, sexual satisfaction, and lower problem intensity than matched control couples (Markman et al., 1988). Participants demonstrated significantly more positive interaction up to 4 years postintervention (Markman et al., 1993). More significantly, clear group differences were obtained up to 4 years following intervention on negative communication patterns (e.g., withdrawal, denial, dominance, negative affect), with PREP couples communicating less negatively than both matched control couples and decliner couples. These kinds of differences are very important because such patterns are strongly correlated with risk for marital distress, violence, and breakup (Gottman & Krokoff, 1989; Holtzworth-Munroe et al., 1995; Markman et al., 1988). The follow-ups with the Denver sample also revealed a statistically greater chance of premarital breakup among control group and decliner couples than PREP couples, with similar though nonstatistically significant trends for divorce and separation 4 to 5 years after training (Markman et al., 1993).

In a pre–post design using random assignment, Blumberg found PREP to be more effective than EE in building positive communication, problem-solving, and support and validation behaviors at postintervention (reported in Renick, Blumberg, & Markman, 1992). Similar research programs in Germany (Hahl-weg & Markman, 1988; Hahlweg, Markman, Thurmaier, Engl, & Eckert, 1997) and Australia (Behrens & Halford, 1994) have demonstrated significant gains in communication, conflict management, and satisfaction posttest, with the former sample showing a maintenance of communication and satisfaction gains at 1- and 3-year follow-ups. Furthermore, the most recent data from the Germany project show that, at the 5-year follow up, PREP couples have a divorce rate of 3%, versus 16% for the control couples (Thurmaier, Engl, & Hahlweg, 1999). A study by Van Widenfelt, Hosman, Schapp, and van der Staak (1996) did not obtain the same kinds of positive findings. However, interpretations of these results are problematic because the PREP couples had been together significantly longer than controls, the PREP couples had been together an average of 9 years before intervention (making generalizations to prevention difficult), and a differential dropout rate led to the control couples being increasingly selected for couples doing well over time.

A large-scale, National Institute of Mental Health–supported research project is under way at the University of Denver. It is designed, among other things, to test the effectiveness of PREP when given by clergy or lay leaders in religious organizations. Preliminary results suggest that couples taking PREP from either their religious leaders or university staff are communicating significantly more positively and less negatively from pre- to postassessment, relative to couples receiving premarital training typically offered in their religious organizations, who are actually communicating more negatively following their premarital training than before it (Stanley, Blumberg, & Markman, 1999). The early evidence also suggests that the religious leaders can deliver the program as effectively as university staff. Couples taking PREP from either type of leader rated their training experience more highly than couples taking the typical offering, although most couples were satisfied with their prevention experiences.

The program is now being used by religious organizations, mental health centers, and therapists; PREP is also used by military chaplains in all branches of the U.S. armed forces, especially in the U.S. Navy.

Summary of Skills-Based Approaches

Taken as a whole, the results from many different outcome studies on these prominent skills-oriented programs suggest great promise for preventive interventions with couples. More research is needed to determine which types of couples respond best to which types of preventive efforts, but it seems reasonable to assert that skills-oriented, preventive education efforts can have positive and lasting effects on couples.

Research Issues

Measurement of effect sizes has become a standard for judging the impact of educational and therapeutic programs (Giblin et al., 1985; Guerney & Maxson, 1990). Educational programs typically show smaller effect sizes than therapeutic programs given to distressed couples (Giblin et al., 1985). This is not surprising considering that the targeted changes are different (maintenance of nondistress versus amelioration of distress) and that distressed couples have greater room for improvement. Premarital (avg. = .53) and family (avg. = .54) programs produce somewhat larger effects than marital (avg. = .42) programs. Specific gains must always be viewed in terms of the overall experience. For instance, couples in RE discussion groups (an alternative to skills practice) gained greater awareness of couple issues but increased in frustration levels, likely because of lack of skills training to address those issues (Ridley, Jorgenson, et al. 1982).

Results of university-based programs such as PREP and RE are consistently greater than results of community-based programs (Renick et al., 1992; Silliman & Schumm, 2000). The latter are infrequently evaluated because they are not typically put on by researchers, and testing interventions in community-based research is inherently difficult (Stanley et al., 1995). Measurement of effects in this field is complicated by interactions of personal and couple factors and modalities of assessment. Ideally, assessment should incorporate both self-report measurement of key variables but also observational coding of couple interaction—especially for programs that target such changes in interaction. As a case in point, studies on PREP that incorporate observational coding generally show strong effects (e.g., Markman, et al., 1993; Hahlweg, et al., 1997; Renick et al., 1992), but those not using observational measurement show few or no group differences (Van Widenfelt et al., 1996; Trathen, 1995).

Studies that track long-term outcomes are particularly valuable in this field.

The desired effects of prevention are, by definition, longer-term effects. Unfortunately, only a few studies provide evidence for duration of impact (e.g., Hahlweg et al., 1997; Markman et al., 1993; Ridley, Avery, Harrell, Haynes-Clements, & McCunney, 1981). Furthermore, findings from long-term studies of program outcomes are susceptible to varying interpretations because of complex selection effects (both those pertaining to group assignment and those caused by differential attrition) as well as loss of statistical power over time (Stanley, 1997b). Future longitudinal studies that address various methodological concerns and that track both couple development and program outcomes can greatly inform the work of prevention.

Criteria for Effective Prevention

Reviews of program outcomes have identified several ingredients as critical to effectiveness. Among these are a clear, consistent theoretical base (Bagarozzi & Rauen, 1981; Fournier & Olson, 1986; Guerney & Maxson, 1990; Schumm & Denton, 1979); realistic and meaningful assessment and evaluation (Larson & Holman, 1994) with valid and reliable instruments (Larson & Olson, 1989); competent, credible leadership by caring trainers or facilitators (Center for Marriage and Family, 1995; Most & Guerney, 1983; Stahmann & Hiebert, 1987); focused and effective marketing and recruitment (Center for Marriage and Family, 1995; Duncan, Box, & Silliman, 1996); appropriate timing and duration of intervention (Fournier & Olson, 1986); and relevant and focused program content (Silliman & Schumm, 1989).

Further, effective prevention programs (a) focus on understanding risks and needed behavior change in a target group; (b) offer new opportunities that alter long-range outcomes; (c) teach coping skills and offer social support; (d) strengthen existing supports in family, community, or school settings; and (e) carefully plot results to document effectiveness and procedures to replicate success (Price et al., 1989).

Practical Issues in Preventive Work With Couples

Seminal issues for practitioners arising from the marriage preparation and education literature include targeting and meeting special needs of audiences, recruiting and screening participants, and delivering and following up to maximize program impact. Much basic and applied research is needed to design effective programs for a variety of couple needs. The next section summarizes what is known to date and suggests profitable directions for future efforts.

Selecting Target Groups

Couples who are doing well and are not currently distressed at any stage of marital and family development would make good targets for prevention. Essentially, any couple interested in learning more about keeping their marriage on track is eligible. In fact, such interest must surely drive a good portion of the self-help market, in which products for helping marriages are plentiful and popular (e.g., Gray, 1992; Smalley, 1996).

Key transition points in marriage and family development are logical points for the work of prevention (Markman et al., 1986). The two transition points that seem of greatest potential for targeting couples with preventive interventions are the transitions to marriage and to parenthood. In addition, there are many opportunities to help couples with marriage enrichment programs regardless of transition or developmental stage.

Postmarriage Enrichment as Prevention

Postmarriage enrichment efforts emerged with Marriage Guidance Centers, founded by David and Vera Mace in the 1950s, and the Marriage Encounter movement, initiated by Father Gabriel Calvo in 1960 (Denton, 1986). Mace and Mace (1976) emphasized support and strengthening of healthy marriages, in contrast to the prevailing problem orientation of marital therapy, hence such enrichment efforts are entirely consistent with the aims of prevention. Hof and Miller (1981) described the key features of this approach as (a) emphasizing preventive, experiential education; (b) facilitating individual and couple growth; (c) encouraging a continuous process of growth; (d) focusing on identifying, sharing, and developing positive aspects of relationships; (e) fostering communication; and (f) modeling growth-oriented skills.

The Transition to Marriage

Most often the couples targeted for prevention are premarital couples. There are at least three reasons for this being such a popular transition to target. First, these couples are, for the most part, truly at a point in time where prevention is the right model—before development of serious relationship distress and damage. Second, religious institutions have the attention of many couples at this time, because most couples get married within a religious organization (e.g., churches, synagogues; Stanley et al., 1995). There is therefore some leverage to "encourage" couples to pay attention to the foundation of their life together. In fact, while experts disagree on whether premarriage is the best time for preventive work with couples, there is no other time where any group or institution has so much leverage with the greatest number of couples. Although it may not be the best time developmentally (and that point is debatable), it is surely the best time to reach the greatest number of couples. From the perspective of a public health model, that is a compelling reason to attempt prevention premaritally.

Third, there is, for many couples, increased motivation to get the marriage off to a good start. Most of the programs or approaches discussed in this chapter have been used with couples in the transition to marriage. In fact, much of the outcome research reported here has taken place with premarital samples. Despite the factors that favor premarital training as a form of prevention, most couples get married in the United States with no premarital preparation to speak of (Stanley & Markman, 1997).

The Transition to Parenthood

Preventive interventions with couples need not be limited to the premarital or general postmarriage periods. As a major developmental transition, the transition to parenthood has an impact on the individual, couple, and family through changes in identities, roles, relationships, abilities, and patterns of behavior (Schumacher & Meleis, 1994). Findings from a growing number of studies indicate that couples' levels of disagreement and conflict increase after the birth of a first child, and both men's and women's satisfaction with their couple relationship decreases from pregnancy into the child-rearing years (e.g., Belsky & Rovine, 1990; Cowan & Cowan, 1992). Because these negative changes occur even in low-risk families, Cowan and Cowan (1995) advocated the development and implementation of universal primary prevention programs for couples becoming parents for the first time. Childbirth education classes, which remain the most common programs for expectant parents, focus on preparation for labor and birth, place fathers in a subordinate, supporting role, and do little to prepare parents for the many life changes that will accompany the birth of a first child (Jordan, 1995a).

As with the transition to marriage, the transition to parenthood is a significant life change that creates a window of opportunity for preventive intervention. Expectant couples tend to be concerned about what will happen and are therefore more open to learning and changing behavior patterns. The transition to parenthood puts couples at risk for tremendous miscommunication and conflict as each individual contends with incorporating the new identity of parent, reorganizing relationships, developing new skills, contending with the multiple expectations of self and partner, as well as assuming responsibility for a dependent being.

The Becoming a Family Project (Cowan & Cowan, 1992) was the first couple-focused, randomized clinical trial of a transition to parenthood primary prevention program. Couples in the intervention group participated in 24 weekly small group meetings from the last 3 months of pregnancy through the first 3 months of parenthood, facilitated by trained leader couples. Group discussions consisted of a structured component that focused on issues identified from the various measures used in the study as well as unstructured time during which couples could address any questions or concerns they had. Declines in marital satisfaction were less severe in intervention couples, and by 18 months postbirth, none of the 24 couples from the intervention group had divorced, while 10 couples from the control groups had separated or divorced.

Pilot studies of structured couple-based primary prevention transition to parenthood interventions have recently been completed. Heavey (1995) and Jordan (1995a) used slightly modified versions of PREP to provide relationship skills training to married couples expecting the birth of a first child. The minor modifications in the PREP content merely adapted the information to expectant parents. Few significant differences were found between intervention and comparison couples over their transition to parenthood using paper-and-pencil measures of individual well-being, couple communication, and marital satisfaction. This could be because of methodology (condensed forms of the intervention, lack of true randomized clinical trials, and failure to use observational measures of couple communication) or could indicate something lacking in the intervention used during this transition.

Despite the limitations of these pilot studies, findings support that couples expecting the birth of a first child are very open to such programs, find them useful, and evaluate them positively. Jordan is currently conducting a randomized controlled clinical trial of a structured comprehensive transition to parenthood intervention built on a foundation of PREP (P. L. Jordan, personal communication, November 17, 1996). Six classes are spread over pregnancy to strengthen the intervention through reinforcement and adequate opportunities for practice; a booster session is provided in the second month after birth. Observational as well as paper-and-pencil measures of communication, satisfaction, and individual well-being are being used.

Recruitment and Screening

Most couples are ill-prepared for the interpersonal and practical challenges of marriage or parenthood, yet few seek educational programs or enrichment groups to master skills correlated with marital success (Arond & Pauker, 1987). Naivete, romance, and self-reliance are often cited as reasons for not seeking marriage education. These factors may have led college students to prefer learning from experience over formal programs or informal help-seeking as a prime approach to marriage preparation (Silliman, Schumm, & Jurich, 1992). Learning from experience can be costly, however, because premarital problems tend to continue and amplify after marriage (Fournier & Olson, 1986). What is hopeful is that a substantial percentage of high school (Silliman, 1996) and college (Silliman & Schumm, 1989) students express interest in prevention programming.

Programs must be perceived as highly relevant to couples if they are expected to divert time and resources from other activities (Stanley, 1997a). Programs with the strongest customer satisfaction (Center for Marriage and Family, 1995; Russell & Lyster, 1992) and behavioral change (Ridley, Jorgenson, et al., 1982; Stanley et al., 1995) present the clearest explanation of their educational or theological rationale to the couples.

Prevention programs to date have attracted White, middle-class, educated couples, especially those motivated to improve already functional relationships. Indeed, cultural differences in couple relationships have been inadequately examined, providing a less than ideal database to inform preventive efforts with diverse groups. However, reviews suggest that while extended kin networks play larger roles in overall cohesion and adaptability in families of color, couple functioning is critical to family strengths across cultures (Taylor, Chatters, Tucker, & Lewis, 1990; Vega, 1990; Woehrer, 1989). Nevertheless, it is likely that preventive efforts will be most effective when tailored to the particular needs and culture of the couples being served. Religious organizations may be in a very strong position for helping couples of all kinds because they tend to be very embedded in the culture in which the couples live (Stanley et al., 1995).

Marketing education and support to couples marrying earlier- or later-than-average and extending support and education through the first 3 years of marriage (the most difficult years of adjustment), with special attention to those whose family and relationship history indicates greater risk of distress, might significantly reduce divorce and domestic violence rates. Adapting awareness messages, programs, and training providers to reach more culturally diverse audiences could extend benefits of existing programs in a more familiar, relevant context.

Delivery

Researchers have not, in general, attempted dismantling studies that could help preventionists know what specifics make for the most effective delivery of prevention programs. However, experience in the field has led prevention experts to draw conclusions about the variables that probably make a difference. For example, clear structure and ground rules that promote a confidential, non-judgmental interaction facilitate a safe learning climate (Olson & Moss, 1980; Stanley et al., 1995). Successful outcomes have been reported for a variety of formats, including weekly and intensive weekend training (Center for Marriage and Family, 1995; Stanley et al., 1995). While typical community-based programs average 2 to 4 hours in duration (Schumm & Denton, 1979), research-based programs that demonstrate knowledge and skills gains range from 12 to

30 hours in length (Markman et al., 1993; Miller et al., 1983; Ridley & Slad-ezek, 1992). Intensive practice and sustained application is fundamental to attitude and behavior change (Markman et al., 1986). Homework, including reflective discussions (Stahmann & Hiebert, 1987) and skills application (Bagarozzi et al., 1984; Markman et al., 1993), is a widely regarded method of extending and reinforcing training, although examination of specific homework effects does not seem to have been done. Younger couples in Russell and Lyster's (1992) study appreciated a more structured approach, while older couples (avg. = 34 years) valued open discussion. Provider competence, confidence, caring, and clarity enhances participant satisfaction (Most & Guerney, 1983).

Follow-Up

Only a few programs show evidence of continued contact, training, or support for couples (Bader, Microys, Sinclair, Willett, & Conway, 1980; Ridley, Jorgen-son, et al., 1982). Despite some evidence of sustained benefits (Hahlweg et al., 1997; Markman et al., 1993), it seems unlikely that prevention programs in-oculate couples from distress like a one-time shot may inoculate a child from one disease indefinitely. Rather, prevention of marital failure may be most like getting a tetanus shot—it is wise to obtain a booster every few years or after specific events such as getting a puncture wound.

Conclusion

Current prevention programs for select groups of couples provide promise for enhancing competence and satisfaction and reducing distress, divorce, and vi-olence in the general population. Prevention scientists can learn much by noting strengths of resilient couples, then assessing if and how replicating such pro-cesses or conditions through programming may have an effect on individuals, couples, or their environment. Greater attention to couple traits (risk status, ethnicity, individual differences), process variables (educational methods or cou-ple interaction), and long-range (cumulative) outcomes in both program and research design will help explain how prevention can be most effective in a variety of circumstances. Social effects such as increased prevention awareness and behavior across communities, reduced costs of distress (health care or legal costs, social stability) or increased benefits from competence (work force pro-ductivity, child adjustment), as well as dyadic effects should be documented. Current, limited investigation of individual, couple, and cultural variables and program effectiveness evidence from one group (White, middle-class, educated volunteers) restricts efforts of practitioners and policy makers to design or tailor more effective programs for a variety of couples.

Psychoeducational programs for dating, married, and remarrying couples have become more available and more widely reported and evaluated in the last two decades. Public awareness of the need for preparation and enrichment (e.g., Denton, 1986; Glieck, 1995; McManus, 1993) and couple participation in church and community-based programs is strong and may be growing (Center for Marriage and Family, 1995; Jones & Stahmann, 1994; McManus, 1993). Popular books, research-based books, workbooks, and educational videotapes for couples and providers expanded dramatically during this period. However, community-based prevention programs for couples remain too scattered, brief in duration, and often lack depth or continuity over time (Jones & Stahmann, 1994; Olson, 1983; Schumm & Denton, 1979). Research on such programs typically lacks systematic implementation, evaluation, and follow-up (Stahmann & Hiebert, 1987). Therefore, although there is reason for hope in the efficacy of some prevention strategies, much work is needed if we are to fully capitalize on opportunities for preventing marital failure.

With continued improvements in the quality of assessments, curricula, and provider training—especially in community settings—we will see a greater impact on marital distress and increasingly positive attitudes toward prevention. For proponents of the prevention perspective, public and professional advocacy as well as educational and research improvements are needed. Media campaigns regarding benefits of functional marriages or relationship education might increase interest and investment in prevention programs for couples. Coalition-building among clergy, teachers, counselors, and other professionals also holds promise. For example, in 1997, the first conference of the Coalition for Marriage, Family and Couples Education was held in Washington, DC. Under the banner of prevention, this coalition brought together most of the major prevention programs and researchers, along with clergy, lay leaders, therapists, and journalists from around the world. Such a meeting holds great promise in that it represents a confluence of trends that support prevention as a worthwhile activity. We suggest that the opportunities for preventing marital distress exist if the right practitioners have access to the right tools to help couples in the most effective ways.

References

Arond, M., & Pauker, S. (1987). *The first year of marriage.* New York: Warner Books.

Avery, A. W., Ridley, C. A., Leslie, L. A., & Milholland, T. (1980). Relationship enhancement with premarital dyads: A six-month follow-up. *American Journal of Family Therapy, 3*(8), 23–30.

Bader, E., Microys, G., Sinclair, C., Willett, E., & Conway, B. (1980). Do marriage preparation programs really work? A Canadian experiment. *Journal of Marital and Family Therapy, 6*(2), 171–179.

Bagarrozi, D. A., Bagarozzi, J. A., Anderson, S. A., & Pollane, L. (1984). Premarital education and training sequence: PETS: A three-year follow-up of an experimental study. *Journal of Counseling and Development, 63*(2), 91–100.

Bagarozzi, D. A., & Rauen, P. I. (1981). Premarital counseling: Appraisal and status. *American Journal of Family Therapy, 9*(3), 13–27.

Behrens, B., & Halford, K. (1994, August). *Advances in the prevention and treatment of marital distress.* Paper presented at the "Helping Families Change" Conference, University of Queensland, Brisbane, Australia.

Belsky, J., & Rovine, M. (1990). Patterns of marital change across the transition to parenthood. *Journal of Marriage and the Family, 52,* 109–123.

Bradbury, T. N. (1995). Assessing the four fundamental domains of marriage. *Family Relations, 44*(4), 459–468.

Center for Marriage and Family. (1995). *Marriage preparation in the Catholic Church: Getting it right.* Omaha, NE: Center for Marriage and Family, University College, Creighton University.

Clements, M., Stanley, S. M., & Markman, H. J. (1997). *Predicting marital failure in a longitudinal study of couples development.* Manuscript in preparation.

Coie, J. D., Watt, N. F., West, S. G., Hawkins, J. D., Asarnow, J. R., Markman, H. J., Ramey, S. L., Shure, M. B., & Long, B. (1993). The science of prevention: A conceptual framework and some directions for a national research program. *American Psychologist, 48*(10), 1013–1022.

Commission on Chronic Illness. (1957). *Chronic illness in the United States* (vol. 1; Published for the Commonwealth Fund). Cambridge, MA: Harvard University Press.

Cowan, C. P., & Cowan, P. A. (1992). *When partners become parents.* New York: Basic Books.

Cowan, C. P., & Cowan, P. A. (1995). Interventions to ease the transition to parenthood: Why they are needed and what they can do. *Family Relations, 44,* 412–423.

Cox, F. (1990). *Human intimacy: Marriage, the family and its meaning.* St Paul, MN: West.

Denton, W. (1986). Starting a local marriage enrichment group. In W. Denton (Ed.), *Marriage and family enrichment* (pp. 69–77). New York: Haworth Press.

Doherty, W. J., Lester, M. E., & Leigh, G. (1986). Marriage Encounter weekends: Couples who win and couples who lose. *Journal of Marital and Family Therapy, 12,* 49–61.

Duncan, S. F., Box, G., & Silliman, B. (1996). Racial and gender effects on perceptions of marriage preparation programs among college-educated young adults. *Family Relations, 45*(1), 80–90.

Eidelson, R. J., & Epstein, N. (1981). Unrealistic beliefs of clinical couples: Their relationship to expectations, goals and satisfaction. *American Journal of Family Therapy, 9*(4), 13–22.

Fincham, F. D., & Bradbury, T. N. (1993). Marital satisfaction, depression, and attributions: A longitudinal analysis. *Journal of Personality and Social Psychology, 64,* 442–452.

Fitzpatrick, M. A. (1987). *Between husbands and wives.* Beverly Hills, CA: Sage.

Forthofer, M. S., Markman, H. J., Cox, M., Stanley, S., & Kessler, R. C. (1996). Associations between marital distress and work loss in a national sample. *Journal of Marriage and the Family, 58*(3), 597–605.

Fournier, D. G., & Olson, D. H. (1986). Programs for premarital and newlywed couples. In R. F. Levant (Ed.), *Psychoeducational approaches to family therapy and counseling* (pp. 194–231). New York: Springer.

Fowers, B. J., & Olson, D. H. (1986). Predicting marital success with PREPARE: A predictive validity study. *Journal of Marital and Family Therapy, 12*(4), 403–413.

Giblin, P., Sprenkle, D. H., & Sheehan, R. (1985). Enrichment outcome research: A meta-analysis of premarital, marital, and family interventions. *Journal of Marital and Family Therapy, 11*(3), 257–271.

Glenn, N. D. (1990). Quantitative research on marital quality in the 1980s: A critical review. *Journal of Marriage and the Family, 52*(4), 818–831.

Glieck, E. (1995, February 27). Should this marriage be saved? *Time Magazine,* 48–56.

Gottman, J. M. (1993). A theory of marital dissolution and stability. *Journal of Family Psychology, 7,* 57–75.

Gottman, J. M. (1994). *Why marriages succeed or fail.* New York: Simon & Schuster.

Gottman, J. M., & Krokoff, L. J. (1989). Marital interaction and satisfaction: A longitudinal view. *Journal of Consulting and Clinical Psychology, 57,* 47–52.

Gray, J. (1992). *Men are from Mars, women are from Venus: A practical guide for improving communication and getting what you want in your relationships.* New York: HarperCollins.

Grych, J. H., & Fincham, F. D. (1990). Marital conflict and children's adjustment: A cognitive–contextual framework. *Psychological Bulletin, 108,* 267–290.

Guerney, B. G., Jr. (Ed.). (1977). *Relationship enhancement.* San Francisco: Jossey-Bass.

Guerney, B. G., Jr. (Ed.). (1987). *Relationship enhancement manual.* Bethesda, MD: Ideal.

Guerney, B. G., Jr., & Maxson, P. (1990). Marital and family enrichment research: A decade review and a look ahead. *Journal of Marriage and the Family, 52*(4), 1127–1135.

Hahlweg, K., & Markman, H. J. (1988). The effectiveness of behavioral marital therapy: Empirical status of behavioral techniques in preventing and alleviating marital distress. *Journal of Consulting and Clinical Psychology, 56,* 440–447.

Hahlweg, K., Markman, H. J., Thurmaier, F., Engl, J., & Eckert, V. (1997). *Prevention of marital distress: Results of a German prospective–longitudinal study.* Manuscript submitted for publication.

Hahlweg, K. D., Revensdorf, D., & Schindler, L. (1984). Effects of behavioral marital therapy on couples' communication and problem-solving skills. *Journal of Consulting and Clinical Psychology, 52,* 553–566.

Heavey, C. L. (1995, November). *Promoting the marital adjustment of first time parents: A pilot test of PREP.* Paper presented at the Association for the Advancement of Behavioral Therapy 29th Annual Convention, Washington, DC.

Heitland, W. (1986). An experimental communication program for premarital dating couples. *School Counselor, 34,* 57–61.

Hof, L., & Miller, W. (1981). *Marriage enrichment: Philosophy, process, and program.* Bowie, MD: Brady.

Holman, T. B., Larson, J., & Harmer, S. L. (1994). The development and predictive validity of a new premarital assessment instrument. *Family Relations, 43*(1), 46–52.

Holtzworth-Munroe, A., & Jacobson, N. S. (1985). Causal attributions of married couples. When do they search for causes? What do they conclude when they do? *Journal of Personality and Social Psychology, 48,* 1398–1412.

Holtzworth-Munroe, A., Markman, H. J., O'Leary, D. K., Neidig, P., Leber, D., Heyman, R. E., Hulbert, D., & Smutzler, N. (1995). The need for marital violence prevention efforts: A behavioral–cognitive secondary prevention program for engaged and newly-married couples. *Applied and Preventive Psychology, 4,* 77–88.

Jacobson, N. S., Follette, W. C., & McDonald, D. W. (1982). Reactivity to positive and negative behavior in distressed and nondistressed couples. *Journal of Consulting and Clinical Psychology, 50,* 706–714.

Jones, E. F., & Stahmann, R. F. (1994). Clergy beliefs, preparation, and practice in premarital counseling. *Journal of Pastoral Counseling, 48*(2), 181–186.

Jordan, P. L. (1995a). The mother's role in promoting fathering behavior. In J. L. Shapiro, M. J. Diamond, & M. Greenberg (Eds.), *Becoming a father: Contemporary, social, developmental, and clinical perspectives.* New York: Springer.

Jordan, P. L. (1995b, November). *PREP pilot: Transition to parenthood.* Paper presented at the Association for the Advancement of Behavioral Therapy 29th Annual Convention, Washington, DC.

Karney, B. R., & Bradbury, T. N. (1995). The longitudinal course of marital quality and stability: A review of theory, method, and research. *Psychological Bulletin, 118*(1), 3–34.

Kitson, G. C., & Morgan, L. A. (1990). The multiple consequences of divorce: A decade review. *Journal of Marriage and the Family, 52*(4), 913–924.

Kurdek, L. A. (1993). Predicting marital dissolution: A 5-year prospective longitudinal study of newlywed couples. *Journal of Personality and Social Psychology, 64,* 221–242.

L'Abate, L., & Lantz, J. (1990). Marriage preparation. In L. L'Abate (Ed.), *Building family competence: Primary and secondary prevention strategies* (pp. 176–186). Newbury Park, CA: Sage.

L'Abate, L., & Weinstein, S. E. (1987). *Structured enrichment programs for couples and families.* New York: Brunner/Mazel.

Laner, M. R., & Russell, J. N. (1994). Course content and change in students: Are marital expectations altered by marriage education? *Teaching Sociology, 22*(1), 10–18.

Larson, A. S., & Olson, D. H. (1989). Predicting marital satisfaction using PREPARE: A replication study. *Journal of Marital and Family Therapy, 15*(3), 311–322.

Larson, D., Sawyers, J. P., & Larson, S. S. (1995). *The costly consequences of divorce.* Rockville, MD: National Institute for Healthcare Research.

Larson, J. H., & Holman, T. B. (1994). Premarital predictors of marital quality and stability. *Family Relations, 43*(2), 228–237.

Larson, J. H., Holman, T. B., Klein, D. M., Busby, D. M., Stahmann, R. F., & Peterson, D. (1995). A review of comprehensive questionnaires used in premarital education and counseling. *Family Relations, 44*(3), 245–252.

Mace, D. (1983). *Prevention in family services.* Beverly Hills, CA: Sage.

Mace, D., & Mace, V. (1976). Marriage enrichment: A preventive group approach for couples. In D. H. Olson (Ed.), *Treating relationships.* Lake Mills, IA: Graphic.

Mack, D. (2000). *Hungry hearts: Evaluating the new curricula for teens on marriage and relationships.* New York: Institute for American Values.

Maneker, J. S., & Rankin, R. P. (1993). Religious homogamy and marital duration among those who file for divorce in California, 1966–1971. *Journal of Divorce and Remarriage, 19*, 1–2, 233–247.

Markey, B., Micheletto, M., & Becker, A. (1985). *Facilitating open couple communication, understanding, and study (FOCCUS).* Omaha, NE: Archdiocese of Omaha.

Markman, H. J., Floyd, F. J., Stanley, S. M., & Lewis, H. (1986). Prevention. In N. Jacobson & A. Gurman (Eds.), *Clinical handbook of marital therapy* (pp. 173–195). New York: Guilford Press.

Markman, H. J., Floyd, F. J., Stanley, S. M., & Storaasli, R. D. (1988). Prevention of marital distress: A longitudinal investigation. *Journal of Consulting and Clinical Psychology, 56*, 210–217.

Markman, H. J., Renick, M. J., Floyd, F. J., Stanley, S. M., & Clements, M. (1993). Preventing marital distress through communication and conflict management training: A 4- and 5-year follow-up. *Journal of Consulting and Clinical Psychology, 61*, 70–77.

Markman, H. J., Stanley, S. M., & Blumberg, S. L. (1994). *Fighting for your marriage: Positive steps for preventing divorce and preserving a lasting love.* San Francisco: Jossey-Bass.

Martin, T. C., & Bumpass, L. L. (1989). Recent trends in marital disruption. *Demography, 26*, 37–51.

Matthews, L. S., Wickrama, K. A. S., & Conger, R. D. (1996). Predicting marital instability from spouse and observer reports of marital interaction. *Journal of Marriage and the Family, 58*, 641–655.

McManus, M. J. (1993). *Marriage savers.* Grand Rapids, MI: Zondervan.

Miller, S., Wackman, D. B., & Nunnally, E. W. (1976). A communication training program for couples. *Social Casework, 57*(1), 9–18.

Miller, S., Wackman, D. B., & Nunnally, E. W. (1983). Couple communication: Equipping couples to be their own best problem solvers. *The Counseling Psychologist, 11*(3), 73–77.

Most, R. K., & Guerney, B. G. Jr. (1983). An empirical evaluation of the training of volunteer lay leaders for premarital relationship enhancement. *Family Relations, 32,* 239–251.

Noller, P. (1984). *Nonverbal communication and marital interaction.* New York: Pergamon Press.

Noller, P., & Fitzpatrick, M. A. (1990). Marital communication in the eighties. *Journal of Marriage and the Family, 52*(4), 832–843.

Olson, D. H. (1983). How effective is marriage preparation? In D. R. Mace (Ed.), *Prevention in family services: Approaches to family wellness* (pp. 65–75). Beverly Hills, CA: Sage.

Olson, D. H., & DeFrain, J. (1994). *Marriage and the family: Diversity and strengths.* Mountain View, CA: Mayfield.

Olson, D. H., Fournier, D. G., & Druckman, J. M. (1989). *PREPARE, PREPARE-MC, ENRICH inventories* (3rd ed.). Minneapolis, MN: PREPARE/ENRICH.

Olson, D. H., & Gravatt, A. E. (1968). Attitude change in a functional marriage course. *Family Coordinator, 17*(1), 89–104.

Olson, T. D., & Moss, J. J. (1980). Creating supportive atmospheres for family life education. *Family Relations, 29*(3), 391–395.

Price, R. H., Cowen, E. L., Lorion, R. P., & Ramos-McKay, J. (1989). The search for effective prevention programs: What we learned along the way. *American Journal of Orthopsychiatry, 59*(1), 49–58.

Popenoe, D. (1993). American family decline, 1960–1990: A review and appraisal. *Journal of Marriage and the Family, 55*(3), 527–555.

PREPARE/ENRICH, Inc. (1997). *PREPARE/ENRICH Newsletter, 2*(1).

Renick, M. J., Blumberg, S., & Markman, H. J. (1992). The Prevention and Relationship Enhancement Program (PREP): An empirically-based preventive intervention program for couples. *Family Relations, 41*(2), 141–147.

Rice, F. (1990). *Intimate relationships, marriages and families.* Mountain View, CA: Mayfield.

Ridley, C. A., Avery, A. W., Harrell, J. E., Haynes-Clements, L. A., & McCunney, N. (1981). Mutual problem-solving skills training for premarital couples: A six-month follow-up. *Journal of Applied Developmental Psychology, 2*(1), 179–188.

Ridley, C. A., Avery, A. W., Harrell, J. E., Leslie, L. A., & Dent, J. (1981). Conflict management: A premarital training program in mutual problem solving. *American Journal of Family Therapy, 9*(4), 23–32.

Ridley, C. A., & Bain, A. B. (1983). The effects of a premarital relationship enhancement program on self-disclosure. *Family Therapy, 1*(10), 13–24.

Ridley, C. A., Jorgensen, S. R., Morgan, A. C., & Avery, A. W. (1982). Relationship enhancement with premarital couples: An assessment of effects on relationship quality. *American Journal of Family Therapy, 10*(3), 41–48.

Ridley, C. A., & Sladezeck, I. E. (1992). Premarital relationship enhancement: Its effects on needs to relate to others. *Family Relations, 41*(2), 148–153.

Russell, C. S., Bagarozzi, D. A., Atilanao, R. B., & Morris, J. E. (1984). A comparison of two approaches to marital enrichment and conjugal skills training: Minnesota Couples Communication Program and structured behavioral exchange contracting. *American Journal of Family Therapy, 12*, 13–25.

Russell, M., & Lyster, R. F. (1992). Marriage preparation: Factors associated with consumer satisfaction. *Family Relations, 41*(4), 446–451.

Schumacher, K. L., & Meleis, A. I. (1994). Transitions: A central concept in nursing. *Image, 26*(2), 119–127.

Schumm, W. R., & Denton, W. (1979). Trends in premarital counseling. *Journal of Marital and Family Therapy, 5*(4), 23–32.

Sheek, B. W. (1984). *A nation for families.* Washington, DC: American Home Economics Association.

Silliman, B. (1996, November). *Adolescents' perceptions of marriage relationships and enhancement programs.* Paper presented to the National Council on Family Relations Annual Conference, Kansas City, MO.

Silliman, B., & Schumm, W. R. (1989). Topics of interest in premarital counseling: Clients' views. *Journal of Sex and Marital Therapy, 15*(3), 199–204.

Silliman, B., & Schumm, W. R. (2000). Marriage preparation programs: A literature review. *Family Journal, 8*(2), 128–137.

Silliman, B., Schumm, W. R., & Jurich, A. P. (1992). Young adults' preferences for premarital preparation program designs. *Contemporary Family Therapy, 14*, 89–100.

Smalley, G. (1996). *Making love last forever.* Dallas: Word.

Stahmann, R. F., & Hiebert, W. J. (1987). *Premarital counseling: The professional's handbook* (2nd ed.). Lexington, MA: Lexington Books.

Stahmann, R. F., & Salts, C. J. (1993). Educating for marriage and intimate relationships. In M. E. Arcus, J. D. Schvaneveldt, & J. J. Moss (Eds.), *Handbook of family life education* (pp. 33–61). Newbury Park, CA: Sage.

Stanley, S. M. (1997a). What's important in premarital counseling? *Marriage and Family: A Christian Journal, 1*, 51–60.

Stanley, S. M. (1997b). Acting on what we know: The hope of prevention. *Threshold, 56*, 6–11.

Stanley, S. M., Blumberg, S. L., & Markman, H. J. (1999). Helping couples fight *for* their marriages: The PREP approach. In R. Berger & M. Hannah (Eds.), *Handbook of preventive approaches in couple therapy* (pp. 279–303). New York: Brunner/Mazel.

Stanley, S. M., Lobitz, W. C., & Dickson, F. (2001). Using what we know: Commitment and cognitions in marital therapy. In W. Jones & J. Adams (Eds.), *Handbook of interpersonal commitment and relationship stability.* New York: Plenum Press.

Stanley, S. M., & Markman, H. J. (1997). *Marriage in the 90s: A nationwide random phone survey.* Denver, CO: PREP.

Stanley, S. M., Markman, H. J., Prado, L. M., Olmos-Gallo, P. A., Tonelli, L., St. Peters, M., Leber, B. D., Bobulinski, M., Cordova, A., & Whitton, S. (2001). Community based premarital prevention: Clergy and lay leaders on the front lines. *Family Relations, 50*(1), 67–76.

Stanley, S. M., Markman, H. J., St. Peters, M., & Leber, D. (1995). Strengthening marriages and preventing divorce: New directions in prevention research. *Family Relations, 44,* 392–401.

Stanley, S. M., & Trathen, D. (1994). Christian PREP: An empirically based model for marital and premarital intervention. *Journal of Psychology and Christianity, 13,* 158–165.

Stanley, S., Trathen, D., McCain, S., & Bryan, M. (1998). *A lasting promise: A Christian guide to fighting for your marriage.* San Francisco: Jossey-Bass.

Taylor, R. J., Chatters, L. M., Tucker, M. B., & Lewis, E. (1990). Developments in research on black families: A decade review. *Journal of Marriage and the Family, 52*(4), 993–1014.

Thurmaier, F., Engl, J., & Hahlweg, K. (1999). Eheglück auf Dauer? Methodik, Inhalte und Effektivität eines präventiven Paarkommunikationstrainings—Ergebnisse nach fünf Jahren. *Zeitschrift für Klinische Psychologie, 28,* 54–62.

Trathen, D. W. (1995). A comparison of the effectiveness of two Christian premarital counseling programs (skills and information-based) utilized by evangelical Protestant churches. (Doctoral dissertation, University of Denver, 1995). *Dissertation Abstracts International, 56/06-A,* 2277.

Van Widelfelt, B., Hosman, C., Schapp, C., & van der Staak, C. (1996). The prevention of relationship distress for couples at risk: A controlled evaluation with nine-month and two-year follow-ups. *Family Relations, 45*(2), 156–165.

Vega, W. A. (1990). Hispanic families in the 1980s: A decade of research. *Journal of Marriage and the Family, 52*(4), 1015–1024.

Wampler, K. S. (1990). An update of research on the Couple Communication Program. *Family Science Review, 3*(1), 21–40.

Woehrer, C. E. (1989). Ethnic families in the circumplex model: Integrating nuclear family with extended family systems. In D. H. Olson, C. S. Russell, & D. H. Sprenkle (Eds.), *Circumplex model: Systemic assessment and treatment of families* (pp. 199–238). New York: Haworth.

Worthington, E. L., Buston, B. G., & Hammonds, T. M. (1989). A component analysis of marriage enrichment: Information and treatment modality. *Journal of Counseling and Development, 67,* 555–560.

CHAPTER 8

Toward a Scientifically Based Marital Therapy

John M. Gottman
Kimberly D. Ryan
Sybil Carrère
Annette M. Erley

Marital dissolution has reached epidemic proportions in the United States. We now know that separation and divorce have deleterious consequences to the mental and physical health of the spouses involved. These negative effects include increased risk for psychopathology; increased rates of automobile accidents (including fatalities); and increased incidence of physical illness, suicide, violence, homicide, and mortality from diseases (for a review see Bloom, Asher, & White, 1978; Burman & Margolin, 1992). Clearly, marital disruption is best conceptualized as both a negative life event and a powerful predictor of such events. In fact, on the commonly used Scale of Stressful Life Events (Holmes & Rahe, 1967), marital disruption weighs heavily among major life stressors in discriminating between those individuals who become ill and those who do not. Although divorce may mark the end of an intolerable marriage, this cursory review suggests that there are high costs, emotionally and physically, associated with marital dissolution. For many distressed couples, it is the possibility of divorce that leads them to enter couple therapy in an effort to increase their marital satisfaction and to stabilize their marriages. Increasingly, researchers have sought to address the effectiveness of these marital therapies.

This chapter reviews the marital therapy research literature, with a focus on outcome studies and the effective components of marital therapy. In addition, we review the longitudinal research on the prediction of divorce, with an emphasis on our findings and those relevant to marital therapy. Third, we discuss our "sound marital house" theory and mathematical model of marital interaction. We then discuss the implications of our model and research for development of more effective marital therapies.

Results of Marital Intervention Studies

The evidence is that marital therapies are able to create statistically significant short-term effects compared to no-treatment control groups. To date, there have been a number of meta-analyses, as well as a summary review of these meta-analyses (Bray & Jouriles, 1995). Hahlweg and Markman's (1988) meta-analysis assessed the effect size of behavioral marital therapies as .95 (an improvement rate of 44%). However, Shadish, Montgomery, Wilson, Bright, and Okwumabua (1993), by adding unpublished dissertations, obtained smaller effect sizes of .74 for behavioral marital interventions (an improvement rate of 35%) and .51 for nonbehavioral marital therapies (an improvement rate of 23%).

Even these treatment effect sizes may not be as powerful as they seem. It is clear that nondirective, nonspecific, and nonorganized treatment with a passive therapist causes people to drop out of marital treatment at high rates. But almost all organized interventions, in the short run, tend to exceed a no-treatment control group. Although the effect sizes in these meta-analyses appear to be encouraging, the effects of intervention may be primarily caused by the deterioration of marriages in the no-treatment control groups. Jacobson and Addis (1993) wrote, "The success that investigators have had establishing these effects for their preferred treatments is not as impressive as first thought. The improvement rate in the absence of treatment is so low that even small changes in an experimental treatment are likely to be statistically significant" (p. 85). Jacobson and Addis reanalyzed data from four behavioral marital studies and concluded that, although 55% of the couples improved after treatment, only 35% were in the nondistressed range at the end of therapy. Furthermore, a pervasive problem that exists for almost all marital therapies that have been systematically evaluated using a long-term follow-up is a ubiquitous relapse effect. Although it is estimated that about 50 to 75% of couples make initial gains, a sizable percentage of these couples relapse within 2 years (Jacobson & Addis, 1993). In summary, the results of outcome research suggest that the majority of couples do not make clinically significant improvements in marital satisfaction immediately following even the best marital therapies, and that when improvements occur they are often short-lived (Jacobson, Follette, & Revenstorf, 1984). Although on the whole these results do not appear to be encouraging, they do suggest that some couples benefit from marital therapy, particularly behavioral marital therapy (BMT).

The Active Ingredients in Treatment Effects

It is important to point out that the effects in BMT are not the result of nonspecific factors, such as the therapeutic alliance, therapist–client rapport, and so on (Jacobson, 1978). But if the effects are not the result of nonspecific factors, what then are the active ingredients? This is not easy to determine from the literature, because most studies have added components to the marital therapy, leading to paradoxical results. The addition of these components appears to contribute nothing to the effects of intervention. The strange conclusion is that every component appears to be as effective as the whole. Why would this be the case? First, enormous similarity exists across so-called "schools" of marital therapy. For instance, the active core ingredient in almost all schools of marital intervention is active listening during conflict resolution. In active listening the listener is asked to listen nondefensively, to not argue for his or her point of view, to paraphrase the speaker, to check the accuracy of their paraphrase with the speaker, and then to genuinely and empathically validate the speaker's feelings. A number of writers have suggested that there is little empirical basis for this intervention and that it may be very difficult to do this when the listener is being criticized by the speaker (Johnson & Greenberg, 1985).

There is one exception in the behavioral marital intervention literature to the pattern that every component is as effective as the whole. This exception is a follow-up of a study by Jacobson (1984) and his students on the combination of behavior exchange and communication skills training. Jacobson, Schmaling, and Holtzworth-Munroe (1987) reported the 2-year follow up results of a BMT in which there were three treatment groups: behavior exchange, communication problem-solving, and complete treatment. After 2 years, the percentage of couples who separated or divorced was 55% in the behavior exchange treatment, 36% in the communication problem-solving treatment, and only 9% in the complete treatment group. Despite the small sample size, the complete treatment couples were reported as significantly less likely to have separated or divorced than either the behavior exchange or communication problem-solving couples ($p < .05$). To summarize, the Jacobson treatment combination stands out from other treatments in terms of its long-term outcomes and is the only behavioral study that has demonstrated lasting effects beyond 2 years of follow-up. It should be noted, however, that the study did not include observational data.

A careful reading of how these components were actually applied in Jacobson's manuals suggests to us that the contracting component of the intervention was aimed at increasing everyday positive affect exchanges in the marriage, while the communication skills training component was aimed at reducing negative affect during conflict. A meta-analysis found the separate immediate effect sizes of these two interventions to be .85 for communication training and .88 for behavior exchange (Shadish, Montgomery, et al., 1993; Shadish, Ragsdale, Glaser-Renita, & Montgomery, 1995). But it is the combination that produces more lasting change. These results suggest that lasting effects in BMT are most likely when interventions are two-pronged in their approach.

Not all marital interventions accomplish these two therapeutic goals. Baucom and Lester (1986) reported that as a result of treatment the only change in marital interaction was the reduction of negativity, not the increase of positivity. Schindler et al. (1983) have conducted the only observational study to date that evaluates this two-pronged approach. They found that active listening only decreased negativity; it did not increase positivity, and there were substantial decreases in initial gains on follow-up. Interestingly, it was the insight-oriented treatment, not the behavioral treatment, of Snyder and Wills (1989) that showed significant gains in positivity. Similarly, Hahlweg, Revenstorf, and Schindler (1984), using a combined behavioral approach to communication and problem-solving training on observational measures, found both increases in positivity and decreases in negativity. Unfortunately, their study included no long-term follow-up.

Insight-Oriented Intervention

There is one other study in the marital intervention literature that has produced lasting effects, and that is the insight-oriented intervention of Snyder, Wills, and Grady (1991a; see Snyder, Cozzi, & Mangrum, chapter 4, this volume, for a discussion of this study). However, the exact nature of the Snyder et al. (1991a) intervention led to a debate between Jacobson (1991) and Snyder, Wills, and Grady (1991b). Jacobson maintained that a careful examination of the insight-oriented manual developed by Snyder et al. (1991a) revealed the insight condition to be nearly identical to Jacobson's combined condition, while the behavioral intervention used by Snyder et al. was similar to the BMTs commonly practiced around 1980. Jacobson (1991) went on to claim that the Snyder et al. intervention and the Jacobson intervention were equivalent across 26 of the 31 separate elements. Snyder and Wills's (1989) own coding of their therapy sessions showed that the behavioral treatment was consistent and specific to the behavioral treatment 82% of the time, while the equivalent percentage for the insight condition was only 49%, suggesting that the insight-oriented intervention may have been eclectic. In the Snyder–Jacobson debate we can see dramatically the importance of the distinction we made previously between clinical interventions and experiments. The clinical intervention used by Snyder et al. (1991a) implemented planned changes that were so complex that even after a remarkably successful study, little was learned about what actually produced the observed changes. Given these methodological complexities, the debate regarding what constitutes effective intervention is likely to continue for some time. We have proposed that the essential feature important in both the Snyder et al. (1991a) and Jacobson interventions is the use of a two-pronged approach that increased positive affect in everyday interaction and decreased negative affect during conflict resolution, with appropriate insights.

Characteristics of Couples That Show Improvement

In the previous sections we delineated some of the key elements of successful marital therapy. However, it is equally important to identify the individual characteristics of those clients who do best in therapy, as well as those at greatest risk. There is some inconsistency across studies (see, for example, Snyder, Mangrum, & Wills, 1993), but the essential pattern is that couples who show the most improvement are less severely distressed and more occupationally advantaged (not unemployed or unskilled). They also tend to be more emotionally engaged, meaning that couples have a higher frequency of sexual intercourse, a greater emphasis on affective communication, and a higher quality of emotional affection. Finally, the couples who do the best show less negative affect before treatment. Extensive life stress (especially depression) is a poor prognostic indicator (but psychopathology and marital satisfaction are generally unrelated). There is some suggestion that greater commitment and active participation in the therapy itself, including the completion of homework, lead to greater improvements in couples seeking treatment and predict greater maintenance of changes following that treatment (Holtzworth-Munroe, Jacobson, DeKlyen, & Whisman, 1989).

There is clearly a need for a developmental epidemiology (Kellam, 1990) of marriage that accompanies any intervention study that can tell us (in some depth) the range of types of couples that exists in the population, as well as comorbid conditions (e.g., depression). This need is dramatized in Jacobson's (1991) reply to Snyder, in which Jacobson showed that a much higher percentage of Snyder et al.'s (1991a) couples were happily married than was the case for Jacobson's couples. This may have been only one salient dimension on which the couples differed across the two studies. Basic information about the couples in these studies is critical to evaluate issues like the permanence of treatment effects. Any information about the couples and the nature of their marriages is lost in all the meta-analytic studies of marital therapy outcomes. Hence, the effect size (or percent effectiveness) summary statistics are inadequate as measures of the therapy's effectiveness without a description of who the couples are. It is remarkable that after more than 20 years of systematic research with a variety of marital interventions, not one specific marital treatment exists that is based on any dimension of the marriage. The view promulgated by every marital therapy proposed is a "one size fits all" marital therapy. Jacobson and Addis (1993) decry this fact and call for attribute x treatment intervention research with marriages. That has yet to occur, and it would be assisted by an epidemiology of marriage that accompanies intervention research with couples.

A Practical and Theoretical Impasse

Generally speaking, current marital therapies are not based on empirical research findings. This is also true of the best researched marital therapies, the BMTs. Instead, most have evolved from the recommendations of respected therapists. For example, consider the evolution of a form of marital therapy called *contingency contracting*. Contingency contracting originated from the writings of Lederer and Jackson (1968), who suggested that the basic problem of distressed marriages was the failure of couples to have "quid pro quo" or equitable exchange agreements. Although their idea went untested, it quickly appeared as a new and popular marital therapy in the behavioral literature (Azrin, Naster, & Jones, 1973). Unfortunately, despite a later finding by Murstein, Cerreto, and MacDonald (1977) that showed quid pro quo arrangements in marriage to be more characteristic of distressed couples than nondistressed couples, contingency contracting continued to be used by practitioners in the field.

Contingency contracting and behavior exchange therapy have undergone a slow evolution as a result of subsequent clinical writing. For instance, following the publication of Stuart's (1996) ideas regarding "love days," behavior exchange became noncontingent and was oriented toward changing the everyday level of positivity instead of focusing on conflict. Hence, behavioral intervention evolved, but these changes were not the result of basic research findings, nor were they based on outcome data. This brief review of one component of marital therapy is true of other components of most marital therapies. Remarkably, the idea of putting marital therapy on an empirical footing is as yet an untried strategy. We are currently experimenting with this strategy in our marital laboratory in an effort to develop an empirically based theory and marital intervention. The remainder of the chapter will focus on this recent work, beginning with a discussion of the basic research on marriage from which it evolved.

Findings From Our Basic Research on Marriage

In our early studies we were particularly interested in predicting which couples would become dissatisfied with their marriages and choose to divorce (Gottman, 1994; Gottman & Levenson, 1992). Moreover, we wanted to identify what was dysfunctional in these ailing marriages. Across all of our research studies on marriage, we have taken a multimethod approach that involves a combination of observational, self-report, interview, and physiological measures. There is much evidence from the existing literature on prospective studies of divorce prediction (Gottman, 1993a, 1994) to suggest that use of self-report measures alone provides only limited validity and reliability (Bentler & Newcomb, 1978; Block, Block, & Morrison, 1981; Constantine & Bahr, 1980; Fowers & Olson, 1986; Kelly & Conley, 1987; Sears, 1977).

The work being conducted with couples in our laboratory revealed that the patterns of affective behaviors that couples used with each other were at the root of dysfunctional marital processes (Gottman & Levenson, 1992). Using an observational coding system, the Rapid Couples Interaction Scoring System (RCISS; Krokoff, Gottman, & Haas, 1989), Gottman and Levenson were able to derive one variable (the slope of a cumulated curve that plotted positive minus negative behaviors) to classify couples into two groups, regulated couples and nonregulated couples.

Regulated couples had positive slopes, indicating that both spouses displayed a significantly greater number of positive problem-solving behaviors (e.g., neutral or positive problem description, assent, humor) than negative problem-solving behaviors (e.g., complaining, criticizing, defensiveness, escalating negative affect). Nonregulated couples were those couples showing a curve of any other shape, the result of at least one spouse exhibiting a greater number of negative rather than positive problem-solving behaviors. This distinction between couples made it possible to predict marital dissolution with 75% accuracy in a short-term, 4-year longitudinal study. It also allowed for the establishment of a trajectory toward divorce, later referred to as the *cascade model of dissolution*.

This trajectory revealed a predictable series of stages leading up to marital dissolution. Those couples who later divorced initially showed marital unhappiness and dissatisfaction followed by thoughts of separation and divorce. This consideration of separation and divorce eventually led to separation and, finally, to divorce. The existence of this trajectory unified research on the correlates of marital dissatisfaction with research on divorce prediction. With our ability to reliably predict the cascade toward divorce, we can now quantify improvement in marital interaction in terms of divorce predictors.

In later work, Gottman (1994) proposed that not all negative behaviors were equally corrosive. He identified four behaviors that together form a cascade he called the *"four horsemen of the apocalypse"*: criticism, contempt, defensiveness, and stonewalling. Using these variables, the prediction of dissolution increased to 85%. Gottman then defined a second cascade that he called the *"distance and isolation cascade."* This model included the following variables: emotional flooding, viewing problems as severe, not wanting to work out problems with the spouse, parallel lives, and loneliness. The addition of these variables increased the prediction of dissolution to more than 90%.

These results showed that a multimethod research perspective was quite successful in predicting divorce and marital stability. The situation, in fact, seemed overdetermined. Wherever we looked, we found predictors of divorce. For instance, using a semistructured interview (oral history interview; Buehlman, Gottman, & Katz, 1992) that assesses a couple's relationship history and their philosophy of marriage, we were able to code for lasting thoughts and attributions about the marriage. These variables alone allowed us to accurately predict divorce at a rate of 94% (Buehlman, Gottman, & Katz, 1992). In many ways the results were unremarkable, with fondness toward one's partner expressed on the oral history interview predicting stability, and contempt in the marital interaction predicting divorce. There were some surprises, however. For example, anger was found to be unrelated to any negative outcome longitudinally—provided that anger was not blended with defensiveness or contempt or delivered in a belligerent manner.

Another of the surprising findings in our longitudinal work was the discovery of three very different types of stable marriages: volatile, validating, and conflict-avoiding. Couples in the volatile type of marriage tend to be high on immediate persuasion attempts, with little direct listening and validation before persuasion attempts begin. In the validating type, couples listen well and reflect back feelings before beginning persuasion attempts. The conflict-avoiding type includes couples who almost never engage in persuasive attempts (Gottman, 1993a, 1994). These classifications, initially made using our RCISS observational coding system, are now made using the Specific Affect Coding System (SPAFF; Gottman, 1996). We have also developed a set of questionnaires that make it possible to reliably classify couples into the three types (Gottman, 1994).

One serendipitous result of this work was the finding that all three types of stable marriages had positive-to-negative ratios not significantly different from 5.0 (compared to a ratio of .80 for unstable couples heading for divorce). Additionally, it allowed for the development of a balance theory of marriage (Gottman, 1993b). This theory suggests that each couple will find a balance, or a steady state, between positive and negative affect. These discoveries support the idea that attribute x treatment interaction intervention studies are both important and relevant to the marital research field (Varda, Avner, & Neeman, 1989; Varda & Hannah, 1991).

The Sound Marital House Theory

Our research across three separate longitudinal studies has demonstrated that we can predict divorce and marital stability with over 90% accuracy (Buehlman, Gottman & Katz, 1992; Gottman, 1994, 1996; Gottman & Levenson, 1992). Additionally, we have been able to predict marital satisfaction among stable couples, and even among newlyweds (Gottman, Coan, Carrere, & Swanson,

1998). More recently, we have moved beyond checklists of marital dysfunction and function to develop a process model of marriage that addresses what is dysfunctional when a marriage is unstable and dissatisfying, what is functional when a marriage is stable and satisfying, and the etiology of dysfunctional patterns. Furthermore, we have proposed a theory of marriage, the *sound marital house theory,* which is designed to provide explanations of mechanisms at work in marital relationships (see Figure 8-1).

The sound marital house theory outlines some of the elements that we have identified in our laboratory as important in building and sustaining a functional marital relationship. This theory has been pivotal in expanding our understanding of the role of positive affect in well-functioning marriages, the etiology of specific negative affects that are predictive of divorce, and the nature of conflict resolution in well-functioning marriages. For instance, our research indicates that satisfaction in marriage is related to a high level of (or increase in) everyday positive affect and a low level of (or reduction in) negative affect, especially during conflict resolution. The use of positive affect during a couple's daily interaction appears to be particularly important. Indeed, positive affect was predictive of marital stability in our newlywed sample and of marital satisfaction among the stable couples we studied. In these stable relationships, positive affect was used to de-escalate conflict and to physiologically soothe one's self and spouse. Surprisingly, it was the absence of positive affect and not the presence of negative affect that predicted the couples who would later divorce (Gottman, 1994).

FIGURE 8-1

CREATING SHARED SYMBOLIC MEANING
DREAMS, NARRATIVES, MYTHS AND METAPHORS
MAKING DREAMS AND ASPIRATIONS COME TRUE (AVOIDING GRIDLOCK)

REGULATING CONFLICT
FOUR PARTS OF EFFECTIVE PROBLEM SOLVING
DIALOGUE WITH PERPETUAL PROBLEMS

CREATING POSITIVE SENTIMENT OVERRIDE
POSITIVE SENTIMENT OVERRIDE

THE MARITAL FRIENDSHIP
TURNING TOWARD VERSUS TURNING AWAY (THE EMOTIONAL BANK ACCOUNT)
FONDNESS AND ADMIRATION SYSTEM AND PHYSIOLOGICAL SOOTHING
LOVE MAPS

The Gottman sound marital house.

The findings reviewed here indicate that positive affect plays a pivotal role in the development of satisfying and lasting relationships. The question that remains, however, is how do couples go about building and sustaining positive affect in their marital interactions? Unfortunately, it is difficult to create positive affect or to recreate it in a distressed marriage that has lost it. The admonition to be positive or the setting up of behavioral exchanges is usually doomed. Vincent, Friedman, Nugent, and Messerly (1979), after a neutral no-instruction condition, asked couples to either fake good or fake bad. While verbal behavior differentiated couples faking from the neutral condition, the positive or negative nonverbal behaviors of couples did not change. Rather than using contingency contracting to create positive affect in the marriage, we have found that building or rebuilding a couple's friendship is the treatment of choice. In particular, this involves creating positive affect and friendship in nonconflict contexts. The first three levels of the sound marital house theory form the foundation needed to establish this sense of friendship that fosters positive affect within the marriage. These levels include (a) love maps, (b) fondness and admiration, and (c) turning toward versus turning away.

Love Maps

It is well-known that over half of all divorces occur in the first 7 years of marriage. Some of this involves a cascade toward divorce that follows the birth of the first child, in which 75% of all couples (mainly wives) experience a precipitous drop in marital satisfaction, while 25% do not. This drop in marital satisfaction is part of the cascade toward divorce. In our longitudinal research with newlyweds we attempted to discover, in the first few months of marriage, what would predict whether a couple would wind up in the 25% group versus the 75% group. Using our oral history interview and the oral history coding system, we found that the amount of "cognitive room" an individual person (particularly a husband) has about the marriage, its history, and the life of their spouse (including the spouse's psychological world) was predictive of marital satisfaction. Those husbands who essentially had a "map" of their wives' worlds and continued to "know" their wives' psychological world wound up in the 25% whose marital satisfaction did not drop as they made the transition to parenthood. We have called this concept of cognitive room the *love map*. Our research clearly shows that the first part of friendship is knowing one's partner.

Fondness and Admiration

The second part of the theory is the *fondness and admiration system*. In our research program it is assessed using our oral history interview. When members of a couple express fondness and admiration for one another they are more likely to have a satisfying, stable marriage (Buehlman, Gottman, & Katz, 1992).

Moreover, we found that the oral history interview variables that tapped the fondness and admiration system were predictive of the longitudinal course of marriages across two separate studies. Our work suggests that the expression of fondness and admiration may also help to buffer couples during stressful or transitional periods (Shapiro & Walker, 1997), and may serve as an antidote for interactions characterized by contempt.

Turning Toward Versus Turning Away

The marital interaction pattern of turning toward versus turning away, or what may be called the *emotional bank account,* makes up the third level of the theory. The concept of turning toward versus turning away has its basis in the everyday, mundane interactions we observe in our apartment laboratory. The idea is that if partners characteristically turn toward one another rather than away, it is "emotional money in the bank." In contrast, too many withdrawals (turning away) will leave the emotional bank account depleted. The following dialogue provides an example of the concept of "turning toward:"

> *Wife:*   Isn't that a beautiful boat?
>
> *Husband:*   (Putting down the newspaper) Yeah, like one of those old schooners.

The turning away scenario is distinctly different, revealing a marital interaction pattern in which members of a couple do not orient or respond to one another.

> *Wife:*   Isn't that a beautiful boat?
>
> *Husband:*   (No response. Husband continues to read the newspaper).

In research terms, the emotional bank account involves relating the ratio of positivity to negativity in nonconflict discussions, and in our apartment lab setting, to the way people interact when resolving conflict. In our 1983 to 1997 study, we predicted the husband and wife ratios in the "conflict conversation" from their ratios in the "events of the day" discussion. Our findings revealed a multiple R of .71, R-squared = .51, $F(2, 62) = 31.99$ ($p = .0000$) for the wife's conflict ratio and a multiple R of .54, R-squared = .29, $F(2, 62) = 12.46$ ($p = .0000$) for the husband's conflict ratio. In other words, the simple ratio of positive-to-negative affect in mundane, everyday conversations sets the stage for the same ratios in conflict conversations, and these ratios in the conflict context predicted divorce. Indeed, over the long run, turning-away behaviors are likely to lead to a sense of distance and isolation that, in turn, is predictive of emotional toxicity and divorce. Marital intervention in this area involves reprogramming the way the couple moves through time together, encouraging connections across fairly mundane and mindless moments of the day.

Positive Sentiment Override

The most consistent discriminator between distressed and nondistressed marriages is *negative affect reciprocity* a sequential pattern in which negative affect by a spouse becomes more likely than his or her baseline level of negative affect would suggest following negativity from the partner. This implies that it is very important that a couple be able to repair the interaction and that they be able to exit a negative affect cycle once they have entered it. Indeed, it may be the sine qua non of effective marital interaction during conflict. We have been studying these repair processes and have discovered that, on average, repair efforts occur about once every 3 minutes. Interestingly, these efforts at repair occur more frequently in distressed couples, and the success of the repair attempts cannot be predicted from any parameter of its delivery, context, or timing. Instead, an honors student in our laboratory discovered that successful repair attempts are determined by a concept called *positive sentiment override* (PSO; Lorber, 1997).

The concept of PSO was first proposed by Weiss (1980). Weiss suggested that reactions during marital interaction may be determined by a global dimension of affection or disaffection rather than by the immediately preceding valence of the stimulus. We extended Weiss's idea of PSO and negative sentiment override (NSO), suggesting that it had its basis in everyday, mundane, nonconflict interaction. These overrides are determined by insider–outsider coding discrepancies. For instance, in PSO a spouse will say something with negative affect (as judged by observers), and it is received as a neutral message, perhaps with italics, meaning that this is an important issue to the spouse. On the other hand, in NSO a neutral message (as judged by observers) is received as if it were negative. Lorber found that the husband's use of PSO was particularly important, for it determined the success of repair attempts during conflict resolution.

More recently, one of our research assistants discovered that a critical variable in PSO was the wife's general perception of her husband's anger (Hawkins, 1997). In marriages that were destined to become happy and stable the wife did not perceive her husband's anger negatively; instead she saw it as neutral. Although the wife noticed and responded to the anger, she did not evaluate it as negative (as determined via our video-recall rating dial.) In marriages headed for unhappiness or divorce, the wife's rating of her husband's anger was negative. It is important to note that this was a categorical and not a minor quantitative difference. Wives in marriages headed for stability and happiness were actually seeing their husbands' anger as neutral, not just as less negative than their counterparts in marriages destined for misery or divorce.

The sound marital house theory suggests that PSO mediates between positive affect in a couple's everyday interaction as well as a couple's ability to regulate negative affect during the resolution of conflict. Hence, in the theory, what determines PSO is positive affect in nonconflict interaction. As described earlier, the use of positive affect in marital interactions can be thought of as an emotional bank account. This model suggests that PSO is determined by the amount of emotional money the couple has in the bank. Thus, PSO is the outcome of the marital friendship going well. Our data support this linkage in the theory.

Effective Problem Solving and Dialogue With Perpetual Problems

In examining the forms of problem solving and communication that couples engage in around areas of disagreement, it is critical to have an understanding of the etiology of dysfunctional patterns of interaction. This is particularly true of interactions in which there are obvious and consistent gender differences. An example of one such pattern during conflict resolution is the demand–withdraw pattern. It has been well-established that among distressed couples women are generally more likely than men to make demands for change, while men are more likely than women to withdraw (e.g., Christensen, 1987, 1988, 1990; Christensen & Heavey, 1990; Cohen & Christensen, 1980). Moreover, it is well-known that women more frequently begin conversations about problems than men (Ball, Cowan, & Cowan, 1995; Oggins, Veroff, & Leber, 1993). Our longitudinal research indicates that during conflict resolution women are also more likely to use criticism than men, while men are more likely than women to stonewall (listener withdrawal). Moreover, these patterns of interaction were shown to be predictive of both early and late divorce (Gottman, 1994).

The etiology of these patterns is important, particularly with regard to patterns that have been used historically to blame women for marital distress. In an effort to address etiology, we assessed couples after they had been apart for at least 8 hours. Couples were then asked to have two discussions, the first an "events of the day" discussion, and the second a "conflict conversation." To index the demand–withdraw pattern, we computed the sum of the differences between men and women on criticism and stonewalling during conflict resolution. We found that this female negative startup pattern during conflict did have an etiology and that it was indeed predicted by the husband's affect during the events of the day nonconflict interaction.

Our research suggests that couples face two types of problems in regulating conflict within the relationship: problems that are resolvable and problems that have no solution. Consider, for instance, our findings regarding the content of the discussions around a major area of continuing disagreement. In only 31% of the discussions that took place in our marital laboratory were couples grappling with a problem that could be considered to have a solution. Thus, in

69% of the discussions, couples were talking about unresolvable problems, what we now call *perpetual problems*. Perpetual problems tend to involve longstanding issues of disagreement, often having to do with fundamental personality differences between spouses.

For the 31% of marital problems that are resolvable, we found a pattern of four skills that predicted the longitudinal course of the marriage in newlyweds. We have discovered, through detailed observational coding and sequential analysis in our newlywed study, that these four components of effective conflict resolution (when the problem has a solution) are (a) softened startup, (b) accepting influence, (c) repair and de-escalation, and (d) compromise (Gottman et al., 1998). The use of positive affect in the service of de-escalation also plays a role. Unfortunately, positive affect during conflict resolution is generally not programmable by intervention. Behavior exchange in the Jacobson intervention is one way of attempting to induce positive affect by changing the everyday interactions of the couple. Changing the nature of the couple's friendship is a conceptualization of this process. We have found, clinically, that positive affect during conflict resolution just happens by itself when PSO is in place. Recent analyses on our newlywed sample show that positive affect and de-escalation are also associated with physiological soothing of the husband by the wife and self-soothing by the husband (Gottman et al., 1998). Physiological soothing (self and partner) is fundamental to both solvable and perpetual problems and is hypothesized to be an important ingredient for avoiding relapse. The couple, and not the therapist, needs to be able to do this soothing to minimize relapse after treatment.

Unfortunately, many conflicts are intractable (Gottman, 1998). However, we discovered that what determined the future of the marriage in the problem-solving domain was not whether a couple solved a perpetual problem but the accompanying affect with which they worked toward resolving the problem. What seems to be important is whether a couple can establish a positive affective dialogue around their perpetual problems that allows them to communicate amusement and affection while seeking change. We have found that if couples cannot establish such a dialogue, the conflict becomes gridlocked, and gridlocked conflict eventually leads either to high levels of negative affect (particularly criticism, defensiveness, contempt, and stonewalling) or lack of affect and emotional disengagement.

These findings on marital interaction and positive affect point to the importance of positive affect within the resolution of conflict. We have now studied the stability of marital interaction over a 4-year period and have discovered remarkable consistency in these interaction patterns, particularly with regard to affect. Moreover, we have found that it is the regulation of most conflicts and not their resolution that is predictive of longitudinal outcomes in marriages. These are also the processes operative in our long-term marriage study with couples in their 40s and 60s (Carstensen, Gottman, & Levenson, 1995; Levenson, Carstensen, & Gottman, 1993, 1994). As such, we suggest that diagnosis and treatment of couples involve an assessment of positive affect in everyday interaction and conflict resolution, as well as an assessment of negativity (e.g., the four horsemen of the apocalypse). Our research indicates that both the absence of positive affect (even during conflict resolution) and the presence of negative affect are indicative of marital dysfunction. The use of such an assessment procedure will be more effective than current methods in identifying problematic marriages that are at the stage of emotional detachment (farther down the distance and isolation cascade). Couples in these emotionally disengaged marriages as well as couples experiencing other forms of gridlocked conflict will benefit from exploring the symbolic meaning of each person's position in the conflict, using our dreams-within-conflict intervention. This intervention involves helping the couple identify the core issues in the marriage.

Creating Shared Symbolic Meaning and Honoring Life Dreams

Gottman discovered clinically that it is the construction of shared meanings that unlocks gridlocked marital conflict. This involves honoring and meshing each spouse's individual life dreams, narratives, myths, and metaphors. It is this meshing of the symbolic meanings attached to aspects of marriage (goals, rituals, roles, symbols) and family that prevents marital gridlock. We have found that the basis of a continued positive affective emotional connection involves the perception of the marriage's effectiveness at making personal life dreams and aspirations come true. Even if the two people come from the same racial, ethnic, and geographic background, the two families they grew up in will be very different, and so their union will always involve the creation of a new world of meaning.

We have developed two salient interviews that tap into these narratives about what life means. The first, the *meta-emotion interview*, is used to determine each person's experience history with the basic emotions such as sadness, anger, fear, love, pride, embarrassment, guilt, and shame. It also assesses the individual's feelings and philosophy about these various emotions. Marchitelli and Levenson (1992, 1994) discovered that emotion metaphors during marital conflict were related to physiological arousal. The second interview is the *meanings interview*. It asks couples to discuss the meaning of everyday rituals, as well as the meaning of fundamental roles in their family of origin and in their own marriage and family. We use this interview to uncover roles, rituals, goals, and symbolic meanings—in effect the interview delineates the family's culture. These two interviews can be viewed as interconnecting the levels of the sound marital house theory in that the exploration of a couple's emotional world and the narratives, dreams, metaphors, and myths they have about marriage enables them to get to know one another more completely and encourages the expression of fondness and admiration and turning toward one's partner. These three components make up the foundation of the theory. We have discovered that emotional disengagement and lack of affect in marriage often occur when couples have not dealt adequately with these levels. Indeed, they make it possible for couples to use positive affect during conflict resolution in the service of de-escalation and physiological soothing, thereby allowing marital conflict to proceed in a healthy and functional manner.

Potential Contributions of the Theory

In addressing the potential contributions of the sound marital house theory, we must first consider how the theory relates to current thinking about marital therapy. Unlike many of the current marital therapies, the theory suggests that intervention not be based solely or primarily on how couples resolve conflict. Instead, it presents a more holistic model regarding intimacy in marriage and its basis. Moreover, it proposes that the effective resolution of conflict itself is based on the first level of the sound marital house, which has its roots in everyday marital interaction and thought and has its effects through PSO. The theory also suggests that, when conflicts have a solution, the conflict resolution skills that most therapies are targeting (active listening) are the wrong targets, and it proposes four alternative targets. Finally, it posits that most marital conflict involves "perpetual problems" that never get resolved and that what matters most is the couple's affect during discussion of and conflict around these intractable problems. Either the couple establishes a dialogue with the perpetual problem and communicates acceptance, or the conflict becomes gridlocked. Our 14-year prospective longitudinal divorce prediction studies suggest that when conflict becomes gridlocked two patterns emerge, depending on the stage of gridlock (Gottman & Levenson, 1992). One pattern occurs early in the relationship, during the first 7 years of marriage (average of 5.2 years) and involves the four horsemen (criticism, contempt, defensiveness, and stonewalling). The other pattern is characterized by emotional disengagement and lack of affect and is predictive of later divorce (average of 16.4 years).

Our hypotheses about what is necessary to create lasting change in marriages developed out of these recent findings. We found that a model emphasizing negative affect during conflict at Time 1 (particularly the four horsemen) predicted earlier divorcing, whereas a model involving the absence or lack of positive affect at Time 1 predicted later divorcing. These two critical time points for intervention are consistent with other findings in the marital research literature. For example, Cherlin (1981) reported that the first 7 years of marriage contain half the divorces. Jacobson and Addis (1993) underscored this point when they wrote, "Because there is a predictable decline in couple satisfaction that occurs after the birth of children, this seems to be an ideal time to intervene" (p. 90). It is also well-known that the low point in marital satisfaction in the life course occurs around the time that a family's first child becomes a teenager (Anderson, Dimidjian, & Miller, 1995). Given the importance of commitment and participation in the therapy process, we hypothesize that couples who have just entered the cascade toward divorce (assessed using the Gottman-Krokoff distance and isolation cascade questionnaires) will benefit more from therapeutic intervention than those couples who are farther along the cascade toward divorce. Indeed, these findings indicate that couples initially higher in overall positive affect and lower in negative affect during conflict will do best in marital therapy. This suggests that both the failure of marital therapy and the marriage, in some way, involve positive and negative processes of interaction; this is consistent with the idea that a two-pronged intervention that increases positivity and reduces negativity is necessary if couples are to make lasting changes in their marital interaction patterns.

The sound marital house theory addresses this lack of positivity and the presence of negativity in the marital relationship and proposes a resolution to gridlocked conflict. The resolution of conflict, like the etiology of conflict, involves the clash of people's life dreams, and clash in the symbolic meaning of people's stands on these issues. This part of the marriage is about a couple's culture. Our approach to culture is not limited to how these processes vary with ethnic and racial groupings; rather, the theory says that we are always dealing with the culture that a couple creates when they marry. This culture is their own unique blend of meanings, symbol systems, metaphors, narratives, philosophy, goals, roles, and rituals. It is this culture that fuels both intimacy and estrangement.

A Mathematical Model of Marital Interaction

An important advance we recently made in our own work was the development of a mathematical model of marital interaction (Cook et al., 1995). With the help of a team of applied mathematicians led by James Murray, we have developed a set of dynamic nonlinear difference equations that model marital interaction and predict longitudinal outcomes. This mathematical model has parameters that constitute a theory of marital functioning. Furthermore, the use of mathematics makes it possible to simulate couple behavior, perception, and physiology under conditions different from those that were used to estimate the parameters of the model.

The mathematical model that we developed suggests that each marriage arrives at a core steady state (or attractor) of behavior, cognition, and physiology in which negativity is balanced by positivity in each of these domains. It further suggests that each person brings an uninfluenced steady state (a function of enduring characteristics such as personality and the past history of the relationship) to every marital interaction As a couple interact, this steady state is changed through an influence process. The influence process can be described by each person's inertia, that is, their resistance to change, and by two influence functions.

As noted earlier, Gottman and Levenson (1992) used one variable, the slope of a cumulated curve that plotted the difference between positive problem-solving behaviors and negative problem-solving behaviors, to predict marital stability or dissolution. Our mathematical model attempted to dismantle this variable into components and parameters that were theoretically meaningful. The purpose of this model was to construct a theoretical language using the balance theory of marriage that would allow us to generate theory regarding marital stability and divorce.

The equations for the mathematical model are presented here, where t is time,

$$W_{t+1} = I_{H \to W}(H_t) + r_1 W_t + a_1 \tag{1}$$

$$H_{t+1} = I_{W \to H}(W_t) + r_2 H_t + a_2 \tag{2}$$

(H_t) is the husband's data and (W_t) is the wife's data. The I's represent the husband's "influence function" on the wife in Equation 1, and the wife's "influence function" on the husband in Equation 2. These functions have distinct shapes and describe the prediction regarding the course of a couple's marriage, or, in mathematical terms, the influence that one partner has on the other partner across a range of point-graph values after controlling for autocorrelation. The r_1 and r_2 are the "emotional inertia" parameters, and the a_1 and a_2 (scaled by $1/(1 - r_1)$) are the "uninfluenced set points." Using these equations, it is possible to compute both an "influenced set point" and the magnitude of discrepancy between influenced and uninfluenced set points.

An examination of the data from a study of 79 couples revealed several differences between unstable and stable marriages (Cook et al., 1995). These differences are summarized in Table 8-1. Compared to stable marriages, unstable marriages showed greater husband and wife inertia and more negative husband and wife uninfluenced set points. Moreover, in unstable marriages the spouse's influence moved the set point toward the negative rather than toward the positive direction. These dysfunctional marriages also showed a mismatch in shape between husband and wife influence functions, whereas the influence functions of stable couples were matched in shape. Finally, for all couples headed for divorce the influenced set point was more negative than the unin-

TABLE 8-1

Differences in mathematical model parameters as a function of marital stability

MARITAL STABILITY	HUSBAND			WIFE		
	INERTIA	UNINFLUENCED SET POINT	INFLUENCED-UNINFLUENCED	INERTIA	UNINFLUENCED SET POINT	INFLUENCED-UNINFLUENCED
STABLE	.29	.44	.17	.20	.55	.10
UNSTABLE	.36	−.16	−.08	.49	−.44	−.10

fluenced set point. For all types of stable marriages (volatile, conflict-avoiding, and validating), the influenced set point was more positive than the uninfluenced set point.

In a closer examination of the three types of stable marriage, the influence functions were shown to be dramatically different. Volatile couples influenced one another only when the interaction had negative values, and their influence was negative. Conflict-avoiding couples, on the other hand, influenced one another only when the interaction had positive values, and their influence was positive. Validating couples influenced one another throughout the range of values. As such, they had a positive influence for positive values and a negative influence for negative values. In a second study using the mathematical model, we have essentially replicated these results with a representative sample of Seattle newlyweds (Gottman et al., 1998).

These early studies used actual data to estimate the shape of the influence functions. Subsequent to this, we began experimenting with a theoretical shape for these functions. We are currently assuming that the theoretical shape of the influence function is an O-Jive, or an S-shaped curve (see Figure 8-2). However, we are also experimenting with differential equations and the hyperbolic tangent shape. The influence function presented here is the mean of the wife's next score across all the time points for which the husband's score has a particular

FIGURE 8-2

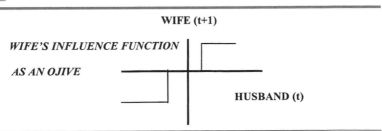

Influence function.

value. The graph shows a function in which the husband has no effect on the wife until he exceeds a certain threshold of positivity, and then he has a constant positive effect on her next behavior. For the negative ranges, he has no effect until he exceeds a threshold of negativity, and then he has a constant negative effect on her next behavior. As the model is modified in subsequent research, individual couples may be shown to have their own thresholds, and the shape of the function could become more complex (for example, we might decide that the more positive the husband's previous behavior, the more positive his impact on the wife's subsequent behavior, so instead of a constant we would have a straight line with a slope).

Using the mathematical model, we can compute and plot what mathematicians call the *null clines* (Cook et al., 1995). Null clines are the steady states of the system (stable and unstable) and are termed *attractors* within the mathematical equation. Steady states allow one to determine where a system will move when perturbed. This information can then be used to describe the system's behavior. It is relatively easy to show mathematically that the null clines for the husband and wife are simply their respective influence functions, translated by the respective uninfluenced set point and scaled by 1 minus the respective inertia. For each couple, we can determine their stable, steady states and then ascertain whether either the steady state or the influence functions have been changed by the intervention.

General systems theory has suggested for the past 30 years that we distinguish between first-order (more superficial) and second-order (deeper) change, but for years these ideas have remained at the level of metaphors and armchair speculation. This is no longer the true. For example, using our influence functions and the model parameters, which determine the null clines, we can now model catastrophic qualitative changes in the marriage following a slow decline of any or both uninfluenced set points. What we find is that after passing a threshold value, the couple suddenly loses all positive, stable, steady states and is left with only negative, unstable steady states.

Contributions of the Mathematical Model

The mathematical model contributes much to the marital therapy research arena in that it gives us a language that we have never before had to talk about marital interaction. Additionally, mathematical models can be fit for each couple, making it possible to computer simulate the couple's interactions. Consider, for instance, that in any observation we only see a couple in a limited set of conditions. If the model is right, we can use that data to predict how this same couple will interact under entirely different conditions without actually having to observe them in these new contexts. Finally, these simulations can suggest relevant hypotheses and experiments, and the results of these experiments can then be used to further test the mathematical model. In other words, we are able to test whether the model actually works in these simulations and, if it does not, perhaps figure out ways to modify it.

Developing an Empirically Based Marital Intervention

As discussed earlier, we believe that one major problem with current marital therapies is that they are not guided by an empirically based theory. We have described one possible theory, the sound marital house theory, and have supplemented this theory with a set of nonlinear difference equations. These equations are based on a balance theory of marriage that has emerged from our laboratory studies of divorce prediction. Our basic marital research has also shown us that there is a clearly identifiable and replicated cascade toward divorce (Gottman, 1994) and that the progression toward divorce essentially forms a Guttman scale. It is possible, therefore, to speculate about what the goals might be of a minimal marital therapy program.

We suggest that a more effective marital therapy may result from relatively simple social psychology intervention studies in which very specific interventions are designed to produce only proximal change, rather than carrying out complex clinical trials that attempt to alter all aspects of the marriage. This makes sense if the goal of the intervention is to target and change specific destructive patterns of marital interaction found to be predictive of divorce in previous prospective, longitudinal research (e.g., social cognitions, attributions, and physiological patterns). The problem, however, is which predictors to select as targets of change. This problem is solved once we have a mathematical model, because we then have a set of parameters that index the fundamental marital processes related to our prediction of the longitudinal course of a marriage. The mathematical model also gives us a theoretical language to discuss the changes in marital interaction required to strengthen marriages. Moreover, this model is also eminently testable and modifiable, allowing us to generate experiments and providing a method for computer simulation of couple behavior under subsequent experimental conditions.

In the proximal intervention studies, instead of trying to create permanent change in the marriage, the goal is only to improve the second of two conflict resolution interactions. These interactions involve two conversations in which couples are asked to discuss at least one longstanding area of disagreement. The disagreement areas to be discussed are selected from a standardized, self-report checklist developed for use in our marital research (see Bray, chapter 5, this volume, for further details). Following these two conversations, we have found that it is possible to determine whether the second conversation is "better" than the first, in the sense that the parameters we derive from the second interaction are less characteristic of couples on a trajectory toward divorce than the parameters in the first interaction.

We have been piloting this research agenda for the past 4 years. Currently, a series of eight studies designed to examine proximal change in marital interaction is under way in our laboratory. These studies are not arbitrary but guided by the sound marital house theory and the mathematical model described here. Our overall goal is to develop a new empirically based marital intervention, with each experiment tapping a different area related to divorce prediction.

Although the experimental interventions are designed only to create proximal change in marriage, the experiments themselves seek to build theory. Unlike clinical trials in marital therapy, our series of controlled experiments changes only a single variable or, in the case of a factorial design, at most two variables at one time. As such, the proximal effects on other variables in the theoretical model can be detected. The distinction between clinical interventions and experiments is an important one. In a clinical intervention the planned changes are so complex that following the intervention it is difficult, if not impossible, to decipher what exactly produced the observed change. This is also true of studies that seek to dismantle a complex intervention into its components (dismantling studies). Indeed, the dismantling strategy has been quite unsuccessful in the marital intervention field because generally (except for two studies) every component has turned out to be equally effective, and as effective as the whole. Moreover, each component remains extremely complex (Baucom & Hoffman, 1986). Finally, in contrast to the outcome research being conducted in the field today, our experimental interventions evaluate the effects when we change a process variable up as well as down. To date, this has been a significant limitation of clinical studies and constitutes a major difference between the proposed experiments and the current therapeutic interventions.

Understandably, therapy programs hold hidden and implicit assumptions that couple interaction needs to change in only one direction, the one that is considered "healthy" or "therapeutic." In our research, we need not impose such limitations. For example, in assessing the effect of an active listening condition in our experiments, we compare it to a control condition as well as contrasting it with its opposite. This so-called *opposite position* is an intervention in which people are encouraged to debate, to argue for their own point of view, and to prepare aggressively for their partner's counterarguments. Surprisingly, our pilot work has found both approaches to be equally effective, depending on the type of couple and the type of problem the couple is dealing with. Preliminary results suggest that the debating approach may be particularly effective when a couple has become emotionally disengaged from one another because of a demand–withdraw pattern. Experimental approaches such as the one we are proposing, therefore, are able to challenge what have become cherished beliefs about therapeutic change supported in large part by clinical folk-lore.

In our pilot work, it has turned out that in a very short time we can dramatically change most distressed marital interactions. We expect these changes to be short-lived, however, with most couples making only temporary gains as a result of these interventions. Thus, the marriage experiments themselves offer us a natural paradigm for studying the relapse effect following intervention. Although we predict that most couples will relapse after successful proximal change, we do not assume that all couples will do so. Indeed, we have been surprised to find that about 30% of the time the changes made in marital interaction seem to last. We are currently following each couple for a period of 1 year in order to assess the effects of each intervention and to address why some couples relapse while others do not. In this and other ways, our marital laboratory is ideally suited to conducting these proximal studies on marital intervention.

The Research Agenda

There are two objectives of the proximal studies: (a) to assess whether our interventions have changed the variables that are predictive of the cascades toward marital dissolution, and (b) to determine if successfully changing behavior to make people less defensive alters physiology and perception. This is a theory-construction and model-building goal that can only be accomplished with empirical studies. Following the completion of these two objectives, a new marital therapy that combines all effective interventions must be created and tested in a clinical trial. This clinical trial must be combined with an epidemiological study so that we can discuss the nature of treatment failures. These analyses will eventually lead to attribute x treatment interaction studies as we learn how to individualize therapy. Coupled with this approach, it would be sensible to design and implement interventions of varying duration and cost—from psychoeducational workshops to intensive, individualized marital therapy—to determine what types of marriages need what types of interventions. Indeed, we are currently experimenting with inexpensive psychoeducationally based couples' weekend workshops that combine all of the experiments as exercises.

Conclusion

This chapter had several specific objectives. First we briefly reviewed the marital therapy literature, focusing on recent findings in the field as well as our own longitudinal research on divorce prediction. Second, we described, in some detail, both our sound marital house theory and our mathematical model of marital interaction. To our knowledge, the work we have done with the mathematical model is unique in psychology because it uses the methods of non-linear dynamic modeling rather than simply relying on its metaphors. We are hopeful that when other researchers see the progress we have made with this modeling that they will follow our lead. We feel strongly that the modeling could benefit a variety of problems in psychology. Furthermore, the marital research field is in desperate need of a theory. Current marital therapies are primarily not based on empirical work, and this is true of even the best researched behavioral marital therapies. In this chapter, we suggest that the development of a scientifically based marital therapy be based on experimental intervention studies that use specifically designed interventions to produce proximal changes in specific destructive patterns of marital interaction. This differs from the previous work in the field, which has attempted to alter all aspects of the marriage simultaneously. Our current research agenda seeks to construct theory that will explain the mechanisms by which marriages travel the high road of satisfaction and function or, conversely, the low road of decay and dissolution. In short, we would like to delineate the elements that support or impede couples in their construction of a sound marital house.

References

Anderson, C. M., Dimidjan, S., & Miller, A. (1995). Redefining the past, present, and future: Therapy with long term marriages at midlife. In N. Jacobson & A. Gurman (Eds.), Clinical handbook of couple therapy (pp. 247–260). New York: Guilford Press.

Azrin, N. H., Naster, B. J., & Jones, R. (1973). Reciprocity counseling: A rapid learning-based procedure for marital counseling. Behaviour Research & Therapy, 11(4), 365–382.

Ball, F. L. J., Cowan, P., & Cowan, C. P. (1995). Who's got the power? Gender differences in partner's perception of influence during marital problem-solving discussions. Family Process, 34, 303–321.

Baucom, D. H., & Hoffman, J. A. (1986). The effectiveness of marital therapy: Current status and application to the clinical setting. In N. Jacobson & A. Gurman (Eds.), Clinical handbook of couple therapy (pp. 597–620). New York: Guilford Press.

Baucom, D. H., & Lester, G. W. (1986). The usefulness of cognitive restructuring as an adjunct to behavioral marital therapy. Behavior Therapy, 17, 385–403.

Bentler, P. M., & Newcomb, M. D. (1978). Longitudinal study of marital success and failure. Journal of Consulting & Clinical Psychology, 45(5), 1053–1070.

Block, J. H., Block, J., & Morrison, A. (1981). Parental agreement–disagreement on child rearing and gender related personality correlates in children. Child Development, 52, 965–974.

Bloom, B., Asher, S., & White, S. (1978). Marital disruption as a stressor: A review and analysis. *Psychological Bulletin, 85,* 867–894.

Bray, J. H., & Jouriles, E. N. (1995). Treatment of marital conflict and prevention of divorce. *Journal of Marital and Family Therapy, 21*(4), 461–473.

Buehlman, K., Gottman, J. M., & Katz, L. (1992). How a couple views their past predicts their future: Predicting divorce from an oral history interview. *Journal of Family Psychology, 5,* 295–318.

Burman, B., & Margolin, G. (1992). Analysis of the association between marital relationships and health problems: An interactional perspective. *Psychological Bulletin, 112,* 39–63.

Carstensen, L. L., Gottman, J. M., & Levenson, R. W. (1995). Emotional behavior in long-term marriage. *Psychology and Aging, 10*(1), 140–149.

Cherlin, A. (1981). *Marriage, divorce, remarriage.* Cambridge, MA: Harvard University Press.

Christensen, A. (1987). Detection of conflict patterns in couples. In K. Hahlweg & M. J. Goldstein (Eds.), *Understanding major mental disorder: The contribution of family interaction research* (pp. 250–265). New York: Family Process Press.

Christensen, A. (1988). Dysfunctional interaction patterns in couples. In P. Noller & M. A. Fitzpatrick (Eds.), *Perspectives on marital interaction* (pp. 31–52). Avon, England: Multilingual Matters.

Christensen, A., & Heavey, C. L. (1990). Gender and social structure in the demand/withdraw pattern of marital conflict. *Journal of Personality and Social Psychology, 59,* 73–81.

Cohen, R. S., & Christensen, A. (1980). A further examination of demand characteristics in marital interaction. *Journal of Consulting and Clinical Psychology, 48,* 121–123.

Constantine, J. A., & Bahr, S. J. (1980). Locus of control and marital stability. *Journal of Divorce, 4*(1), 11–22.

Cook, J., Tyson, R., White, J., Rushe, R., Gottman, J., & Murray, J. (1995). The mathematics of marital conflict: Qualitative dynamic mathematical modeling of marital interaction. *Journal of Family Psychology, 9,* 110–130.

Fowers, B. J., & Olson, D. H. (1986). Predicting marital success with PREPARE: A predictive validity study. *Journal of Marital and Family Therapy, 12,* 403–413.

Gottman, J. M. (1993a). The roles of conflict engagement, escalation, or avoidance in marital interaction: A longitudinal view of five types of couples. *Journal of Consulting and Clinical Psychology, 61,* 6–15.

Gottman, J. M. (1993b). A theory of marital dissolution and stability. *Journal of Family Psychology, 7,* 57–75.

Gottman, J. M. (1994). *Why marriages succeed or fail.* New York: Simon & Schuster.

Gottman, J. M. (Ed.). (1996). *What predicts divorce?: The measures.* Hillsdale, NJ: Erlbaum.

Gottman, J. M. (1998). Psychology and the study of the marital processes. *Annual Review of Psychology, 49,* 169–197.

Gottman, J. M., Coan, J., Carrere, S., & Swanson, C. (1998). Predicting marital happiness and stability from newlywed interactions. *Journal of Marriage and the Family, 60*(1), 5–22.

Gottman, J. M., & Levenson, R. W. (1992). Marital processes predictive of later dissolution: Behavior, physiology, and health. *Journal of Personality and Social Psychology, 63,* 221–233.

Hahlweg, K., & Markman, H. J. (1988). Effectiveness of behavioral marital therapy: Empirical status of behavioral techniques in preventing and alleviating marital distress. *Journal of Consulting and Clinical Psychology, 56*(3), 440–447.

Hahlweg, K. L., Revenstorf, D., & Schindler, L. (1984). The Munich marital therapy study. In K. Hahlweg & N. S. Jacobson (Eds.), *Marital interaction: Analysis and modification* (pp. 3–26). New York: Guilford Press.

Hawkins, M. W. (1997). *Sentiment override: The effect of perception on marital conflict.* Unpublished manuscript.

Holmes, T. H., & Rahe, R. H. (1967). The social readjustment rating scale. *Journal of Psychosomatic Research, 11,* 213–218.

Holtzworth-Munroe, A., Jacobson, N. S, DeKlyen, M., & Whisman, M. A. (1989). Relationship between behavioral marital therapy outcome and process variables. *Journal of Consulting and Clinical Psychology, 57*(5), 658–662.

Jacobson, N. S. (1978). Specific and nonspecific factors in the effectiveness of a behavioral approach to the treatment of marital discord. *Journal of Consulting and Clinical Psychology, 46*(3), 442–452.

Jacobson, N. S. (1984). A component analysis of behavioral marital therapy: The relative effectiveness of behavior exchange and communication/problem-solving training. *Journal of Consulting and Clinical Psychology, 52*(2), 295–305.

Jacobson, N. S. (1991). Behavioral versus insight-oriented marital therapy: Labels can be misleading. *Journal of Consulting and Clinical Psychology, 59*(1), 142–145.

Jacobson, N. S., & Addis, M. E. (1993). Research on couple therapy: What do we know? Where are we going? *Journal of Consulting and Clinical Psychology, 61*(1), 85–93.

Jacobson, N. S., Follette, W. C., & Revenstorf, D. (1984). Psychotherapy outcome research: Methods for reporting variability and evaluating clinical significance. *Behavior Therapy, 15*(4), 336–352.

Jacobson, N. S., Schmaling, K., & Holtzworth-Munroe, A. (1987). Component analysis of behavioral marital therapy: 2-year follow-up and prediction of relapse. *Journal of Marital and Family Therapy, 13,* 187–195.

Johnson, S. M., & Greenberg, L. S. (1985). Differential effects of experiential and problem-solving interventions in resolving marital conflict. *Journal of Consulting and Clinical Psychology, 53*(2), 175–184.

Kellam, S. G. (1990). Developmental epidemiological framework for family research on depression and aggression. In G. R. Patterson (Ed.), *Depression and aggression in family interaction* (pp. 11–48). Hillsdale, NJ: Erlbaum.

Kelly, E. L., & Conley, J. J. (1987). A prospective analysis of marital stability and marital satisfaction. *Journal of Personality and Social Psychology, 52*(1), 27–40.

Krokoff, L. J., Gottman, J. M., & Haas, S. D. (1989). Validation of a rapid couples interaction coding system. *Behavioral Assessment, 11,* 65–79.

Lederer, W. J., & Jackson, D. D. (1968). *The mirages of marriages.* New York: Norton.

Levenson, R. W., Carstensen, L. L., & Gottman, J. M. (1993). Long-term marriage: Age, gender, and satisfaction. *Psychology and Aging, 8*(2), 301–313.

Levenson, R. W., Carstensen, L. L., & Gottman, J. M. (1994). The influence of age and gender on affect, physiology and their interrelations: A study of long-term marriages. *Journal of Personality and Social Psychology, 67,* 56–68.

Lorber, M. (1997). *Repair attempts in marital conflict.* Unpublished manuscript.

Marchitelli, L., & Levenson, R. W. (1992, Oct.). *When couples converse: The language and physiology of emotion.* Paper presented at the Society for Psychophysiological Research, San Diego.

Marchitelli, L., & Levenson, R. W. (1994, Oct.). *Heat, pressure, and other angry things: The psychophysiology of anger metaphors.* Paper presented at the Society for Psychophysiological Research, Atlanta.

Murstein, B. L., Cerreto, M., & MacDonald, M. G. (1977). A theory and investigation of the effect of exchange-orientation on marriage and friendship. *Journal of Marriage and the Family, 39*(3), 543–548.

Oggins, J., Veroff, J., & Leber, D. (1993). Perceptions of marital interaction among Black and White newlyweds. *Journal of Personality and Social Psychology, 65,* 494–511.

Sears, R. R. (1977). Sources of life satisfaction of the Terman gifted men. *Journal of Personality, 39,* 1135–1148.

Shadish, W. R., Montgomery, L. M., Wilson, P., Bright, M. R., & Okuwambua, T. (1993). Effects of family and marital psychotherapies: A meta-analysis. *Journal of Consulting and Clinical Psychology, 61*(6), 992–1002.

Shadish, W. R., Ragsdale, K., Glaser-Renita, R., & Montgomery, L. M. (1995). The efficacy and effectiveness of marital and family therapy: A perspective from meta-analysis. *Journal of Marital and Family Therapy, 21*(4), 345–360.

Shapiro, A. F., & Walker, K. (1997, April). *Marital satisfaction: Predicting changes over the transition to parenthood.* Paper presented at the biennial meeting of the Society for Research in Child Development, Washington, DC.

Snyder, D. K., Mangrum, L. F., & Wills, R. M. (1993). Predicting couples' response to marital therapy: A comparison of short- and long-term predictors. *Journal of Consulting and Clinical Psychology, 61*(1), 61–69.

Snyder, D. K., & Wills, R. M. (1989). Behavioral versus insight-oriented marital therapy:

Effects on individual and interspousal functioning. *Journal of Consulting and Clinical Psychology, 57*(1), 39–46.

Snyder, D. K., Wills, R. M., & Grady, F. A. (1991a). Long-term effectiveness of behavioral versus insight-oriented marital therapy: A 4-year follow-up study. *Journal of Consulting and Clinical Psychology, 59*(1), 138–141.

Snyder, D. K., Wills, R. M., & Grady, F. A. (1991b). Risks and challenges of long-term psychotherapy outcome research: Reply to Jacobson. *Journal of Consulting and Clinical Psychology, 59*(1), 146–149.

Stuart, R. B. (1976). An operant interpersonal program for couples. In D. H. L. Olson (Ed.), *Treating relationships* (pp. 119–132). Lake Mills, IA: Graphic.

Varda, S. S., Avner, R., & Neeman, R. (1989). You're changed if you do and changed if you don't: Mechanisms underlying paradoxical interventions. *Journal of Consulting and Clinical Psychology, 57*(5), 590–598.

Varda, S. S., & Hannah, M. T. (1991). Client–treatment interaction in the study of differential change processes. *Journal of Consulting and Clinical Psychology, 59*(2), 217–225.

Vincent, J. P., Friedman, L. C., Nugent, J., & Messerly, L. (1979). Demand characteristics in observations of marital interaction. *Journal of Consulting and Clinical Psychology, 47,* 557–566.

Weiss, R. L. (1980). Strategic behavioral marital therapy: Toward a model for assessment and intervention. In J. P. Vincent (Ed.), *Advances in family intervention, assessment and theory* (Vol. 1, pp. 229–271). Greenwich, CT: JAI Press.

PART 4

Advances in Family Intervention Research

Toward Prevention and Clinical Relevance: A Preventive Intervention Model for Family Therapy Research and Practice

William M. Pinsof

Alexandra B. Hambright

This chapter aims to increase the relevance of family therapy process and outcome research by presenting a new, integrative research model. *Family therapy* is defined as any type of psychotherapy with an explicit and primary goal of changing some aspect of a family or intimate system. This model targets two types of relevance: prevention and clinical. *Prevention relevance* refers to the extent to which the findings of family therapy research facilitate the prevention of major mental disorders and psychosocial problems. *Clinical relevance* refers to the extent to which practitioners let research have an impact on their practice. This model increases prevention relevance by formally integrating core concepts and methods from epidemiology, particularly the concepts of behavioral risk and protective factors. It increases clinical relevance by integrating two related traditions from psychotherapy process research: the specific descriptive and the task analytic traditions. Our thesis is that this new model simultaneously enhances the clinical and prevention relevance of family therapy research.

The Problem

Family therapy research has focused on becoming more relevant within the new health care market by demonstrating to insurance companies, managed care organizations, government agencies, and mental health policy makers that family therapy is an effective treatment that should be part of any package of basic

Alexandra B. Hambright's work on this chapter was supported by the John J. B. Morgan Fellowship grant from the Burton D. Morgan Foundation. The authors would like to thank Erika Lunkenheimer for her work as a research assistant for this chapter.

mental health services. As part of this initiative, a special issue of the *Journal of Marital and Family Therapy* pulled together the data on the efficacy and effectiveness of marital and family therapy for the treatment of major mental disorders and psychosocial problems (Pinsof & Wynne, 1995a). That special issue as well as other recent reviews (Lebow & Gurman, 1995; Pinsof, Wynne, & Hambright, 1996) demonstrated that there is good scientific evidence to support the efficacy, and in certain cases, the superiority of conjoint treatments for various serious mental disorders and problems (Pinsof & Wynne, 1995b).

To make new family therapy research more relevant to health policy makers, managed care providers, and clinical service administrators, Pinsof and Wynne (1995b) have advocated the inclusion of cost-effectiveness measures in family therapy research. They have also encouraged family therapy research to become more focused on patient satisfaction, as well as research that looks at family therapy's effectiveness in real-life clinical settings. This initiative and the specific findings and recommendations that result from it pertain to a third type of relevance: the *market relevance* of family therapy research.

The problem with this initiative and the growing body of research theory and practice that emanates from it is that, although increasing in market relevance, they still lack clinical and prevention relevance. The research lacks clinical relevance because it does not speak to the moment-to-moment concerns of practicing family therapists. As researchers have lamented over the last two decades, the findings of family therapy research (and psychotherapy research in general) have been irrelevant to clinicians. It has not generated a process knowledge that affects what therapists actually do with their patients.

This body of research lacks prevention relevance in that it does not aim to prevent major mental illnesses and problems. This research and the treatments it has studied target disorders and problems after they have already achieved acute, and in certain cases, chronic status. For epidemiology, this is tertiary prevention research. If family therapy is to achieve its clinical potential, it must focus more on preventing disorders and problems before they disable and disease. It must target the early detection and treatment of preacute disorders.

Process and Outcome Research: The Failure to Achieve Clinical Relevance

Process and outcome research links what goes on in therapy with the outcome of therapy. Three types of phenomena occur in family therapy: (a) therapist behaviors (e.g., confrontation, support), (b) patient behaviors (e.g., conflict, sadness), and (c) interactive behaviors that include the therapist and patient (e.g., arguing, laughing). *Behavior* includes overt action as well as experience —cognition and emotion—and can be measured by observers with an observational methodology or by participants with a self-report methodology (Pinsof, 1981). Minimally, outcome is measured on relevant patient indices at the beginning and end of therapy. Greenberg and Pinsof (1986) have described this pre−post outcome design as the "big O," as opposed to designs that repeatedly measure outcomes during therapy—the "little o's."

The Failure to Find Process and Outcome Linkages

Family therapy process and outcome research has enjoyed a short and not illustrious career. Since Pinsof's (1981) initial review of pre-1980 research, researchers have had difficulty demonstrating any kind of consistent relationship between in-therapy behaviors and patient outcomes. "A consistent relationship" means that a process and outcome finding has been confirmed in at least two distinct studies, ideally from different research programs, and there have been no negative findings. Possible exceptions to this conclusion are (a) findings of a positive relationship between the therapeutic alliance (an interactive variable measured through patient self-report) and outcome (Friedlander, Wildman, Heatherington, & Skowron, 1994; Pinsof, 1994), and (b) Chamberlain and Patterson's (Chamberlain, Patterson, Reid, Kavanagh, & Forgatch, 1984; Stoolmiller, Duncan, Bank, & Patterson, 1993) linking the failure to achieve a curvilinear pattern of (maternal) resistance in parent training therapy to poorer outcomes with youths with conduct disorders.

Furthermore, meta-analytic studies have not found any consistent outcome differences between different family therapy approaches (Shadish et al., 1993; Shadish, Ragsdale, Glaser, & Montgomery, 1995). Thus, although the field now has empirically validated family treatments that all appear to be effective (Baucom, Shoham, Mueser, Daiuto, & Stickle, 1998), when applied to the same problem none of these treatments appears to be superior.

If therapists confined themselves to practicing according to confirmed research findings, their treatment would be profoundly truncated. They would include parents in the treatment of most childhood disorders (Estrada & Pinsof, 1995), but that would be it. After assembling the "family" group in the room, they would have nothing to say. Beyond the value of conjoint treatment (including intimate others in treatment), the research has virtually nothing definitive to say about what interventions to use with whom at which points in therapy. Once the door to the therapy room closes, today's family therapist proceeds without any kind of empirically validated map. The most frightening conclusion to be drawn from the failure to find consistent linkages between therapist technique and outcomes is that technique does not matter. This conclusion simultaneously invalidates the experience of most therapists as well as the family therapy training industry. Fortunately, there are plausible rival hypotheses to explain this lack of consistent process and outcome findings.

The primary rival hypothesis asserts that this failure originates from the nature of the research as opposed to a lack of linkages. Most process research in family therapy in the last 15 years has been adherence or verification research intended to determine whether the therapists in a particular study, usually a clinical trial, actually did what the treatment manual prescribed. The research has not asked which aspects of the process, particularly therapist behavior, correlated with outcome. If the data showed that the therapists followed the treatment manual, that was the process inquiry.

Unfortunately, the proliferation of adherence rating systems has almost completely usurped the use of more descriptively specific coding systems in family therapy research. Adherence ratings lack specificity (Pinsof, 1981, 1989). The knowledge that can be derived from studies that rely on adherence ratings as the only process measure is about the overall treatment, rather than about specific interventions at specific points in time in the context of specific patient behaviors. It is impossible to discern which specific components of the treatment process accounted for the outcome variance. Adherence-based process research only characterizes treatment at the level of the therapy (or the phase or the session), not the more molecular levels of the intervention or the operation (a series of interventions) where most clinicians work and conceptualize therapy.

Toward Clinically Meaningful Process and Outcome Research

Two psychotherapy process research traditions emerged within the last 20 years that together provide a clear pathway toward more clinically meaningful research that is also more likely to find process and outcome linkages: the specific descriptive tradition and the task analytic tradition.

The Specific Descriptive Tradition in Process Research

The *specific descriptive tradition* (Alexander, Newell, Robbins, & Turner, 1995; Gurman, 1988; Patterson & Chamberlain, 1988; Pinsof, 1981, 1988, 1989) provides a behaviorally specific description of some aspect of the therapy process in a temporal sequence. It describes who did what when. Most specific and descriptive process analysis systems have been observational as opposed to self-report. Within this tradition, evaluation does not occur in the coding of the behavior but in the data analysis. The coder does not evaluate the behavior on some evaluative dimension, such as empathic understanding or therapeutic skillfulness; the behavior is described and quantified, usually on some kind of nominal as opposed to ordinal scale. The evaluation occurs when the data are statistically related to patient change scores on an outcome measure. Data from specific descriptive studies can be analyzed sequentially (Hahlweg, 1988; Pinsof, 1989).

Furthermore, the more specific the coding system, the greater the likelihood that the patient and therapist's behavior can be reconstructed in some kind of clinically meaningful form from the coded data (Pinsof, 1989). As Alexander et al. (1995) have detailed, observational coding systems of family therapy can be organized according to inference and content—meaning. They can also be organized along the continuum of specificity—from molecularity to molarity. Dichotomous systems like Sigal et al.'s drive—interpretation (Postner, Guttman, Sigal, Epstein, & Rakoff, 1971) or Alexander's (1973) supportive—defensive fall at the molar pole, whereas Pinsof's family therapist coding system (FTCS; Pinsof, 1981, 1986) and Benjamin et al.'s structural analysis of social behavior (SASB; Benjamin, Foster, Roberto, & Estroff, 1986) fall at the molecular pole. The more molecular systems permit the therapist's behavior (FTCS) or the patient's behavior (SASB) to be meaningfully reconstructed from code data.

With FTCS, Pinsof (1986) found that beginning and advanced therapists behaved differently in initial interviews with families with child problems. Advanced therapists began with a relatively low level of disagree—disapprove (DD) behavior, increased it threefold in the middle third of the interview, and returned to the initial level at the end. With DD, the therapist disagrees with or disapproves of a family member's behavior. In contrast, beginning therapists reduced DD by almost half in the middle third of the interview and then returned to their initial level at the end. During the middle phase, the advanced therapists' DD level was 10 times higher than the beginners'. Both beginning and advanced therapists increased S-Support behavior over the course of the interview.

These data paint the following picture: As they became more supportive from the first to the second third of the interview, advanced therapists became much more confrontational and disapproving. They continued increasing support from the second to the last third of the interview as they decreased confrontational and disapproving behavior. In contrast, beginners became less confrontational as they became more supportive in the first two thirds of the interview and then increased their confrontational behaviors back to their initial level as they continued increasing support in the last third.

These data provide a clinically meaningful picture of therapist activity. The advanced therapists actively engaged the families, particularly their negative behaviors. However, this confrontational engagement was phased to slowly increase and then decrease over the course of the interview. It was also moderated "anesthetically" by growing levels of supportive behaviors. In contrast, the beginners did not directly challenge the families; their behavior was primarily supportive. Unfortunately, this initial session process study did not evaluate the outcome of the session or the therapy.

The primary problem with specific descriptive analyses of process data is that they are very time- and labor-intensive. Coders need to be extensively trained; video or audiotaped data need to be transcribed or segmented; data need to be coded at least at the level of the speech (what one person says between the utterances of one or more other people); and ultimately, the data need to be entered into a computer program that respects their sequential nature. Coding a 15-minute segment of family therapy with FTCS or SASB can take close to an hour, whereas listening to or watching the same segment and then rating it on an adherence scale can take as few as 16 minutes (15 to listen and one to rate).

The Task Analytic Tradition in Process Research

Rice and Greenberg (1984) originated the theory and methodology of psychotherapy task analysis within individual therapy. Task analysis focuses on *events*, "an interactional sequence between client and therapist . . . that has a beginning, an end, and a particular structure that gives it meaning as an island of behavior" (Greenberg, 1984b, p. 138). An event has three components: a *marker* or client performance pattern that reveals some kind of unresolved affective issue as well as the client's readiness to work on it; *interventions* in which the therapist gains access to the underlying affective issue; and the *subsequent client process* that ideally reveals some kind of resolution of the affective issue.

Borrowing from Gestalt therapy, Greenberg (1984a) initially focused his task analytic research on *splits,* markers in which the client expresses intrapersonal conflict. Drawing on client-centered therapy, Rice focused her task analysis on *problematic reaction points,* a marker in which "the client recognizes that his or her own reaction to a particular situation is problematic" (Rice & Saperia, 1984, p. 33). Recently, Greenberg and colleagues have started task analyses of couple therapy (Greenberg, 1995; Greenberg, Heatherington, & Friedlander; 1995) that focus on episodes in which one partner pursues and blames the withdrawing partner. Using observational and self-report process analysis methods (SASB, the Experiencing Scale, and interpersonal process recall), they identified four stages or components of the operation that successfully resolves a blame–withdrawal sequence: escalation, de-escalation, testing, and mutual openness.

Task analysis adds to the specific descriptive tradition theory as well as providing focus and a more direct link to proximal or "little o" outcomes (e.g., successful resolution of an episode). In Greenberg et al.'s (1995) task analysis of couple therapy, specific descriptive measures are brought to bear on an "event" to test the emergent theory about the underlying affective process and its resolution. What emerges from this integration of specific descriptive methods and task analysis is clinically meaningful. Every couple therapist struggles with blame–withdrawal sequences. Research that identifies the steps involved in their successful resolution and the interventions that facilitate those steps speaks directly to the moment-to-moment concerns of practicing therapists.

Family Therapy, Research, and Prevention Science

By and large, family therapy and family therapy research have been oblivious to epidemiology, "the study of the distribution and determinants of disease frequency" (Hennekens & Buring, 1987, p. 3), as well as to epidemiology's intervention science—prevention (Coie et al., 1993). Epidemiologists distinguish primary, secondary, and tertiary prevention, depending on where intervention occurs in the disease process. *Primary prevention* "keeps disease from occurring at all, by removing its causes" (Fletcher, Fletcher, & Wagner, 1996, p. 166) and aims "to prevent the development of a disease in a person who is well" (e.g., polio immunization and the chlorination of water; Gordis, 1996, p. 5). *Secondary prevention* "detects disease early, when it is asymptomatic and when early treatment can stop it from progressing" (e.g., mammograms; Fletcher et al., 1996, p. 167). *Tertiary prevention* occurs after the disease has emerged and aims to reduce its effects (e.g., chemotherapy).

Primary prevention has been rare within family therapy because of its roots in a psychotherapeutic framework, which becomes activated when patients seek help for emergent or full-blown problems. The few primary prevention initiatives within family therapy have emphasized education and relational skill building for nonclinical populations, primarily couples seeking some kind of premarital or marital growth experience. The family therapy pioneer in primary prevention has been Bernard Guerney (1977), who has applied his Relationship Enhancement model to nonclinical couples for close to 20 years. More recently, Markman and colleagues developed the Prevention and Relationship Enhancement Program (PREP; Markman, Renick, Floyd, Stanley, & Clements, 1993), and Olson and colleagues created the Premarital Personal and Relationship Evaluation (PREPARE) and Enriching Relationship Issues, Communication, and Happiness (ENRICH; Flowers & Olson, 1986; Olson, Fournier, & Druckman, 1987) to help premarital couples avoid marital distress and reduce divorce.

For the same reason, *secondary prevention* in family therapy, which focuses on at-risk populations with early signs of a disorder, has also been rare. Several recent secondary initiatives include Tolan et al's program to understand and address the early (pubertal) determinants of adolescent aggression in populations that are racially and socioeconomically at risk (Gorman-Smith, Tolan, Zelli, & Huesmann, 1996; Tolan, 1987) and the Fast Track multisite demonstration project, which uses comprehensive, family-focused interventions to improve parenting, parent–teacher interaction, and child academic performance for elementary schoolchildren at risk for conduct disorder (Bierman, 1996;

McMahon & Slough, 1996). Aiming even earlier, Webster-Stratton (1994) has developed and demonstrated the efficacy of videotape-based parent training for preschool children with conduct problems and their families.

Although most family therapy is tertiary prevention and not preventive in regard to the presenting problems, family therapists have long believed that it is preventive in terms of its impact on nonsymptomatic family members. The successful treatment of a couple experiencing acute distress reduces the likelihood that their children will suffer a variety of problems; similarly, the successful transformation of a family of an adolescent male with conduct disorder creates a healthier environment for his or her younger siblings. Lastly, premarital couple therapy aims to prevent more serious problems later in the relationship by either improving the relationship or facilitating its termination.

Family therapy research (Pinsof & Wynne, 1995b) has clearly established family therapy as an effective tertiary prevention for a variety of mental disorders and problems. Now family therapy should turn its attention to secondary and primary prevention. Because primary prevention usually occurs outside the clinical setting, addresses nonclinical populations, and generally does not require highly trained therapists, family therapy is most appropriately and most likely to be used as a secondary prevention.

Risk and Protective Factors: The Targets of Prevention

Risk refers to "the likelihood that people who are exposed to certain factors ('risk factors') will subsequently develop a particular disease" (Fletcher et al., 1996, p. 94). As epidemiologists have studied mental disorders and behavior problems, they have expanded the risk factor concept to include characteristics of individuals or groups that are associated with "a high probability of onset, greater severity, and longer duration of major mental health problems" (Coie et al., 1993, p. 1013). Risk factors can be inherent within an individual or group, in which case they are usually genetic. They can also be environmental (physical or emotional factors that increase risk for certain diseases or problems) as well as behavioral or interactional (activities that a person engages in alone or with others that increase risk).

A *behavioral risk factor* is a behavior in which a person engages while they are alone or that does not require the presence of another (e.g., smoking, self-mutilation, and drug abuse). An *interactional risk factor* is a behavior that requires the presence of another (e.g.. defiance, conflict, and physical aggression). Psychotherapists are interested primarily in behavioral and interactional risk factors because they are more accessible and malleable than inherent or environmental risk factors. Family therapists are particularly interested in interactional risk factors because they are social and systemic.

Although not widely discussed in epidemiology, there is a second type of factor that predicts who will suffer a disease or problem. A *protective factor* is a characteristic of an individual or a group that decreases the likelihood that they will suffer a disease or problem. As Coie et al. (1993) observed, "Protective factors may decrease dysfunction directly, interact with the risk factor to buffer its effects, disrupt the mediational chain through which the risk factor operates . . . or prevent the initial occurrence of the risk factor" (Coie et al., 1993, p. 1014). Protective factors can be inherent, environmental or behavioral–interactional, with the latter being of particular interest to therapists because of the capacity for access and change. Strong parent–child bonding, careful parental monitoring of children, and a high ratio of positive–negative marital interactions exemplify interactional protective factors. Compared to the attention devoted to the study of risk factors, the study of protective factors is virtually nonexistent. They are not even mentioned in three of the most widely used epidemiology textbooks (Fletcher et al., 1996; Gordis, 1996; Hennekens & Buring, 1987). Protective factors constitute the next frontier for prevention science.

Preventive interventions target the antecedents of disease and health: risk and protective factors. They aim to decrease risk factors and to increase protective factors in populations that are at risk "in order to disrupt processes that contribute to human dysfunction" (Coie et al., 1993, p. 1014). To mount empirically based prevention programs, researchers in health disciplines must first identify the risk and protective factors associated with particular diseases and problems that will become the primary targets of their preventive interventions.

Epidemiological Research Designs for Identifying Risk and Protective Factors

Three types of epidemiological research design identify risk and protective factors: case-control, cross-sectional, and cohort (Gordis, 1996; Fletcher et al., 1996). All three are observational as opposed to experimental. For ethical and humanitarian reasons, epidemiological research cannot manipulate exposure to risk or protective factors but instead takes advantage of nature's intervention.

The *case-control* design retrospectively compares one group of individuals who have a disease or disorder—the cases—to another group that is as similar as possible but does not have the disease—the controls. Case-control studies are compromised by a host of design factors (e.g., reliability of retrospection), but they can help in the initial identification of potential risk and protective factors

Cross-sectional designs compare two or more groups at a one point in time on disease or disorder measures and on risk and protective factor measures.

Although overcoming the problem of retrospection, cross-sectional designs are unable to embrace time and sequence. Differences may be found between cases and controls on risk factors, but the causal link cannot be established. Cross-sectional studies can be useful in identifying potential risk and protective factors, but not in determining the causal linkages.

Cohort studies involve prospective, longitudinal designs that target one group who has been or is being exposed to a risk or protective factor and one group who has not; the groups are then studied over time to determine the incidence of the disorder. The primary problem with cohort studies is also their strength: their longitudinality. The time lag between exposure to the risk or protective factor and emergence of the full-blown disease or disorder is often lengthy and requires a long-term research project with minimal participant attrition. Despite this weakness, cohort studies are methodologically superior to case-control and cross-sectional studies and are the "next best design" to randomized clinical trials, which are ethically contraindicated in epidemiological research (Fletcher et al., 1996, p. 237). When they include additional groups that receive different levels of the risk or protective factor, cohort studies get close to demonstrating causal relationships between risk or protective factors and diseases or disorders.

The Four-Stage Preventive Intervention Model for Clinically and Prevention-Relevant Research

Family therapy research is on the brink of a new era. Lines of inquiry are possible now that were not available before. Clinically relevant research strategies have emerged in process and outcome research like the small "o," the specific descriptive, and the task analytic. Some large-scale longitudinal cohort studies are beginning to produce findings that, in concert with the process research strategies, provide a new foundation for clinically and prevention-relevant research. This section delineates that foundation with the four-phase relevance research model, outlined in Exhibit 9-1.

Phase I: Identifying Risk and Protective Factors Through Longitudinal Family Interaction Research

After selecting the disorder or problem to be addressed, the first phase of the model involves identifying the interactional risk and protective factors for that disorder or problem. To find interactional risk and protective factors, family therapy research must rely on research that examines the interaction patterns of families with or at risk for particular disorders or problems. Most family interaction research has used cross-sectional or case-control designs to identify

EXHIBIT 9-1

Four-phase model for clinically and prevention-relevant process and outcome research in family therapy

PHASE I	Cross-sectional and longitudinal family interaction research identifies risk and protective factors for major problems or disorders
PHASE II	Identification of in-therapy patient risk and protective markers that are the Stage I factors themselves or that are highly associated with those factors
PHASE III	Identification of therapist interventions associated with a reduction in risk markers and an increase in protective markers and preliminary construction of a change model (task analysis)
PHASE IV	Testing of intervention–client–therapist factor hypotheses generated in Stage III in larger samples and clinical trials with long-term follow-up of disease or disorder rates in experimental and comparison groups

characteristics of individuals or groups that might constitute risk and protective factors. Alexander and colleagues have found that families with a lower ratio of supportive–defensive (SD) communications are more likely to have an adolescent with a delinquency problem than families with higher SD ratios. A host of studies have found that families of children with schizophrenia and high levels of expressed emotion (EE) have higher rates of schizophrenic symptomatology and rehospitalization than families with lower levels of EE (Goldstein & Miklowitz, 1995). This research identifies potential risk factors but does not substantiate the SD ratio as a risk factor for delinquency or EE as a risk factor for schizophrenia. Expressed emotion predicts higher levels of rehospitalization and symptoms (Hooley, Rosen, & Richters, 1995), not whether a child will have schizophrenia, just as SD does not predict whether a child will be delinquent.

To substantiate a variable as a risk or protective factor, the research must be longitudinal. There have been relatively few studies or bodies of research within family therapy that have examined a group of participants, no less two groups, over time and in regard to a particular disease or disorder. However, within the last 15 years, a number of high quality longitudinal cohort-type research projects have emerged that are beginning to remedy this deficit. Two longitudinal research programs in particular have started to identify the specific type of interactional risk and protective factors that clinically and prevention-relevant family therapy research requires.

Studying more than 300 nonclinical couples over time, Gottman and colleagues (Gottman, 1993, 1994; Gottman & Levenson, 1992) have identified a set of interactive behaviors that predict whether a couple will divorce within 4 years. The first two behaviors are *criticism*, particularly criticism that aims at the person, not the behavior; and *defensiveness*. The next two behaviors are *contempt*, generally on the part of the wife; and *stonewalling*, or refusing to overtly communicate, generally on the part of the husband. Together these behaviors make up the *four horsemen of the apocalypse* (see Gottman, Ryan, Carrère, & Erley, chapter 8, this volume). None of these behaviors alone powerfully predicts divorce, but their simultaneous presence dramatically increases the probability of it. Together they constitute a clear interactional risk marker for divorce.

Gottman has also identified a potential interactional protective factor that decreases the likelihood of divorce: the ratio of positive-to-negative interactions. Couples with a positive-to-negative ratio of 5:1, regardless of the amount of nonphysical conflict, have a lower divorce rate as well as higher levels of marital satisfaction than couples with a ratio of 1:1 or lower. This ratio is one of the first family interaction research findings about a specific pattern of behavior that appears to confer some degree of immunity to a problem.

In the second longitudinal research program, O'Leary and colleagues (O'Leary et al., 1989; O'Leary, Malone, & Tyree, 1994) evaluated over 250 nonclinical newlywed couples three times over the first 30 months of marriage: 1 month before, and 18 and 30 months after. At the premarital assessment, at least one member of 58% of the couples reported some degree of physical partner aggression in the previous year. By 30 months, approximately half of those couples reported being nonviolent within the preceding year. By far, the single strongest predictor of which couples would report violence at 30 months was premarital physical aggression. Additionally, couples that were violent initially tended to get more violent by 30 months.

O'Leary's research identifies premarital physical aggression as the single strongest risk factor for marital violence. In contrast to Gottman's observational research, O'Leary's aggression data were self-report (using the Conflict Tactics Scale) about behavior outside of the laboratory. Nevertheless, his research has identified an interactional risk factor, evident at the time of marriage, for one of the most dangerous and destructive family problems: partner violence.

These two research programs exemplify longitudinal family interaction research that identifies risk and protective factors that are potential targets of family therapy prevention programs. Fortunately, there are other research programs that are starting to produce similar types of data for adolescent aggression (Gorman-Smith, Tolan, Zelli, & Huesmann, 1996), stepfamily problems (Bray and Berger, 1993), postdivorce adjustment (Heatherington, 1993). and other problems, but much more work is needed. The molecular study of families over time to identify interactional risk and protective factors is the best methodology for laying the foundation for clinically and prevention-relevant family therapy research.

Phase II: Identifying In-Therapy Risk and Protective Markers

The second phase in this research model identifies the *in-therapy markers* that represent the risk and protective factors previously identified. In-therapy markers constitute the direct targets of intervention as well as outcome variables for the therapy. They are what the therapist has most direct access to and the greatest capacity to change. Task analytic research lacks prevention relevance because it has not selected in-therapy markers that represent interactional risk or protective factors from longitudinal family research.

In certain situations, the in-therapy risk and protective markers will be the actual interactional risk and protective factors identified in the preceding phase. For instance, every marital therapist knows Gottman's four horsemen. In therapy, couples criticize, become defensive, express contempt, and stonewall. Little translation needs to occur from the family interaction research identification of these risk factors to their identification as markers in therapy.[1]

It is not as easy to transfer the 5:1 positive-to-negative ratio into a protective marker. It is a summary variable derived from a quantitative analysis of periods of couple interaction, as opposed to a discrete set of events like the four horsemen. Nevertheless, the therapist's "sense" of the ratio with a particular couple can be an important signal for particular interventions.

A risk factor like physical aggression in young couples needs to be translated into an in-therapy marker. Seldom will couples, even violent couples, become physically aggressive in a therapy session. Researchers need to find the in-therapy markers for out-of-therapy physical aggression. Potential candidates might be reports about out-of-therapy violence or verbally abusive confrontations in therapy.

It is not enough to translate an interactional factor into an in-therapy marker. The link should be empirically tested in proximal situations like the four horsemen and established in more distal situations like physical violence. There are two research strategies for establishing the empirical link. The first correlates the factor's frequency in families' out-of-therapy and in-therapy behavior; the second correlates risk marker reductions or protective marker increases with comparable changes in the factor in families' out-of-therapy behavior.

The more specific and discrete the marker, the stronger its clinical rele-

---

[1]Gottman's four horseman were identified in laboratory studies with the Rapid Couples Interaction Scoring System (RCISS). In coding therapy with RCISS, we found that the system did not fit therapy interaction because of the presence of the therapist and the nature of the interaction. Even though risk factors from interaction research like the four horseman have "face validity" in therapy interaction, the actual jump from one context to the other may be more problematic.

vance. When a clinician can easily identify a marker in patients' behavior, that marker readily takes on clinical significance. Consequently, clinically significant markers make it easier for the clinician to learn new, alternative interventions when confronted with those markers in therapy or training.

Phase III: Identifying Therapist Behaviors Associated With Marker Change

The third phase of the model identifies therapist behaviors associated with decreases in risk factors and increases in protective factors. Therapist behaviors can be scaled on a continuum, ranging from small, discrete interventions, such as a directive (e.g., "Why don't you sit over there?") to a series of linked interventions—in other words, an operation (e.g., a confrontation that involves a series of steps including supportive interventions). Larger-scale behaviors range from an episode (a task-linked series of operations), such as repairing a tear in the therapeutic alliance, through a distinct phase of therapy with specific tasks, up to a whole therapy. The most clinically and epidemiologically relevant levels on the continuum start with the operation and proceed up to an episode.

The strategy for identifying therapist behaviors integrates the specific descriptive and task analytic traditions. After the markers have been identified, the first step of this third phase, *identifying good therapies,* examines the therapies of specific patients (or phases within particular therapies) in which the markers changed in the expected directions (in-therapy change) and in which patients also improved (out-of-therapy change). With couples at risk for divorce, this might entail identifying cases in which the four horsemen (or at least some of them) decreased and in which the couples improved.

Once the "good" therapies or "good" phases have been selected, the next step, *event selection*, identifies specific events that commence with the emergence of the marker. In regard to couples at risk for divorce, this would involve locating specific therapy episodes in which one or more of the four horsemen have emerged. It is not particularly important at this point whether the events involve risk factor reduction or protective factor augmentation; in fact, a selection of "differentially resolved" events is ideal.

The third step, *microanalysis*, analyzes a number of events to delineate the process in well- and poorly resolved events. Microanalysis examines the therapist and patient behaviors that followed the emergence of the risk or protective factor marker. With couples at risk for divorce, this would entail specific description of what the therapist and patients did after the emergence of the horsemen. For example, what did the therapist say and what did the wife and husband do after the wife verbalized her contempt for her husband?

In the fourth step, *change model building*, the researcher constructs a model of the successful marker change process. This abstracts a set of principles and intervention guidelines from the microanalysis of well- and poorly resolved events that constitutes a model for successfully reducing the risk marker or increasing the protective marker. With couples who are at risk, the researcher might develop a theory of the successful resolution of contempt events.

The fifth and last step, *change model testing*, tests the model against a series of "fresh events." This refines the model in preparation for the last phase. With couples who are at risk, this might entail finding fresh contempt events from other good therapies and evaluating the change model against them. Do the therapist and patient behaviors in these new events fit the model? If they do not, the model should be modified to accommodate the new data.

In this research model, Rice and Greenberg's concept of a marker has changed. For them, a marker revealed an unresolved affective issue and the patient's readiness to address it. In the relevance model, the marker may but does not have to reflect an unresolved affective issue. It must be linked to a risk or protective factor and must be as specific and discrete as possible. The marker also does not have to reflect patient readiness. To some extent, the patients have indicated a general readiness by electing to come for therapy. However, some markers emerge under conditions in which key patients might not want to address the underlying issues.

Phase IV: Testing the Change Process Model

The last phase of the relevance research model formally tests the marker and intervention model. The typical progression in this phase begins by testing the model idiographically in a series of single case studies in which the same therapist responds with the model change process to randomly selected markers in the therapy of a particular family. This type of research is most easily implemented when the markers occur relatively frequently and discretely. Before a session or a series of sessions, the therapist can be instructed to respond differently to marker emergence in experimental and control events.

The next level idiographically examines multiple therapists with multiple cases. The change process model is tested in different patient–therapist dyads in a series or set of single case studies. This expansion of the evaluation refines hypotheses about what works with whom under what conditions. The model now differentiates more patient, therapist, and phase variables.

Ultimately, the change process model needs to be tested nomothetically. In this larger scale, clinical trial group testing, patients are randomly assigned to intervention and comparison conditions and to therapists within those conditions. The outcome analysis in these nomothetic studies needs to evaluate the risk and protective factor changes in the experimental and comparison groups. Also, long-term follow-up needs to test the extent to which patients who received the preventive intervention actually have a lower incidence of the disorder or problem.

Conclusion

The goal of this chapter has been to make the case for a model of process and outcome research that has strong clinical and prevention relevance. This relevance model integrates family interaction research, new traditions in psychotherapy process and outcome research, and core concepts and methods from epidemiological research. The model "preventionizes" task analysis by linking in-therapy markers to risk and protective factors for major problems and disorders. The value of this model for family therapy research and practice is that it simultaneously has high clinical and prevention relevance: It kills two birds with one stone. In doing so, it makes family therapy research more meaningful to more people (therapists and patients) and creates new empirically derived forms of family therapy that can have greater and more lasting impact.

References

Alexander, J. F. (1973). Defensive and supportive communications in normal and deviant families. *Journal of Consulting and Clinical Psychology, 40,* 223–241.

Alexander, J. F., Newell, R. M., Robbins, M. S., & Turner, C. W. (1995). Observational coding in family therapy process research. *Journal of Family Psychology, 9*(4), 355–365.

Baucom, D., Shoham, V., Mueser, K., Daiuto, A., & Stickle, T. (1998). Empirically supported couple and family interventions for marital distress and adult mental health problems. *Journal of Consulting and Clinical Psychology, 66,* 53–88.

Benjamin, L. S., Foster, S. W., Roberto, L. G., & Estroff, S. E. (1986). Breaking the family code: Analysis of videotapes of family interactions by structural analysis of social behavior (SASB). In L. Greenberg & W. Pinsof (Eds.), *The psychotherapeutic process: A research handbook* (pp. 391–438). New York: Guilford Press.

Bierman, K. L. (1996). Integrating social skills training interventions with parent training and family focused support to prevent conduct disorder in high risk populations: The Fast Track multi-site demonstration project. In C. Ferris & T. Grisso (Eds.), *Understanding aggressive behavior in children. Annals of the New York Academy of Sciences* (Vol. 794, pp. 256–264). New York: New York Academy of Sciences.

Bray, J., & Berger, S. (1993). Developmental issues in the StepFamilies Research Project: Family relationships and parent–child interactions. *Journal of Family Psychology, 7*(1), 76–90.

Chamberlain, P., Patterson, G. R., Reid, J. B., Kavanagh, K., & Forgatch, M. S. (1984). Observation of client resistance. *Behavior Therapy, 15,* 144–155.

Coie, J., Watt, N., West, S., Hawkins, D., Asarnow, J., Markman, H., Ramey, S., Shure, M., & Long, B. (1993). The science of prevention: A conceptual framework and some directions for a national research program. *American Psychologist, 48*(10), 1013–1022.

Estrada, A., & Pinsof, W. M. (1995). The effectiveness of family therapy in the treatment of selected disorders of childhood. *Journal of Marital and Family Therapy, 21*(4), 403–440.

Fletcher, R. H., Fletcher, S. W., & Wagner, E. H. (1996). *Clinical epidemiology: The essentials* (3rd ed.). Baltimore: Williams & Wilkins.

Flowers, B., & Olson, D. (1986). Predicting marital success with PREPARE: A predictive validity study. *Journal of Marital and Family Therapy, 12,* 403–413.

Friedlander, M., Wildman, J., Heatherington, L., & Skowron, E. (1994). What we do and don't know about the process of family therapy. *Journal of Family Psychology, 8*(4), 390–416.

Goldstein, M., & Miklowitz, D. (1995). The effectiveness of psychoeducational family therapy in the treatment of schizophrenic disorders. *Journal of Marital and Family Therapy, 21*(4), 361–376.

Gordis, L. (1996). *Epidemiology.* Philadelphia: Saunders.

Gorman-Smith, D., Tolan, P. H., Zelli, A., & Huesmann, L. R. (1996). The relation of family functioning to violence among inner-city minority youths. *Journal of Family Psychology, 10*(2), 115–129.

Gottman, J. M. (1993). The roles of conflict engagement, escalation, or avoidance in marital interaction: A longitudinal view of five types of couples. *Journal of Consulting and Clinical Psychology, 61,* 6–15.

Gottman, J. M. (1994). *Why marriages succeed or fail.* New York: Simon and Schuster.

Gottman, J. M., & Levenson, R. W. (1992). Marital processes predictive of later dissolution: Behavior, physiology, and health. *Journal of Personality and Social Psychology, 63,* 221–233.

Greenberg, L. S. (1984a). Task analysis: The general approach. In L. Rice & L. Greenberg (Eds.), *Patterns of change* (pp. 124–148). New York: Guilford Press.

Greenberg, L. S. (1984b). A task analysis of intrapersonal conflict resolution. In L. Rice & L. Greenberg (Eds.), *Patterns of change* (pp. 67–123). New York: Guilford Press.

Greenberg, L. S. (1995). The use of observational coding in family therapy research: Comment on Alexander et al. (1995). *Journal of Family Psychology, 9*(4), 366–370.

Greenberg, L. S., Heatherington, L., & Friedlander, M. (1995). The events based approach to couples and family therapy research. In D. Sprenkle & S. Moon (Eds.), *Family therapy research: A handbook of methods.* New York: Guilford Press.

Greenberg, L. S., & Pinsof, W. M. (1986). Process research: Current trends and future perspectives. In L. Greenberg & W. Pinsof (Eds.), *The psychotherapeutic process: A research handbook* (pp. 3–22). New York: Guilford Press.

Guerney, B. G. (1977) *Relationship enhancement: Skill training for therapy, problem prevention and enrichment.* San Francisco: Jossey-Bass.

Gurman, A. S. (1988). Issues in the specification of family therapy interventions. In L. Wynne (Ed.), *The state of the art of family therapy research: Controversies and recommendations* (pp. 125–138). New York: Family Process Press.

Hahlweg, K. (1988). Statistical methods for studying family therapy process. In L. Wynne (Ed.), *The state of the art of family therapy research: Controversies and recommendations* (pp. 235–248). New York: Family Process Press.

Heatherington, M. (1993). An overview of the Virginia Longitudinal Study of divorce and remarriage with a focus on early adolescence. *Journal of Family Psychology, 7*(1), 39–56.

Hennekens, C. H., & Buring, J. E. (1987). *Epidemiology in medicine.* Boston: Little, Brown.

Hooley, J., Rosen, L., & Richters, J. (1995). Expressed emotion: Toward clarification of a critical construct. In G. A. Miller (Ed.), *The behavioral high-risk paradigm in psychopathology* (pp. 88–120). New York: Springer-Verlag.

Lebow, J., & Gurman, A. (1995) Research assessing couple and family therapy. *Annual Review of Psychology, 46,* 27–57.

Markman, H. J., Renick, M. J., Floyd, F. J., Stanley, S. M., & Clements, M. (1993). Preventing marital distress through communication and conflict management training: A 4- and 5-year follow-up. *Journal of Consulting and Clinical Psychology, 61,* 70–77.

McMahon, R. J., & Slough, N. (1996). Family based intervention in the Fast Track Program. In R. Peters & R. McMahon (Eds.), *Preventing childhood disorders, substance abuse, and delinquency. Banff International Behavioral Science Series* (Vol. 3, pp. 90–110). Thousand Oaks, CA: Sage.

O'Leary, K. D., Barling, J., Arias, I., Rosenbaum, A., Malone, J., & Tyree, A. (1989). Prevalence and stability of physical aggression between spouses: A longitudinal analysis. *Journal of Consulting and Clinical Psychology, 57,* 263–268.

O'Leary, K. D., Malone, J., & Tyree, A. (1994). Physical aggression in early marriage: Prerelationship and relationship effects. *Journal of Consulting and Clinical Psychology, 62,* 594–602.

Olson, D., Fournier, D., & Druckman, J. (1987). *Counselor's manual for PREPARE/ENRICH* (Rev. ed.). Minneapolis, MN: PREPARE/ENRICH.

Patterson, G. R., & Chamberlain, P. (1988). Treatment process: A problem at three levels. In L. Wynne (Ed.), *The state of the art of family therapy research: Controversies and recommendations* (pp. 189–223). New York: Family Process Press.

Pinsof, W. M. (1981). Family therapy process research. In A. S. Gurman & D. P. Kniskern (Eds.), *Handbook of family therapy* (pp. 699–741). New York: Brunner/Mazel.

Pinsof, W. M. (1986). The process of family therapy: The development of the family therapist coding system. In L. Greenberg & W. Pinsof (Eds.), *The psychotherapeutic process: A research handbook* (pp. 201–284). New York: Guilford Press.

Pinsof, W. M. (1988). Strategies for the study of family therapy process. In L. Wynne (Ed.), *The state of the art of family therapy research: Controversies and recommendations* (pp. 159–174). New York: Family Process Press.

Pinsof, W. M. (1989). A conceptual framework and methodological criteria for family therapy process research. *Journal of Consulting and Clinical Psychology, 57,* 53–59.

Pinsof, W. M. (1994). An integrative systems perspective on the therapeutic alliance: Theoretical, clinical and research implications. In A. Horvath & L.Greenberg (Eds.), *The working alliance: Theory, research and practice* (pp. 173–198). New York: Wiley.

Pinsof, W., & Wynne, L. (Eds.). (1995a). Family therapy effectiveness: Current research and theory [AAMFT Special Monograph]. *Journal of Marital and Family Therapy, 21*(4).

Pinsof, W., & Wynne, L. (1995b). The efficacy of marital and family therapy: An empirical overview, conclusions and recommendations. *Journal of Marital and Family Therapy, 21*(4), 585–614.

Pinsof, W., Wynne, L., & Hambright, A. (1996). The outcomes of couple and family therapy: Findings, conclusions, and recommendations. *Psychotherapy, 33,* 321–331.

Postner, R. S., Guttman, H., Sigal, J., Epstein, N., & Rakoff, V. (1971). Process and outcome in conjoint family therapy. *Family Process, 10,* 451–474.

Rice, L. N., & Greenberg, L. S. (1984) The new research paradigm. In L. Rice & L. Greenberg (Eds.), *Patterns of change* (pp. 7–26). New York: Guilford Press.

Rice, L. N., & Saperia, E. P. (1984). Task analysis of the resolution of problematic reactions. In L. Rice & L. Greenberg, (Eds.), *Patterns of change* (pp. 29–66). New York: Guilford Press.

Shadish, W., Montgomery, L., Wilson, P., Wilson, M., Bright, I., & Okwumubua, T. (1993). The effects of family and marital psychotherapies: A meta-analysis. *Journal of Consulting and Clinical Psychology, 61,* 992–1002.

Shadish, W., Ragsdale, K., Glaser, R., & Montgomery, L. (1995). The efficacy and effectiveness of marital and family therapy: A perspective from meta-analysis. *Journal of Marital and Family Therapy, 21*(4), 345–360.

Stoolmiller, M., Duncan, T., Bank, L., & Patterson, G. R., (1993). Some problems and solutions in the study of change: Significant patterns in client resistance. *Journal of Consulting and Clinical Psychology, 61*(6), 920–928.

Tolan, P. (1987). Implications of age of onset for delinquency risk identification. *American Journal of Community Psychology, 15,* 47–65.

Webster-Stratton, C. (1994). Advancing videotape parent training: A comparison study. *Journal of Consulting and Clinical Psychology, 62,* 583–593.

CHAPTER 10

Family-Focused Prevention Research: "Tough but Tender"

Patrick H. Tolan

In a seminal conceptual paper on prevention research and its policy role, Emory Cowen (1973) noted that such research can be characterized as a combination of a tender sentiment, the desire to improve the quality of life for children who are at risk, with the tough standard for empirical verification. As Cowen noted, such work requires the often uneasy blend of the desire to do good with the desire to meticulously control and measure how that good is done. Although often implicit in prevention research, these values often remain unarticulated or imbalanced, which impedes the quality and impact of prevention research. Indeed, there has been a general and sentimental lauding of prevention in the field that has, ironically, undermined it as a full member of the clinical intervention science and led to its underemphasis in family intervention research.

At the same time, this has left uncontested the inadequate recognition among prevention researchers of the value of a family focus. Because essentially everyone within the fields of prevention and family systems interventions can

Based on invited presentations to the APA Conference on Family and Marital Process and Outcome Research, Philadelphia, PA, May 5, 1995; and to the National Institute of Mental Health Workshop on Linking Violence Risk and Prevention Research, September 27, 1994, Washington, DC. The development and writing of this chapter was conducted with the support from NIMH grants R1848034 and RO148248, NICHD grant HS35415, CDC grant R49/CCR512739, SAMHSA/CSAP grant CCR512379, NSF grant SPR-9601157, and a University of Illinois at Chicago Great Cities Institute Faculty Scholar Award. Although the author is responsible for all of the viewpoints presented, this work has benefited from the collaborations with Drs. Deborah Gorman-Smith, David Henry, Mary McKay, Nancy Guerra, and numerous others who have worked or currently work on the Metropolitan Area Child Study, the Chicago Youth Development Study, and the SAFEChildren project. Finally, the families, children, and community representatives who have aided our work are to be thanked for their belief in these studies and for their continuing patience in trying to help me to understand.

agree in principle with the social good of prevention, there has not been adequate critical discussion about the specific value of prevention efforts within family-systems circles or about the role of families in prevention efforts. The purpose of this chapter is to link these two areas and to suggest an approach to family-focused prevention that can organize and advance our knowledge and help us to express our "tender sentiments" through tough scientific standards.

The chapter is organized in five sections. The first provides a review of the current typology for distinguishing level of prevention and implications for design and evaluation. Theoretical and practical characteristics that differentiate prevention from treatment interventions are then described and used to provide a framework for family-focused prevention research. Next, the reasons for the underemphasis on family in child-oriented prevention research are discussed. Different types of family-focused intervention are then reviewed, with exemplars noted. Finally, a suggested framework for integrating these two areas is presented, including benefits and limitations of family-focused prevention research, suggested research priorities, and related design considerations.

Prevention Design Based on the Type of Population Focus

The historical perspective on prevention distinguishes three levels: primary, secondary, and tertiary (Affifi & Breslow, 1994). In this public health schema developed to combat biologically induced disease, all prevention is distinguished from treatment by two major features: (a) intervening before the disease, problem, or syndrome develops rather than ameliorating the ailment or minimizing its symptoms; and (b) focusing on populations rather than individuals (Coie et al., 1993). The goal is to decrease the rate (incidence or prevalence) of a disease or disorder among the target population rather than curing or easing the ailment of specific patients (Caplan, 1964). The value of the intervention depends on changes in these rates, primarily the rates of onset or new incidence of a disorder subsequent to the intervention (Lorion, Price, & Eaton, 1989). Although this schema has been regularly applied to psychopathology and social adaptation, it has been difficult to clearly distinguish the levels of prevention and to distinguish prevention from different stages and levels of treatment. Extended discussions and complex definitions were developed to help make this biomedical definition fit well in behavioral areas, but none seems to provide the needed clarity (Cowen, 1973; Lorion et al., 1989; Price & Lorion, 1989; Steinberg & Silverman, 1987).

More recently, behavioral prevention has adopted a variation on the primary, secondary, and tertiary distinction (Gordon, 1983). This approach distinguishes preventive interventions that target everyone in a given population, labeled *universal prevention*, from efforts targeted to select subpopulations of heightened risk, labeled *selective prevention*. The differentiation was pioneered by Gordon (1983) and has been adopted by the Institute of Medicine (Mzarek & Haggerty, 1994) and the National Institute of Mental Health.

Selective interventions often target subgroups with some shared characteristic (e.g., first-grade children from families with parents who are illiterate are selected for reading skills interventions). This approach is distinguished from the third type, labeled *indicated prevention*, which targets only the portion of the sample that shows specific risk, usually because of individual differences. Thus, this approach distinguishes which portion of the population is targeted and the relative risk of that portion (Gordon, 1983). The distinction is not determined primarily by etiology, which is the basis for implementing primary, secondary, or tertiary prevention; however, there are implications about how risk is carried in the targeted population.

It is important to note that Gordon's interest and this schema were predicated on the fact that prevention does not rest on patient consent—it is applied based on risk or benefits, not by help-seeking or other indications of interest from clients (Caplan, 1964). This distinction reflects as well as engenders a different approach to determining resource allocation and the type of social contract between provider and client. For example, rather than engaging clients who identify a problem and seek treatment, the prevention researcher engages clients who are at risk or have some characteristic related to targeting (Tolan & McKay, 1996). The client may not understand that characteristic as denoting risk, may have difficulty understanding the risk, and may not agree with the implications. Thus, the participation agreement can be less specific and may require different types of engagement (Hanish & Tolan, in press; Tolan & McKay, 1996).

Gordon's schema implies differentiating several aspects of the design and understanding the prevention effort. The following sections outline the implications for intervention and design of Gordon's schema.

Differentiating Universal, Selective, and Indicated Prevention

The goal of universal intervention is to prevent the onset of disorder. Such efforts often include attempts to increase resources, competencies, and skills to inoculate against general risk (Kazdin, Bass, Ayers, & Rodgers, 1990). Family-focused examples could include public education campaigns to improve parental awareness of curfew, or parenting classes as part of the general prenatal classes. In most cases, these interventions are mass distributed and have low cost and intensity. Effects are likely to be general. Their public health benefit may be dramatic, however, because they lower risk slightly for large numbers of persons. Similarly, they are generally likely to have limited risk.

An implicit assumption is that risk is relatively evenly distributed within the population and that population characteristics are the main determinants of risk. Also, there is an implicit assumption that intervention effects may be shared equally or that self-selection serves those in need without harming those not in need. In other words, what is provided probably can help everyone and will hurt no one (Lorion et al., 1989). Because universals are intended to affect the overall rate of the problem in the population, the most direct measure of effect is the incidence rate.

In general, the outcomes of interest are categorical, although in some instances the interest is in reducing the average (mean or median) on a scale representing the extent of a problem (e.g., attitudes favorable toward drug use). Because universals are often large-scale and given to entire populations, comparison to a matched population may be the optimal balance of control and external validity. Random assignment within a population may not be plausible because of the mass distribution of the intervention and the likelihood of uncontrollable or unmeasurable "contamination" of control groups. When a random assignment or a matched community is not possible, prior cohort comparison is necessary (Tolan & Brown, 1998).

Selective programs differ from universals by focusing on a subgroup or population that is exposed to or shares risk factors. This approach is useful when risk is not evenly distributed and the risk is related to some group membership. An example would be an intervention to smooth adaptation to school in families with a child entering first grade and who live in low-income neighborhoods. The risk for school failure and later behavior problems is seen as being caused by exposure to neighborhood and school contexts, and tutoring and family intervention are intended to inoculate against the risk (Tolan, Gorman-Smith, & Henry, in press).

Selective interventions usually focus on a theoretical model of risk development and the empirically identified elements of risk. However, they also focus on group rather than individual risk. Because a subpopulation is targeted, selective interventions are usually more intensive than universals and are therefore costlier and have a higher risk of negative impact. Accurately identifying the risk group and the degree of elevated risk attributable to the shared characteristics is important in determining when to use selective interventions (Loeber, Dishion, & Patterson, 1984). If identification is reasonably accurate and there is substantial attributable risk, selective programs may have lower overall costs than an indiscriminately or inappropriately applied general program (Lorion et al., 1989).

In the context of evaluation, selective programs differ from universal programs in how effects are measured. The statistical interest is in lowering the rate of the problem among those in the subgroup exposed to the intervention compared with those not exposed. The clinical interest, however, is in approximating the incidence among the low-risk portions of the general population. From a developmental perspective, the interest is having the treated high-risk subgroup approximate the trajectories of the low-risk group (Coie et al., 1993). Including those not in need (false positives) as well as excluding those in need (false negatives, treating them as low risk) can increase error in the estimate of the impact. In a cross-sectional analysis or pre–post comparison, the results apply only to a given point in time. If linear measures of a characteristics are examined (that is, as one measure increases, the other does as well, and the relationship does not change), an effective selected intervention is one that attenuates distribution among the overall population (Brown, 1993a, 1993b).

The third type of preventive intervention, indicated interventions, focuses on individual risk rather than population risk. These interventions are intended to lessen seriousness, chronicity, or continuation of symptoms and disorder (Lorion et al., 1989). As originally defined, the focus was on persons who are asymptomatic of the specific outcome of interest but show "clinically demonstrative abnormality" (Gordon, 1983). In practical terms, such programs focus on serving individuals with early signs of problems or early manifestations of problems, such as early aggression predicting later delinquency (Gordon, 1983). They are designed to curtail or eliminate the long-term consequences of the disorder (Caplan, 1964). Thus, the focus is on altering the natural course of the problem to lessen its harmful impact (Kellam, 1990).

Indicated population programs, like selective programs, rely on epidemiology and screening to determine who is included, but inclusion is usually based on the presence of specific symptoms or behaviors; accurate identification is critical (Kellam, 1990). Their application is viable when risk is carried by individuals and the individuals must be changed to reduce risk. The interventions should have a greater intensity than other prevention programs and would be expected to have a greater impact on individuals. Accordingly, they are usually more costly per person than other prevention programs, and they have greater probability of iatrogenic effects. *Iatrogenic effects* are unintended negative effects as a result of treatment (e.g., when a cancer treatment makes someone worse in another way or unintentionally leads to greater risk). These concerns are balanced, however, by the high probability of worsening or continued serious problems without intervention, the greater costs of managing more serious and chronic forms of the problem, and the need for an immediate response. They may be the most cost-effective prevention when risk is concentrated in a small portion of the population and the risk carriers can be accurately identified (Lorion et al., 1989).

For indicated population interventions, the logical outcomes of interest are control of the disorder, desistance of symptoms or undesired behaviors, and lessened duration or arrested development of a disorder. Evaluation of such efforts should focus on decreasing the seriousness and duration of problems compared with untreated individuals with similar preintervention risk.

In evaluating indicated interventions, the primary comparison is to others in the risk group who do not receive the intervention; random assignment is thus a viable design for such studies (Tolan & Brown, 1998). One may be interested in reducing the extent of the problem (e.g., number of incidents of acute psychosis) or in changing the relative position in the population distribution of those with the problem. At a population level, the interest is in changing the incidence rate of categorically defined problems and attenuating the distribution of problems measured as extent of symptoms. Interpreting the benefits of an indicated program can be quite misleading if one assumes that the effect should approximate the developmental trajectory of low-risk populations or affect the group average.

Implications for Family-Focused Prevention

The differences noted earlier suggest that quite different methods, targeting, implementation, and evaluation criteria are appropriate depending on the relation of risk factors to the outcome and distribution of such characteristics among the population of interest (Brown, 1993a). Family prevention efforts that take account of such differences and incorporate these implications in program design are more likely to have the intended impact, be adequately implemented, and have appropriate evaluation applied. As in other areas of prevention, the distinction is not about which type of prevention is better, but which is more useful and justified for a given goal to prevent a given problem. In addition to differentiating type of prevention, family focused prevention has several important characteristics that differ from those of family-focused treatment. However, these differences have not usually been specified and often impede the effects of prevention.

Differences Between Prevention and Treatment Research and Programming

A common criticism of prevention designs, particularly indicated interventions, is that they do not differ from treatment. This may be because of the fact that much of what is called prevention is, by these standards, treatment (it ameliorates symptoms or noxious effects of symptoms), and much of what is called treatment is intended to prevent (impact is defined in terms of lessened risk in the future; Cowen, 1973). However, design and implementation can differentiate family-focused treatment and prevention interventions. First, the focus of prevention is on populations, whereas treatment focuses on the individual; the interest of prevention in individuals is only part of a population. Samples in prevention are valid to the extent that they include all individuals who are qualified or in need in a population with defined characteristics (Kellam, 1990). In treatment, other than symptom verification or problem definition (e.g., someone is depressed), the interest is in an aggregate of individuals. This has implications for how efficacy is judged, for adjusting interventions prescriptively to the needs of the family, and for case management (Brown, 1993a).

Judging Efficacy

An important distinction of prevention from other types of intervention research is how efficacy or effectiveness is evaluated. In prevention research, the evaluation interest is not in immediate effects. Also, the effects are interpreted differently. The clinical interest is not, as it is in treatment, in reducing clinical levels of problems to normal levels (Kendall, Marrs-Garcia, Nath, & Sheldrick, 1999). Instead, prevention focuses on lowering rates of later occurrence of the targeted outcome; the interest in immediate effects depends on the theoretical relationship of proximal effects to the ultimate outcome (Kellam, 1990). Also, there is no presumption of equal need or receptivity among the sample; heterogeneity is expected, as is meaningful variation in intervention impact (Brown, 1993b). It is also not uncommon in prevention research to expect and find variations in impact depending on preintervention risk status, varying characteristics, or timing and setting of intervention (Brown, 1993a, 1993b; Coie et al., 1993; Kellam, 1990; Metropolitan Area Child Study Group, 2000). Thus, a primary focus in assessing outcome is the rate of problems not occurring by some specified point in the future. Also, the meaning of finding no immediate differences between treated and untreated groups may vary depending on the theoretical contentions about the relationship between proximal risk markers and eventual status (Tolan & Brown, 1998).

One important difference is the relationship between proximal (or immediate) postintervention effects and distal (or later) effects (Brown, 1993a; Kellam, 1990). In most treatment programs, the most basic question is, Are there immediate effects, and if so, are they maintained? The follow-up effects are often secondary in indicating efficacy, and follow-up is undertaken to maintain initial impact. In prevention, the immediate effects are of interest to the extent that they help explain distal effects. The status immediately postoutcome may tell us little about the value of the intervention. For example, age 25 is apparently when risk ceases for initiating involvement in serious antisocial behavior. Thus, any preventive efforts carried out in childhood cannot be fully judged until the population reaches that age.

Measurement Emphasis

This difference in measurement emphasis affects more than outcome analysis. Measurement may vary when individuals represent subgroups or constituents within a population (rather than interchangeable representatives of the population). For example, when characterizing how individuals with different characteristics fare, it may be more appropriate to organize them through clustering patterns across measures of pertinent characteristics than to examine the linear combination of relative scores on such measures (Tolan, Gorman-Smith, Henry, Chung, & Hunt, 2000). Also, because of the inherent longitudinal nature of measuring effects, developmental issues must be considered, often causing substantial complications in measuring effects; one must measure impact against a normative model of change informed by a longitudinal measurement model (Patterson & Bank, 1989). For example, changing measurement reliability caused by developmental changes may obscure intervention effects (Muthen & Curran, 1997).

Intervention Design

Program design also differs in treatment as opposed to prevention efforts. In treatment studies, the approach is usually tailored and structured to test a specific protocol, but with the understanding that the approach is a prototype that is to be modified when case characteristics change and when the prototype is implemented by practitioners. Variation in activities, degree, and staff orientation and responsiveness to client needs are undesirable rather than optimal. It is also explicitly acknowledged in treatment studies that not all will benefit. This may require that clinically oriented staff rethink "case management" and no longer intensify efforts with the least responsive cases. In prevention design, the efficacy test rests on the understanding that, although other issues may arise, adherence to the protocol is critical. This difference is not absolute but is present as a relative difference in weighing prescriptive response versus specific program application.

Importance of the Relationship of Proximal to Distal Effects

Prevention can also be differentiated from treatment by the importance placed on proximal effects and distal status. In turn, this relationship must be consistent with the type of prevention selected and the targets during the intervention. It is uncommon for treatments to rest on articulated theory, other than maintenance of effect. However, because prevention is focused on status at some point in the future, the type of prevention, inclusion criteria, and the methods to be used must be based on a theoretical (and it is hoped empirically demonstrated) relationship between the risk factors identified, the targets of intervention, the intervention activities, and the proximal and distal outcomes (Kellam, 1990; West, Aiken, & Todd, 1993). Thus, like treatment, one needs to articulate a theory about the program's immediate impact and how it will lead to long-term effects (Lorion, Tolan, & Wahler, 1987; Lorion et al., 1989). Inherently, this requires a developmental model of the psychopathology or problem mapped onto a model of normal development (Coie et al., 1993). Increasingly, it is recognized that a developmental model must also be placed in context so that the focus is on developmentally targeted interventions that are ecologically sound (Elliott & Tolan, 1999; Tolan, Guerra, & Kendall, 1995).

Implementation

The third difference is that participation is not decided primarily by those receiving the intervention. Although, of course, participation is usually voluntary to some degree, prevention is offered based on need and benefit, not choice. In reality, there is a complicated and difficult process of getting clients (or their gatekeepers) to agree on the value of the intervention (Tolan & McKay, 1996). In addition, if participation is based on some inclusion criteria related to relative risk, that risk must be able to be reliably determined, and the risk must determine inclusion more than motivation for help. This not only adds another wrinkle to evaluation, but it adds considerable complexity to how programs are set up and where they should be located, how participation is solicited, and how participation rates affect validity (Tolan & Brown, 1998). The programs may need to be offered through venues other than traditional mental health and social service agencies, given that these settings can confer stigma. In most cases, it means soliciting persons who have not been identified as needing intervention and may not be experiencing specific distress. They may not accept or understand the risk and its relation to later problems.

The Underemphasis on Families in Prevention

In addition to these substantial conceptual and implementations issues, prevention efforts have not been family-focused, particularly when the child's functioning is the outcome of interest. The theoretical models of individual development and risk identification are far more advanced and have much more extensive empirical support than their counterparts for families (Coie et al., 1993; Tolan, Gorman-Smith, Zelli, & Huesmann, 1997). Also, costs of delivery and difficulty in securing adequate rates of prevention for confidence in judging effects are greater when families rather than individuals are the focus of prevention. Defining risk becomes much more complicated because there are many more covariates to consider (Tolan & McKay, 1996). In addition, parents of children who are at risk are often least able or interested in participating (Reid, 1988). Nonparticipation may be caused by other factors apart from risk. Economic demands, work schedules, disruptive family events, and other impediments can influence participation, as well as drug abuse, illiteracy, and psychopathology (Tolan & McKay, 1996).

Family prevention, like other family intervention, introduces measurement complexities as well (Dakof, 1996; Tolan, Gorman-Smith, Huesmann, & Zelli, 1997). Families can be conduits for intervention effects, they can induce risk through problematic family processes, or they can be intervention resources to develop and support skills and processes designed to prevent the undesirable outcome (Combrinck-Graham, 1989). If the family is merely a venue for targeting prevention to an individual (e.g., families are present while a cognitive–behavioral training is performed with a child who is impulsive), it is important to measure the family's support of the program, but it may not be critical to measure their systemic characteristics (Kumpfer, 1989). If family processes are implicated as causes of risk or as important protective factors, they must be measured in a manner that reflects family-level constructs, not merely as a collection of individual measures (Tolan et al., in press). If family is the unit of intervention focus (e.g., one wants to make families less abusive with each other), it is necessary to show how change in the family will be measured, and proximal and distal outcomes must be defined as more than parallel analyses of individuals (Shadish et al., 1993). There are also theoretical complications in targeting families that are not present in interventions aimed at individuals (Liddle & Dakof, 1995; Pinsof & Wynne, 1995). For example, how does one evaluate an intervention that makes mothers more able to monitor and discipline their sons but does not affect fathers? Is it a failure, a partial success, or a full success if this is enough to reduce risk substantially among the population?

School and other institutional-based prevention is also more common than family-focused prevention because it provides ease of access to recipients, and scheduling can be simplified to accommodate efficient delivery. Multiple family groups provide a more efficient method than working with each family individually, but still can be relatively costly compared with other prevention services (Tolan & McKay, 1996). However, when focusing on peers and school factors, family interventions can also ease complications because parents do not have to attend extra school meetings and the like and do not feel coerced by principals, judges, or special education teams.

Examples of Family-Focused Prevention

Family-focused prevention can take many forms and can vary greatly in how family is viewed. A review of the literature suggest three primary types of family-focused prevention activities, particularly in regard to children (Pinsof & Wynne, 1995). First, and most common, are studies that focus on the family, particularly parenting practices, as the direct causes of risk (Patterson, Reid, & Dishion, 1992). In such interventions, the family relationships and practices are the direct targets, with impact thought to depend on the extent to which such family characteristics are changed (Tolan & McKay, 1996; Shadish et al., 1993). There are numerous examples of such programs (see Tolan & McKay, 1996). For example, Webster-Stratton and colleagues (Webster-Stratton, 1991; Webster-Stratton, Kolpacoff, & Hollinsworth, 1988) have provided universal and selective interventions with parents of preschool children and early elementary-age children to reduce the later incidence of oppositional defiant disorder and conduct disorder. They have shown reduction in rates of these conditions, long-term effects, and favorable cost–benefit comparisons (Webster-Stratton et al., 1988).

Although there have been many family prevention programs, particularly related to disruptive behavior problems, there have been few such studies about other types of child and adolescent psychopathology and social problems (Chamberlain & Rosicky, 1995; Liddle & Dakof, 1995). In addition, many of the studies have not focused on measuring family processes other than parenting practices (Tolan & Guerra, 1996; Tolan et al., 1997). Even fewer have evaluated the process by which the effects were found; those under way show promising results, however. For example, in the Metropolitan Area Child Study family intervention (Tolan & McKay, 1996), we have explored how increasing parenting skill and the child's compliance with parent directives affects child aggression. Our results suggest that parenting is the path of effects and that change in parenting practices is related to an alliance with the intervention provider (Tolan, Hanish, Mckay, & Dickey, 2000). However, a second study suggests that there is different reaction to the intervention depending on initial parenting skills, family systemic relationships, and child aggression level (Hanish & Tolan, in press).

A second type of family-focused prevention addresses families with children who are medically ill (Campbell & Patterson, 1995; Goldstein & Milklowitz, 1995). The focus is on developing and supporting a family's capacity to maintain and support the child over time, although some interventions focus on reducing pathogenic family processes. Research suggests that there are multiple dimensions of family functioning that are important; in most cases the focus is on improving family skills for managing the illness and retaining needed social support. For example, Kliewer and Lewis (1995) found that when there was more emotional cohesion and better parental coping, children with sickle-cell anemia showed more active and positive coping.

As with interventions that focus on family processes, there are several limitations that have not been sufficiently investigated. In particular, it may be that family-focused health service delivery or psychoeducational and family support adjuncts to necessary health care may be particularly valuable in lessening symptomology or the severity of acute episodes. Evaluations of universal prevention programs, such as family-focused health promotion efforts, are also needed.

The third type of family-focused prevention views the family not as a direct cause of problems or as a moderator of risk but as a venue for enhancing prevention services (Combrinck-Graham, 1989). For example, one can increase child compliance with needed medical care by focusing on family involvement in treatment and by incorporating medical needs into family routines and plans (Kliewer, 1997). Although less researched than other types of family-focused prevention, this area of prevention research may provide some of the most important information about the benefits of prevention, given that it tends to shed light on how service should be delivered as well as the efficacy of specific activities. Thus, for example, one can test the impact of a family-based approach to reading practice versus a traditional individual practice method for children with poor initial reading skills to determine whether one is more effective and whether there are cost benefits (Combrinck-Graham, 1989).

There are probably several other areas of family prevention that could be distinguished. However, these are the areas with the most activity to date. Even here, however, there has been little extensive work and even less evidence of the necessary sophistication as suggested in the initial review of prevention types. A review of the literature suggests increasing sophistication, but much basic work is still needed.

Conclusion

Family-focused prevention is an area of great promise for providing a harmonious melding of public good with strong scientific scrutiny (Cowen, 1973; Shadish et al., 1993). The emerging evidence is that family-focused prevention may be quite effective and may have greater cost benefits than treatment and other forms of prevention for children (Tolan & Guerra, 1994; Shadish et al., 1993). However, such prevention efforts are a complex enterprise with many theoretical and practical problems. Among the complexities is the need to locate intervention design and targeting within epidemiologic, risk, and intervention technology research as well as within the ecological factors that affect service delivery and effects (Tolan & McKay, 1996; Tolan & Guerra, 1996). We can currently identify the limitations of present paradigms and borrowed methods, and we are quickly defining the structure of prevention science and developing more appropriate models and methods for family-focused prevention (Coie et al., 1993). There is a trade-off, however, between exciting possibilities and simple, clear direction.

Within these qualifications and general conclusions, there are some guidelines that merit consideration in developing, designing, implementing, and evaluating prevention efforts that involve the family.

1. *Clarifying the type of prevention is more than a nicety.* Distinguishing the type of population to be included based on the distribution of risk among the population, the expected costs and benefits of inclusion or exclusion, and the likely population benefits of a given prevention approach is an advance over the previous typology borrowed from biomedical epidemiology. Universal, selective, and indicated interventions differ not only in which portion of the population is included but in specific design and evaluation features. Failure to adequately consider these or to follow the implications for inclusion methods, program design, or evaluation can lead to erroneous and perhaps misleading evaluation.

2. *In prevention, base rates are critical in determining which type of intervention is warranted, the likely risk markers, and the degree of population effect that can be expected.* In concert with cost–benefit analyses, these statistics help guide the level of advisable prevention. This is different from a concrete application of risk models. For example, there is evidence that parental hostility relates to delinquency. A prevention program may thus aim to reduce the relative level of hostility within a target population. However, one may reduce the mean hostility in a population substantially with no effect on prevalence if the relationship is between extreme hostility and delinquency rather than the lower but more common levels of hostility.

3. *It is critical that any prevention effort articulate a relationship between proximal and distal outcomes and that it is done within a developmental model that pays due attention to developmental timing effects and contextual influences.* Without such specification, the rationale for intervention components is usually weak, and any relationship to long-term effects may be indeterminable. The nature of effects and variations on meaningful subgroups of participants will also be difficult to clarify.

4. *Families likely represent the most optimal intervention target for many disorders and social problems in children and adults.* However, compared with prevention focused on individuals, rigorous construct assessment and developmental models to guide such prevention are lacking. Similarly, it is important to distinguish family prevention efforts that focus on family processes as risk factors, family processes and skills as moderators of risk–outcome links, and those that aim to benefit by providing services in a family-friendly way. All three areas merit investigation and can contribute to the field of family intervention science as well as aiding in the cost-effective delivery of needed services to families and children.

References

Afifi, A. A., & Breslow, L. (1994). The maturing paradigm of public health. *Annual Review of Public Health, 15*, 223–235.

Brown, C. H. (1993a). Statistical methods for preventive trials in mental health. *Statistics in Medicine, 12*, 289–300.

Brown, C. H. (1993b). Analyzing preventive trials with generalized additive models. *American Journal of Community Psychology, 21*, 635–664.

Campbell, T. L., & Patterson, J. (1995). The effectiveness of family interventions in the treatment of physical illness. *Journal of Marital and Family Therapy, 21*, 545–584.

Caplan, G. (1964). *Principles of preventive psychiatry.* New York: Basic Books.

Chamberlain, P., & Rosicky, J. G. (1995). The effectiveness of family therapy in the treatment of adolescents with conduct disorders and delinquency. *Journal of Marital and Family Therapy, 21*, 441–460.

Coie, J. D., Watt, N. F., West, S. G., Hawkins, J. D., Asarnow, J. R., Markham, H. J., Ramey, S. L., Shure, M. B., & Long, B. (1993). The science of prevention: A conceptual framework and some directions for a national research program. *American Psychologist, 48*, 1013–1022.

Combrinck-Graham, L. (1989). *Children in family contexts.* New York: Guilford Press.

Cowen, E. L. (1973). Baby-steps toward primary prevention. *American Journal of Community Psychology, 5*, 1–22.

Dakof, G. (1996). Meaning and measurement of family. *Journal of Family Psychology, 10*, 142–146.

Elliott, D., & Tolan, P. H. (1999). Overview of adolescent violence from a lifespan–ecological perspective. In D. Flannery & R. Hoff (Eds.), *Youth violence: A volume in the psychiatric clinics of North America* (pp. 3–46). Washington, DC: American Psychiatric Association.

Goldstein, M. J., & Milklowitz, D. J. (1995). The effectiveness of psychoeducational family therapy in the treatment of schizophrenic disorders. *Journal of Marital and Family Therapy, 21*, 361–377.

Gordon, R. (1983). An operational definition of prevention. *Public Health Reports, 98*, 107–109.

Hanish, L., & Tolan, P. H. (in press). Patterns of response to a family aggression prevention program. *Journal of Marriage and Family Therapy.*

Kazdin, A. E., Bass, D., Ayers, W. A., & Rodgers, A. (1990). Empirical and clinical focus of child and adolescent psychotherapy research. *Journal of Consulting and Clinical Psychology, 58*(6), 729–740.

Kellam, S. G. (1990). Developmental epidemiological framework for family research on depression and aggression. In G. R. Patterson (Ed.), *Depression and aggression in family interaction* (pp. 11–48). Hillsdale, NJ: Erlbaum.

Kendall, P. C., Marrs-Garcia, D., Nath, S. R., & Sheldrick, R. C. (1999). Normative comparison for the evaluation of clinical significance. *Journal of Consulting and Clinical Psychology, 67,* 285–299.

Kliewer, W. (1997). Children coping with chronic illness. In S. A. Wolchik & I. N. Sandler (Eds.), *Handbook of children's coping* (pp. 275–300). New York: Plenum Press.

Kliewer, W., & Lewis, H. (1995). Family influences on coping processes in children and adolescents with sickle cell disease. *Journal of Pediatric Psychology, 20,* 511–525.

Kumpfer, K. L. (1989). Prevention of alcohol and drug use: A critical review of risk factors and prevention. In D. Shaffer, I. Philips, N. B. Enzer, & M. M. Silverman (Eds.), *Prevention of mental disorders, alcohol, and other drug use in children and adolescents* (pp. 309–371). Rockville, MD: Office for Substance Abuse Prevention.

Liddle, H. A., & Dakoff, G. A. (1995). Family therapy for drug abuse: Promising but not definitive efficacy evidence. *Journal of Marital and Family Therapy, 21,* 511–544.

Loeber, R., Dishion, T. J., & Patterson, G. R. (1984). Multiple-gating: A multistage assessment procedure for identifying youths at risk for delinquency. *Journal of Research in Crime and Delinquency, 21,* 7–32.

Lorion, R. P., Price, R. H., & Eaton, W. E. (1989). The prevention of child adolescent disorders: From theory to research. In D. Shaffer, I. Philips, N. B. Enzer, & M. M. Silverman (Eds.), *Prevention of mental disorders, alcohol, and other drug use in children and adolescents* (pp. 55–96). Rockville, MD: Office for Substance Abuse Prevention.

Lorion, R. P., Tolan, P. H., & Wahler, R. G. (1987). Prevention. In H. C. Quay (Ed.), *Handbook of juvenile delinquency* (pp. 383–416). New York: Wiley.

Metropolitan Area Child Study Group. (2000). *A cognitive–ecological approach to prevention of aggression in urban children.* Manuscript submitted for publication.

Muthen, B. O., & Curran, P. (1997). General growth modeling of individual differences in experimental designs: A latent variable framework for analysis and power estimation. *Psychological Methods, 2,* 311–402.

Mrazek, P. J., & Haggerty, R. J. (1994). *Reducing risks for mental disorders: Frontiers for preventive intervention research.* Washington, DC: National Academy Press.

Patterson, G. R., & Bank, L. (1989). Some amplifying mechanisms for pathologic processes in families. In M. R. Gunnar & E. Thalen (Eds.), *Systems and development: The Minnesota Symposium on Child Psychology* (Vol. 22, pp. 167–209). Hillsdale, NJ: Erlbaum.

Patterson, G. R., Reid, J. B., & Dishion, T. J. (1992). *Antisocial boys: A social interactional approach* (Vol. 4). Eugene, OR: Castalia.

Pinsof, W. M., & Wynne, L. C. (1995). The effectiveness of marital and family therapy: An empirical overview, conclusions and recommendations. *Journal of Marital and Family Therapy, 21,* 585–613.

Price, R. H., & Lorion, R. P. (1989). Prevention programming as organizational reinvention: From research to implementation. In D. Shaffer, I. Philips, N. B. Enzer, &

M. M. Silverman (Eds.), *Prevention of mental disorders, alcohol and other drug use in children and adolescents.* [OSAP Prevention Monograph 2] (pp. 97–123). Rockville, MD: Office for Substance Abuse Prevention.

Reid, J. B. (1988). Involving parents in the prevention of conduct disorder: Rationale, problems, and tactics. *Community Psychologist, 24,* 28–30.

Shadish, W. R., Montgomery, L. M., Wilson, P., Wilson, M. R., Bright, I., & Okumabua, T. (1993). The effects of family and marital psychotherapies: A meta-analysis. *Journal of Consulting and Clinical Psychology, 61,* 992–1002.

Steinberg, J. A., & Silverman, M. M. (Eds.). (1987). *Preventing mental disorders: A research perspective.* Washington, DC: U.S. Government Printing Office.

Tolan, P. H., & Brown, C. H. (1998). Methods for evaluating intervention and prevention efforts. In. P. K. Trickett & C. Schellenbach (Eds.), *Violence against children in the family and the community* (pp. 439–464). Washington, DC: American Psychological Association.

Tolan, P. H., Gorman-Smith, D., & Henry, D. (in press). The developmental–ecology of influences on urban youth violence: Community, neighborhoods, parenting and deviant peers. *Developmental Psychology.*

Tolan, P. H., Gorman-Smith, D., Henry, D., Chung, S., & Hunt, M. (2000). *The effects of coping styles of urban youth on social competence and symptomology.* Manuscript submitted for publication.

Tolan, P. H., Gorman-Smith, D., Huesmann, L. R., & Zelli, A. (1997). Assessment of family relationship characteristics: A measure to explain risk for antisocial behavior and depression in youth. *Psychological Assessment, 9,* 212–223.

Tolan, P. H., & Guerra, N. G. (1994). *What works in reducing adolescent violence: An empirical review of the field.* Monograph prepared for the Center for the Study and Prevention of Youth Violence. Boulder: University of Colorado.

Tolan, P. H., Guerra, N. G., & Kendall, P. (1995). A developmental–ecological perspective on antisocial behavior in children and adolescents: Towards a unified risk and intervention framework. *Journal of Consulting and Clinical Psychology, 63,* 579–584.

Tolan, P. H., Hanish, L., McKay, M., & Dickey, M. (2000). *Measures for evaluating process in child and family interventions: An example in the prevention of aggression.* Manuscript submitted for publication.

Tolan, P. H., & McKay, M. (1996). Preventing serious antisocial behavior in inner-city children: An empirically based family prevention program. *Family Relations, 45,* 148–155.

Webster-Stratton, C. (1991). Strategies for helping families with conduct disordered children [annotation]. *Journal of Child Psychology and Psychiatry, 32,* 1047–1062.

Webster-Stratton, C., Kolpacoff, M., & Hollinsworth, T. (1988). Self-administered videotape therapy for families with conduct-problem children: Comparison with two cost-effective treatments and a control group. *Journal of Consulting and Clinical Psychology, 56,* 558–566.

West, S. G., Aiken, L. S., & Todd, M. (1993). Probing the effects of individual components in multiple component prevention programs. *American Journal of Community Psychology, 21,* 571–605.

CHAPTER 11

Toward Family-Level Attribute x Treatment Interaction Research

Michael J. Rohrbaugh

Varda Shoham

Melissa W. Racioppo

The idea that "different folks benefit from different therapeutic strokes" makes intuitive sense, yet several decades of individually focused attribute x treatment interaction (ATI) research (Cronbach & Snow, 1977) have yielded few firm empirical guidelines for matching clients to treatments (Shoham & Rohrbaugh, 1995; Stiles, Shapiro & Elliot, 1986). As the "common factors" perspective gains popularity in therapy research, one senses growing skepticism that research on specific interventions will tell us much useful or interesting about what works for whom. In the alcoholism field, for example, recent results from Project MATCH have dampened enthusiasm about client–treatment matching to the point that an *APA Monitor* headline concluded that "Tailoring Treatments for Alcoholics Is Not the Answer" ("Tailoring Treatments," 1997). Unfortunately, like most ATI studies, Project MATCH disregarded developments in family psychology by focusing almost exclusively on characteristics of individual alcoholics undergoing individual treatments (Project MATCH Research Group, 1997). In this chapter we propose that pessimism about ATI research and client–treatment matching is premature—at least when treatments involve more than one person. We summarize new evidence indicating that meaningful ATIs can be obtained when treatments differ clearly on dimensions that are theoretically relevant to the hypothesized moderator variables and when the

The research used to illustrate relational moderators of treatment response was supported by Grant No. AA08970 from the National Institute on Alcohol Abuse and Alcoholism. We are indebted to Larry E. Beutler, the project's principal investigator; to Theodore Jacob, coprincipal investigator; and to the many students and project staff who made this work possible. We dedicate this chapter to our friend and mentor, the late Richard E. Snow.

scope of potential moderators expands beyond the individual patient to attributes of his or her close (family) relationships.

The chapter has three sections: First, in a brief overview and critique of the ATI paradigm, we suggest that ATI research has focused on overly narrow client moderator attributes and overly broad treatments. To understand what works for whom in couple and family therapies, researchers will need to consider relational as well as individual moderators of response to different treatments. The second section illustrates this point with findings from an investigation of several couple-level attributes we hypothesized would moderate response to cognitive–behavioral versus family systems therapies for couples in which the male partner was alcoholic. The hypothesized moderator variables were demand–withdraw interaction, couple affect, nonverbal dyadic synchrony, and a construct we called *symptom–system fit*. Despite some conceptual and empirical overlap, several of these variables appeared to make independent contributions to predicting differential response to the two treatments. The last section of the chapter then considers the limitations and implications of our work and some directions for further research. Here we note that the ATI paradigm challenges family researchers to investigate differential indications for minimalist versus multicomprehensive treatments and to identify conditions under which more focused, parsimonious interventions may be sufficient. We also suggest examining another type of contextual moderation relevant to therapy integration—namely, whether specific interventions retain their original efficacy when transported from one therapeutic context (or model) to another.

Toward Family-Level ATI Research

The most definitive method of studying what works for whom involves ATI research (Cronbach & Snow, 1977; Snow, 1991). The *attribute* (A) in the ATI paradigm—modified in therapy research from the original use of *aptitude* in educational psychology—represents any client or problem characteristic that may moderate the effects of *treatment* type (T) on *outcome* (O). *Interaction* (I) indicates simply that A moderates the relationship between T and O. At minimum, an ATI finding requires two treatments and one moderator: Showing that a given client characteristic (e.g., anxiety, impulsivity, or a stable marriage) predicts response to one treatment provides useful information but stops short of demonstrating that the intervention is *differentially* indicated because other interventions could have worked for these clients just as well (Smith & Sechrest, 1991; Snow, 1991). To appreciate this, consider Jacobson, Follette, and Pagel's (1986) report that behavioral marital therapy (BMT) is more beneficial for symmetrical, "egalitarian" couples than for those in a marriage organized according to traditional gender roles. Even if this finding is robust, we would need to know that the moderator variable—egalitarian versus traditional relationship —operates differently for some *other* form of marriage therapy in order to conclude that BMT is differentially indicated.

The ATI paradigm looks beyond the so-called "dodo bird" verdict that different therapies have equivalent outcomes ("everyone has won and all must have prizes"; Luborsky, Singer, & Luborsky, 1975, p. 995). Although equivalence findings predominate in comparative psychotherapy outcome research, the large variability in outcome typically found within treatments may obscure systematic individual differences in how clients respond to different treatments. The promise of ATI research has been to show how outcome depends on the match or mismatch between specific attributes of clients and the treatments they receive (Beutler, 1991; Shoham-Salomon & Hannah, 1991). Although dodo-bird equivalence findings have convinced many in the field to pursue "common factors" across therapies (Garfield, 1990), ATI proponents believe it is too soon to abandon investigations of why specific treatments work and for whom they are most and least helpful.

Unfortunately, solid ATI results in psychotherapy research are hard to find: Many findings are post hoc, few are theory-driven, and some have proved difficult to replicate (Beckham, 1990; Dance & Neufeld, 1988; Smith & Sechrest, 1991; Stiles et al., 1986). As noted earlier, the most recent disappointment in this regard was the widely publicized report of the Project MATCH Research Group (1997), which found that client–treatment matching did not improve outcomes for individuals who abused alcohol. In perhaps the largest randomized therapy study ever undertaken, alcoholic outpatients ($N = 1,726$) received 12 sessions of one of three manualized treatments: cognitive–behavioral therapy (CBT), motivational enhancement therapy (MET), and 12-step facilitation (TSF). Despite careful a priori attention to selecting potential moderator variables, the results confirmed only 1 of 16 matching hypotheses (patients without "psychopathology" benefited more from TSF than CBT), and even some promising, previously reported ATI findings (e.g., Kadden, Cooney, Getter, & Litt, 1989; Longabaugh, Wirtz, Beattie, Noel, & Stout, 1995) did not replicate in Project MATCH. On the average, clients in all three groups showed significant and sustained improvements in the year following treatment, a finding consistent with results of a recent multisite, naturalistic study comparing naturally occurring CBT and TSF in Veterans Administration medical centers (Ouimette, Finney, & Moos, 1997).

Should results such as these bring down the curtain on ATI research and client–treatment matching? In our view, it is too soon to discount potentially important contributions of the ATI paradigm, even to the treatment of alcohol problems. The main reason is that moderator variables in the vast majority of ATI studies—including Project MATCH—deal only with attributes of individual clients undergoing individual treatments; the possibility that a client's current intimate relationships may predict differential treatment response remains virtually uninvestigated. Such an individualistic focus seems especially short-sighted in the alcoholism field, where research indicates that drinking problems are inextricably interwoven with the intimate contexts in which they occur (Jacob & Leonard, 1988; McCrady & Epstein, 1995) and that couple and family interventions typically have better outcomes than individual counseling (Baucom, Shoham, Mueser, Daiuto, & Stickle, 1998; O'Farrell, Cutter, & Floyd, 1985). In fact, recent reviews of empirically supported treatments conclude that the only viable efficacy evidence so far available for outpatient alcohol treatment comes from studies that involve spouses or spouses and significant others (Baucom et al., 1998). Furthermore, even as clients change in individual therapy, their spouses and significant others often act (or react) in ways that facilitate or hinder therapeutic progress—and as research described later will illustrate, the direction of this influence may depend on the fit (or lack thereof) between couple interaction patterns and particular approaches to intervention.

Because theories of change underpinning most psychotherapies focus almost exclusively on the thoughts, behavior, or psychodynamics of the individual patient, it is not surprising that these are the main foci of measurement in psychotherapy research. Only rarely do researchers assess attributes of the individual's spouse or marriage and family relationships, and when they do, these relational variables are usually measured from only the patient's view. At the same time, psychotherapy researchers have understandably invested a great deal of effort in developing and improving measures of the therapeutic relationship, yet as Coyne and Liddle (1992) pointed out, "the psychotherapeutic relationship is only one among many in the patient's life and usually not the most important one" (p. 48).

Although we are most concerned here with ATI applications in couple and family therapy, it is not difficult to imagine how naturally occurring relationship patterns might even moderate response to different individual therapies. For example, relevant relational moderator variables might be whether an individual client is actually involved in a committed relationship with a partner and whether the client comes to therapy around the time of an important family life cycle transition (e.g., within 6 months of birth, marriage, children leaving home, divorce, etc.). Researchers often record this type of information to describe their clinical samples, but they rarely analyze it as a moderator of treatment process and outcome. We would not be surprised, however, if future studies show better outcomes for cognitive–behavioral than psychodynamic therapies with relationally "committed" clients, and perhaps an opposite pattern for single clients, or, if supportive and problem-solving interventions prove more effective than psychodynamic therapies around the time of a family life cycle transition, with perhaps the opposite true when the patient's family life is not in transition. To our knowledge, the only ATI study of individual therapy that begins to look beyond the individual patient was reported by Longabaugh and colleagues, who found limited evidence that alcoholics' self-reported investment in social networks, as well as their perceived social support for abstinence, may moderate response to different combinations of individual treatments (Longabaugh et al., 1995).

Hypotheses about relational moderators are easier to discern in the literature on couple and family therapy. Based on clinical experience, some authors have proposed guidelines for how a therapist might intervene differently depending on relational patterns such as a couple or family's level of conflict, distress, or "readiness" (see review by Carlson, Sperry, & Lewis, 1997). None of these proposals has been investigated in systematic ATI research, however. Hypotheses about relational ATIs also come from the empirical literature. For example, studies of couple therapy give reason to predict that partners in symmetrical, egalitarian relationships may benefit more from therapies emphasizing direct negotiation of behavior exchange and communication skills (Jacobson et al., 1986), while clients in rigidly complementary systems may do better with strategic interventions designed to challenge problematic transactions less directly (Goldman & Greenberg, 1992) or with interventions designed to promote "acceptance" rather than behavior change (Christensen, Jacobson, & Babcock, 1995). Other examples can be gleaned from research on schizophrenia and depression, which links family-level variables such as expressed emotion and affective style to treatment outcomes as well as exacerbations of symptoms (Hooley, 1986). Some investigators have called for ATI designs that will improve our ability to match different schizophrenia patients to different treatments (Bellack & Meuser, 1993)—and considering expressed emotion itself as a potential moderator variable would be a good place to start. One possibility is that patients from families that are high in expressed emotion may respond best to treatments that avoid confrontation and use normalizing and supportive interventions, whereas patients from families that are low in expressed emotion may be amenable to more direct cognitive–behavioral interventions and skill training.

More generally, family ATI research might also draw on family theoretical frameworks such as Olson's (1986) circumplex model, which offers well-developed client self-report and clinician observation scales to locate families on the orthogonal dimensions of cohesion (enmeshed versus disengaged) and adaptability (rigid versus chaotic). One could speculate that clients from enmeshed families might benefit most from treatments that emphasize intra- or interpersonal boundary definition, while those from disengaged families may be better served by techniques oriented to establishing or participating more effectively in close relationships. Similar predictions might be made about differential indications of structured and unstructured (e.g., directive versus nondirective) therapies for clients from rigid as opposed to chaotic families.

Given these rich possibilities, it is striking that the treatment (T) variable in the few relevant published studies we know of consists simply of providing (versus not providing) some form of supplement to the same treatment, rather than contrasting different treatments whose effects may be moderated by relational factors. For example, Barlow, O'Brien, and Last (1984) found that including (versus not including) the husbands of agoraphobic women in exposure therapy improved outcomes when the patient's marital satisfaction was low but not when it was high. Similarly, in a recent study of BMT with and without additional couples relapse prevention sessions, O'Farrell, Choquette, and Cutter (1998) found that alcoholics with more severe marital problems benefited more from adding the relapse prevention sessions to BMT, while their BMT-only counterparts had fewer abstinent days and showed a steep decline in abstinence during 30 months of follow-up. Several other investigations of behavioral couples therapy for alcohol problems also suggest that couple attributes such as marital distress and relational commitment predict response to treatment (Epstein, McGrady, Miller, & Steinberg, 1994; O'Farrell et al., 1985), although prediction did not address differential (moderated) response to clearly distinguishable treatments. Still, even the Barlow et al. and O'Farrell et al. studies may not meet the strict definition of ATI research because they did not investigate moderated response to two or more *different* treatments.

In any case, the main empirical generalization from the studies of relational predictors reported so far seems to be that supplementary couple-level interventions work best for couples who need them most. Although hardly a startling conclusion, finding relational variables that predict whether adding relapse prevention or including a spouse will improve outcome is clearly a useful step in the right direction. This also sets the stage for investigating the more intriguing possibility that relationship variables can predict not only whether a couple-level intervention will improve outcome, but also the type of intervention likely to produce the best results.

An Investigation of Relational Moderators

We tested hypotheses about relational moderators in the framework of a larger project (Beutler et al., 1993; Beutler, Shoham, Jacob, & Rohrbaugh, 1997) comparing manualized CBT (Wakefield, Williams, Yost, & Patterson, 1996) and family systems therapy (FST; Rohrbaugh, Shoham, Spungen & Steinglass, 1995) for couples in which the male partner was alcoholic. The hypothesized moderator constructs, assessed before treatment began, were (a) demand–withdraw couple interaction (Christensen & Heavey, 1993), particularly the pattern of wife demand–husband withdraw; (b) the balance of positive to negative affect observed when the couple discussed a disagreement (Gottman, 1994); (c) nonverbal synchrony, a nonreactive indicator of dyadic rapport (Bernieri & Rosenthal, 1991); and (d) a more complex construct we call *symptom–system fit,* which attempts to capture whether drinking is syntonic or dystonic to the couple's relationship (Rohrbaugh, Shoham, Racioppo, & Stickle, 1996). Each of these potential moderators is relevant not only to the clinical problems of alcohol-involved couples but also to the main differences between the CBT and FST treatments, as explained next.

The project was based at the University of California, Santa Barbara, where 63 randomly assigned couples meeting the project's inclusion criteria participated in up to 20 sessions of either CBT or FST. To be included, male participants had to meet criteria for alcoholism and had to have been in a committed couple relationship for at least 1 year with a female partner. The therapists were master's-level clinicians who had at least 1 year of previous experience working with substance abuse clients. The therapists were trained by the authors of the respective treatment manuals, and supervisors regularly reviewed videotapes of therapy sessions to ensure the integrity of the two protocols.

The design, methodology, and results are described in detail elsewhere (Shoham, Rohrbaugh, Stickle, & Jacob, 1998). Suffice it to say here that we compared CBT and FST to each other rather than to a control group and attached less importance to main-effect differences in overall group means than to statistical interactions (ATIs), indicating that the two treatments were differentially effective as a function of the various relational moderator variables. Assessment of prospective moderators was based on reliable observational ratings of a videotaped pretreatment marital interaction task in which each couple discussed (a) an area of conflict in their relationship other than drinking, and (b) the problem of drinking itself. Some parallel questionnaire measures of relational patterns were available as well, but these proved less useful than the observational ratings in ATI analyses.

The primary dependent variables were (a) the number of therapy sessions attended by at least one member of the couple; (b) whether the identified drinker completed the full 20-session treatment program; and (c) ratings of the drinker's abstinence from alcohol at termination, based primarily on administrations of the time line followback interview (Sobell & Sobell, 1992). Although drinking outcomes were also assessed 6 and 12 months after termination, the follow-up results are compromised by high attrition from measurement. The available data are thus sufficient to identify immediate ATIs based on retention, but they offer less definitive information about ATIs related to drinking outcomes and cannot support conclusions regarding the durability of these effects.

Although both were conducted in a couple format, the CBT and FST treatments differed sharply on two dimensions relevant to our relational moderator hypotheses: (a) the level of demand treatment placed on the drinker (and significant others) for abstinence and change; and (b) the treatment's relative emphasis on the thoughts, behaviors, or psychopathologies of the individual drinker as opposed to the system of specific relationships and interaction patterns that help to maintain the problem. In general, Wakefield et al.'s (1996) CBT focused primarily on the individual drinker and drinking per se in the context of high demand for abstinence, while the low-demand FST (Rohrbaugh et al., 1995) addressed mainly the systemic interactional processes in which the drinking was embedded. Cognitive–behavioral therapy aimed to teach the drinking individual cognitive strategies and behavioral skills to facilitate abstinence, and also to help him and his spouse maintain sobriety by addressing relationship issues, social skills deficits, and alcohol-related life problems. Treatment followed a structured format, emphasizing therapist guidance, exploration of contingencies and vulnerabilities, didactic training in basic communication skills, and practice in the development of new coping and mastery strategies by both the drinker and spouse (Wakefield et al., 1996). In contrast, the systemic FST approach focused on problem drinking as an aspect of ongoing marital and family relationships, aiming to alter interactions that maintain drinking as well as the meanings attributed to drinking by the partners as a couple. Rather than requiring abstinence, FST began with a consultation phase, throughout which the therapist remained neutral about change until the clients as a couple explicitly chose to pursue a change goal related to drinking. This approach also incorporated strategic and structural techniques to anticipate and deal with clients' reluctance to change (Rohrbaugh et al., 1995). A crucial difference between the treatments was that CBT took a firm stance about expected abstinence from alcohol and used adjunctive breathalyzer tests to ensure compliance. Family systems therapy was more permissive in this respect, using both direct and indirect strategies to work with client resistance and promote drinking cessation. Thus, although both treatments viewed drinking as a primary target for change, they sought to alter different aspects of client functioning and differed substantially in their handling of noncompliance and resistance to change.

To confirm that the CBT and FST treatments were indeed different in their implementation and distinct from each other in the manner anticipated, we trained graduate students to rate therapy tapes on the key process dimensions of therapist demand and systemic (relationship versus individual) focus. As expected, CBT received higher ratings than FST on the therapist demand dimension, while the FST focused more on the couple's relationship than CBT. In fact, the distributions of averaged judges' scores for the two treatments showed very little overlap on either dimension. We used these process ratings not only to confirm treatment distinctiveness, but also to determine if these dimensions of therapist behavior could effectively replace treatment assignment in the ATI equation.

Demand–Withdraw Interaction

Our first test of relational moderation (Shoham et al., 1998) focused on demand–withdraw (DW) interaction, a common pattern in troubled couples where one partner pursues, criticizes, nags, or demands while the other distances, defends, avoids, or withdraws (Christensen & Heavey, 1990, 1993; Watzlawick, Beavin, & Jackson, 1967). Clinicians report that this pattern has special relevance when one of the partners has a drinking problem (Bepko & Krestan, 1985). Thus, a nondrinking wife may pursue, criticize, or request change from her alcoholic husband, who then withdraws or defends himself, which leads to more demands by the wife, and so on. Similar patterns have been noted in observational research, where alcoholic husbands seem especially likely to deflect or avoid confrontation and respond negatively to their wives problem-solving attempts (Jacob & Leonard, 1988; McCrady & Epstein, 1995).

Although studies of nonalcoholic couples (see review by Christensen & Heavey, 1993) indicate that DW roles vary by gender, with the "wife demand–husband withdraw" (WdHw) pattern typically more prevalent than "husband demand–wife withdraw" (HdWw), mean differences favoring WdHw over HdWw can be reduced (Heavey, Layne, & Christensen, 1993) and even reversed (Klinetob & Smith, 1996) when couples talk about a problem or issue of greater concern to the husband than the wife. Thus, when a husband has an alcohol problem, one might expect the wife to pursue change and the husband to resist or avoid it—especially when they discuss the husband's drinking.

In terms of our treatments, we hypothesized that a therapy high in demand for change (e.g., abstinence) would be a poor fit for high DW couples, especially those high on WdHw, because it replicates the problem pattern by providing "more of the same" ineffective solution (Watzlawick, Weakland, & Fisch, 1974): An alcoholic husband may thus withdraw from a high-demand therapy in the same way he withdraws from a demanding wife, and conversely, a treatment that addresses specific interaction patterns around the drinking should be relatively more successful when DW is high. We thus predicted that high-DW couples would respond less favorably to CBT than to FST, but that FST would be equally beneficial for high and low levels of DW. In other words, we expected DW to correlate negatively with outcome among CBT but not FST cases. More specifically, because moderation may depend on the wife attempting to influence the husband to change (and him resisting), we hypothesized that ATIs would be stronger (a) when the wife demands and the husband withdraws, compared to the opposite (HdWw) pattern; and (b) when the couple discusses the husband's drinking as compared to another area of conflict in their relationship.

The retention and abstinence results generally supported these predictions. Observational and report measures of pretreatment DW (see Christensen &

Heavey, 1993) produced significant ATIs, indicating that couples higher on DW attended fewer sessions, less often completed therapy, and tended to have poorer drinking outcomes in CBT, while DW levels made little difference in FST. An especially vivid illustration of this moderation emerged in the treatment completion rates for identified alcoholics in couples above and below the median on the observational measure of total DW (WdHw + HdWw): In the 11 high-DW couples who entered CBT, *none* of the male drinkers completed the full 20 sessions. This contrasted with a completion rate of 60% for low-DW CBT couples and rates of 39% and 61% for the low- and high-DW FST cases, respectively.

Of particular interest were predictions about which specific DW pattern— WdHw or HdWw—would most moderate response to the two treatments. As we had hypothesized, the main analyses linking treatment and retention found stronger moderation (ATIs) for the WdHw pattern than the HdWw pattern, especially when DW was rated during the couple's discussion of the husband's drinking. This supports the idea that WdHw may have special prognostic significance because it foreshadows the drinker's reluctant response to a demanding treatment—and WdHw is most relevant when the couple discusses drinking, because in this context the wife may more often demand change.

Couple Affect

Although the DW results suggest that moderation of treatment response was to some extent specific to the WdHw pattern assessed during the drinking discussion, we also considered the possibility that the general quality of a couple's relationship might moderate response to CBT versus FST as much or more than specific patterns of DW. Indeed, there are suggestions in both the empirical and clinical literature (e.g., Goldman & Greenberg, 1992; Todd, 1986) that systemic and strategic couple therapies may be generally advantageous with highly troubled or resistant couples. If so, couple attributes such as communication quality or the ratio of positive to negative couple affect—which according to Gottman (1994) predicts divorce—might predict differential response to our two treatments just as well as DW.

To test this idea, we repeated the ATI analyses using as moderator variables (a) the ratio of positive to negative affect expressed during the conflict and drinking discussions, based on codes from the Marital Interaction Coding System (MICS; Weiss & Summers, 1983); and (b) a pretreatment questionnaire measure of "constructive communication" (Heavey, Larson, Christensen, & Zumtobel, 1996) completed by both partners. The direction of results from these analyses paralleled those obtained for DW, although ATIs were statistically robust only for couple affect observed during the drinking discussion and not for the conflict discussion or for the report measure of communication quality (Shoham et al., 1998). However, in a related thesis project investigating predictors of treatment dropout in this same data set, Stickle (1997) was able to obtain a substantial moderation effect (strong prediction of dropout in CBT and none in FST) using a composite measure of couple affect that included global observational ratings and self-report items in addition to the MICS data.

The couple affect results thus leave open the possibility that relational moderation in this project was not limited to specific DW patterns, but was more broadly relevant to troubled (versus successful) couple functioning. This may not be surprising, given that DW is widely regarded as a key marker of troubled relationships—and in fact, the observational DW and negative affect measures were moderately correlated in the couples we studied. If having a troubled relationship is a *general* moderator of treatment response, however, we might expect ATIs to occur across discussion contexts, which they did not. Other behavioral markers of relational quality might therefore be worth examining as well.

Interactional Synchrony

Several years ago we became interested in *interactional synchrony,* an indicator of dyadic rapport characterized by nonverbal coordination in rhythm, simultaneous movement, and behavioral meshing (Bernieri & Rosenthal, 1991; Tickle-Degnen & Rosenthal, 1990). So far, nonverbal synchrony has been studied primarily in complementary dyads (e.g., mother–child, physician–patient). Given its conceptual and operational definition, however, we suspected that interactional synchrony between partners in a committed relationship might complement more transparent self-report measures of relational quality and correlate with other behavioral measures such as observed DW and couple affect. Furthermore, in line with the ATI hypotheses described earlier, we also suspected that couples low on interactional synchrony would benefit less from CBT than from FST.

Interactional synchrony is unique because its measurement relies solely on partners' nonverbal behavior. Synchrony differs from most other dyadic relationship measures in that (a) it is purely relational, addressing the way partners coordinate their interaction rather than coding separately what each partner says or does toward the other; and (b) it is largely nonreactive, because interactants typically have little awareness of the nonverbal dimensions being assessed. In the alcohol project, trained raters were able to code synchrony reliably from silent videotapes of the pretreatment marital interaction tasks, so that we had this additional measure of couple functioning to examine as a potential moderator of treatment response.

To our surprise, interactional synchrony was essentially unrelated to the measures of DW, constructive communication, and the ratio of positive to negative affect used in previous ATI analyses. At the same time, we found that synchrony as a relational moderator produced significant ATIs for both retention and drinking outcomes. The pattern was similar to the ATI for DW, except here the regression lines crossed, indicating that high-synchrony couples benefited more from CBT, while those lower in synchrony tended to do better in FST (Trost, Shoham, & Rohrbaugh, 1997). Because synchrony was uncorrelated with DW, it was also possible to compare the moderating effects of these two relational variables in the same regression equations. The results suggested that nonverbal synchrony and DW made independent contributions to predicting differential response to the two treatments.

Thus, the synchrony analyses further highlight the importance of relational moderators in ATI research and support our general finding that high-demand CBT was a poor match for difficult, distressed, disconnected couples. The results also underscore the potential value of nonreactive, nonverbal measures of couple interaction: Nonverbal synchrony apparently captures a different facet of a couple relationship than other observational measures that focus on DW or the positivity or negativity of couple affect.

Symptom–System Fit

The last relational moderator construct we investigated, called *symptom–system fit* (SSF), is perhaps the most interesting conceptually but also the most difficult to measure. We based the construct on observations that alcohol abuse sometimes has adaptive relational consequences for couples and families that can, in effect, reinforce and perpetuate problem drinking (Jacob & Leonard, 1988; Steinglass, Bennett, Wolin, & Reiss, 1987; Steinglass, Davis, & Berenson, 1977). For example, in clinical observations of conjointly hospitalized "alcoholic couples" during sobriety and intoxication, Steinglass et al. (1977) noted apparent benefits of "wet" (intoxicated) family interaction compared to "dry" (sober) interaction (e.g., increased or decreased intimacy or affect) that varied from couple to couple. More rigorous documentation of adaptive consequences comes from daily diary studies showing that the spouses of some (but not all) alcoholics report *decreased* marital satisfaction following reductions in drinking (Dunn, Jacob, Hummon, & Seilhamer, 1987) and from experimental evidence that some (but not all) couples actually show improved problem-solving behavior when the problem drinker is intoxicated (Jacob & Leonard, 1988). Whether drinking has positive or negative relational consequences may vary with the pattern (steady versus episodic) and location of consumption, as well as characteristics of the drinker (Leonard, 1990), although evidence on these points has not been consistent.

From our perspective, an implication of the heterogeneous links between drinking and marital interaction is that alcohol-involved couples vary considerably in the extent to which drinking "fits" (i.e., helps to maintain and support) their relational system. For some—perhaps most—couples with an alcoholic partner, drinking is clearly an invader or irritant to the relationship; yet for others drinking appears to be more of a friend or ally—a kind of lubricant that promotes positive relational stability, at least in the short run, but a stability that may ultimately be dysfunctional. We reasoned that placing couples along such a continuum of SSF might help to predict how they would respond to different treatments. For couples to whom drinking is "relationship syntonic" (high SSF), it may be especially important to address systemic relationship patterns (cf. Steinglass et al., 1987) and to anticipate that drinking cessation may be disruptive and require realignment of family relationships. On the other hand, when drinking is "relationship dystonic" (low SSF), a more direct, drinker-focused approach should be at least as effective as a therapy focusing on couple and family relationships. We therefore predicted that SSF should moderate response to CBT and FST, such that high SSF (syntonic) couples should benefit more from FST than from CBT, but that the treatments should do equally well for (dystonic) couples low on SSF.

Although an ATI hypothesis about SSF seemed to make good sense, finding a satisfactory operational definition of this moderator construct was another matter. It was not possible to have clients drink in the laboratory before entering treatment or even to collect the kind of intensive diary data that could document associations between drinking and marital functioning. It also seemed that direct, self-report approaches to measuring SSF would risk socially desirable responses (and no such measures were available), so we opted to do content analyses of how each couple discussed the husband's drinking problem in the pretreatment marital interaction task. Trained raters reviewed tapes and transcripts of these discussions and coded references to positive and negative consequences of drinking and not drinking, both for the partners individually and as a couple. In this way, we were able to generate a reliable, couple-level measure of SSF to use in the ATI analyses. As it turned out, the judges found much more evidence of the dystonic than the syntonic SSF pattern, but they coded at least some adaptive relational consequences of drinking for about half of the couples.

The ATI results were inconclusive. As expected, SSF scores were not strongly related to the other moderator dimensions (DW, couple affect, and synchrony). Unfortunately, although means and correlations were in the expected direction, the predicted ATI effects all fell short of statistical significance. Thus, we could not confirm the hypothesis that relational SSF moderated response to the two treatments.

Conclusion

The main lesson from this research is that attributes of couple and family re-lationships can predict differential response to clearly distinctive couple treat-ments for alcohol abuse. We believe this finding illustrates a promising new direction for ATI research and, in the wake of Project MATCH, provides a useful counterpoint to the new skepticism about matching alcoholic clients to treat-ments. Although family psychologists will not be surprised by evidence that "context matters," the psychotherapy and substance abuse fields have been slow to look beyond the individual client when offering guidelines for selecting dif-ferent treatments. Basing recommendations for matching on unreplicated find-ings would of course be premature. If substantiated, however, our results would suggest that clinicians exercise caution in using high-demand treatments with highly distressed, alcohol-involved couples embroiled in DW interaction cycles.

Some limitations of this study of relational moderators deserve comment: First, high levels of missing data, especially at follow-up, makes it difficult to draw firm conclusions about drinking outcomes or the durability of ATIs. Still, the clear ATIs for dropout and number of sessions completed are notable in their own right, and retention appears to be a meaningful proxy for favorable longer-term response to alcoholism treatments (Stark, 1992). A second question that is pertinent to generalizability concerns the extent to which our CBT and FST treatments are representative of other treatments carrying the "cognitive–behavioral" and "family systems" brand names. Indeed, some cognitive and behavioral therapies (e.g., Miller, Zweben, DiClemente, & Rychtarik, 1992; Christensen et al., 1995) incorporate low-demand intervention techniques, and some alcohol treatments based on family systems principles (e.g., Liepman, Nirenberg, & Begin, 1989) are undoubtedly more confrontational than Rohr-baugh et al.'s (1995) brand of FST. The representativeness question may be most important for CBT, where the relational variables we studied were most prognostic of treatment response. Based on process ratings and a careful reading of treatment manuals, we suspect that the Wakefield et al. (1996) CBT used here may have placed less emphasis on relationship issues and altering alcohol-related interactions than the evidence-based behavioral couple therapies for alcoholism developed by O'Farrell et al. (1985) and McCrady et al. (1986). The CBT may also have been more cognitive than O'Farrell's and McCrady's treat-ments. In most respects, however, we believe our CBT and FST treatments were faithful to their respective traditions.

Our examination of multiple moderator constructs leaves ambiguous the question of how much the observed ATIs reflected specific couple interaction patterns such as the WdHw sequence, as opposed to more general aspects of couple functioning. On one hand, the specific WdHw pattern appeared to mod-erate how these couples responded to the two treatments much more strongly than the opposite HdWw pattern. But there was also some evidence that more general indicators of relationship quality such as nonverbal synchrony and couple affect predicted differential treatment response, while SSF—a relational construct concerned with type rather than level of dysfunction—did not. Future findings that measures of general couple functioning produce ATIs would be consistent with a central theme in the clinical literature on matching and tailoring couple and family interventions to client attributes (Carlson et al., 1997) —namely that severity of *relationship problems* should guide decisions about what to do for whom.

One might also wonder how the various moderator variables interacted with each other in predicting differential outcome. Of the four moderator constructs we examined, only DW and couple affect were substantially correlated, and at least two of the four moderators appeared to make independent (unique) contributions to ATIs. We did not attempt to identify higher-order interactions because of the modest sample size and our own limited capacity for interpreting complexity. As Cronbach (1975) put it: "Once we attend to interactions, we enter a hall of mirrors that extends to infinity. However far we carry our analysis —to third order or fifth order or any other—untested interactions of a still higher order can be envisioned" (p. 119). Such potential complexity is a downside of ATI research and may contribute to replication failures because replications inevitably entail some variation in client or family characteristics. And of course these characteristics can interact with each other regardless of whether we measure (Shoham-Salomon & Hannah, 1991).

Where might family ATI research go from here? To this point we have emphasized expanding the "A side" of the paradigm to capture relevant relational moderator variables, but should also note that ATI studies of individual therapy have given much more attention to client attributes than to what specific treatments those attributes should interact with. In fact, the "T" in psychotherapy research is often a large, multifaceted package (like our own CBT and FST) that incorporates a variety of therapeutic components. Yet as Shulman (1981) pointed out some time ago, "Why should we expect to find generalizable interactions (ATIs) when we measure aptitudes with a micrometer and treatments with a divining rod?"

Elsewhere we have suggested that ATI researchers distinguish treatment models or packages ("big T's") from specific treatment interventions or techniques ("little t's") and concentrate on the latter (Shoham & Rohrbaugh, 1995). Despite some notable big T applications, the most promising ATI results in individual psychotherapy research have come from little t designs, where the little t's were clearly operationalized specific interventions that were conceptually linked to specific client attributes (cf. Daldrup, Beutler, Engle, & Greenberg, 1988; Ost, Jerremalm, & Johansson, 1984; Shoham-Salomon, Avner, & Neeman, 1989). Most of these were also relatively short-term interventions, with outcomes assessed after only a few sessions. The same (little t) focus should be a promising direction for couple and family ATI research, although our own (big T) study is perhaps not the best example of how to do this. It would be better, in our view, to investigate differential indications for such little t's as problem- versus solution-focused interviewing, relational- versus diagnosis-centered reframing of the presenting complaint, acceptance interventions versus problem-solving training, and emotion-focused (arousing) versus defocused (calming) interventions for couples.

The prospect of studying little t's runs counter to the idea that we should investigate integrative, broad-band, multicomponent treatment packages that combine relational, individual, and even biological and community interventions, particularly for problems such as substance abuse, schizophrenia, and conduct disorder (Liddle & Dakof, 1995; Pinsoff, 1995; Pinsoff & Wynne, 1995). With such difficult problems, the argument goes, no single approach to intervention is likely to be sufficient; thus more treatment (in terms of both type and amount) should be necessary for optimal results. Interest in comprehensive, integrative treatments is an understandable reaction against the ideological excesses and parochialism of brand-name therapies. And more important, several multicomponent, integrative packages—including treatments for substance abuse (Henggler et al., 1991; Liddle & Dakof, 1995) and schizophrenia (Goldstein & Miklowitz, 1995) have well-documented efficacy. From a scientific perspective, however, such broad-band, "kitchen sink" approaches to treatment pose several problems. For example, without dismantling designs or some other strategy for intramodel comparisons (Jacobson & Addis, 1993), it is difficult to know which aspects of the integrative package make a difference for whom or how the various components (alone or in combination) actually work.

It is also possible that, for some clients, a more minimal treatment will be as effective, or even more effective, than an intensive or comprehensive one. The alcohol treatment literature provides several hints of this, dating from Orford and Edward's (1977) classic study showing that for some (nongamma) alcoholics, a single session of brief advice was more beneficial than extensive treatment (cf. Babor & Grant, 1992). In a study relevant to possible relational moderation, Azrin, Sisson, Meyers, and Godley (1982) compared various levels of treatment comprehensiveness that ranged from brief, spouse-involved "disulfiram assurance" (contracting to use Antabuse) to a multicomponent package involving not only Antabuse and behavior therapy but extensive training of the drinker's family members and friends following Azrin's community reinforcement approach. Whereas single alcoholics benefited most from the full package, those who were married did just as well with minimalist, spouse-involved Antabuse contracting as with the far more extensive and costly community reinforcement approach (cf. Baucom et al., 1998). Similarly, in our own clinical work with alcohol-involved couples, we sense that the brief problem- and solution-focused therapy approaches described by Berg and Miller (1992) and Fisch (1986) may be more useful for some cases than for others—and the ATI paradigm challenges us to identify conditions under which such parsimonious interventions may be sufficient.

A related direction for family ATI research concerns the empirical foundations for therapy integration. Proponents of integration believe that "by integrating the best constructs, clinical strategies, and techniques from the various psychotherapeutic orientations, we will advance the comprehensiveness of our effective treatments" (Wolfe, 1994, p. 165). But how do we know what the "best constructs, clinical strategies, and techniques" really are? And how will we know which interventions and techniques are best for whom? The answer, of course, is through ATI research. Furthermore, the distinction between little t's and big T's might help to clarify what seems to us a fundamental issue in therapy integration—namely, the extent to which an intervention from one therapy model (or conceptual context) can be imported to another (integrative) context without compromising its effectiveness (Shoham & Rohrbaugh, 1996). In our view, this is an important but unanswered empirical question. For example, do little t interventions like solution-focused interviewing, couple communication training, or relational reframing retain their effectiveness for a particular type of patient or problem, regardless of the larger (big T) context in which they are applied?

If statistical interaction between little t's and big T's reveals evidence of *contextual moderation,* such that the effectiveness of a specific intervention depends on the larger model or package in which it is applied, one would wonder about the empirical legitimacy of decontextualizing specific intervention (little t) techniques by using them in other (big T) contexts. On the other hand, the absence of contextual moderation would place the practice of technical eclecticism on firmer ground. In the study described here, we found tentative evidence that therapist demandingness—a key process dimension that clearly distinguished the two treatments—had a different relationship with outcome in CBT from what it did in FST. Ironically, within the low-demand FST treatment, relatively higher levels of demand predicted better response, while the opposite tended to be true for high-demand CBT. Although therapist demandingness per se is not a little t intervention, this intriguing finding suggests that dimensions of therapist behavior cannot be reliably substituted for treatments in the ATI equation and that the meaning and impact of specific therapist behaviors may depend on the broader framework in which they are applied.

To summarize, we have presented evidence that context matters in family intervention science, not only in understanding problems in contextual (systemic) terms, but also in predicting what will work for whom. How clients respond to different interventions may depend on attributes of their couple and family relationships as much or more as it depends on their attributes as individuals. Even for alcohol problems, where individual-focused ATI research has yielded few dividends, attending to relational moderators appears to hold promise for matching clients to treatment—at least when the unit of treatment involves more than one person.

References

Azrin, N. H., Sisson, R. W., Meyers, R., & Godley, M. (1982). Alcoholism treatment by disufiram and community reinforcement therapy. *Journal of Behavior Therapy and Experimental Psychiatry, 13,* 105–112.

Babor, T. F., & Grant, M. (1992). Combined analysis of outcome data: The cross-national generalizability of brief interventions. Report on phase II: A randomized clinical trial of brief interventions in primary health care. *WHO collaborating investigators project on identification and management of alcohol-related problems* (Technical report). Copenhagen: World Health Organization.

Barlow, D. H., O'Brien, F. T., & Last, C. G. (1984). Couples treatment of agoraphobia: Initial outcome. In K. D. Craig & R. J. McMahon (Eds.), *Advances in clinical behavior therapy.* New York: Brunner/Mazel.

Baucom, D. H., Shoham, V., Mueser, K. T., Daiuto, A. D., & Stickle, T. R. (1998). Empirically supported couple and family interventions for adult mental health problems. *Journal of Consulting and Clinical Psychology, 66,* 53–88.

Beckham, E. E. (1990). Psychotherapy of depression research at a crossroads: Directions for the 1990s. *Clinical Psychology Review, 10,* 207–228.

Bellack, A. S., & Meuser, K. T. (1993). Psychosocial treatment for schizophrenia. *Schizophrenia Bulletin, 19,* 317–336.

Bepko, C., & Krestan, J. (1985). *The responsibility trap: A blueprint for treating the alcoholic family.* New York: Free Press.

Berg, I. K., & Miller, S. D. (1992). *Working with the problem drinker: A solution-focused approach.* New York: Norton.

Bernieri, F. J., & Rosenthal, R. (1991). Coordinated movement in human interaction. In R. S. Feldman & B. Rime (Eds.), *Fundamentals of nonverbal behavior* (pp. 401–431). New York: Cambridge University Press.

Beutler, L. E. (1991). Have all won and must all have prizes? Revisiting Luborsky et al.'s verdict. *Journal of Consulting and Clinical Psychology, 59,* 226–232.

Beutler, L. E., Patterson, C., Jacob, T., Shoham, V., Yost, L., & Rohrbaugh, M. J. (1993). Matching treatment to alcoholism subtypes. *Psychotherapy, 30,* 463–472.

Beutler, L. E., Shoham, V., Jacob, T., & Rohrbaugh, M. J. (1997). *Family versus behavioral treatment of alcoholism.* A final report on Grant No. 1 RO 11108486. Washington, DC: National Institute on Alcoholism and Alcohol Abuse.

Carlson, J., Sperry, L., & Lewis, J. A. (1997). *Family therapy: Ensuring treatment efficacy.* Pacific Grove, CA: Brooks/Cole.

Christensen, A., & Heavey, C. L. (1990). Gender and social structure in the demand/withdraw pattern of marital interaction. *Journal of Personality and Social Psychology, 59,* 73–81.

Christensen, A., & Heavey, C. L. (1993). Gender differences in marital conflict: The demand/withdraw interaction pattern. In S. Oskamp & M. Costanzo (Eds.), *Gender issues in contemporary society* (pp. 113–141). Newbury Park, CA: Sage.

Christensen, A., Jacobson, N. S., & Babcock, J. C. (1995). Integrative behavioral couple therapy. In N. S. Jacobson & A. S. Gurman (Eds.), *Clinical handbook of couple therapy* (pp. 31–64). New York: Guilford Press.

Coyne, J. C., & Liddle, H. A. (1992). The future of systems therapy: Shedding myths and facing opportunities. *Psychotherapy, 29,* 44–50.

Cronbach, L. (1975). Beyond the two disciplines of scientific psychology. *American Psychologist, 30,* 116–126.

Cronbach, L. J., & Snow, R. E. (1977). *Aptitudes and instructional methods: A handbook for research on interactions.* New York: Irvington.

Daldrup, R. J., Beutler, L. E., Engle, D., & Greenberg, L. S. (1988). *Focused expressive psychotherapy: Freeing the overcontrolled patient.* New York: Guilford Press.

Dance, K. A., & Neufeld, R. W. J. (1988). Aptitude–treatment interaction research in the clinical setting: A review of attempts to dispel the "patient uniformity" myth. *Psychological Bulletin, 104,* 192–213.

Dunn, N. J., Jacob, T., Hummon, N., & Seilhamer, R. A. (1987). Marital stability in alcoholic-spouse relationships as a function of drinking pattern and location. *Journal of Abnormal Psychology, 96,* 99–107.

Epstein, E. E., McGrady, B. S., Miller, K. J., & Steinberg, M. (1994). Attrition from conjoint alcoholism treatment: Do dropouts differ from completers? *Journal of Substance Abuse, 6,* 249–265.

Fisch, R. (1986). The brief treatment of alcoholism. *Journal of Strategic and Systemic Therapies, 5,* 40–49.

Garfield, S. L. (1990). Issues and methods in psychotherapy research. *Journal of Consulting and Clinical Psychology, 58,* 273–280.

Goldman, A., & Greenberg, L. (1992). Comparison of integrated systemic and emotionally focused approaches to couples therapy. *Journal of Consulting and Clinical Psychology, 60,* 962–969.

Goldstein, M. J., & Miklowitz, D. J. (1995). The effectiveness of psychoeducational family therapy in the treatment of schizophrenic disorders. *Journal of Marital and Family Therapy, 21,* 361–376.

Gottman, J. M. (1994). *What predicts divorce? The relationship between marital processes and marital outcome.* Hillsdale, NJ: Erlbaum.

Heavey, C. L., Larson, B., Christensen, A., & Zumtobel, D. C. (1996). The communication patterns questionnaire: The reliability and validity of a constructive communication subscale. *Journal of Marriage and the Family, 58,* 796–800.

Heavey, C. L., Layne, C., & Christensen, A. (1993). Gender and conflict structure in marital interaction: A replication and extension. *Journal of Consulting and Clinical Psychology, 61,* 16–27.

Henggeler, S. W., Borduin, C. M., Melton, G. B., Mann, B. G., Smith, L. A., Hall, J. A., Cone, L., & Fucci, B. R. (1991). Effects of multisystemic therapy on drug use and abuse in serious juvenile offenders: A progress report from two outcome studies. *Family Dynamics of Addiction Quarterly, 1,* 40–51.

Hooley, J. M. (1986). Expressed emotion and depression: Interactions between patients high versus low EE spouses. *Journal of Abnormal Psychology, 95,* 237–246.

Jacob, T., & Leonard, K. (1988). Alcoholic-spouse interaction as a function of alcoholism subtype and alcohol consumption interaction. *Journal of Abnormal Psychology, 97,* 231–237.

Jacobson, N. S., & Addis, M. E. (1993). Research on couples and couples therapy: What do we know? Where are we going? *Journal of Consulting and Clinical Psychology, 61,* 85–93.

Jacobson, N. S., Follette, W. C., & Pagel, M. (1986). Predicting who will benefit from behavioral marital therapy. *Journal of Consulting and Clinical Psychology, 54,* 518–522.

Kadden, R. M., Cooney, N. L., Getter, H., & Litt, M. D. (1989). Matching alcoholics to coping skills or interactional therapies: Posttreatment results. *Journal of Consulting and Clinical Psychology, 57,* 698–704.

Klinetob, N. A., & Smith, D. A. (1996). Demand–withdraw communication in marital interaction: Test of interspousal contingency and gender role hypotheses. *Journal of Marriage and the Family, 58,* 945–957.

Leonard, K. E. (1990). Marital functioning among steady and episodic alcoholics. In R. L. Collins, K. E. Leonard, & J. S. Searles (Eds.), *Alcohol and the family: Research and clinical perspectives* (pp. 220–243). New York: Guilford Press.

Liddle, H. A., & Dakof, G. A. (1995). Family therapy for drug abuse: Promising but not definitive. *Journal of Marital and Family Therapy, 4,* 511–544.

Liepman, M. R., Nirenberg, T. D., & Begin, A. M. (1989). Evaluation of a program designed to help family and significant others to motivate resistant alcoholics into recovery. *American Journal of Drug and Alcohol Abuse, 15,* 209–221.

Longabaugh, R., Wirtz, P. W., Beattie, M. C., Noel, N., & Stout, R. (1995). Matching treatment focus to patient social investment and support: 18-month follow-up results. *Journal of Consulting and Clinical Psychology, 63,* 296–307.

Luborsky, L., Singer, B., & Luborsky, L. (1975). Comparative studies of psychotherapies: Is it true that "everyone has won and all much have prizes"? *Archives of General Psychiatry, 32,* 995–1008.

McCrady, B. S., & Epstein, E. E. (1995). Directions for research on alcoholic relationships: Marital- and individual-based models of heterogeneity. *Psychology of Addictive Behaviors, 9,* 157–166.

McCrady, B. S., Noel, N. E., Abrams, D. B., Stout, R. L., Nelson, H. G., & Hay, W. M. (1986). Comparative effectiveness of three types of spouse involvement in outpatient behavioral alcoholism treatment. *Journal of Studies on Alcohol, 47,* 459–467.

Miller, W. R., Zweben, A., DiClemente, C. C., & Rychtarik, R. G. (1992). *Motivational enhancement therapy manual: A clinical research guide for therapists treating individuals with alcohol abuse and dependence.* NIAAA Project MATCH Monograph (Vol. 2), DHHS Publication No. (ADM) 92-1894. Washington, DC: U.S. Government Printing Office.

O'Farrell, T. J., Choquette, K. A., & Cutter, H. S. G. (1998). Couples relapse prevention sessions after behavioral marital therapy for alcoholics and their wives: Outcomes during three years after starting treatment. *Journal of Studies on Alcohol, 59,* 357–370.

O'Farrell, T. J., Cutter, H. S. G., & Floyd, F. J. (1985). Evaluating behavioral marital therapy for male alcoholics: Effects on marital adjustment and communication from before to after treatment. *Behavior Therapy, 16,* 147–167.

Olson, D. H. (1986). Circumplex model VII: Validation studies and FACES III. *Family Process, 25,* 337–351.

Orford, J., & Edwards, G. (1977). *Alcoholism: A comparison of treatment and advice within a study of the influence of marriage.* London: Oxford University Press.

Ost, L., Jerremalm, A., & Johansson, J. (1984). Individual response pattern and the effects of different behavioral methods in the treatment of agoraphobia. *Behaviour Research and Therapy, 22,* 697–707.

Ouimette, P. C., Finney, J. W., & Moos, R. H. (1997). Twelve-step and cognitive–behavioral treatment for substance abuse: A comparison of treatment effectiveness. *Journal of Consulting and Clinical Psychology, 65,* 230–240.

Pinsof, W. M. (1995). *Integrative problem-centered therapy: A synthesis of biological, individual, and family therapies.* New York: Basic Books.

Pinsof, W. M., & Wynne, L. C. (1995). The efficacy of marital and family therapy: An empirical overview, conclusions, and recommendations. *Journal of Marital and Family Therapy, 21,* 585–613.

Project MATCH Research Group. (1997). Matching alcoholism treatments to client heterogeneity: Project MATCH posttreatment drinking outcome. *Journal of Studies on Alcohol, 58,* 7–29.

Rohrbaugh, M., Shoham, V., Racioppo, M., & Stickle, T. (1996, June). *Relational moderators of engagement in systemic versus cognitive–behavioral therapy for problem drinking.* Paper presented at meeting of the Society for Psychotherapy Research, Amelia Island, FL.

Rohrbaugh, M. J., Shoham, V., Spungen, C., & Steinglass, P. (1995). Family systems therapy in practice: A systemic couples therapy for problem drinking. In B. Bongar & L. E. Beutler (Eds.), *Comprehensive textbook of psychotherapy: Theory and practice* (pp. 228–253). New York: Oxford University Press.

Shoham, V., & Rohrbaugh, M. J. (1995). Aptitude x treatment interaction (ATI) research: Sharpening the focus, widening the lens. In M. Aveline & D. Shapiro (Eds.), *Research foundations for psychotherapy practice* (pp. 73–95). Sussex, England: Wiley.

Shoham, V., & Rohrbaugh, M. J. (1996). Promises and perils of empirically supported psychotherapy integration. *Journal of Psychotherapy Integration, 6,* 191–206.

Shoham, V., Rohrbaugh, M. J., Stickle, T. R., & Jacob, T. (1998). Demand–withdraw couple interaction moderates retention in cognitive–behavioral vs. family-systems treatments for alcoholism. *Journal of Family Psychology, 12,* 557–577.

Shoham-Salomon, V., Avner, R., & Neeman, R. (1989). You are changed if you do and changed if you don't: Mechanisms underlying paradoxical interventions. *Journal of Consulting and Clinical Psychology, 57,* 590–598.

Shoham-Salomon, V., & Hannah, M. T. (1991). Client–treatment interactions in the study of differential change processes. *Journal of Consulting and Clinical Psychology, 59,* 217–225.

Shulman, L. S. (1981, August). *Educational psychology returns to school (G. Stanley Hall Series).* Paper presented at the 89th Annual Convention of the American Psychological Association, Los Angeles.

Smith, B., & Sechrest, L. (1991). Treatment of aptitude x treatment interactions. *Journal of Consulting and Clinical Psychology, 59,* 233–244.

Snow, R. E. (1991). Aptitude–treatment interaction as a framework for research on individual differences in psychotherapy. *Journal of Consulting and Clinical Psychology, 59,* 205–216.

Sobell, L. C., & Sobell, M. B. (1992). Timeline followback: A technique for assessing self-reported alcohol consumption. In R. Litten & J. Allen (Eds.), *Measuring alcohol consumption.* Totowa, NJ; Numana Press.

Stark, M. J. (1992). Dropping out of substance abuse treatment: A clinically oriented review. *Clinical Psychology Review, 12,* 93–116.

Steinglass, P., Bennett, L. A., Wolin, S. J., & Reiss, D. (1987). *The alcoholic family.* New York: Basic Books.

Steinglass, P., Davis, D. I., & Berenson, D. (1977). Observations of conjointly hospitalized "alcoholic couples" during sobriety and intoxication: Implications for theory and therapy. *Family Process, 16,* 1–16.

Stickle, T. R. (1997). *Does what predicts divorce predict dropout from couples alcoholism treatment? The role of couple affect.* Unpublished master's thesis, University of Arizona.

Stiles, W. B., Shapiro, D. A., & Elliot, R. K. (1986). Are all psychotherapies equivalent? *American Psychologist, 41,* 165–180.

Tailoring Treatments for Alcoholics Is Not the Answer. (1997, February). *APA Monitor, 6,* 1.

Tickle-Degnen, L., & Rosenthal, R. (1990). The nature of rapport and its nonverbal correlates. *Psychological Inquiry, 1,* 285–293.

Todd, T. C. (1986). Structural–strategic marital therapy. In N. S. Jacobson & A. S. Gurman (Eds.), *Clinical handbook of marital therapy* (pp. 71–105). New York: Guilford Press.

Trost, S., Shoham, V., & Rohrbaugh, M. J. (1997, December). *Interactional synchrony between partners moderates response to couple therapies.* Paper presented at the meeting of the North American Society for Psychotherapy Research, Tucson, AZ.

Wakefield, P., Williams, R. E., Yost, E., & Patterson, K. M. (1996). *Couples therapy for alcoholism: A cognitive–behavioral treatment manual.* New York: Guilford Press.

Watzlawick, P., Beavin, J., & Jackson, D. D. (1967). *Pragmatics of human communication.* New York: Norton.

Watzlawick, P., Weakland, J. H., & Fisch, R. (1974). *Change: Principles of problem formation and problem resolution.* New York: Norton.

Weiss, R. L., & Summers, K. J. (1983). Marital Interaction Coding System-III. In E. E. Filsiger (Ed.), *A sourcebook of marriage and family assessment* (pp. 85–115). Beverly Hills, CA: Sage.

Wolfe, B. E. (1994). Adapting psychotherapy outcome research to clinical reality. *Journal of Psychotherapy Integration, 4,* 160–166.

CHAPTER 12

Linking Basic and Applied Research in a Prevention Science Process

Marion S. Forgatch
Nancy M. Knutson

> "If you want to understand something, try to change it."
>
> —Walter Fenno Dearborn

When prevention science reflects an integration of basic research and practical application within a theoretical model, scientific method, intervention procedures, and theory all benefit. Such approaches make it possible to test both the efficacy of an intervention program and the theoretical model on which the intervention is based (Reid & Eddy, 1997). The outcomes of these experimental manipulations yield confirmations, disconfirmations, surprises, and puzzles, which lead to future refinements in knowledge and method through an iterative process.

The early stages in any scientific process tend to be crude. Beginning studies are exploratory, hypotheses are broadly defined, methodology is rough, and intervention trials are weak tests. With progress, the theory is refined: Hypotheses that survive early trials are better specified, erroneous hypotheses are purged, and alternative hypotheses are added. Intervention procedures are also shaped through iteration: Some components are eliminated and some promising dimensions are introduced. At the same time, the research methods improve: Measurement strategies become more precise, robust, and generalizable; and analytic procedures become more focused and advanced. This iterative process with clinical studies to treat mental health problems began several decades ago with substantial government research funding. Support for preventing mental health problems is more recent. For example, the first National Institute of

Support for this project was provided by Grant Nos. RO1 MH38318, RO1 MH54703, and P50 MH46690 from the Child and Adolescent Treatment and Preventive Intervention Research Branch, Division of Services and Intervention Research, National Institute of Mental Health, U.S. Public Health Service.

Mental Health (NIMH) Prevention Intervention Research Center (PIRC) was funded in 1983 (Mrazek & Haggerty, 1994). This chapter describes ways in which the group at Oregon Social Learning Center (OSLC) has linked basic research and practical application within prevention science.

Lessons Learned From Clinical Efforts

In the 1950s, Gerald Patterson worked with youngsters in a residential treatment setting using procedures based on psychoanalytic theory. Although the children learned to behave appropriately in the highly structured institutional setting, recidivism was a serious problem. The home environment seemed implicated in the children's adjustment difficulties. Influenced by the exciting new work of Barker (1951, 1963), Patterson and his colleagues went into the homes of maladjusted youngsters to discover what mechanisms might be involved. This field observation in the naturalistic environment led to advances in observational methodology and treatment procedures (Reid, 1970, 1978). The observations suggested that parents directly (although inadvertently) train their youngsters in the behaviors involved in their maladjustment. The combination of direct observation of family process and treatment of clinical problems stimulated growth in three areas: hypothesis development, treatment techniques, and methodology to evaluate the process and outcome of intervention. Thus, the OSLC model of basic research, theory, and practical application began within the context of a focused set of mental health problems (i.e., conduct and co-occurring problems).

During the 1960s, several teams of investigators began to develop behaviorally based parent management training procedures for families of children with conduct disorders (Hawkins, Peterson, Schweid, & Bijou, 1966; Patterson & Brodsky, 1966; Wahler, Winkle, Peterson, & Morrison, 1965). Since then, this approach to treatment has flourished. Reviews of the literature agree that parent management training for conduct problems has produced positive effects that are consistently replicated (Dumas, 1989; Kazdin, Esveldt-Dawson, French, & Unis, 1987; Lipsey & Wilson, 1993; McMahon & Wells, 1989). However, it has proved extremely expensive to treat conduct disorders once they are well established (Bank, Marlowe, Reid, Patterson, & Weinrott, 1991). This fact coupled with a general change in the zeitgeist among mental health professionals has resulted in a noticeable shift from treatment to prevention.

A Social Interactional Learning Model

The theoretical model that emerged through the clinical science process is the link between basic research and practical application in prevention science at

OSLC. The model represents the merging of two theoretical streams: social interaction and social learning. Both perspectives emphasize the influence of the social environment on an individual's overall adjustment. The social interactional dimension describes connections among family members at microsocial levels. The focus on conduct problems as a research question has led to detailed studies of coercive interpersonal processes. The social learning dimension addresses the question of how behavioral patterns become established (e.g., reinforcing contingencies). A macro model based on positive parenting practices was constructed to address this issue. The key assumption is that these positive parenting practices control the reinforcing contingencies that occur in families. At a more molar level, the model incorporates contexts that influence parenting practices and thereby indirectly influence child outcomes. This ecological perspective is treated through mediational analyses. Thus, background contexts are presumed to affect youngsters' adjustment through their impact on parenting practices.

As shown in Figure 12-1, the adjustment of youngsters is enveloped in two layers of context, one provided by parents and one by contextual factors. The most proximal layer is expressed in terms of positive and coercive parenting practices, which are presumed to shape the adjustment of the youngsters. On the left-hand side of the shield are positive parenting practices (i.e., discipline, monitoring, positive involvement, problem solving, and skill encouragement). Each practice is presumed to make a unique contribution to adjustment and to operate in concert with one another. On the right-hand side are coercive parenting practices (i.e., negative reciprocity, escalation, and negative reinforcement) that erode healthy adjustment. The layer of parenting practices is surrounded by contexts that can affect youngsters by influencing the quality of parenting. Thus, the contexts are more distal to youngsters' adjustment than are parenting practices.

Parenting Practices

Parents determine the social environment at home and influence the social settings their children will experience away from home. Parental management of social environments consist of the set of positive practices that the interventions seek to strengthen. Longitudinal analyses using multiple-method assessment and path modeling have shown that deficits in these parenting skills predict conduct problems and other adjustment difficulties for children and adolescents. These negative outcomes include antisocial behavior, academic failure, deviant peer association, delinquency, and depressed mood (Capaldi, 1992; Conger, Patterson, & Ge, 1995; DeGarmo & Forgatch, 2000; DeGarmo, Forgatch, & Martinez, 1999; Dishion, Andrews, & Crosby, 1995; Forgatch & DeGarmo, 1999, in press).

FIGURE 12-1

A Social Interactional Learning Model

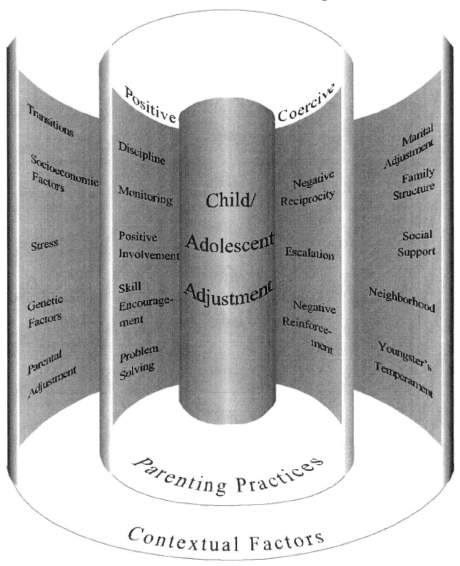

A social interactional learning model.

The positive parenting skills and their applications have been described in detail elsewhere (e.g., Chamberlain, 1994; Dishion & Patterson, 1996; Forgatch & Patterson, 1989; Patterson & Forgatch, 1987). Briefly, *skill encouragement* promotes prosocial development through scaffolding techniques (e.g., breaking behavior into small steps, prompting appropriate behavior) and contingent positive reinforcement (Forgatch & DeGarmo, 1999, in press). *Discipline* decreases deviant behavior through the appropriate and contingent use of mild sanctions (Patterson, 1986). *Monitoring* protects youngsters from involvement in risky activities and association with deviant peers. This skill requires keeping track of youngsters' activities, associates, and whereabouts and arranging for appropriate supervision (Patterson & Forgatch, 1987). *Problem-solving* skills help family members negotiate disagreements, establish rules, and specify consequences for following or violating rules (Forgatch & Patterson, 1989). *Positive involvement* reflects the many ways parents provide their youngsters with loving attention (Forgatch & DeGarmo, in press).

Coercive parenting, shown on the right-hand side of the parenting practices layer in Figure 12-1, has a destructive effect on relationships in general and child adjustment in particular. For this reason, the interventions attempt to weaken coercive family process. Coercion is a complex process in which people are inadvertently shaped to become increasingly hostile. In distressed relationships, coercive processes become overlearned, automatic, and take place with little or no cognitive awareness (Patterson, 1982).

Social interactional patterns are learned and practiced within families (e.g., between siblings, parents, and parents and children). A balance favoring coercion can entrap family members in interactional styles that disrupt interpersonal relationships outside the family (e.g., with teachers, peers, coworkers). When parents tolerate and reinforce certain patterns of social interaction more than others, they provide the training ground for habitual behavioral patterns. Coercive patterns then generalize from the settings in which they are learned to other social environments (e.g., from home to school; DeBaryshe, Patterson, & Capaldi, 1993). Coercive parenting practices have been described in detail elsewhere (Forgatch & DeGarmo, in press; Patterson, 1982; Snyder, Edwards, McGraw, Kilgore, & Holton, 1994; Snyder, Peterson, & St. Peter, 1997). Three coercive patterns are particularly lethal: *negative reciprocity, escalation,* and *negative reinforcement.*

Reciprocity reflects in-kind reactions, both positive and negative, between individuals (e.g., husband and wife embrace, parent and adolescent argue about curfew, siblings hit each other). When negative reciprocity becomes highly predictable, it is a sign of distress in families (Patterson, 1982) and in married couples (Hooley & Hahlweg, 1989). Although positive reciprocity characterizes both healthy and distressed relationships, only negative reciprocity appears to be a problem (Patterson, 1982).

Escalation involves the exchange of hostile behavior until someone increases the intensity of the response, say from criticism to humiliation, or from shouting to hitting. Escalation ultimately concludes the negativity bout, and one person wins with the last word, blow, or otherwise aversive behavior. Herein lies yet another mechanism of coercion theory: negative reinforcement.

A familiar example of negative reinforcement is the buzzing seatbelt that silences when the two ends are fastened. In this way, compliance with seatbelt regulations is secured by terminating the aversive stimulus of the buzz. This is escape conditioning. The pain stops when the expected behavior is performed. The buzzing seatbelt also shapes up avoidance behavior in subsequent trials so that people fasten their belts immediately on entering the car. These escape and avoidance conditioning bouts take place in family interactions. A common example is when parents direct their children to do homework. This direction is like the buzzing seatbelt: It is an aversive stimulus for the child who hates homework. If the child lies and says there is no homework and the parent allows the child to watch television, the child learns that lying terminates the parental demand. Thus, the child is negatively reinforced for lying.

The positive and coercive parenting practices that are the primary targets of the OSLC interventions have been identified through basic research. The basic research also identified the contexts that make it so hard for parents to change. For example, in earlier clinical research studies, we found that parental adjustment (e.g., antisocial behavior, depression) was a context associated with resistance to the parent training procedures (Patterson & Chamberlain, 1988). Thus, context is relevant to the intervention.

Contextual Factors

Background factors can enhance or diminish parenting quality. If a family lives in a high-crime neighborhood, extraordinary levels of monitoring may be necessary to protect children from harm, deviant peer exposure, and delinquency (Wilson, 1980). Divorce is a context associated with increases in coercive discipline (Forgatch, Patterson, & Ray, 1996; Furstenberg & Seltzer, 1986; Hetherington, Cox, & Cox, 1985). A child's intraindividual qualities (e.g., genetic and temperamental) can challenge parenting skills that might have sufficed under ordinary circumstances (Lykken, 1993). Social advantage can benefit parenting through increased availability of resources. The role that background contexts play with respect to a youngster's adjustment is presumed to be mediated through parenting. Thus, each context can function as a direct risk factor for parenting practices and an indirect risk for child and adolescent adjustment.

This mediational model has been supported in a series of cross-sectional and longitudinal studies that used multiple-method assessment and structural equations models. For example, in a cross-sectional study of two independent samples of single-mother families, the impact of social disadvantage and antisocial maternal qualities on child antisocial behavior was mediated by maternal discipline and monitoring (Bank, Forgatch, Patterson, & Fetrow, 1993). Another cross-sectional study with a new sample of single-mother families tested direct and indirect effects of maternal education, occupation, and income on child achievement and school behavior (DeGarmo et al., 1999). The relation between social disadvantage factors and child achievement and behavior was primarily mediated, with some exceptions. Maternal occupation had a direct and indirect path to child achievement, and mothers' predivorce income had a direct and indirect relation to child behavior. In a cross-sectional analysis with a sample of mixed family structures, a strong linear relationship was found between family structure transitions and child adjustment problems; that relationship was mediated by parental monitoring and involvement (Capaldi & Patterson, 1991). In a longitudinal design, Larzelere and Patterson (1990) demonstrated that monitoring and discipline mediated the relationship between social disadvantage and delinquency. In a series of cross-sectional and longitudinal analyses with a sample of divorced mothers, Forgatch et al. (1996) found the risk factors of stress, maternal depression, and repartnering to be mediated by maternal monitoring, discipline, and problem solving. Other cross-sectional and longitudinal analyses with single-mother samples showed the relationship of adult confidant support and child adjustment to be mediated by parenting practices (DeGarmo & Forgatch, 1997; Forgatch & DeGarmo, 1997). Overall, these studies support the hypothesis that certain contexts place children at risk for antisocial behaviors because they interfere with effective parenting. The analysis of contextual effects suggests new risk populations that may become foci for future preventive efforts.

The Social Interactional Learning Model continues to be refined and expanded. In the last decade, the model has addressed developmental questions (Patterson, 1992, 1993; Patterson & Yoerger, 1993, 1997). For example, Why do some people start a particular trajectory? What factors contribute to the timing of onset or the severity and chronicity of deviancy? Does the form of deviancy change as youngsters mature? What are the mechanisms of initiation, continuity, and change? When basic research using careful measurement and longitudinal analysis addresses such developmental issues, interventions can be tailored accordingly.

How Does Prevention Differ From Treatment?

There are subtle and not-so-subtle differences between clinical and prevention research. To adapt clinical programs for prevention, several distinctions must be taken into account. In clinical trials, participants are screened to ensure the presence of diagnosed problems. By contrast, in prevention trials, the samples are heterogeneous in topography and intensity of problem behaviors (Coie et al., 1993). Clinical trials are designed primarily to reduce specific symptoms (Kazdin, 1993). Prevention programs often have multiple goals: (a) to ameliorate existing problems, (b) to prevent new problems, (c) to promote new prosocial development, and (d) to prevent the decay of existing prosocial behavior (Coie et al., 1993). To achieve statistically significant effects, prevention trials require substantial power (large samples) and relatively long follow-up periods (Goldklang, 1989). Furthermore, effect sizes for the distal variables are likely to be smaller in prevention than in clinical trials (Durlak & Wells, 1997). Thus, homogeneity, singularity of purpose, and intensity of the treatment make it possible to achieve greater effects with smaller samples in clinical compared to prevention trials.

Treatment programs attempt to reduce clearly identified problems to within a nonclinical range. Prevention programs operate along a continuum of problem severity, adjusting the level of intervention accordingly. Thus, prevention strategies include universal, selected, and indicated programs (Mrazek & Haggerty, 1994; National Institute of Mental Health Prevention Steering Committee, 1993; Tolan & Guerra, 1994). In general, these strategies vary according to the targeted population (risk characteristics and selection of participants), intensity of the intervention (cost and allocated resources), and the timing of the intervention in terms of the level of problem development. Universal programs are directed toward broad populations and use economical and minimal interventions. An example of a universal program is the use of a media campaign and community involvement to reduce tobacco availability and use by teenagers (Biglan et al., 1995). Selected programs target risk populations, use a screening procedure to ensure presence of the risk, and provide interventions relevant to the risk factor. The Oregon Social Learning Center has developed several selected intervention programs: an intervention in schools in high-crime neighborhoods (Reid, Eddy, Fetrow, & Stoolmiller, 1999); a program for middle-school youth at risk for multiple dimensions of dysfunctional adjustment (Dishion & Andrews, 1994); and an intervention to help mothers and sons in divorcing families (Forgatch & DeGarmo, 1999, in press). Indicated programs are for populations in need of an extensive intervention to correct a current problem and prevent its reoccurrence. For example, work with delinquent adolescents might have goals to (a) break the trajectory of delinquency, (b) prevent the return to delinquency during adolescence, and (c) prevent adult criminal behavior (Tolan & Guerra, 1994). The treatment foster care program for adolescents who are delinquent and disturbed represents an elegant transformation of parent management training for this population of youths (Chamberlain & Reid, 1998). Combining all three strategies (universal, selected, and indicated) within one program can be accomplished through the use of multiple gating

(Dishion, Kavanagh, & Kiesner, in press). This tiered strategy assigns participants to each level of intervention, titrating need to the level of support provided to parents to reduce the overall prevalence of risk. Pinsof & Hambright (chapter 9, this volume) discuss in more detail the different types of prevention programs.

Passive longitudinal studies provide the basic research that benefits both treatment and prevention programs. The correlational data generated by this program of research form the basis for experimental studies that are the lifeblood of intervention, because the data suggest mechanisms for adjustment problems. For example, the use of coercive discipline by parents has been found to be associated with children's antisocial behavior in passive longitudinal studies (Forgatch et al., 1996; Patterson & Bank, 1989). Because these data were only correlational, however, discipline could not be identified as causing the antisocial behavior. Only a controlled experimental manipulation can address questions of cause and effect. Interventions within clinical and prevention programs are ideal for such experimental tests of theoretical relationships. Tests of causal status can be achieved through randomized experimental designs in which one group receives and one group does not receive an intervention that targets the putative mechanism. Thus, the intervention, which is an experimental manipulation, provides a test of the model. In the discipline and antisocial behavior example, parents in the experimental condition are taught to reduce coercive discipline while the control parents continue with no discipline intervention. If there is differential change by group for discipline (i.e., the experimental group improves while the control does not) and that improvement is associated with a commensurate improvement in antisocial behavior, the theoretical model is supported.

Each level of intervention (i.e., universal, selected, indicated) may be used as an experimental test of a theory as long as several conditions are met: (a) random assignment to experimental and control groups, (b) effective delivery of the intervention, (c) benefits to the experimental group relative to the control, and (d) demonstration that the putative mechanisms contributed to these benefits. In selected studies, the type of risk is a critical factor in determining the focus, sequence, and format of the intervention. For example, divorce is a risk factor for many aspects of adjustment for youngsters (e.g., academic failure, peer relationship problems, externalizing behavior, and internalizing problems; Chase-Lansdale, Cherlin, & Kiernan, 1995; Hetherington & Clingempeel, 1992; Zill, Morrison, & Coiro, 1993). However, most youngsters from divorced families are likely to escape these problems. Thus, the challenge to achieve positive child outcomes requires (a) an intervention that operates on multiple outcomes, (b) a large sample of divorcing families or screening to ensure that youngsters have incipient levels of one or more of these problems, and (c) an intervention that effectively alters the putative mechanism (Forgatch & DeGarmo, in press).

Some Oregon Social Learning Center Prevention Programs

The improvement of parenting practices is the component present in all OSLC interventions. In the Social Interactional Learning Model, parents are most proximal to child development; therefore, parents are targeted in the intervention. This requires that the parenting practices be malleable. Treatment studies have repeatedly demonstrated that parenting practices can be taught (Dadds, Schwartz, & Sanders, 1987; Griest et al., 1982; Kazdin et al., 1987; Patterson, Chamberlain, & Reid, 1982). More recently, the studies have advanced to show that changes in parenting practices account for commensurate changes in children's adjustment outcomes (Dishion, Patterson, & Kavanagh, 1992; Forgatch, 1991; Forgatch & DeGarmo, 1999, in press; Patterson & Forgatch, 1995). Thus, the core of the OSLC intervention requires the teaching of effective parenting.

Other components may be added to parent training to enhance the program's effectiveness, depending on the nature of the risk factors for a given sample. For example, populations at risk for both marital distress and child behavior problems appear to benefit from a marital enhancement component. This was demonstrated in research by Dadds and colleagues (Dadds, Sanders, Behrens, & James, 1987), who recruited a sample of families with child behavior problems in which half of the families were also experiencing marital problems. Families were blocked on marital problems and assigned to parent management training alone or parent management training plus partner support training. Both groups had improved parenting and significant reductions in child behavior problems at termination. At 6-month follow-up, the child outcome improvements were lost for families in which the couples were maritally distressed and received parent management training alone. Maritally distressed families who received the enhanced parent management training maintained positive outcomes. In the marriage and parenting in stepfamilies preventive intervention currently under way at OSLC (Forgatch & Rains, 1997), a marital enhancement program has been added to the parent training core to help the biological and stepparents work together effectively in their child-rearing strategies.

A selected program designed by Dishion and colleagues focused on middle-school youngsters at risk for antisocial behavior and substance abuse (Dishion & Andrews, 1995). An enhancement component taught prosocial skills to teens in peer groups. Random assignment was made to five conditions: parent education groups (12 sessions), teen skills training groups (12 sessions), parent–teen groups combined (12 sessions), a self-directed program with written and videotaped materials, and a control condition. Parent and teen interventions resulted in immediate improvements in observed family conflict. The parent intervention also yielded immediate beneficial effects in teacher-reported behavior problems at school (Dishion & Andrews, 1995). Parents in the experimental group improved their discipline practices relative to the controls from baseline to termination. Discipline practices at termination contributed to the reductions in youngsters' antisocial behavior (Dishion et al., 1992).

Another selected prevention program, the Oregon Divorce Study, was conducted with recently separated single mothers with an elementary school-aged son. The boys were at risk for problems associated with their parents' separation (e.g., internalizing problems, externalizing problems, school failure). The intervention was designed to prevent and ameliorate maternal and child problems by teaching mothers strategies to enhance parenting practices and personal adjustment through a series of 14 parent information groups. Children did not participate in the intervention. This design provided a stringent test of parenting practices as mechanisms of child adjustment. Findings were based on multiple method and agent assessments at baseline (within the first 25 months of marital separation) and at 6, 12, 18, and 30 months postbaseline.

As expected, the intervention produced significant benefits to parenting practices for mothers in the experimental group relative to those in the control. Coercive discipline (negative reinforcement, negative reciprocity, and ineffective discipline) and positive parenting (i.e., skill encouragement, monitoring, positive involvement, and problem-solving outcome) showed classic prevention effects: The control group deteriorated over 30 months, whereas the experimental group showed no decrement. The benefits to parenting practices produced commensurate benefits to child outcomes for experimental group boys relative to their control counterparts in several areas of functioning. Benefits were found for teacher ratings of delinquency, aggression, externalizing, adaptive functioning, and prosocial behavior at school; laboratory tests for reading achievement; boys' self-report of depression, peer relations, and association with deviant peers; and noncompliant behavior observed in the laboratory (DeGarmo & Forgatch, 2000; Forgatch & DeGarmo, 1999, in press; Martinez & Forgatch, in press). Mothers in the experimental group benefited relative to control mothers with greater reduction in depression and financial stress. Families in the experimental group also experienced some relief from poverty, with more per capita monthly income and a trend for families to rise above poverty thresholds (Forgatch & DeGarmo, 2000). The data supported the theoretical model and showed broad-ranging positive effects of the intervention.

Theoretical perspectives may suggest additional components, as in the universally delivered prevention trial carried out by Reid et al. (1999). Youngsters were at risk for antisocial behavior problems because their elementary school was in a high-crime neighborhood; no other risk factors were specified. Schools were randomly assigned to experimental or control conditions, and the intervention was conducted in the school setting. In addition to six parent information groups, components included problem-solving training in the classroom, behavior management on the playground, and the introduction of a telephone line to the classrooms to facilitate communication between parents and teachers. Immediate benefits were obtained, with significant decreases in aggressive and other antisocial behaviors for experimental compared to control children as reported by teachers, parents, peers, and trained observers who scored behavior on the playground during recess (Reid et al., 1999). Furthermore, families in the experimental group showed immediate improvements in problem-solving outcomes relative to controls, and this change was associated with commensurate improvements in children's problem behaviors over 3 years as rated by teachers (DeGarmo & Forgatch, in press).

Some well-implemented interventions yield unpleasant surprises. Theoretically based programs occasionally produce iatrogenic effects (i.e., the intervention has negative side effects). In one study, the investigators were dismayed to find that an enhancement condition added to the core parent training procedures made things worse (Dishion & Andrews, 1995; Dishion et al., 1992). When social skills were taught in groups to teens who were at risk, the youngsters actually increased their tobacco smoking. Their teachers also reported an increase in externalizing problems relative to teens in the other conditions. Apparently, group treatment of youths who are at risk inadvertently strengthens deviant peer association and promotes deviant behavior.

Processes of Intervention

As a program becomes established, investigation can be directed toward the process of change within the intervention. This can include testing methods of transmitting information (e.g., parent groups, family sessions, books, audio and videotapes) or studying interpersonal process observed during intervention. Learning how to deliver interventions to families with troubled youngsters and studying the processes that interfere with change can pave the way for programs designed to prevent problems before they begin or to ameliorate incipient problems.

A focus of the applied research at OSLC has been the study of therapy process. With the development of coding systems to describe therapist and client behaviors observed during treatment sessions, the OSLC group has embarked on a series of studies to better understand why it is so hard to help people to change (Patterson & Chamberlain, 1988; Patterson & Forgatch, 1985; Stoolmiller, Duncan, Bank, & Patterson, 1993). It seemed paradoxical that families seeking advice frequently responded to suggestions for change with "I can't" or "I won't" (Patterson & Forgatch, 1985). The studies revealed that predictors of these resistant responses came from antecedent therapist behaviors and family characteristics.

In one study, an experimental manipulation based on sequential analyses showed that two therapist behaviors (i.e., teach and confront) appeared to elicit resistance (Patterson & Forgatch, 1985). Using an ABAB reversal design, therapists engaged in teach and confront in the A conditions and desisted in the B conditions. Client resistance was high during A conditions and low during the B conditions, supporting the hypothesis that therapist teach and confront elicited client resistance. This suggested a paradox for the didactic approach in which teaching leads to client verbal behavior indicating "I can't" and "I won't."

One might ask, Is it feasible to remove all teach and confront from the didactic process? As shown in one study with an OSLC treatment sample (Stoolmiller et al., 1993), the timing of teach and confront and the resolution of resistance by treatment termination were critical to long-term outcomes. Latent growth curve modeling was used to describe levels of resistance observed at the beginning, midpoint, and end of treatment. An increase in resistance at the midpoint of therapy followed by a decrease by termination was associated with reduced police arrests for the youngsters more than 2 years after termination. This finding supports a "struggle and work through" hypothesis (e.g., Patterson & Chamberlain, 1988). The idea is that the first phase of therapy requires the therapist to form a relationship with the family. Confrontation is not appropriate during this period, and teaching is limited in scope. Once a good relationship is established, the therapist uses that bond to challenge the parents to change their child-rearing practices. During this phase (the midpoint of therapy), more resistance is expected, and is in fact appropriate. But by the time therapy reaches its end, this struggle should be resolved as the parents use the procedures and receive therapeutic support for creating change in their families. Should therapists avoid teaching and confronting altogether? No, but they should be careful in their timing.

Conclusion

In this chapter, we have described a process linking basic and applied prevention research within a context of pragmatic programmatic investigations. The work of OSLC treatment investigators was used as an exemplar of how clinical efforts can be modulated for prevention science. We discussed the spectrum of intervention strategies including universal, selected, and indicated and provided some examples of recent prevention programs at OSLC. Germane to this body of work is the use of a clearly articulated theoretical framework to guide bidirectional processes between basic research and practical application.

In the new millennium, prevention science must move out of the ivory tower and into the real world to disseminate empirically validated programs. Communities need readily accessible effective programs. Fortunately, a new science of dissemination is emerging that can promote advancement, not regression. It is interesting to note that pioneers in the art and science of dissemination recommend the same iterative process that we have described between basic research and practical application for clinical and prevention programs (Carnine, 1998; Sanders, 1998). If scientific rigor is applied during dissemination efforts, every step in the process can benefit.

As in any new science, we can expect problems at the beginning. Our early work in dissemination science will be exploratory, our methodology rough, and our trials weak tests of our hypotheses. To place programs that were developed within narrow confines into broader community settings, we must change them while retaining their integrity—a process that will provide us with new levels of understanding. But we can only learn if we retain the link between basic research and practical application.

References

Bank, L., Forgatch, M. S., Patterson, G. R., & Fetrow, R. A. (1993). Parenting practices of single mothers: Mediators of negative contextual factors. *Journal of Marriage and the Family, 55,* 371–384.

Bank, L., Marlowe, J. H., Reid, J. B., Patterson, G. R., & Weinrott, M. R. (1991). A comparative evaluation of parent-training interventions of families of chronic delinquents. *Journal of Abnormal Child Psychology, 19*(1), 15–33.

Barker, R. G. (1951). *One boy's day.* New York: Harper & Row.

Barker, R. G. (1963). The stream of behavior as an empirical problem. In R. G. Barker (Ed.), *The stream of behavior: Explorations of its structure and content* (pp. 1–22). New York: Appleton-Century-Crofts.

Biglan, A., Henderson, J., Humphrey, D., Yasui, M., Whitman, R., Black, C., & James, L. (1995). Mobilising positive reinforcement to reduce youth access to tobacco. *Tobacco Control, 4,* 42–48.

Capaldi, D. M. (1992). Co-occurrence of conduct problems and depressive symptoms in early adolescent boys: A 2-year follow-up at grade 8. *Development and Psychopathology, 4,* 125–144.

Capaldi, D. M., & Patterson, G. R. (1991). Relation of parental transition to boys' adjustment problems: Mothers at risk for transitions and unskilled parenting. *Developmental Psychology, 27*(3), 489–504.

Carnine, D. (1998, June). *Advancing the adoption of empirically supported preventive practices.* Paper presented at the Meeting of the Society for Prevention Research, Park City, UT.

Chamberlain, P. (1994). *Family connections: A treatment foster care model for adolescents with delinquency* (Vol. 5). Eugene, OR: Castalia.

Chamberlain, P., & Reid, J. B. (1998). Comparison of two community alternatives to incarceration for chronic juvenile offenders. *Journal of Consulting and Clinical Psychology, 66*(4), 624–633.

Chase-Lansdale, P., Cherlin, A. J., & Kiernan, K. E. (1995). The long-term effects of parental divorce on the mental health of young adults: A developmental perspective. *Child Development, 66,* 1614–1634.

Coie, J. D., Watt, N. F., West, S. G., Hawkins, J. D., Asarnow, J. R., Markman, H. J., Ramey, S. L., Shure, M. B., & Long, B. (1993). The science of prevention: A conceptual framework and some directions for a national research program. *American Psychologist, 48*(10), 1013–1022.

Conger, R. D., Patterson, G. R., & Ge, X. (1995). It takes two to replicate: A mediational model for the impact of parents' stress on adolescent adjustment. *Developmental Psychology, 66,* 80–97.

Dadds, M. R., Sanders, M. R., Behrens, B. C., & James, J. E. (1987). Marital discord and child behavior problems: A description of family interactions during treatment. *Journal of Clinical Child Psychology, 16*(3), 192–203.

Dadds, M. R., Schwartz, S., & Sanders, M. R. (1987). Marital discord and treatment outcome in behavioral treatment of child conduct disorders. *Journal of Consulting and Clinical Psychology, 55*(3), 396–403.

DeBaryshe, B. D., Patterson, G. R., & Capaldi, D. M. (1993). A performance model for academic achievement in early adolescent boys. *Developmental Psychology, 1993*(29), 795–804.

DeGarmo, D. S., & Forgatch, M. S. (1997). Confidant support and maternal distress: Predictors of parenting practices for divorced mothers. *Personal Relationships, 4,* 305–317.

DeGarmo, D. S., & Forgatch, M. S. (2000, November). *Preventing the "early start" within transitional divorce families: An experimental test of precursors influencing antisocial behavior and delinquency.* Paper presented at the American Society of Criminology Annual Meeting: Crime and Criminology in the Year 2000, San Francisco.

Degarmo, D. S., & Forgatch, M. S. (in press). Putting problem solving to the test: Replicating experimental interventions for preventing youngsters' problem behaviors. In R. D. Conger, F. O. Lorenz, & K. A. S. Wickrama (Eds.), *Continuity and change in family relations: Theory, methods, and empirical findings.* Mahwah, NJ: Erlbaum.

DeGarmo, D. S., Forgatch, M. S., & Martinez, C. R. Jr. (1999). Parenting of divorced mothers as a link between social status and boys' academic outcomes: Unpacking the effects of SES. *Child Development, 70*(5), 1231–1245.

Dishion, T. J., & Andrews, D. W. (1994). *Preventing escalation in problem behaviors with high-risk adolescents: Immediate and 1-year outcomes.* Unpublished manuscript, Oregon Social Learning Center, Eugene, OR.

Dishion, T. J., & Andrews, D. W. (1995). Preventing escalation in problem behaviors with high-risk young adolescents: Immediate and 1-year outcomes. *Journal of Consulting and Clinical Psychology, 63*(4), 538–548.

Dishion, T. J., Andrews, D. W., & Crosby, L. (1995). Antisocial boys and their friends in early adolescence: Relationship characteristics, quality, and interactional processes. *Child Development, 66,* 139–151.

Dishion, T. J., Kavanagh, K., & Kiesner, J. (in press). Prevention of early adolescent substance use among high-risk youth: A multiple gating approach to parent intervention. In R. S. Ashery (Ed.), *Research meeting on drug abuse prevention through family interventions.* National Institute on Drug Abuse Research Monograph.

Dishion, T. J., & Patterson, S. G. (1996). *Preventive parenting with love, encouragement, and limits: The preschool years.* Eugene, OR: Castalia.

Dishion, T. J., Patterson, G. R., & Kavanagh, K. A. (1992). An experimental test of the coercion model: Linking theory, measurement, and intervention. In J. McCord & R. Tremblay (Eds.), *The interaction of theory and practice: Experimental studies of intervention* (pp. 253–282). New York: Guilford Press.

Dumas, J. E. (1989). Treating antisocial behavior in children: Child and family approaches. *Clinical Psychology Review, 9,* 197–222.

Durlak, J. A., & Wells, A. M. (1997). Primary prevention mental health programs for children and adolescents: A meta-analytic review. *American Journal of Community Psychology, 25*(2), 115–152.

Forgatch, M. S. (1991). The clinical science vortex: A developing theory of antisocial behavior. In D. Pepler & K. H. Rubin (Eds.), *The development and treatment of childhood aggression* (pp. 291–315). Hillsdale, NJ: Erlbaum.

Forgatch, M. S., & DeGarmo, D. S. (1997). Adult problem solving: Contributor to parenting and child outcomes in divorced families. *Social Development, 6*(2), 238–254.

Forgatch, M. S., & DeGarmo, D. S. (1999). Parenting through change: An effective prevention program for single mothers. *Journal of Consulting and Clinical Psychology, 67*(5), 711–724.

Forgatch, M. S., & DeGarmo, D. S. (2000, November). *Accelerating recovery from poverty: Prevention effects for divorcing mothers.* Manuscript submitted for publication.

Forgatch, M. S., & DeGarmo, D. S. (in press). Extending and testing the social interaction learning model with divorce samples. In J. B. Reid, G. R. Patterson, & J. Snyder (Eds.), *The Oregon Model: Understanding and altering the delinquency trajectory.* Washington, DC: American Psychological Association.

Forgatch, M. S., & Patterson, G. R. (1989). *Parents and adolescents living together: Vol. 2. Family problem solving.* Eugene, OR: Castalia.

Forgatch, M. S., Patterson, G. R., & Ray, J. A. (1996). Divorce and boys' adjustment problems: Two paths with a single model. In E. M. Hetherington & E. A. Blechman (Eds.), *Stress, coping, and resiliency in children and families* (pp. 67–105). Mahwah, NJ: Erlbaum.

Forgatch, M. S., & Rains, L. (1997). *MAPS: Marriage and parenting in stepfamilies* [parent training manual]. Eugene, OR: Oregon Social Learning Center.

Furstenberg, F. F., Jr., & Seltzer, J. A. (1986). Divorce and child development. *Sociological Studies of Child Development, 1,* 137–160.

Goldklang, D. S. (1989). Research workshop on prevention of depression with recommendations for future research. *Journal of Primary Prevention, 10*(1), 41–49.

Griest, D. L., Forehand, R., Rogers, T., Breiner, J., Furey, W., & Williams, C. A. (1982). Effects of parent enhancement therapy on the treatment outcome and generalization of a parent training program. *Behavior Research and Therapy, 20,* 429–436.

Hawkins, R. P., Peterson, R. F., Schweid, E., & Bijou, S. W. (1966). Behavior therapy in the home: Amelioration of problem parent–child relations with the parent in a therapeutic role. *Journal of Experimental Child Psychology, 4,* 99–107.

Hetherington, E. M., & Clingempeel, G. (1992). Coping with marital transitions. *Monographs of the Society for Research in Child Development* (Vol. 57, Nos. 2–3, Serial No. 227). Chicago: University of Chicago Press.

Hetherington, E. M., Cox, M., & Cox, R. (1985). Long-term effects of divorce and remarriage on the adjustment of children. *Journal of the American Academy of Child Psychiatry, 24*(5), 518–530.

Hooley, J. M., & Hahlweg, K. (1989). Marital satisfaction and marital communication in German and English couples. *Behavioral Assessment, 11,* 119–133.

Kazdin, A. E. (1993). Psychotherapy for children and adolescents: Current progress and future research directions. *American Psychologist, 48*(6), 644–657.

Kazdin, A. E., Esveldt-Dawson, K., French, N. H., & Unis, A. S. (1987). Effects of parent management training and problem-solving skills training combined in the treatment of antisocial child behavior. *American Academy of Child and Adolescent Psychiatry, 26*(3), 416–424.

Larzelere, R. E., & Patterson, G. R. (1990). Parental management: Mediator of the effect of socioeconomic status on early delinquency. *Criminology, 28,* 301–324.

Lipsey, M. W., & Wilson, D. B. (1993). The efficacy of psychological, educational and behavioral treatment: Confirmation from meta-analysis. *American Psychologist, 48*(12), 1181–1209.

Lykken, D. T. (1993). Predicting violence in the violent society. *Applied and Preventive Psychology, 2,* 13–20.

Martinez, C. R., Jr., & Forgatch, M. S. (in press). Preventing problems with boys' noncompliance: Effects of a parent training intervention for divorcing mothers. *Journal of Consulting and Clinical Psychology.*

McMahon, R. J., & Wells, K. C. (1989). Conduct disorders. In E. J. Mash & R. A. Barkley (Eds.), *Treatment of childhood disorders* (pp. 73–132). New York: Guilford Press.

Mrazek, P. J., & Haggerty, R. J. (1994). *Reducing risks for mental disorders: Frontiers for preventive intervention research.* Washington DC: National Academy Press.

National Institute of Mental Health Prevention Steering Committee. (1993). *The prevention of mental disorders: A national research agenda* [Executive summary]. Bethesda, MD: Author.

Patterson, G. R. (1982). *A social learning approach: Coercive family process* (Vol. III). Eugene, OR: Castalia.

Patterson, G. R. (1986). Performance models for antisocial boys. *American Psychologist, 41,* 432–444.

Patterson, G. R. (1992). Developmental changes in antisocial behavior. In R. D. Peters, R. J. McMahon, & V. L. Quinsey (Eds.), *Aggression and violence throughout the life span* (pp. 52–82). Newbury Park, CA: Sage.

Patterson, G. R. (1993). Orderly change in a stable world: The antisocial trait as a chimera. *Journal of Consulting and Clinical Psychology, 61*(6), 911–919.

Patterson, G. R., & Bank, L. (1989). Some amplifying mechanisms for pathologic processes in families. In M. R. Gunnar & E. Thelen (Eds.), *Systems and development: The Minnesota symposia on child psychology* (Vol. 22, pp. 167–209). Hillsdale, NJ: Erlbaum.

Patterson, G. R., & Brodsky, G. (1966). A behaviour modification programme for a child with multiple problem behaviours. *Journal of Child Psychology and Psychiatry, 7,* 277–295.

Patterson, G. R., & Chamberlain, P. (1988). Treatment process: A problem at three levels. In L. C. Wynne (Ed.), *The state of the art in family therapy research: Controversies and recommendations* (pp. 189–226). New York: Family Process Press.

Patterson, G. R., Chamberlain, P., & Reid, J. B. (1982). A comparative evaluation of a parent-training program. *Behavior Therapy, 15,* 144–155.

Patterson, G. R., & Forgatch, M. S. (1985). Therapist behavior as a determinant for client noncompliance: A paradox for the behavior modifier. *Journal of Consulting and Clinical Psychology, 53*(6), 846–851.

Patterson, G. R., & Forgatch, M. S. (1987). *Parents and adolescents living together: The basics* (Vol. I). Eugene, OR: Castalia.

Patterson, G. R., & Forgatch, M. S. (1995). Predicting future clinical adjustment from treatment outcome and process variables. *Psychological Assessment, 7*(3), 275–285.

Patterson, G. R., & Yoerger, K. (1993). Developmental models for delinquent behavior. In S. Hodgins (Ed.), *Crime and mental disorders* (pp. 140–172). Newbury Park, CA: Sage.

Patterson, G. R., & Yoerger, K. (1997). A developmental model for late-onset delinquency. In D. W. Oswood (Ed.), *Motivation and delinquency: Nebraska symposium on motivation* (Vol. 44, pp. 119–177). Lincoln: University of Nebraska Press.

Reid, J. B. (1970). Reliability assessment of observation data: A possible methodological problem. *Child Development, 41,* 1143–1150.

Reid, J. B. (Ed.). (1978). *A social learning approach to family intervention: Observation in home settings.* Eugene, OR: Castalia.

Reid, J. B., & Eddy, J. M. (1997). The prevention of antisocial behavior: Some considerations in the search for effective interventions. In D. M. Stoff, J. Breiling, & J. D. Master (Eds.), *Handbook of antisocial behavior* (pp. 343–356). New York: Wiley.

Reid, J. B., Eddy, J. M., Fetrow, R. A., & Stoolmiller, M. (1999). Description and immediate impacts of a preventive intervention for conduct problems. *American Journal of Community Psychology, 27*(4), 483–517.

Sanders, M. (1998, June). *Enhancing the well-being of children and families: The importance of effective dissemination at a national level.* Paper presented at the Fifth Annual Summer Institute of the Family Research Consortium II, Blaine, WA.

Snyder, J. J., Edwards, P., McGraw, K., Kilgore, K., & Holton, A. (1994). Escalation and reinforcement in mother–child conflict: Social processes associated with the development of physical aggression. *Development and Psychopathology, 6,* 305–321.

Snyder, J., Peterson, L., & St. Peter, C. (1997). Origins of antisocial behavior: Negative reinforcement and affect dysregulation of behavior as socialization mechanisms in family interaction. *Behavior Modification, 21*(2), 187–215.

Stoolmiller, M., Duncan, T. E., Bank, L., & Patterson, G. R. (1993). Some problems and solutions in the study of change: Significant patterns of client resistance. *Journal of Consulting and Clinical Psychology, 61*(6), 920–928.

Tolan, P. H., & Guerra, N. G. (1994). Prevention of delinquency: Current status and issues. *Journal of Applied and Preventive Psychology, 3,* 251–273.

Wahler, R. G., Winkle, G. H., Peterson, R. F., & Morrison, D. C. (1965). Mothers as behavior therapists for their own children. *Behaviour Research and Therapy, 3,* 113–124.

Wilson, H. (1980). Parental supervision: A neglected aspect of delinquency. *British Journal of Criminology, 20,* 203–235.

Zill, N., Morrison, D. R., & Coiro, M. J. (1993). Long-term effects of parental divorce on parent–child relationships, adjustment, and achievement in young adulthood. *Journal of Family Psychology, 7*(1), 91–103.

CHAPTER 13

Mental Health Services Research and Family-Based Treatment: Bridging the Gap

Sonja K. Schoenwald
Scott W. Henggeler

In recent years, substantial changes in the health care delivery system have raised serious questions about the clinical and cost-effectiveness of mental health services available to youths and families. Policy makers, consumers, and payers are demanding to know which psychotherapies are effective (U.S. Surgeon General, 1999). In response to this demand, researchers have started to catalog those treatments shown to be efficacious with delineated populations. These treatments are generally developed and tested in accordance with university-based research protocols, hence the term *research treatment* has been used to describe them (Weisz, Weiss, & Donenberg, 1992). It appears, however, that treatments with demonstrated efficacy are seldom deployed by practitioners in community settings. Surveys of community-based mental health practitioners suggest that the predominant treatment of children is general counseling of the child and parent in accordance with psychodynamic or eclectic theoretical orientations (Kazdin, Siegel, & Bass, 1990). Moreover, the nature of treatment is determined by what clinicians know and philosophically prefer rather than by the nature of the presenting problem and circumstances of the family. Although the knowledge base on psychotherapies delivered in community settings is slim, available evidence suggests that they are not effective (Weisz, Han, & Valeri, 1997). Documented differences between "clinic" and "research" treatments include (a) greater severity and heterogeneity of problems presented by clinic cases; (b) higher caseloads of community-based clinicians; and (c) a relative lack of training of clinicians in specific treatment protocols and monitoring of

Preparation of this manuscript was supported in part by National Institute on Drug Abuse Grant DA-08029 and by National Institute of Mental Health Grants ME-51852 and R24MH53558-01.

treatment adherence in community settings (Weisz, Donenberg, Han, & Kauneckis, 1995; Weisz, Donenberg, Han, & Weiss, 1995). The continued parallel but independent production of psychotherapy and services research has contributed to the significant gap between research and clinical practice (Jensen, Hoagwood, & Petti, 1996; Weisz et al., 1997). In addition, the inherent difficulties of conducting randomized trials in field settings renders rigorous evaluation of existing community-based mental health services difficult (Bickman & Rog, 1995).

Bridging the gap between efficacious treatment and real-world services effectiveness has emerged as a priority on the research agendas of mental health services and treatment researchers alike. Among the recommended strategies to do so are developing treatment models that address co-occurring problems in youth and families, testing the effectiveness of these models in community-based settings, and developing research methodologies to examine the "transportability" of efficacious interventions from university- to community-based service settings and sectors (Hoagwood, Hibbs, Brent, & Jensen, 1995; Kazdin & Weisz, 1998; Liddle, 1996). Executing these strategies requires that treatment researchers become familiar with the focus of and methods used in mental health services research.

This chapter has two broad goals. The first is to acquaint researchers engaged in the emergent family intervention science (Liddle, 1996) and treatment development (Azar, 1994) paradigms with a mental health services research perspective. The second is to describe multisystemic therapy (MST; Henggeler & Borduin, 1990; Henggeler, Schoenwald, Borduin, Rowland, & Cunningham, 1998) as an example of the interface between treatment and services research.

Children's Mental Health Services Research

Children's mental health services research differs from clinical research in two broad ways: extensionality and contextuality (Hoagwood & Hohman, 1994). *Extensionality* reflects the reality that, in contrast with participants in clinical trials of psychotherapy, youths and families seeking treatment in the community receive it in a variety of settings, including community health and mental health clinics, public or private hospitals, schools, and facilities operated by or through public mental health, juvenile justice, or child welfare agencies. *Contextuality* refers to the factors that affect the delivery of treatments and services in community settings, such as location, caseload, cost, financing strategies, political factors, and so on. As Hoagwood and Hohman have stated, "services research for children and adolescents is characterized by investigations of the interrelated conditions within which services to children, adolescents, and their families are provided [in community settings]" (1994, p. 260).

Two genres of inquiry are subsumed within child and adolescent mental health services research. One focuses on service systems; the other on the use and effectiveness of various services delivered within those systems. For the last decade, service systems research has focused primarily on organizational aspects (Oswald & Singh, 1996), that is, on the way in which agencies and systems work together to coordinate services, on reducing barriers to coordination through the integration (administrative and fiscal) of services across service sectors (e.g., mental health, education, juvenile justice, child welfare), and on the impact of systems integration on mental health outcomes. With respect to children's services, a major thrust of service system research has been the development and evaluation of a model known as a *continuum of care* (Hoagwood, 1997), in which a range of services, the intensity of which varies in accordance with the needs of the youth, is made available across a variety of community settings. When embedded within a service system characterized by high levels of interagency integration (administrative and, to the extent possible, fiscal) and designed in accordance with a set of principles emphasizing family-focused and highly individualized services, such a continuum is described as a *system of care* (Stroul & Friedman, 1994). Two comprehensive and rigorous evaluations of systems of care have been completed. Results from the Fort Bragg (Bickman, 1996) and Stark County (Bickman, Summerfelt, Firth, & Douglas, 1997) projects indicated that system-level changes such as increased access to services, continuity of care, client satisfaction, and use of less restrictive service environments were achieved, while improvements in clinical outcomes were not (Bickman et al., 1997; Lambert & Guthrie, 1996). Moreover, the integrated system of care was more expensive than the traditional service system (Foster, Summerfelt, & Saunders, 1996).

The second major thrust of mental health services research focuses on service use and effectiveness. Research on use includes epidemiological studies that examine the nature of the population in need of services (i.e., number and demographic characteristics of youths and families, nature of their mental health needs, types of services available and used) and studies of factors (geographic location, cost, reimbursement methodologies) that affect use of those services in general and among particular populations (e.g., foster children; youths with co-occurring disorders of alcohol, drug abuse, and mental disorder; youths from various cultural and ethnic backgrounds).

Effectiveness research focuses on which services work in real-world conditions for whom, in which service settings and service sectors, and at what cost. Since the inception of the federal Child and Adolescent Service Systems Program (CASSP) in 1986, the development of community-based alternatives to traditional office-, residential-, and inpatient-based models of service delivery has been a primary focus of this research. Such alternatives include family preservation services, therapeutic foster care, individualized or "wraparound" services, respite care, crisis care, family support services, and intensive case management (for a review, see Burns, Hoagwood, & Mrazek, 1999). Research on the effectiveness of these new community-based service models is in its infancy, and controlled studies of these services are rare (Jensen et al., 1996). Unfortunately, descriptions of the clinical interventions implemented in these various community-based models are also rare. The sobering findings regarding the failure of system of care initiatives to differentially affect clinical outcomes, however, have drawn attention to the relative neglect of the clinical practices used in such initiatives (Henggeler, Schoenwald, & Munger, 1996; Hoagwood, 1997; Weisz et al., 1997).

Psychotherapy research, on the other hand, is concerned primarily with clinical interventions. Such research focuses on questions of efficacy, namely which well-specified treatments work for whom, under structured and relatively well-controlled conditions, and typically with relatively homogenous samples. Controlled clinical trials that compare the efficacy of certain family therapies with small samples of adolescent substance abusers are illustrative of this modus operandus (for a review, see Liddle & Dakof, 1995). Unfortunately, treatment modalities that have demonstrated promise in university-based efficacy studies have, with rare exceptions, failed to demonstrate lasting effects with problems such as serious antisocial behavior and adolescent substance abuse (Henggeler, Smith, & Schoenwald, 1994), are not often used in community settings, and have rarely been tested with the populations seen and under the conditions that characterize those settings.

Treatment research has the potential to enhance service effectiveness, particularly if it undertakes specification of more complex models of treatment and evaluation of such models with samples in community-based settings. The framework for family-based treatment of adolescents and family intervention science articulated by Liddle (1996) may produce effective alternatives in this regard, particularly if the alternatives incorporate some of the lessons learned in services research. Specifically, studies of family treatments delivered in different service settings (e.g., outpatient, home-based, inpatient) and service sectors (juvenile justice, mental health) and the field's increasing focus on family therapy as one component in a more comprehensive, multicomponent intervention package (Liddle & Dakof, 1995) should enhance the relevance and effectiveness of family therapy research to questions of clinical and cost-effectiveness.

Bridging Family Therapy and Services Research: Multisystemic Therapy

Multisystemic therapy is an example of a family-based treatment that embodies the strengths of university-based treatments (e.g., theory-driven, well-specified interventions, considerable attention to treatment fidelity) and addresses the pragmatic, logistic, and fiscal concerns that are pertinent to community-based mental health services (Henggeler, Schoenwald, & Pickrel, 1995; Hoagwood et al., 1995). It addresses the multiple known correlates of serious antisocial behavior in youths (i.e., individual, family, peer, school, and community factors; Loeber & Farrington, 1998) in a comprehensive yet individualized fashion, in the naturalistic settings where the problems occur (e.g., home, school, and community). Importantly, MST has achieved noteworthy outcomes in several randomized trials (for a review, see Halliday-Boykins & Henggeler, in press).

Throughout the development and validation of MST, considerable attention has been devoted to issues of external validity and ecological validity—the applicability of the treatment model to real-world clinical populations seen in community settings by public sector mental health professionals. Such attention has led to favorable long-term outcomes in treating serious antisocial behavior in youths and to several ongoing projects to extend this success to other populations of children, adolescents, and families that present serious clinical problems.

Treatment Theory

Consistent with pragmatic (as opposed to aesthetic; see Alexander, Holtzworth-Munroe, & Jameson, 1994; Henggeler, Borduin, & Mann, 1993) models of the family and family therapy, MST embodies systems theory and assumptions of multicausality and views families as systems within which interaction processes are reciprocal, repetitive, and associated with the behavioral and psychological functioning of all family members. This view is also consistent with applied behavior analytic and social learning models of treatment for child behavior problems, which inform the emergent behavioral family intervention framework (Sanders, 1996).

In contrast with the classic family therapy paradigm, however, intrafamilial relations are not the sole target of MST interventions. Indeed, the "treatment theory" (Lipsey, 1988) underlying MST draws on both social ecological (Bronfenbrenner, 1979) and family systems (Haley, 1976; Minuchin, 1974) models of behavior. Consistent with Bronfenbrenner's (1979) theory of social ecology, MST views individuals as being nested within a complex of interconnected systems that encompass individual (e.g., biological, cognitive), family, and extrafamilial (i.e., peer, school, neighborhood) factors. Importantly, this ecological view of child and adolescent behavior problems is strongly supported by multivariate correlational and longitudinal studies of delinquency and adolescent substance abuse (for a review, see Henggeler, 1997). These studies indicate that a combination of family (inadequate parental monitoring of youth whereabouts, high conflict, low warmth, inconsistent or harsh discipline practices, and parental problems), peer (association with deviant peers), school (low family–school bonding, problems with academic and social performance), and neighborhood (transience, disorganization, criminal subculture) factors predict the development of delinquency and adolescent substance abuse. Thus, MST views behavior problems as maintained by problematic transactions within and between any one or a combination of the systems in which youths and families are embedded. Targets of MST intervention, therefore, include interactions within the family and between the family and other systems in the natural (e.g., peers, neighborhood, workplace) and service (e.g., mental health, juvenile justice, education, child welfare) ecologies (Schoenwald, Borduin, & Henggeler, 1997). Because MST views family interaction as just one of several targets of intervention, it is better described as a "family-based" treatment (Liddle & Dakof, 1995) than as a type of family therapy.

Therapy Characteristics

Nine treatment principles (see Exhibit 13-1) guide the development and implementation of MST interventions, the overarching goal of which is to em-

EXHIBIT 13-1

MST treatment principles

Principle 1: The primary purpose of assessment is to understand the "fit" between the identified problems and their broader systemic context.

Principle 2: Therapeutic contacts should emphasize the positive and should use systemic strengths as levers for change.

Principle 3: Interventions should be designed to promote responsible behavior and decrease irresponsible behavior among family members.

Principle 4: Interventions should be present-focused, action-oriented, and target specific and well-defined problems.

Principle 5: Interventions should target sequences of behavior within and between multiple systems that maintain the identified problems.

Principle 6: Interventions should be developmentally appropriate and fit the developmental needs of the youth.

Principle 7: Interventions should be designed to require daily or weekly effort by family members.

Principle 8: Intervention efficacy is evaluated continuously from multiple perspectives, with providers assuming accountability for overcoming barriers to successful outcomes.

Principle 9: Interventions should be designed to promote treatment generalization and long-term maintenance of therapeutic change by empowering care givers to address family members' needs across multiple systemic contexts.

power parents with the skills and resources needed to address the inevitable difficulties that arise in raising adolescents and to empower youths to cope with family, peer, school, and neighborhood problems. The volume that introduced MST to the field of family therapy (Henggeler & Borduin, 1990) has been augmented by a manual for practitioners that details the ongoing and interrelated assessment and intervention practices that characterize MST (Henggeler et al., 1998). As indicated in Principle 1, the objective of the ongoing MST assessment process is to understand the "fit" of identified behavior problems with their systemic context rather than at arriving at a diagnosis and, as such, it rarely uses formal assessment tools. Although implemented within a broad social–ecological clinical paradigm, MST interventions are both individualized and consistent with those treatment models (i.e., behavioral, cognitive–behavioral, pragmatic family systems) that demonstrate the largest effect sizes in the meta-analytic literature (Lipsey, 1992; Weisz & Weiss, 1993). Treatment sessions are active, highly focused, and held as often as every day early in treatment and as infrequently as once a week later in treatment.

The MST clinician training and supervision protocol brings a level of clinical rigor to community settings that is similar in intensity to that used in clinical trials conducted in university settings (Weisz et al., 1995). This protocol includes intensive training, quarterly booster training, weekly on-site supervision, and weekly treatment integrity checks through consultation with an expert in MST (see Henggeler et al., 1998). Ongoing attention to treatment fidelity, engagement, and overcoming obstacles to the attainment of positive outcomes is consistent with empirical literature on the relationship of treatment adherence and outcome (Henggeler, Melton, Brondino, Scherer, & Hanley, 1997; McGrew, Bond, Dietzen, & Salyers, 1994; Weisz et al., 1995) and with a philosophical stance in which the clinician, supervisor, and provider organization are held accountable for achieving positive outcomes.

Model of Service Delivery

To date, MST has been provided within a "family preservation" or home-based model of service delivery. The family preservation model is one in which a variety of counseling and concrete service interventions are implemented in the homes and communities of referred families. Family preservation services have increasingly been recommended by clinical child psychology and mental health services researchers as desirable alternatives to the use of restrictive and expensive placements for youths with serious behavioral and emotional problems. Within the last decade, family preservation programs have proliferated, distinct practice models have emerged, and target populations have diversified to include youths and families referred by juvenile justice and mental health agencies (for reviews, see Fraser, Nelson, & Rivard, 1997). Discussion of the common and distinctive elements of family preservation programs and of research on their effectiveness with various populations is beyond the scope of this chapter and appears elsewhere (see Schoenwald & Henggeler, 1997). Consistent with the family preservation model, MST as delivered in community-based clinical trials is (a) provided in home, school, neighborhood, and community settings; (b) intense (2 to 15 hours of service provided per family per week); (c) flexible (clinicians were available 24 hours per day, 7 days per week); (d) time-limited (4 to 6 months) and (e) characterized by low caseloads (4 to 6 families per clinician).

University- and Community-Based Clinical Trials

Multisystemic therapy was originally developed in a university research setting, with early clinical trials supporting its short-term efficacy in treating delinquent inner-city adolescents (Henggeler, Rodick, Borduin, Hanson, Watson, & Urey, 1986), maltreating families (Brunk, Henggeler, & Whelan, 1987), and a small sample of juvenile sex offenders (Borduin, Henggeler, Blaske, & Stein, 1990). In these early clinical trials, clinicians were doctoral-level students in clinical psychology. Treatment fidelity was monitored through weekly clinical group supervision and review of treatment logs. Posttreatment measures of youth behavior problems and family functioning (Brunk et al., 1987; Henggeler et al., 1986) as well as the recurrence of offending (Borduin et al., 1990) indicated that MST was significantly more effective as compared with usual community treatments (Henggeler et al., 1986), behavioral parent training (Brunk et al., 1987), and individual outpatient counseling (Borduin et al., 1990), respectively.

Subsequent studies demonstrating the longer-term effectiveness of MST were conducted under the auspices of university (Borduin et al., 1995) and public service sector (Henggeler, Melton, & Smith, 1992; Henggeler, Melton, Smith, Schoenwald, & Hanley, 1993) settings. These studies were characterized by similarities in design (randomized, two groups, pre- and posttest, follow-up for recidivism), participants (serious juvenile offenders and their families), treatment intensity, clinical supervisory practices, treatment fidelity, and favorable outcome (see Henggeler et al., 1995). The university-based study took place in Columbia, Missouri, and compared MST with individual therapy (IT). Participants were 200 12- to 17-year-old juvenile offenders and their families referred from the local department of juvenile justice office and randomly assigned to receive either MST ($n = 92$) or IT ($n = 84$). The MST therapists were six doctoral students in clinical psychology who provided home-based services, whereas the IT therapists were six master's-level therapists who provided outpatient mental health services. The juvenile offenders were involved in extensive criminal activity as demonstrated by their average of 4.2 previous arrests ($SD = 1.3$) and the fact that 63% had been previously incarcerated. The youths' average age was 14.8 years (SD = 1.6); 67% were male; 70% were Caucasian, and 30% African American; 65% were from families characterized by low socioeconomic status; and 53% lived with two parental figures. At posttreatment, families receiving MST reported and showed more positive changes in dyadic family interactions than did IT families. Families who received MST reported increased cohesion and adaptability and showed increased supportiveness and decreased conflict and hostility during family discussions as compared with IT families. Parents in the MST group showed greater reductions in psychiatric symptomatology than did parents in the IT condition. Most important, results from a 4-year follow-up of recidivism showed that youths who received MST were significantly less likely to be rearrested than youths who received IT. Youths who completed MST treatment had a recidivism rate of 22.1%, as compared with the rate of 71.4% that characterized youths who completed IT. Moreover, youths who dropped out of the MST condition (n = 15) had recidivism rates of 46.6%, while rates of recidivism were identical—71.4%—for both dropouts (n = 21) and completers (n = 63) of IT. Examination of recidivists from each group revealed that MST youths who were arrested during follow-up were arrested less often and for less serious offenses than IT youths arrested during follow-up. Follow-up data also revealed that MST youths had a significantly lower rate of substance-related arrests than IT youths (4% versus 16%; Henggeler et al., 1991) and a lower rate of arrests for violent crimes (e.g., rape, attempted rape, sexual assault, aggravated assault, assault and battery) relative to IT youths. The effectiveness of MST was not moderated by adolescent age, race, social class, gender, or pretreatment arrest history.

The community-based study was conducted in Simpsonville, South Carolina, and compared MST with usual services (e.g., court-ordered curfew, school attendance, probation services, referral to other community agencies). Participants were 84 violent and chronic juvenile offenders, of whom 54% had been arrested for violent crimes (half the remainder self-reported that they had committed at least one violent crime during the previous 6 months); their mean number of arrests was 3.5, and they averaged 9.5 weeks of previous placement in correctional facilities. The average age of the youths was 15.2 years; 77% were male; 56% were African American, 34% Caucasian; the average Hollingshead (1975) social class score was 25 (i.e., semiskilled workers), and 26% lived with neither biological parent. In this study, MST therapists were three master's-level counselors employed by the local department of mental health with an average of 2 years of previous experience in mental health.

In the Simpsonville study, youths receiving MST had significantly fewer arrests (M = .87 versus 1.52), weeks incarcerated (M = 5.8 versus 16.2), and self-reported offenses (M = 2.9 versus 8.6) than did youths receiving usual services at the 59-week postreferral follow-up. At posttreatment, families receiving MST reported more cohesion, whereas cohesion decreased in the usual services condition. Families also reported decreased adolescent aggression with peers, while such aggression remained the same for youths receiving usual services. A 2.4-year follow-up (Henggeler, Melton, Smith, Schoenwald, & Hanley, 1993) showed that MST doubled the percentage of youths not rearrested in comparison with usual services. Moreover, the relative efficacy of MST was neither moderated by demographic characteristics (race, age, social class, gender, arrest, and incarceration history) nor mediated by psychosocial variables (family relations, peer relations, social competence, behavior problems, and parental symptomatology). Thus, MST was equally effective with youths and families of divergent backgrounds. Finally, a comparison of cost (Henggeler et al., 1992) indicated that the cost per client for treatment in the MST group was about $3,500, which compares favorably with the average cost of institutional placement in South Carolina of $17,769 per offender, the use of which was significantly greater for youths in the usual services condition.

Ongoing Clinical Trials

The success of MST with serious juvenile offenders and their families has led to evaluations of the effectiveness of MST with other populations presenting serious problems. For example, data from an ongoing randomized trial with 118 substance abusing or dependent adolescent offenders suggest that MST is effective in reducing soft and hard drug use at posttreatment as well as incarceration and out-of-home placement at an approximately 1-year follow-up (Henggeler, Pickrel, & Brondino, 1999). Moreover, cost analyses have shown that the costs of MST were nearly offset by savings accrued as a result of reductions in days of out-of-home placement (hospitalization, residential treatment) in the MST condition, relative to the usual services condition, at 1 year following referral. Assuming that the youths in the MST condition continue to benefit from fewer out-of-home placement days for the remainder of the study, MST will yield cost savings (Schoenwald, Ward, Henggeler, Pickrel, & Patel, 1996).

Posttreatment outcomes from a recently completed randomized trial suggest that MST is a more effective and less costly strategy than psychiatric hospitalization for addressing the mental health emergencies of adolescents with severe emotional disturbances (Henggeler, Rowland, et al., 1999; Schoenwald, Ward, Henggeler, & Rowland, 2000). Importantly, a pilot study conducted within this project illuminated the interface of treatment and services research relevant to tailoring MST to better serve youths with serious emotional disturbance, prompting significant changes in the project's clinical procedures, organization, and supervisory processes, as well as in the project's interface with existing community resources. This project provides an example of the ways in which the continued development, replication, and dissemination of MST requires the application of both services and psychotherapy research tools.

The success of MST when implemented by community-based therapists under the auspices of the public mental health service sector (Henggeler et al., 1992, 1993) also led to a study of the relative effectiveness of MST with juvenile offenders when delivered in urban and rural community mental health settings (Henggeler et al., 1997). This study examined the effects of MST in treating violent and chronic juvenile offenders and their families in the absence of on-going treatment fidelity checks. Across two public sector mental health centers, 155 chronic and violent juvenile offenders and their families were randomly assigned to receive MST versus usual juvenile justice services. Although MST improved adolescent symptomatology at posttreatment and decreased incarceration 47% at a 1.7-year follow-up, findings for decreased criminal activity were not as favorable as observed in other recent trials of MST. Analyses of parent, adolescent, and clinician reports of MST treatment adherence, however, indicated that outcomes were substantially better in cases where treatment adherence ratings were high. These results highlight the importance of maintaining treatment fidelity when implementing complex family-based services in community settings. In light of these findings and subsequent experiences disseminating MST, a comprehensive package of quality control mechanisms for use in community sites has been developed.

Dissemination to the Service Delivery Community

Since 1994, dissemination of MST has also occurred outside the context of clinical trials at the request of public agencies and providers of mental health and juvenile justice services in and outside of South Carolina. Initially, the MST training and consultation protocol focused almost exclusively on clinicians, following the precedent established when clinicians participating in clinical trials were trained by the developers of MST. However, early experiences with community-based provider organizations seeking to establish MST programs suggested that several factors presented barriers to provider implementation of MST. These barriers occurred at the level of the clinician, organization, and community and economic context in which the organization operated (see Exhibit 13-2). Some of these factors are similar to those examined in the context of service system (Glisson & Hemmelgarn, 1998) and technology transfer research (Backer & Davis, 1994; Brown, 1995). This research suggests that effectiveness alone does not pave the way for successful dissemination of innovative interventions, because policy makers, public and private payers, service provider organizations, and clinicians need to perceive the innovation as relevant, credible, and acceptable to make the multiple changes required to implement innovations.

EXHIBIT 13-2
Some factors related to the successful implementation of MST

Clinician Strengths
Intelligence, flexibility, creativity, common sense; ability to conceptualize the family and ecology as client; receptive to ongoing peer clinical supervision; feeling accountable for outcomes; voluntarily participating in MST; some experience with empirically validated treatments.

Clinician Weaknesses
Wedded to non–empirically-based theories; exclusively child-focused; not receptive to ongoing peer clinical supervision; not feeling accountable for outcomes; conscripted to participation in MST.

Provider Organization
Clearly articulated "fit" of MST with goals and mandates; MST a distinct program with dedicated staff; all staff who can influence treatment are trained in, and support, MST; concrete support of the treatment team (e.g., personnel, salary, and administrative support of staff doing MST).

Community and Economic Factors
Community referrals sufficient to sustain MST program; existence of third-party public or private reimbursement for MST with no strong financial disincentives; provider organization has collaborative relationships with referral and community agencies.

Training Organization
Clear agreement regarding objectives of training and roles and responsibilities of training organization and provider organization; clear commitment to and engagement in full and continuing training and consultation experience, viewing it from a "continuous quality improvement" perspective.

In his review of the empirical literature on technology transfer, Brown (1995) identified six factors that appear to affect the use of behavioral science innovations in the service delivery community:

1. *Relevance*—the extent to which a novel intervention is viewed as consistent with the mission of the organization and its perceptions of the needs of the population it serves. The primary goals of MST (reducing youth criminal activity, reducing other antisocial behavior such as drug use, and achieving outcomes at a cost savings) are consistent with the missions of juvenile justice and mental health systems in most, if not all, communities.

2. *Timeliness*—(a) the availability of research findings regarding the intervention early in the planning and decision-making processes of policy makers (and payers), and (b) reducing the lapse between

identifying a problem and developing and testing a research-based solution. Research findings on MST clearly address the relevant needs of policy makers and provide them with a currently available treatment alternative that is both clinically and cost-effective with juvenile offender populations.

3. *Clarity*—use of language and format that makes findings accessible (rarely found in peer-reviewed research journals). Information about MST has been made accessible through brochures designed for the general public that summarize past research findings, the treatment approach, the model of service delivery, training, and ongoing controlled outcome studies of the treatment model, and four brief MST online fact sheets were developed in collaboration with the Consortium on Children, Families and the Law (1999). Practice manuals for therapists and supervisors and a program manual for administrators are available to MST provider organizations.

4. *Credibility*—the apparent objectivity and status of the message and of the message-giver. A history of support for MST at the federal, state, and community levels, as demonstrated through research funding, project sponsorship, and ongoing dissemination lend credibility to both the message and the message-giver.

5. *Replicability*—the extent to which interventions studied and found to be efficacious in one setting are replicable in other settings. The research on MST has demonstrated that the treatment model is effective across various settings. The developers of MST have conducted both university- and community-based research in collaboration with representatives from public service agencies that serve children and by collaborating with other professionals and independently evaluating MST programs in various community settings.

6. *Acceptability*—the extent to which organizations and the individuals within them are ready to accept the new intervention and the programmatic change it will entail. With the emergence of managed behavioral health care systems, the demands for increased levels of fiscal and outcome-related accountability on policy makers and providers make many organizations and individuals ready to accept the types of programmatic change necessary to successfully implement MST in a community.

In addition, however, our experiences in implementing MST in different communities indicate that these constructs may be operationalized differently for clinicians, provider organizations, and community agencies. Moreover, some variables that appear to influence successful dissemination of MST are not represented in Brown's framework. These factors (see Exhibit 13-2) and the relevance of Brown's framework to different stakeholders are described next.

Clinician Factors

Our experience suggests that relevance, credibility, and acceptability all operate at the level of the individual clinician. An organization's decision to adopt MST typically requires that clinicians experience new learning and develop additional work skills. Most of these clinicians (generally master's-level social workers, counselors, and psychologists) are midcareer professionals who have practiced relatively autonomously for many years and, consistent with findings in the technology transfer literature (Brown, 1995), they have viewed themselves, and have been viewed by others, as capable and productive. If clinicians perceive the introduction of MST as questioning their competencies and contributions, psychological readiness to adopt MST must be actively cultivated. Thus, consistent with recommendations in the technology transfer literature and with the strengths and focus of the MST treatment model itself, efforts are made to capitalize on clinicians' existing skills and experiences while helping them to develop the skills needed to implement MST.

We have also developed some anecdotal impressions regarding clinician factors that may facilitate readiness to adopt and adhere to MST principles and practices. These impressions are based on experiences in providing training and ongoing consultation to approximately 120 clinicians in 25 programs. Desirable personal characteristics of clinicians include intelligence, flexibility, creativity, open-mindedness, and a serious work ethic. Professional training and experience consistent with MST in terms of treatment focus (family, ecology), epistemology underlying the treatment model (empirically based), and emphasis on measurement of and accountability for clinical outcome appear to enhance clinician adoption of MST practices. Conversely, clinician training and experience that focuses on the individual child is informed primarily by nonempirically based treatment models, and eschews measurement of and individual accountability for outcomes appear to interfere with clinician adoption of MST principles and practices. At this time, neither the specific level of postbaccalaureate training (e.g., doctoral versus master's) nor the specific discipline (e.g., counseling psychology, social work, clinical psychology) seems to predict clinician adoption of or adherence to the treatment model. Within the context of an ongoing multisite study funded by the National Institute of Mental Health (Schoenwald, PI), we are now investigating relations between such variables as clinician training, professional experience, and theoretical orientation with adherence and outcomes.

Provider Organization

The results of a recently completed study of children's service systems highlight the importance of organizational factors to the attainment of positive outcomes (Glisson & Hemmelgarn, 1998). The quasi-experimental study examined the quality and outcomes of the services provided to 250 children placed in the custody of public children's service agencies in 12 counties with service integration and coordination teams and 12 matched control counties. The investigators examined relationships among organizational variables, service system variables, quality of service, and service outcomes for these youths. Findings indicated that organizational variables were more important than service system variables in predicting children's improved psychosocial functioning. Specifically, organizational climate—a construct composed of fairness, cooperation, job satisfaction, several aspects of role definition, and personalization—was significantly related to improved child psychosocial functioning, while the coordination of services throughout the service system was not.

The findings from this study are consistent with our anecdotal observations of organizational and individual clinician variables that appear to affect the successful implementation of MST. As suggested under the "Provider Organization" heading in Exhibit 13-2, several organizational factors seem to be linked with the successful dissemination of MST—such as "articulation of the fit of MST with the organization's goals and mandates" and "concrete support of treatment team"—and can be conceptualized as measures of organizational readiness to adopt innovation. Items that describe team structure and supervisorial authority; consonance of leadership and clinician perceptions of MST; the involvement of all staff influencing treatment; and concrete support of staff through pay, flexible hours, staff cooperation, staff roles, and status are exemplars of organizational factors thought to influence service system outcomes, but these are rarely examined in the context of either psychotherapy or mental health services research.

Community and Economic Factors

Factors that influence a provider organization's capacity to sustain MST include its relationships with referral agencies, providers of other services, and third-party payers. Clinicians and provider organizations that have established collaborative relationships with other agencies can more readily obtain those agencies' sanctions to take the lead in clinical decision making. The clinician's license to take the lead, in turn, is critical to her or his capacity to retain accountability for achieving clinical outcomes—a central tenet of MST. In addition, financing strategies and fiscal incentives (e.g., reimbursement methodologies and rates generated by third-party payers, availability of flexible funding) influence provider motivation to develop an MST program as well as referral patterns to the program. For example, when therapeutic services rendered within the context of a residential treatment program are reimbursed at higher rates than home-based services, service providers have little incentive to shift from residential to home-based service. Or, when referral agencies must pay for a portion of treatment delivered by providers of home-based services trained in MST but not for treatment delivered by providers of other services (e.g., outpatient, residential, training facilities), referral rates for providers trained in MST are low, which in turn threatens the economic viability of the MST program.

Training Organization–Provider Organization Interface

Studies of the use of research-based substance abuse treatment programs suggest that interpersonal contact between the developers of the technology and its potential users encourages successful technology transfer (Brown, 1995). To date, MST experts have provided training and telephone clinical consultation to clinicians in provider organizations, thus ensuring ongoing interpersonal contact between the developers and the users of MST. Communications between the provider and training organizations also address the programmatic, organizational, and community factors related to the successful implementation of MST in community-based settings. In addition, efforts are made to establish clear mutual expectations and agreements regarding objectives of ongoing MST training and the roles and responsibilities of the training and provider organization in meeting those objectives.

Among the responsibilities that have emerged for the training organization is the development of a more comprehensive package of quality assurance mechanisms to address more proactively potential clinician, organizational, and community barriers to the implementation of MST. Accordingly, the MST training and consultation protocol has been expanded to address the organizational and extraorganizational factors that influence successful program development. Further specification of supervision and organizational practices that support MST program implementation has been made possible as a result of federal funding from the Office of Juvenile Justice and Delinquency Prevention (OJJDP) intended to advance the dissemination of MST to juvenile justice systems nationally. A manual for supervisors has been written (Henggeler & Schoenwald, 1998), a measure of supervisory practices has been validated, and training specific to MST supervision has been developed and implemented. In addition, a manual that describes organizational conditions and procedures conducive to the establishment of MST programs has been written. This manual includes discussion of interagency agreements and reimbursement strategies conducive to the sustainability of MST programs. Finally, a multisite study funded by the National Institute of Mental Health (Schoenwald, PI) is examining the linkages among contextual variables (organizational and extraorganizational), therapist adherence, and child outcomes.

Implications for Family Intervention Science

The success of MST is instructive with respect to treatment and service delivery issues that should be considered in the development and validation of effective, family-based treatments that can be implemented in community-based service settings by community-based practitioners. Consistent with the family preservation model of service delivery, MST is characterized by a philosophical commitment to the empowerment of families and by service delivery characteristics (e.g., home-based, flexible, intensive, time-limited) that reduce the barriers to access and effectiveness that often characterize more traditional models of service delivery (e.g., traditional outpatient, residential treatment, inpatient). The treatment theory that guides MST is specified not only in accordance with a broad theory (e.g., social ecology), but also in terms of the specific factors in the youth's ecology shown to cause or maintain the antisocial behavior being targeted for treatment.

Whereas classic, pragmatic family therapies address the connections between family interactions and behavior problems and are demonstrating some promise with adolescents who have substance abuse problems (see Liddle & Dakof, 1995) and in engaging families of various ethnic backgrounds (Santisteban et al., 1996; Szapocznik et al., 1988), these family therapies may ultimately prove to be no more effective than other well-conceived, empirically validated treatments (e.g., parent behavior management training, social problem-solving skills training, and treatments combining these components) that have yet to demonstrate effectiveness with serious behavior problems in community-based treatment settings. To this end, the focus of family therapies on intrafamilial interactions may be too narrow to achieve significant and sustainable gains with youths who exhibit serious antisocial behavior such as delinquency and substance abuse. The increasingly ecological focus of family-based treatment for adolescents (Liddle, 1996) and family intervention science (Liddle & Bray, chapter 1, this volume) is consistent with empirical evidence for the multidetermined nature of serious clinical problems.

Similarly, over-reliance on office-based models of service delivery may limit the effectiveness of empirically validated family therapies with youths and families facing practical challenges such as work schedules, availability of child care, and transportation problems. Increased attention to and investigation of such issues as engagement of families of different ethnicities and therapist and process variables associated with resistance to treatment (Patterson & Chamberlain, 1994) are important strides toward increasing treatment relevance to and retention of various real-world client populations. Engagement and retention in treatment, however, may also be related with the accessibility to and ecological validity of the treatment in question. As suggested elsewhere (Henggeler et al., 1995), combining treatment models that are characterized by construct validity with models of service delivery that are characterized by ecological validity may be essential to providing effective, community-based services to youths with serious clinical problems and their families. The construct validity of family-based models of treatment for adolescents has been enhanced by recent accommodations of the empirical evidence regarding the multidetermined nature of such problems (Liddle, 1996). Models of service delivery, however, and issues pertaining to the service community (e.g., practitioners, service provider organizations, community context, financing strategies) and the interfaces of researchers with the service community have not yet been addressed in that literature.

The emergent family intervention and treatment development paradigms are quite consistent with the family-centered focus of children's mental health service system reform efforts (Stroul & Friedman, 1994). Family therapy and family-based treatment research are more likely to have an impact on the service delivery community, and therefore youths and families in need of treatment, if therapy researchers (a) attend to service delivery issues not as nuisance variables but as targets of intervention; (b) broaden the focus of classic family therapies tested in university-based studies to better reflect the multidetermined and often co-occurring nature of serious clinical problems; (c) conduct treatment outcome research in ways that more closely reflect the real-world conditions that families and clinicians face in community-based settings; and (d) attend to the individual, organizational, and community factors that influence transfer of behavioral science technology to service delivery communities.

Conclusion

A growing coalition of mental health services and treatment researchers contend that the development and dissemination of effective mental health services for children and families will require both treatment and mental health services research. Factors pertaining to treatment models (theory, interventions, therapists, supervisory practices), service delivery models (caseload, service site, intensity, frequency, duration, locus of accountability for outcomes), target population (antisocial behavior, abuse and neglect, substance abuse), service sectors (mental health, juvenile justice, child welfare, education, private sector), and fiscal issues must be examined together. The development and dissemination of clinically and cost-effective treatments to the service settings and service sectors in which youths and families with complex problems are most likely to be seen may require a transformation of the models of treatment, service delivery, and service systems developed to date.

The simultaneous or sequential examination of the intervention, service, and system variables that have an impact on treatment efficacy with heterogeneous populations is likely to require that both psychotherapy and services researchers develop new skills. In straddling the treatment and services research worlds, significant effort must be invested in developing and maintaining active collaborations with both the leadership and the line staff in public service sector, agency, and provider organizations. This ongoing investment has been critical to the empirical validation and initial dissemination of MST and to its early dissemination outside the context of clinical trials. The development and evaluation of our dissemination protocol also required collaboration across university-based researchers and various, state, county, and provider-level entities. For example, the federal Office of Juvenile Justice and Delinquency Prevention funded a project to specify clinical supervisory and organizational structures necessary to develop and maintain effective MST programs as well as measurement methods necessary to promote treatment fidelity and to evaluate programs. Those measures were developed and tested in collaboration with several different provider sites. Colleagues in a variety of disciplines (public health, economics, criminal justice) who participated in the Consortium on Children, Families, and Society collaborated with us on the effort to make information about MST accessible and comprehensible to a wide range of stakeholders (see Consortium on Children, Families and the Law, 1999). Learning the constructs and methodologies associated with cost analyses has been necessary to examine the cost-effectiveness of MST, which, in turn, has been of utmost interest to the funding agencies in our state and others in which providers of mental health services are reimbursed by public funds or managed care entities. Such skills are not typically acquired or valued by the traditional treatment research community. These skills are necessary, however, to answer satisfactorily the questions raised by policy makers, practitioners, and consumers regarding the clinical and cost-effectiveness of mental health services delivered in the real world.

References

Alexander, J. F., Holtzworth-Munroe, A., & Jameson, P. (1994). The process and outcome of marital and family therapy: Research review and evaluation. In A. E. Bergin & S. L. Garfield (Eds.), *Handbook of psychotherapy and behavior change* (pp. 595–630). New York: Wiley.

Azar, B. (1994, July). Initiatives broaden addiction research. *APA Monitor,* p. 4.

Backer, T. E., & David, S. L. (1994). Synthesis of behavioral science learnings about technology transfer. *Reviewing the behavioral science knowledge base on technology transfer.* National Institute on Drug Abuse Monograph Series, No. 155, U.S. Department of Health and Human Services, National Institutes of Health, National Institute on Drug Abuse, Rockville, MD.

Bickman, L. (1996). A continuum of care: More is not always better. *American Psychologist, 51,* 689–701.

Bickman, L., & Rog, D. J. (Eds.). (1995). *Children's mental health services: Research, policy, and evaluation.* Thousand Oaks, CA: Sage.

Bickman, L., Summerfelt, W. T., Firth, J. M., & Douglas, S. (1997). The Stark County Evaluation Project: Baseline results of a randomized experiment. In C. Nixon & D. Northrup (Eds.), *Evaluating mental health services: How do programs for children "work" in the real world* (pp. 231–258). Thousand Oaks, CA: Sage.

Borduin, C. M., Henggeler, S. W., Blaske, D. M., & Stein, R. (1990). Multisystemic treatment of adolescent sexual offenders. *International Journal of Offender Therapy and Comparative Criminology 34,* 105–113.

Borduin, C. M., Mann, B. J., Cone, L. T., Henggeler, S. W., Fucci, B. R., Blaske, D. M., & Williams, R. A. (1995). Multisystemic treatment of serious juvenile offenders: Long-term prevention of criminality and violence. *Journal of Consulting and Clinical Psychology, 63,* 569–578.

Bronfenbrenner, U. (1979). *The ecology of human development: Experiments by nature and design.* Cambridge, MA: Harvard University Press.

Brown, B. S. (1995). Reducing impediments to technology transfer in drug abuse programming. *Reviewing the behavioral science knowledge base on technology transfer.* National Institute on Drug Abuse Monograph Series, No. 155, U.S. Department of Health and Human Services, National Institutes of Health, National Institute on Drug Abuse, Rockville, MD.

Brunk, M., Henggeler, S. W., & Whelan, J. P. (1987). A comparison of multisystemic therapy and parent training in the brief treatment of child abuse and neglect. *Journal of Consulting and Clinical Psychology, 55,* 311–318.

Burns, B. J., Hoagwood, K., & Mrazek, P. J. (1999). Treatment for mental disorders in children and adolescents. *Clinical Child and Family Psychology Review, 2,* 199–254.

Consortium on Children, Families and the Law. (1999). *Fact sheets on multisystemic therapy* [Online]. Available: http://virtual.clemson.edu/groups/ifnl/consortium.htm.

Foster, E. M., Summerfelt, W. T., & Saunders, R. C. (1996). The costs of mental health services under the Fort Bragg Demonstration. *Journal of Mental Health Administration, 23,* 92–106.

Fraser, M. W., Nelson, K. E., & Rivard, J. C. (1997). The effectiveness of family preservation services. *Social Work Research, 21,* 138–152.

Glisson, C., & Hemmelgarn, A. (1998). The effects of organizational climate and interorganizational coordination on the quality and outcomes of children's service systems. *Child Abuse and Neglect, 22,* 401–421.

Haley, J. (1976). *Problem solving therapy.* San Francisco: Jossey-Bass.

Halliday-Boykins, C. A., & Henggeler, S. W. (in press). Multisystemic therapy: Theory, research and practice. In E. Walton, P. A. Sandau-Beckler, & M. Mannes (Eds.), *Setting direction for family-centered services in child welfare into the twenty-first century: Theory, practice, policy and research.* New York: Columbia University Press.

Henggeler, S. W. (1997). The development of effective drug abuse services for youth. In J. A. Egertson, D. M. Fox, & A. I. Leshner (Eds.), *Treating drug abusers effectively* (pp. 253–279). New York: Blackwell-North America/Milbank Memorial Fund..

Henggeler, S. W., & Borduin, C. M. (1990). *Family therapy and beyond: A multisystemic approach to treating the behavior problems of children and adolescents*. Pacific Grove, CA: Brooks/Cole.

Henggeler, S. W., Borduin, C. M., & Mann, B. J. (1993). Advances in family therapy: Empirical foundations. In T. H. Ollendick & R. J. Prinz (Eds.), *Advances in clinical child psychology* (Vol. 15, pp. 207–241). New York: Plenum Press.

Henggeler, S. W., Borduin, C. M., Melton, G. B., Mann, B. J., Smith, L. A., Hall, J. A., Cone, L., & Fucci, B. R. (1991). Effects of multisystemic therapy on drug use and abuse in serious juvenile offenders: A progress report from two outcome studies. *Family Dynamics of Addiction Quarterly, 1,* 40–51.

Henggeler, S. W., Melton, G. B., Brondino, M. J., Scherer, D. G., & Hanley, J. H. (1997). Multisystemic therapy with violent and chronic juvenile offenders and their families: The role of treatment fidelity in successful dissemination. *Journal of Consulting and Clinical Psychology, 65,* 821–823.

Henggeler, S. W., Melton, G. B., & Smith, L. A. (1992). Family preservation using multisystemic therapy: An effective alternative to incarcerating serious juvenile offenders. *Journal of Consulting and Clinical Psychology, 60,* 953–961.

Henggeler, S. W., Melton, G. B., Smith, L. A., Schoenwald, S. K., & Hanley, J. (1993). Family preservation using multisystemic therapy: Long-term follow-up to a clinical trial with serious juvenile offenders. *Journal of Child and Family Studies, 2,* 283–293.

Henggeler, S. W., Pickrel, S. G., & Brondino, M. J. (1999). Multisystemic treatment of substance abusing and dependent delinquents: Outcomes, treatment fidelity, and transportability. *Mental Health Services Research, 1,* 171–184.

Henggeler, S. W., Rodick, J. D., Borduin, C. M., Hanson, C. L., Watson, S. M., & Urey, J. R. (1986). Multisystemic treatment of juvenile offenders: Effects on adolescent behavior and family interaction. *Developmental Psychology, 22,* 132–141.

Henggeler, S. W., Rowland, M. D., Randall, J., Ward, D. M., Pickrel, S. G., Cunningham, P. B., Miller, S. L., Edwards, J., Zealberg, J., Hand, L. D., & Santos, A. B. (1999). Home based multisystemic therapy as an alternative to the hospitalization of youths in psychiatric crisis: Clinical outcomes. *Journal of the American Academy of Child and Adolescent Psychiatry, 38,* 1331–1339.

Henggeler, S. W., & Schoenwald, S. K. (1998). *The MST supervisory manual: Promoting quality assurance at the clinical level*. Charleston, SC: MST Institute.

Henggeler, S. W., Schoenwald, S. K., Borduin, C. M., Rowland, M. D., & Cunningham, P. B. (1998). *Multisystemic treatment for antisocial behavior in youth*. New York: Guilford Press.

Henggeler, S. W., Schoenwald, S. K., & Munger, R. L. (1996). Families and therapists achieve clinical outcomes, systems of care mediate the process. *Journal of Child and Family Studies, 5,* 177–183.

Henggeler, S. W., Schoenwald, S. K., & Pickrel, S. G. (1995). Multisystemic therapy: Bridging the gap between university- and community-based treatment. *Journal of Consulting and Clinical Psychology, 63,* 709–717.

Henggeler, S. W., Smith, B. H., & Schoenwald, S. K. (1994). Key theoretical and methodological issues in conducting treatment research in the juvenile justice system. *Journal of Clinical Child Psychology, 23,* 143–150.

Hoagwood, K. (1997). Interpreting nullity: The Fort Bragg Experiment—A comparative success or failure? *American Psychologist, 52,* 546–550.

Hoagwood, K., Hibbs, E., Brent, D., & Jensen, P. (1995). Introduction to the special section: Efficacy and effectiveness in studies of child and adolescent psychotherapy. *Journal of Consulting and Clinical Psychology, 63,* 683–687.

Hoagwood, K., & Hohman, A. A. (1994). Child and adolescent services research at the National Institute of Mental Health: Research opportunities in an emerging field. *Journal of Child and Family Studies, 2,* 259–268.

Hollingshead, A. B. (1975). *Four factor index of social status.* Unpublished manuscript, Yale University, New Haven, CT.

Jensen, P. S., Hoagwood, K., & Petti, T. (1996). Outcomes of mental health care for children and adolescents: II. Literature review and application of a comprehensive model. *Journal of the American Academy of Child and Adolescent Psychiatry, 35,* 1064–1077.

Kazdin, A. E., Siegel, T. C., & Bass, D. (1990). Drawing upon clinical practice to inform research on child and adolescent psychotherapy: A survey of practitioners. *Professional Psychology: Research and Practice, 21,* 189–198.

Kazdin, A. E., & Weisz, J. R. (1998). Identifying and developing empirically supported child and adolescent treatments. *Journal of Consulting and Clinical Psychology, 66,* 19–36.

Lambert, E. W., & Guthrie, P. R. (1996). Clinical outcomes of a children's mental health managed care demonstration. In L. Bickman (Ed.), The evaluation of the Fort Bragg Demonstration [Special issue]. *Journal of Mental Health Administration, 23,* 51–68.

Liddle, H. A. (1996). Family-based treatment for adolescent problem behaviors: Overview of contemporary developments and introduction to the special section. *Journal of Family Psychology, 10,* 3–11.

Liddle, H. A., & Dakof, G. A. (1995). Efficacy of family therapy for drug abuse: Promising but not definitive. *Journal of Marital and Family Therapy, 21,* 511–543.

Lipsey, M. W. (1988). Juvenile delinquency intervention. In H. S. Bloom, D. S. Cordray, & R. J. Light (Eds.), *Lessons from selected program and policy areas: New directions for program evaluation* (pp. 63–84). San Francisco: Jossey-Bass.

Lipsey, M. W. (1992). Juvenile delinquency treatment: A meta-analytic inquiry into the variability of effects. In T. D. Cook, H. Cooper, D. S. Cordray, H. Hartman, L. V. Hedges, R. J. Light, T. A. Louis, & F. Mosteller (Eds.), *Meta-analysis for explanation: A casebook* (pp. 83–127). New York: Russell Sage Foundation.

Loeber, R., & Farrington, D. P. (Eds.). (1998). *Serious and violent juvenile offenders: Risk factors and successful interventions.* Thousand Oaks, CA: Sage.

McGrew, J. H., Bond, G. R., Dietzen, L., & Salyers, M. (1994). Measuring the fidelity of implementation of a mental health program model. *Journal of Consulting and Clinical Psychology, 62,* 670–678.

Minuchin, S. (1974). *Families and family therapy.* Cambridge, MA: Harvard University Press.

Oswald, D. P., & Singh, N. N. (1996). Emerging trends in child and adolescent mental health services. In T. H Ollendick & R. J Prinz (Eds.), *Advances in Clinical Child Psychology* (Vol. 18, pp. 331–365). New York: Plenum Press.

Patterson, G. R., & Chamberlain, P. (1994). A functional analysis of resistance during parent training therapy. *Clinical Psychology: Science and Practice, 1,* 53–70.

Sanders, M. R. (1996). New directions in behavioral family intervention with children. In T. H. Ollendick & R. J. Prinz (Eds.), *Advances in clinical child psychology* (Vol. 18, pp. 293–330). New York: Plenum Press.

Santisteban, D. A., Szapocznik, J., Perez-Vidal, A., Kurtines, W. M., Murray, W. J., & LaPerriere, A. (1996). Engaging behavior problem drug abusing youth and their families into treatment: An investigation of the efficacy of specialized engagement interventions and factors that contribute to differential effectiveness. *Journal of Family Psychology, 10,* 35–44.

Schoenwald, S. K., Borduin, C. M., & Henggeler, S. W. (1997). Changing the natural and service ecologies of adolescents and their families. In M. H. Epstein, K. Kutash, & A. Duchnowski (Eds.), *Outcomes for children and youth with emotional and behavioral disorders and their families. Programs and evaluation best practices* (pp. 485–512). Austin, TX: Pro-ed.

Schoenwald, S. K., & Henggeler, S. W. (1997). Combining effective treatment strategies with family preservation models of service delivery: A challenge for mental health. In R. J. Illback, H. Joseph, Jr., & C. Cobb (Eds.), *Integrated services for children and families: Opportunities for psychological practice* (pp. 121–136). Washington, DC: American Psychological Association.

Schoenwald, S. K., Ward, D. M., Henggeler, S. W., Pickrel, S. G., & Patel, H. (1996). MST treatment of substance abusing or dependent adolescent offenders: Costs of reducing incarceration, inpatient, and residential placement. *Journal of Child and Family Studies, 4,* 431–444.

Schoenwald, S. K., Ward, D. M., Henggeler, S. W., & Rowland, M. D. (2000). MST vs. hospitalization for crisis stabilization of youth: Placement outcomes 4 months post referral. *Mental Health Services Research, 2,* 3–12.

Stroul, B. A., & Friedman, R. M. (1994). *A system of care for children and youth with severe emotional disturbance.* Washington, DC: Georgetown University Child Development Center.

Szapocznik, J., Perez-Vidal, A., Brockman, A. L., Foote, F. H., Santisteban, D., Hervis, O., & Kurtines, W. (1988). Engaging adolescent drug abusers and their families in treatment: A strategic structural systems approach. *Journal of Consulting and Clinical Psychology, 56,* 552–557.

U.S. Surgeon General. (1999). *Mental health: A report of the Surgeon General.* Washington, DC: U.S. Department of Health and Human Services.

Weisz, J. R., Donenberg, G. R., Han, S. S., & Kauneckis, D. (1995). Child and adolescent psychotherapy outcomes in experiments versus clinics: Why the disparity? *Journal of Abnormal Child Psychology, 23,* 83–106.

Weisz, J. R., Donenberg, G. R., Han, S. S., & Weiss, B. (1995). Bridging the gap between laboratory and clinic in child and adolescent psychotherapy. *Journal of Consulting and Clinical Psychology, 63,* 688–701.

Weisz, J. R., Han, S. S., & Valeri, S. M. (1997). More of what? Issues raised by the Fort Bragg study. *American Psychologist, 52,* 541–545.

Weisz, J. R., Weiss, B., & Donenberg, G. R. (1992). The lab versus the clinic: Effects of child and adolescent psychotherapy. *American Psychologist, 47,* 1578–1585.

Weisz, J. R., & Weiss, B. (1993). *Effects of psychotherapy with children and adolescents.* New York: Sage.

CHAPTER 14

Challenges in a 30-Year Program of Research: Conduct Disorders and Attention Deficit Hyperactivity Disorder, the Marital Discord and Depression Link, and Partner Abuse

K. Daniel O'Leary

In writing this chapter, I was asked to present information about my research career and the ways in which it was shaped. In turn, I was asked to describe how my research influenced the field. The research journey is divided into three components that depict the three major areas in which I have worked: conduct disorders and attention deficit hyperactivity disorder (ADHD), the marital discord and depression link, and partner abuse.

Conduct Disorders and Attention Deficit Hyperactivity Disorder

Graduate school was a great period of my life, for there was a sense that we were part of a theoretical "changing of the guard." The psychodynamic conceptualization might be replaced by a new view called *behavior modification* or *behavior therapy*. The most dramatic evidence of this change was represented in the now classic work, *Case Studies in Behavior Modification,* written by Leonard Ullmann (one of my professors at the University of Illinois) and Leonard Krasner (the director of clinical training at the State University of New York at Stony Brook; Ullman & Krasner, 1965). About the same time, I had heard of the work of Sidney Bijou and his colleagues, who had used a token reinforcement program with a classroom of children with mental challenges (e.g., Birnbauer, Bijou, Wolf, & Kidder, 1965). The changes he found in both social and academic behavior were dramatic. A visit to the classroom of children who were emotionally disturbed revealed 17 third-grade children who were very unruly—

verbal and physical aggression were rampant. It seemed logical to my advisor and me to apply a token reinforcement approach in this setting. With the aid of my research mentor, Wesley Becker, I was able to establish baseline observations of the children over 10 days; 76% of the time these students were engaged in inappropriate behavior such as talking out of turn, walking around the room without permission, and bothering a neighbor. The program was described to the children in the following manner (or some minor variant thereof): You know how your parents and older people work to earn money. You are going to be able to earn certain things by behaving well and working hard in your subjects. You will be able to earn things like special pencils, erasers, pens, candy, pennants, comics, tablets. You can even earn larger prizes (e.g., kites or perfume) if you work for a long period. Small notebooks were placed on the corner of each child's desk, and ratings varying from 1 to 10 were placed in the notebook at the end of each academic period in the afternoon (when the children were most unruly). Miss Drake, the teacher, was asked to praise the children frequently for completing academic work and for behaving well. The concept of shaping gradual approximations to the final desired goal was central to what we were doing, both with regard to the use of praise and the use of points for good work and appropriate behavior. The teacher was also asked to ignore as much disruptive behavior as possible and to give soft reprimands to the children (reprimands audible only to the child being reprimanded). Rules were posted on a chart at the front of the room, and they were reviewed daily. As the program progressed, the frequency of teacher ratings (token reinforcers) as well as the frequency of backup reinforcers decreased to a 4-day delay of reinforcement.

With the introduction of the token reinforcement program, the children's behavior changed dramatically almost immediately, and across time, the frequency of tangible reinforcers was reduced. Even when the children were receiving tangible rewards only on a weekly basis, the disruptive behavior was markedly reduced relative to the baseline. Overall, the average percentage of deviant behavior decreased from 76% in baseline to 10% during the token reinforcement period.

This work was published in 1967 in *Exceptional Children,* and it was probably one of the most influential research publications I have ever had (K. D. O'Leary & Becker, 1967). The article was reprinted in full in at least 10 books and was discussed in many more. Basically, we demonstrated that explicit incentive (token reinforcement) programs could be used effectively in classrooms for children with behavioral and emotional problems. As we are into the 21st century and visit such classroom facilities, it appears that token reinforcement programs or variants thereof are here to stay. A close look at several recent books on discipline and classroom management reveals that rewards and token reinforcement programs are covered in those texts (cf. Dornbush & Pruitt,

1995; Goldstein, 1995; Reiff, 1995). The exact nature of the type of rewards that should be used is open to debate in these texts, and there is emphasis on initial limit setting, responsibility training, and reinforcers that are natural to the classroom, such as preferred activities, so that the teachers do not have to purchase tangible reinforcers. It is my impression from visits to many local schools that positive notes that are sent home, commendation letters, and daily report cards are used especially with classes that address children with special needs. In the 1970s, we had advocated the transition to "natural reinforcers" because of the difficulty of withdrawing tangible rewards such as pens and small educational incentives, and this practice is clearly in place.

Let me now turn to a discussion of the status of behavior modification in the late 1960s, when I began my first job at the State University of New York at Stony Brook.

In 1967, no behavior modification and behavior therapy clinics existed on Long Island, where Stony Brook is located, and it is probably fair to say that no such programs existed almost anywhere in the United States. The prevailing views of children's problems were based on psychodynamic conceptualizations, and, in 1972, because of the lack of information about behavioral procedures for teachers, my wife, Susan O'Leary, and I published an edited book, *Classroom Management: The Successful Use of Behavior Modification* (K. D. O'Leary & O'Leary, 1972). In addition, in 1977 we published a second edition of this book with new articles that exemplified how behavioral principles could be used in classrooms (K. D. O'Leary & O'Leary, 1977). Based on sales, this text was well received, and it filled a void in this area.

During my first few years at Stony Brook, with graduate students Ronald Drabman, Ruth Kass, Ken Kaufman, Ronald Kent, and Robert Spitalnik, I evaluated the effects of different components of a token reinforcement program (e.g., reward and cost, rules, praise) and illustrated how self-control procedures could be combined with these programs to enhance the maintenance of positive effects. We also showed that soft reprimands (i.e., reprimands made audible only to the child being reprimanded) were more effective than reprimands audible to many children in the class. With Rita Poulos and Vernon Devine, I explicated how reinforcers were not bribes in an article, *Tangible Reinforcers: Bonuses or Bribes* (K. D. O'Leary, Poulos, & Devine, 1972). However, in all of the work we completed on various means of motivating children in classrooms, we emphasized the moment-to-moment feedback by teachers and parents. This point seemed especially critical for anyone who was using some form of a token reinforcement program, because as the frequency of the token and backup reinforcers decreased, the need for more subtle forms of feedback and encouragement would become more important. This point seems as crucial today as it did 25 years ago.

During the first decade of my research, I developed behavior therapy programs for children with attention deficit and hyperactivity and their parents and teachers. With the help of graduate students William Pelham, Alan Rosenbaum, and Gloria Price, and a pediatrician, Rolf Jacob, I designed behavioral programs in the classroom leading to changes in attending and work completion that appeared to be as great as those produced by the psychostimulant Ritalin (K. D. O'Leary, Pelham, Rosenbaum, & Price, 1976). More specifically, the decreases in inattention and disruptive behavior as assessed by the Conners Teacher Rating Scale were as great as those seen in studies evaluating the effects of Ritalin on hyperactive children. To try to make certain that pediatricians, who are the most likely prescribers of Ritalin, would know of these findings, we published the first study in *Clinical Pediatrics* (K. D. O'Leary et al, 1976). In turn, Susan O'Leary and William Pelham gradually weaned ADHD children off Ritalin and showed that their behavior remained remarkably similar to their behavior on Ritalin with a program of highly specific academic and social goals. Again to illustrate the impact of behavior therapy procedures on pediatricians, this work was published in the journal *Pediatrics* (S. G. O'Leary & Pelham, 1978). One central aspect of these programs was a daily note home or feedback system to parents in which they were encouraged to provide positive feedback and reinforcement for reaching daily and later weekly goals.

In 1980, I summarized my views in a somewhat polemic article entitled *Pills or Skills for Hyperactive Children* (K. D. O'Leary, 1980). Basically, except for extremely inattentive and overactive children, I argued that children with attentional and behavioral problems should receive help in learning social and academic skills through education and behavioral interventions with parents and teachers as a first approach. If such interventions are not effective, then the use of Ritalin seems quite appropriate. Clinically, this advice still seems to be prudent, although one can cogently argue for the use of psychostimulant medication with ADHD children as an initial approach to the treatment of such problems (MTA Cooperative Group, 1999). In a major multisite study with more than 500 children, for most ADHD symptoms, children in a combined behavioral treatment and medication management group showed significantly greater improvement than those given intensive behavioral treatment and community care. Nonetheless, in keeping with the idea that it is necessary to teach skills to such children, only the combined treatment showed greater benefit than community care on outcome domains such as achievement, parent–child relations, and social skills.

Whatever I may have contributed to the impact of research from our group, it is also important to note that I was at the right place at the right time to influence the development of behavior therapy. The field had been opened conceptually by others a few years before I completed graduate school by writers such as Skinner, Ullmann and Krasner, Wolpe, Bijou and Baer, and Bandura. By 1978, I had been listed among the 100 most cited psychologists in the

English-speaking world (Endler, Rushton, & Roediger, 1978). In part, this citation impact of journal articles was caused by the rapidly increasing interest in behavior therapy and to the writing of several texts (e.g., K. D. O'Leary & O'Leary, 1972; K. D. O'Leary & Wilson, 1975).

While conducting research on interventions that would influence the disruptive behavior of children with conduct problems and hyperactivity (now called ADHD), a significant personal event happened that influenced the substance of my research. My wife, Susan O'Leary, was in a tenure track position at Stony Brook, and when she came up for her first 3-year renewal, questions arose about the independence of our work, although we only had collaborated on one article and one book at that time. In order that there not be any question in the future about the independent work of Susan when she came up for tenure, it seemed wise not to do more work together, at least temporarily. Interestingly, other than revising our book, *Classroom Management,* Susan and I never published together again, although we certainly have reviewed each other's work. This prompted me to leave the child area, because that was Susan's interest and because I had become interested in the influence of marital problems on childhood problems. More specifically, with Ronald Kent (Kent & O'Leary, 1976) I had shown that a consultation program for parents and teachers of children with aggression had a significant effect seen in follow-up of the treated children (as compared to a nontreated control group). However, in collecting the follow-up data, we made repeated observations that children in homes fraught with marital problems and other stressors were most likely to show relapse from the treatment. Thus, I started to work more with adults, focusing on the interaction between marital and childhood problems, with several graduate students: Tom Oltmanns, Joan Broderick, Robert Emery, and Beatrice Porter. This work consistently showed a relation between marital and childhood problems, although the strength of the relation depended on whether one collected data from a clinical or a community sample (K. D. O'Leary & Emery, 1983). Although I am not centrally involved in this area of research now, I am happy to say that several people who have worked with me continue to give direction and expansion to the area (e.g., Emery, 1994; Grych & Fincham, 1990).

In the second and third decades of my research, the focus has been largely on (a) the relation of marital discord and depressive symptomatology, and (b) the etiology and treatment of physical aggression in intimate relationships.

The Marital Discord and Depression Link

Many professionals, especially psychiatrists and biologically oriented psychologists, believe that depression, especially a major depressive disorder, is biologically caused and that antidepressant medication is the first choice of treatments (American Psychiatric Association, 1993). My own view is that both twin and family studies show that major depressive disorders have some genetic basis but that what is inherited is not the disorder per se but a vulnerability to develop depression (Beach, Sandeen, & O'Leary, 1990; Wilson, Nathan, O'Leary, & Clarke, 1996). The evidence certainly supports the view that genetics are important, but for the nonhospitalized individual with a major depressive episode—a population that psychologists see most often in outpatient clinics—the role of environmental factors appears to be more important than with depressive disorders that are more severe (Kendler, Heath, Martin, & Eaves, 1987; Torgersen, 1986). For the record, let me also make clear that I am aware that when one or both partners are depressed, marital discord can rapidly develop. As Coyne (1999) has emphasized, depressed people can have a measurable negative impact on others. Further, he has challenged the field to come to grips with the evidence that depression is often a recurrent, episodic disorder but also to attempt to understand how interpersonal factors might explain why such individuals are not depressed.

Let me now turn to a discussion of how we became involved with the marital discord and depression link. In a number of marital cases that came to our university clinic, one or the other partner often appeared to be depressed or had elevated depressive symptomatology. In fact, when we assessed consecutive cases that appeared in our marital clinic, we found that mild to moderate levels of depressive symptomatology were present in more than 50% of the couples—one or the other partner had a Beck Depression Inventory (BDI) score that was greater than 14 (Beach, Jouriles, & O'Leary, 1985).

In a longitudinal study of 241 couples assessed at 6 month and 18 months after marriage, we found that marital discord was predictive of later depressive symptomatology (Beach & O'Leary, 1993). The first-order concurrent correlations between marital discord and depressive symptomatology were clearly significant. For wives, the correlations were, at premarriage, .33; at 6 months, .47; at 18 months, .52. For husbands, the correlations were, at premarriage, .34; at 6 months, .38; at 18 months, .50. The increases in the correlations between marital satisfaction and depression from premarriage to 18 months were significant for both husbands and wives. Hierarchical regression analyses were then conducted, and we found that marital discord predicted later depressive symptomatology, even after controlling for previous levels of depressive symptomatology. Almost 20% of the variance in depressive symptomatology at 18 months, beyond the effect of premarital level of depression, was uniquely attributed to marital discord or interactions with marital discord. One interest in this study was to learn if there were certain individuals for whom marital discord had particularly strong predictive effects for later depressive symptomatology. Thus, the sample was divided into individuals with chronic levels of dysphoria

($n = 407$) and those without dysphoria ($n = 75$). The dysphoric group was found to be more reactive to increases in marital discord. These results were interpreted as evidence for the hypothesis that those who are chronically dysphoric are more vulnerable to stress within the marriage than those without dysphoria. (To be judged dysphoric, an individual had to score in the upper quartile of the depression scores at premarriage and 6 months after marriage.)

A different look at the same community population of married couples at 18 and 30 months after marriage was provided by applying cutoff scores to the group on standardized measures of marital discord and depressive symptomatology and by analyzing the link between marital discord and depressive symptomatology. A Locke-Wallace Marital Adjustment Test score of less than 100 and a BDI score of 14 or fewer were the criteria used to examine the association between the two variables. (With BDI scores of 19 to 20, the averages for this group, Craighead, Craighead, DeRosa, and Allen [1993] found that half of such individuals met the criteria for major depressive disorder.) The odds for depressive symptomatology increased approximately tenfold if the marriage was discordant (odds ratio was 9.5). Because there is some possibility that the association between depressive symptomatology and marital discord in one gender is influenced by the association in the other gender, loglinear models that control for the association of marital discord and depressive symptomatology in the spouse yielded basically the same results as those reported in the earlier odds ratios. The odds ratio is a symmetrical measure of the association between two dichotomized variables derived from a fourfold table, and thus the odds for depressive symptomatology given marital discord will be identical to the odds of being discordant given depressive symptomatology. As such, we needed to garner additional data to show the relative impact of marital discord on depressive symptomatology, and vice versa.

To examine the possibility that negative events in marriage would directly lead to women becoming clinically depressed, we assessed women who had a negative event in their marriage within the last month and excluded women who had ever been depressed in the past. The primary types of events reported were discovery of a husband's infidelity, a separation or divorce initiated by the husband, or a separation or divorce initiated by the wife because of infidelity or marked violence by the husband. Thirty-eight percent of the women became clinically depressed following such events, even though they had never been depressed before. Statistical models showed that marital discord (e.g., problems in the marriage such as communication difficulties, lack of affection) predicted later depressive symptoms in these women but that depressive symptoms did not predict later marital discord. Moreover, being depressed was not related to whether their family members (mother, father, siblings) had ever been depressed (Christian-Herman, O'Leary, & Avery-Leaf, in press), demonstrating that the negative events played a much more important role than a genetic predisposition to depression in these women. Further, to our surprise, infidelity or anticipated loss of a partner were more important causes of depression than being the victim of physical violence.

In a second study of the role of negative events in marriage and depression of women, we again assessed the impact of events such as infidelity of the partner, anticipated loss of a partner, and physical aggression against the wife. In this study, we also assessed women who had experienced highly negative marital events but did not exclude women who had previously been depressed. These women were compared to a control group who had not had a negative marital event in the past month. In this study, 72% of the women who had experienced a negative event became clinically depressed within a month after the event, whereas only 12% of the women who had not experienced a highly negative marital event became depressed (Cano & O'Leary, 2000). As in our earlier research, there was no relationship between becoming depressed and a history of depression in other family members of the women.

In brief, our research has explicitly shown that certain negative events in marriage, especially those that prompt women to devalue their sense of worth, lead directly to clinical depression. In general, women who experience highly negative events in their marriage must be considered at high risk for depression, especially if they had been previously depressed.

Some related longitudinal work confirms the view that marital discord can lead to depressive symptomatology. Fincham, Beach, Harold, and Osborne (1997) followed 116 newly married couples over an 18-month period. Using three different causal models, they found that for women, marital discord was predictive of later depressive symptomatology. For example, using a cross-lagged stability model, they found that there was a significant link between marital discord and later depressive symptomatology but that there was no significant link between depressive symptomatology and later marital discord. The cross-lagged stability model allows one to examine the longitudinal relation between constructs while accounting for the stability of the constructs, in this case marital discord and depressive symptomatology. For men, marital discord was again associated with later depressive symptomatology, but in addition, initial depressive symptomatology was associated with later marital discord.

One additional study provides evidence for the marital discord and depression link. Whisman and Bruce (1999) used the epidemiological catchment area data from New Haven ($N = 904$) and looked at men and women assessed at two points in time, 1 year apart. They had Likert ratings of levels of marital discord and satisfaction, and they had interviewer-diagnosed major depression at both assessments. Odds ratios showed that individuals had an approximately twelvefold higher risk of being depressed at Time 2 if they were maritally dissatisfied at Time 1. For individuals with previous mild marital distress, there was an approximately twofold risk of becoming depressed.

In summary, I believe that there is convincing data indicating that marital discord can lead to later depression. However, generalizations across different types of populations must be made with caution. More specifically, one cannot reasonably use community and general population samples with changes in depressive symptomatology to reach conclusions regarding major depressive episodes. Such data from community samples (without some indication or assessment of clinical problem levels) provide leads to pursue with populations that can be assessed with clinical instruments. As Straus (1992) has very aptly argued in the marital violence area, it is easy to be duped into making clinical versus representative fallacy errors, and the same caution needs to be applied when studying the marital discord and depression link.

Treatment of Marital Discord and Coexisting Depression

Given our evolving view that marital discord can lead to clinical depression, with the aid of Steve Beach, I developed a marital treatment for depressed women and their maritally discordant spouses that reduced depression and increased marital satisfaction. In contrast, the comparison treatment, Beck's individual cognitive behavior therapy, only was associated with a reduction in depression (Beach & O'Leary, 1992; K. D. O'Leary & Beach, 1990). Fortunately, there is other research that confirms the effectiveness of the aforementioned type of marital treatment for depression of women and coexisting marital discord (Jacobson, Dobson, Fruzzetti, Schmaling, & Salusky, 1991). In terms of the impact of this research, I have been very pleased to see that the American Psychiatric Association's (1993) guidelines for treating major depressive disorder included a recommendation that marital therapy be considered when the depression occurs in the context of marital discord. More specifically, they cited the treatment studies of K. D. O'Leary and Beach (1990) and Jacobson et al (1991) and stated that marital therapy "may reduce depressive symptoms and reduce the risk of relapse in patients with marital and family problems" (1993, p. 8).

Etiology and Treatment of Partner Aggression

In 1981 we focused on characteristics of physically abusive men as contrasted with men in maritally discordant relationships and, in turn, each of the aforementioned groups was contrasted with men in satisfactory marriages with no physical aggression (Rosenbaum & O'Leary, 1981). Data were collected on women and men who attended therapy and support sessions at a local domestic violence center. That research showed that physically abusive men had poor communication skills (lack of assertiveness); they were more likely to have witnessed violence; and they were more likely to have been abused as children than men in discordant, nonabusive relationships. As might be expected, the physically abusive men also differed from men in satisfactory marriages on these measures. In addition, for men who would not attend therapy sessions at the facility that provided services to their wives, alcoholism and conservatism were more likely.

In one of my first studies in the partner abuse area, we obtained longitudinal data from a fairly large community sample of engaged partners ($N = 272$) showing that approximately 35% of men *and* women engaged in physical aggression against their partner in the year before marriage (and somewhat less in the 2 years after marriage). These data were not believed by some who thought that few people in a community sample, especially women, would hit, slap, or kick their engaged partner. Others felt that the context must be taken into account when interpreting such data. In fact, Julian Barling, Ileana Arias, Alan Rosenbaum, and I interviewed the couples about the aggression (or lack thereof) and found that most individuals felt that the aggression was not likely to occur in the future, that it was not physically injurious, or that they provoked their partner to engage in the behavior (K. D. O'Leary et al., 1989). Since our presentation of the longitudinal study in 1989, a number of individuals working at Stony Brook have been looking into the prevalence and context of physical aggression in men and women in high school, college, and marital clinic samples. It is clear that *in these samples* both men and women engage in rates of physical aggression that are quite similar, but the consequences of the aggression by males usually are more deleterious than those by women. For example, women are approximately seven times more likely to be injured than men (Cantos, Neidig, & O'Leary, 1994; Cascardi, Langhinrichsen, & Vivian, 1992; Stets & Straus, 1990).

There has been grassroots and professional opposition to couple treatment because of concern that any couple treatment would lead to fights between partners and that women treated with their partners would attribute increased blame to themselves for the marital problems and physical abuse. We addressed these issues in a recent treatment outcome study to reduce wife abuse that compared gender-specific treatments for men and women with a couple treatment. The couple treatment was not generic marital therapy, but a specific couple treatment that focused on the reduction of psychological and physical aggression. In addition, the therapists were alerted to the need for spending time after any treatment session with a client when it was noticed that any man was becoming angry and might not be able to control his anger following the session. Further, if there still was any concern, the therapist was to call the home of the clients after they returned home following the treatment session. With these treatment precautions, there was no difference between the gender-specific and couple treatment in terms of aggressive interchanges that appeared to the clients to be related to the content of the treatment session (K. D. O'Leary,

Heyman, & Neidig, 1999). Further, there was no increase in the extent to which women attributed blame to themselves in the treatments. In fact, there was a slight reduction in self-blaming.

My belief is that many of the differences of opinion about partner violence spring from a failure to meaningfully distinguish between different types and levels of physical aggression against a partner. In a sample of 11,000 randomly selected military personnel, we found that there were differences between predictors of moderate and severe physical aggression (Pan, Neidig, & O'Leary, 1994). Specifically, reported problems with drugs and alcohol were differentially predictive of severe physical aggression. Predictive of both moderate and severe physical aggression against a partner were marital discord, age (younger ages being more aggressive), depressive symptomatology, spouse concerns about finances, and pay grade. Relatedly, Vivian and Malone (1997) found that marital dissatisfaction, depressive symptomatology, and beliefs that their partners could not change were significantly greater in severely aggressive relationships than in moderately aggressive relationships. Of particular interest, however, were the frequent absences of differences between those in discordant, physically non-aggressive relationships from those in discordant, moderately physically aggressive relationships. In summary, it is my hope that it becomes recognized that the etiology and consequences of mild and severe forms of physical aggression are different. As just noted, individuals in moderately physically aggressive relationships often do not differ on individual or relationship measures. In turn, the types of treatment ultimately will take some of these different forms of aggression into account.

Conclusion

Whatever the impact of our work, the interaction with graduate students and postdoctoral fellows has been a great source of pleasure, and I was happy to have been chosen to write an article on mentoring in *Clinical Psychologist* (O'Leary, 1993). As I stated in that article several years ago, numerous graduate students have had important influences on me throughout my career. I have thrived on their input, and I expect that to continue.

The influence of the computer, the availability of software, and the ability to test models about the etiology of a problem have also influenced my colleagues and me, and we have been attempting to evaluate multifactorial models in college students (Riggs & O'Leary, 1996) and in married partners (K. D. O'Leary, Malone, & Tyree, 1994). Further, in more applied settings, we have assessed risk factors for moderate and severe abuse in 11,000 military personnel. In all of these cases, there is an attempt to provide a quantitative measure of the relative predictive value of any of our independent measures.

As I look back, in each of the areas that I did research I worked at both trying to unravel some of the etiological factors associated with the problem and trying to develop a treatment program that successfully changed the behavior. Although I feel quite positive about showing significant changes and even in some cases quite meaningful clinical changes, gaining perspective about relapse rates across the disorders and problems I have treated gives me cautious optimism about the changes that one can make. Aggression is a very difficult problem to treat.

Ultimately, an important criterion about one's work and life is whether you have fun doing what you do. I did and do.

References

American Psychiatric Association. (1993). Practice guideline for major depressive disorder in adults. *American Journal of Psychiatry, 150*(Suppl. 4).

Beach, S. R. H., Jouriles, E. N., & O'Leary, K. D. (1985). Extramarital sex: Impact on depression and commitment in couples seeking marital therapy. *Journal of Sex and Marital Therapy, 11,* 99–108.

Beach, S. R. H., & O'Leary, K. D. (1992). Treating depression in the context of marital discord: Outcome and predictors of response for marital therapy vs. cognitive therapy. *Behavior Therapy, 23,* 507–528.

Beach, S. R. H., & O'Leary, K. D. (1993). Marital discord and dysphoria: For whom does the marital relationship predicts depressive symptomatology. *Journal of Social and Personal Relationships, 10,* 405–420.

Beach, S. R. H., Sandeen, E. E., & O'Leary, K. D. (1990). *Depression in marriage.* New York: Guilford Press.

Birnbauer, J. S., Bijou, S. W., Wolf, M. M., & Kidder, J. D. (1965). Programmed instruction in the classroom. In L. Ullmann & L. Krasner (Eds.), *Case studies in behavior modification* (pp. 358–363). New York: Holt, Rhinehart & Winston.

Cano, A., & O'Leary, K. D. (2000). Infidelity and separations precipitate major depressive episodes and symptoms of non-specific depression and anxiety. *Journal of Consulting and Clinical Psychology, 68,* 774–781.

Cantos, A. L., Neidig, P. H., & O'Leary, K. D. (1994). Injuries of women and men in a treatment program for domestic violence. *Journal of Family Violence, 9,* 113–124.

Cascardi, M., Langhinrichsen, J., & Vivian, D. (1992). Marital aggression: Impact injury and health correlates for husbands and wives. *Archives of Internal Medicine, 152,* 1178–1184.

Christian-Herman, J., O'Leary, K. D., & Avery-Leaf, S. (in press). The impact of severe negative events in marriage on depression. *Journal of Social and Clinical Psychology, 20.*

Coyne, J. (1999). Thinking interactionally about depression: A radical restatement. In

T. Joiner & J. C. Coyne (Eds.), *The interactional nature of depression* (pp. 365–392). Washington, DC: American Psychological Association.

Craighead, L. W., Craighead, W. E., DeRosa, R., & Allen, H. (1993, August). *Interview and self-report data for college students: A review of the issues and some new data.* Paper presented in the symposium "Assessment of Major Depression" at meetings of the American Psychological Association, Los Angeles.

Dornbush, M. P., & Pruitt, S. K. (1995). *Teaching the tiger.* Duarte, CA: Hope Press.

Emery, R. (1994). *Renegotiating family relationships: Divorce, child custody, and mediation.* New York: Guilford Press.

Endler, N. S., Rushton, J. P., & Roediger, H. L. (1978). Productivity and scholarly impact (citations) of British, Canadian, and U.S. Departments of Psychology (1975). *American Psychologist, 33,* 1064–1082.

Fincham, F. D., Beach, S. R. H., Harold, G. T., & Osborne, L. N. (1997). Marital satisfaction and depression: Different causal relationships for men and women? *Psychological Science, 8,* 351–357.

Goldstein, S. (1995). *Understanding and managing children's classroom behavior.* New York: Wiley.

Grych, J. H., & Fincham, F. D. (1990). Marital conflict and children's adjustment: A cognitive–contextual framework. *Psychological Bulletin, 108,* 267–290.

Jacobson, N. S., Dobson, K., Fruzzetti, A. E., Schmaling, K. B., & Salusky, S. (1991). Marital therapy as treatment for depression. *Journal of Consulting and Clinical Psychology, 59,* 547–557.

Kendler, K. S., Heath, A. C., Martin, N. G., & Eaves, L. J. (1987). Symptoms of anxiety and symptoms of depression: Same genes, different environments? *Archives of General Psychiatry, 44*(5), 451–457.

Kent, R. N., & O'Leary, K. D. (1976). A controlled evaluation of behavior modification with conduct problem children. *Journal of Consulting and Clinical Psychology, 44,* 586–595.

MTA Cooperative Group. (1999). Treatment strategies for attention-deficit/hyperactivity disorder. *Archives of General Psychiatry, 56,* 1073–1086.

O'Leary, K. D. (1980). Pills or skills for hyperactive children. *Journal of Applied Behavior Analysis, 13,* 191–204.

O'Leary, K. D. (1993). Mentoring graduate students in clinical psychology. *Clinical Psychologist, 46,* 141–149.

O'Leary, K. D., Barling, J., Arias, I., Rosenbaum, A., Malone, J., & Tyree, A. (1989). Prevalence and stability of marital aggression between spouses: A longitudinal analysis. *Journal of Consulting and Clinical Psychology, 57,* 263–268.

O'Leary, K. D., & Beach, S. R. H. (1990). Marital therapy: A viable treatment for depression and marital discord. *American Journal of Psychiatry, 147,* 183–186.

O'Leary, K. D., & Becker, W. C. (1967). Behavior modification of an adjustment class: A token reinforcement program. *Exceptional Children, 33,* 637–642.

O'Leary, K. D., & Emery, R. E. (1983). Marital discord and childhood behavior problems. In M. D. Levine & P. Satz (Eds.), *Middle childhood: Development and dysfunction* (pp. 345–364). Baltimore: University Park Press.

O'Leary, K. D., Heyman, R. E., & Neidig, P. H. (1999). Treatment of wife abuse: A comparison of gender specific and conjoint approaches. *Behavior Therapy, 30,* 475–505.

O'Leary, K. D., Malone, J., & Tyree, A. (1994). Physical aggression in early marriage: Pre-relationship and relationship effects. *Journal of Consulting and Clinical Psychology, 62,* 594–602.

O'Leary, K. D., & O'Leary, S. G. (1972). *Classroom management: The successful use of behavior modification.* New York: Pergamon Press.

O'Leary, K. D., & O'Leary, S. G. (1977). *Classroom management: The successful use of behavior modification* (Rev. ed.). New York: Pergamon Press.

O'Leary, K. D., Pelham, W. E., Rosenbaum, A., & Price, G. H. (1976). Behavioral treatment of hyperkinetic children: An experimental evaluation of its usefulness. *Clinical Pediatrics, 15,* 510–515.

O'Leary, K. D., Poulos, R. W., & Devine, V. T. (1972). Tangible reinforcers: Bonuses or bribes. *Journal of Consulting and Clinical Psychology, 38,* 1–8.

O'Leary, K. D., & Wilson, G. T. (1975). *Behavior therapy: Application and outcome* (2nd ed). Englewood Cliffs, NJ: Prentice Hall.

O'Leary, S. G., & Pelham, W. E. (1978). Behavior therapy and withdrawal of stimulant medication in hyperactive children. *Pediatrics, 61*(2), 211–217.

Pan, H., Neidig, P. H., & O'Leary, K. D. (1994). Predicting mild and severe husband to wife aggression. *Journal of Consulting and Clinical Psychology, 62,* 975–981.

Reiff, S. (1995). *How to reach ADD/ADHD children.* West Nyack, NY: Center for Applied Research in Education.

Riggs, D. S., & O'Leary, K. D. (1996). Aggression between heterosexual dating partners: An examination of a causal model of courtship aggression. *Journal of Interpersonal Violence, 11,* 519–540.

Rosenbaum, A., & O'Leary, K. D. (1981). Marital violence: Characteristics of abusive couples. *Journal of Consulting and Clinical Psychology, 49,* 63–71.

Stets, J. E., & Straus, M. A. (1990). Gender differences in reporting marital violence and its medical and psychological consequences. In M. A. Straus & R. J. Gelles (Eds.), *Physical violence in American families: Risk factors and adaptations to violence in 8,145 families* (pp.151–165). New Brunswick, NJ: Transaction.

Straus, M. A. (1990). Injury and frequency of assault and the "representative sample fallacy" in measuring wife beating and child abuse. In M. A. Straus & R. J. Gelles (Eds.), *Physical violence in American families: Risk factors and adaptations to violence in 8,145 families* (pp. 75–89). New Brunswick, NJ: Transaction.

Torgersen, S. (1986). Genetic factors in moderately severe and mild affective disorders. *Archives of General Psychiatry, 43,* 222–226.

Ullmann, L. P., & Krasner, L. (1965). *Case studies in behavior modification.* New York: Holt, Rinehart, & Winston.

Vivian, D., & Malone, J. (1997). Relationship factors and depressive symptomatology associated with mild to severe husband-to-wife physical aggression. *Violence and Victims, 12,* 3–18.

Whisman, M. A., & Bruce, M. L. (1999). Marital distress and incidence of major depressive episode in a community sample. *Journal of Abnormal Psychology, 108,* 674–678.

Wilson, G. T., Nathan, P. N., O'Leary, K. D., & Clarke, L. A. (1996). *Abnormal Psychology.* Needham, MA: Allyn & Bacon.

PART 5

Contextual Considerations in Family Intervention Research

Conceptualizing Gender in Marital and Family Therapy Research: The Gender Role Strain Paradigm

Ronald F. Levant
Carol L. Philpot

Despite a body of clinical and theoretical literature that addresses gender issues in marital and family therapy (e.g., Goldner, 1985; Hare Mustin, 1987; Hare Mustin & Marecek, 1990; McGoldrick, Anderson, & Walsh, 1989; Walters, Carter, Papp, & Silverstein, 1988), the empirical literature on the process and outcome of marital and family therapy is notable for the lack of attention given to gender. Not only is the literature on gender in relationship to process and outcome very sparse, but what does exist is based on outmoded conceptual models. From our point of view this is quite unfortunate. As scholars and practitioners who have specialized in the area of gender and marital and family treatment, we view gender[1] as a central construct in family relationships and believe that it should loom much larger in the empirical literature. In fairness to the therapy research community, it should also be noted that gender has not been well-integrated into basic research on the family either. For example, Thompson and Walker (1995) noted that "In most domains authors consider gender to be irrelevant to their understanding of family life" (p. 847; see also Ferree, 1990).

The goals of this chapter are to: (a) introduce a contextual approach to conceptualizing gender to the marital and family therapy research community;

An earlier version of part of this chapter was presented at the First National Conference on Marital and Family Therapy Process and Outcome Research, sponsored by Temple University, Divisions 42 and 43 of the American Psychological Association, and the Philadelphia Child Guidance Center, May 5–7, 1995, Philadelphia, PA.

[1]We will follow the current convention in gender studies and use the word *sex* to refer to biological differences between males and females and *gender* to refer to culturally prescribed norms and roles for men and women.

(b) systematically develop this approach for women; and (c) consider the implications of this approach for family intervention and intervention research.

Review of Empirical Literature

Alexander, Holtzworth-Munroe, and Jameson (1993), in the first major review of the process and outcome research literature to include a focus on gender issues, made several relevant observations about gender and marital therapy research that we will use as a point of departure. First, they observed that the findings on the relationship between gender roles, power differentials, and marital therapy outcome are quite mixed. On the one hand, Jacobson, Follette, and Pagel (1986) found that the only pretreatment variable that significantly predicted outcome was traditional role patterns of affiliation in women and independence in men (assessed by the Edwards Personal Preference Schedule): More traditional couples were less likely to benefit from behavioral marital therapy. However, other studies have shown the opposite: That wives' pretreatment femininity (as measured by the Bem Sex Role Inventory; Baucom & Aiken, 1984) and the couple's pretreatment stereotypical power inequality (assessed by the Verbal Content Coding System; Whisman & Jacobson, 1990) were both associated with positive outcomes (Margolin, Talovic, Fernandez, & Onorato, 1983; Jacobson, 1983).

Second, Alexander et al. (1993) concluded that we may have reached the limit of our ability to help couples with therapy models based on our current understanding of marriage and recommended enlarging the perspective by incorporating longitudinal, developmental, and contextual considerations such as race, ethnicity, class, sexual orientation, and gender. In regard to the contextual consideration of gender, they cited investigators who have started to examine gender differences in such areas as affiliation maintenance (Bell, Daley, & Gonzalez, 1987), the demand–withdraw pattern of marital conflict and its relationship to socialized gender roles and power differentials (Christensen & Heavey, 1990; Christensen & Shenk, 1991), and physiological reactions during marital interaction (Gottman, 1991). They critiqued the "one size fits all" approach for ignoring contextual issues, citing authors who have called for greater attention to gender (e.g., Margolin et al., 1983, p. 143, who observed that behavioral marital therapy has "paid inadequate attention to sex role stereotyping") and greater awareness of sexism in marital therapy research (Rampage, 1989; Witkin, 1989a, 1989b). In specific regard to the treatment of domestic violence, they cited critiques of traditional couples therapy techniques and research methods for obscuring both the violence and the responsibility for perpetuating it by defining problems in strictly relational terms that erroneously assume power equality and shared responsibility (Avis, 1992; Bograd, 1992; Kaufman, 1992). Finally, following Jacobson (1983), they observed that the failure to deal explicitly with power issues may account for the temporary nature of marital therapy's successes (where half of the couples who improve relapse at follow-up) as well as its failures. The methods used in most couples therapy temporarily shifts the power imbalance in favor of the wife, but only temporarily. The measured improvement might be related to this power shift and thus will be maintained only as long as the therapist is part of the system.

From our perspective, the sparse literature, the conflicting findings, and the critiques from feminist and antisexist perspectives strongly indicate that marital and family therapy research is in need of a better developed conceptual framework on gender, one based on the most up-to-date thinking in the field of gender studies. Such a framework must recognize (a) the realities of power differences between men and women, (b) the differential socialization of female and male children into adults whose roles and psychological skill profiles match the power differences, and (c) the recent changes in gender roles and relations that have reduced to some extent these power inequities and bifurcated roles. Before we present our plan for addressing these issues we will briefly discuss the field of gender studies.

Gender Studies

The field of gender studies had its origins within the individual differences research tradition in psychology, when investigators in the 1930s began to focus on what was then termed *sex differences in personality* (Terman & Miles, 1936) and, later, in *cognitive and perceptual attributes* (see Anastasi, 1958, for an early review). Thus the field began with a focus on traits thought to reside in the individual, what Deaux (1984) called the "sex as a subject variable" approach (p. 105). This approach dominated the field for over 50 years. In the 1980s the approach shifted to viewing gender differences as a product of the inter-action between people in a social context in which gender-related beliefs play an important role (Archer, 1996; Deaux, 1984). The marital and family therapy research literature has not incorporated this shift in perspective, judging from the fact that the few studies that do assess gender variables tend to operationalize them as personality traits, most often measured using the Bem Sex Role Inventory (Baucom & Aiken, 1984; Baucom, Notarius, Burnett, & Haefner, 1990; Bradbury, Campbell, & Fincham, 1995) but sometimes using other personality trait instruments (Jacobson et al., 1986). That the therapy research community has not yet incorporated this shift in perspective on studying gender probably reflects the lag time in the diffusion of newer perspectives from one field to another, but it is somewhat ironic, because the shift to a more contextual, systemic perspective would seem to be very congruent with the very heart of the family therapy field. On the other hand, once this perspective becomes more widely known among family intervention researchers it may be quickly adopted because it is so congruent with family systems perspectives.

The Gender Role Strain Paradigm

There are several variations of the contextual approach to conceptualizing gender; however, we will focus on only one: the *gender role strain paradigm* (Pleck, 1981). This model, based in social constructionism, was originally formulated to conceptualize the male gender as part of a corrective (initiated by feminist social scientists) to the prevailing trend in the social sciences to view males as if they had no gender and could in fact serve as a proxy for the human species. Given its origins, the paradigm has been well-developed in its application to men but has only sporadically been applied to women. Because the work on men has been summarized elsewhere (Levant, 1996; Levant & Pollack, 1995; Pleck, 1995) we will not review it here. However, because it has not been well-developed for women, we will offer the first systematic discussion of the application of this paradigm to them. Because this paradigm is new to the field of family intervention, the literature is at a very early stage of development.

The social constructionist perspective on gender views gender roles not as biological or even social "givens," but rather as psychologically and socially constructed entities that bring certain advantages and disadvantages and, most importantly, can be changed. This perspective acknowledges the biological differences between men and women but argues that it is not the biological differences of sex that make for "masculinity" and "femininity." These notions are socially constructed from biological, psychological, and social experience to serve particular purposes. Traditional constructions of gender serve patriarchal purposes; nontraditional constructions, such as those that Gilmore (1990) described among the Tahitians and the Semai, serve more equalitarian purposes.

The gender role strain paradigm, originally formulated by Joseph Pleck in *The Myth of Masculinity* (1981), is a social constructionist perspective on gender that is amenable to empirical investigation. Pleck demonstrated that the paradigm that had dominated the research on gender for 50 years (1930 to 1980)— the *gender role identity paradigm*—not only poorly accounts for the observed data but also promotes the bifurcation of society on the basis of stereotyped gender roles. The identity paradigm assumed that people have an inner psychological need to have a gender role identity and that optimal personality development hinged on its formation. The extent to which this "inherent" need is met is determined by how completely a person embraces his or her traditional gender role. From such a perspective, the development of appropriate gender role identity is anxiously sought by parents, teachers, and family physicians, and failure is dreaded. Failure for men to achieve a masculine gender role identity is thought to result in homosexuality, negative attitudes toward women, or defensive hypermasculinity. For women, faulty gender role socialization is thought to be manifested by a failure to marry and have children, dislike of men, or a lesbian lifestyle. This paradigm springs from the same philosophical roots as the "essentialist" or "nativist" view of sex roles—the notion that there is a clear masculine (or feminine) "essence" that is historically invariant.

In contrast, the gender role strain paradigm proposes that appropriate gender roles are determined by the prevailing gender ideology (which can be assessed through an examination of gender role stereotypes and norms) and are imposed on the developing child by parents, teachers, physicians, and peers—the cultural transmitters who subscribe to the prevailing gender ideology. The imposition of gender roles is thought to result in gender role strain because (a) contemporary gender roles are contradictory and inconsistent; (b) the proportion of persons who violate gender roles is high; (c) violation of gender roles leads to condemnation and negative psychological consequences; (d) actual or imagined violation of gender roles leads people to over-conform to them; and (e) certain prescribed gender role traits (such as male aggression) are often dysfunctional. As noted earlier, this paradigm springs from the philosophical roots of social constructionism—the perspective that notions of "masculinity" and femininity" are relational, socially constructed, and subject to change.

Gender Ideology

Gender ideology is a central construct in the strain paradigm. It is a very different construct from the older notion of gender (or sex role) orientation. Gender orientation arises out of the identity paradigm and "presumes that masculinity is rooted in actual differences between men and women" (Thompson & Pleck, 1995, p. 130). This approach has attempted to assess the *personality traits* more often associated with men or women, using such instruments as the Bem Sex Role Inventory (Bem, 1974) and the Personal Attributes Questionnaire (Spence & Helmreich, 1978). In contrast, studies of gender ideology take a *normative* approach, in which masculinity or femininity is viewed as a socially constructed gender ideal for men or women. Whereas the masculine male in the orientation and trait approach is one who *possesses* particular personality traits, the traditional male in the ideology and normative approach "is one who endorses the ideology that men should have sex specific characteristics (and women should not have these characteristics)" (Thompson & Pleck, 1995, p. 131). Thompson and Pleck (1995) adduced evidence to support the notion that gender orientation and gender ideologies are independent and have different correlates.

Types of Gender Role Strain

Pleck (1995), in an update on the gender role strain paradigm, pointed out that his original formulation of the paradigm stimulated research on three varieties of gender role strain, which he called *discrepancy strain, dysfunction strain,* and *trauma strain.* Discrepancy strain results when one fails to live up to one's internalized gender ideal. Dysfunction strain results even when one fulfills the requirements of the gender code, because many of the characteristics viewed as desirable in men (or women) can have negative side effects on the men (or women) themselves and on those close to them. Trauma strain can result from many sources, one of which is the ordeal of the gender role socialization process, which is now recognized as inherently traumatic because of its effects in truncating males' natural emotionality (Levant & Kopecky, 1995).

The Gender Role Strain Paradigm and Women

Although Joseph Pleck (1981) originally proposed the gender role strain model as a paradigm for studying masculinity, the model also can be applied to women. We recognize that, in proposing to extend a model developed for men to women, some may worry that we are repeating the mistakes of the past, in which research on males was assumed to apply to women. However, it should be noted that the older literature did not consider gender as a variable and simply generalized findings from samples of men to humanity. Our proposal, in contrast, builds on and is consistent with feminist scholarship because of our emphasis on the social construction of gender and our recognition of the power differences between men and women in patriarchal societies.

Femininity Ideology

Although feminist scholars have been studying, critiquing, and revising femininity ideology for over three decades, a search of the literature did not reveal an organized framework for conceptualizing either traditional or "new woman" femininity ideology. Various authors (i.e., Bloom, Glitter, Gutwill, Kogel, & Zaphiropoulous, 1994; Chodorow, 1978; Dowling, 1982; French, 1985; Frieze, Parsons, Johnson, Ruble, & Zellman, 1978; Gilligan, 1982; Gutwill, 1994; Hare-Mustin & Marecek, 1990; Hochschild, 1989; Horney, 1973; Kolbenschlag, 1981; Miller, 1986; Root, 1990; Russianoff, 1981; Tavris, 1992; Wolf, 1991) have addressed certain aspects of femininity ideology, for the most part emphasizing the negative effects that cultural expectations have on women's lives or proposing a modification of patriarchal values to include those that are stereotypically associated with femininity. Most of the research conducted with regard to femininity has emerged from the gender identity paradigm and has used such instruments as the Bem Sex Role Inventory (Bem, 1974) and the Personal Attributes Questionnaire (Spence & Helmreich, 1978) to assess stereotypical feminine personality traits. Other instruments have been designed to study attitudes toward sex roles, such as the MacDonald Sex Role Inventory (as cited in King, King, Carter, & Surface, 1994) and the Sex-Role Egalitarianism Scale (Beere, King, Beere, & King, 1984). In her extensive review of 211 instruments that measure aspects of gender, Carole Beere (1990) categorized the existing instruments into those that measure gender roles, children and gender, stereotypes, marital and parental roles, employee roles, multiple roles, and attitudes toward gender role issues. Only four of these instruments mention ideology in the title; one of these measures attitudes toward women's liberation, one attitudes toward sexuality, and the other two attitudes toward sex roles. Most of the instruments Beere reviewed have been used in one to three studies, the notable exceptions being the Bem inventory (Bem, 1974) and the Personal Attributes Questionnaire (Spence & Helmreich, 1978). Additionally, research has looked at the results of adhering to the prevailing femininity ideology in specific areas such as body image (Unger & Crawford, 1992), career orientation (Komarovsky, 1982), fear of success (Horner, 1972, 1978), external locus of control (Doherty & Baldwin, 1985), role overload (Hochschild, 1989), depression (McGrath, Keita, Strickland, & Russo, 1990), and domestic violence (Walker, 1989). However, to our knowledge, only one instrument, which is still in the development stage, is designed to directly investigate femininity ideology: the Femininity Ideology Scale (Tolman, personal communication, November 1996). The motivation to develop this instrument derives from an intervention project with pregnant adolescent girls. This scale is divided into three subscales entitled (a) *self in relationships,* (b) *relationship to one's body,* and (c) *social practices and identities* and is intended to be suitable for multicultural use.

A Proposed Model

Given the apparent lack of a coherent and inclusive model of femininity ideology and associated instruments, we propose a beginning framework that we hope will stimulate continued exploration of femininity ideology that parallels that found in the new psychology of men. We take, as a starting point, the work of Marilyn French, who delineated what she called the *masculinity and femininity principles* in her book *Beyond Power* (French, 1985). According to her conceptualization, the femininity principle includes a cluster of discrete values that derive from a basic primary value of affiliation. These include cooperation, nurturance, equalitarianism, emotional expressivity, spontaneity, compassion, submission, and empowerment of self and others. These values are presented as being different from those of the masculinity principle, which encompasses a cluster of values based on a root value of autonomy. The masculine values, according to this model, are competition, aggression, hierarchical organization, rational control over emotion and behavior, reliance on abstract principles, domination, and power over others. Based on these contributions of French and many of the other previously mentioned scholars, there appear to be several enduring dimensions of traditional femininity ideology that remain true across time and cultures. Even so, some of these expectations seem contradictory, such as the dictate to be sexual and "pure" simultaneously. In addition, the ideology of the "new woman" adds further dimensions that conflict with the traditional, a situation that in some ways parallels the disparate messages bombarding the "new man."

Traditional Femininity Ideology

A "traditional woman" was expected to be beautiful, sexy, seductive, pure, nurturing, compassionate, sensitive, emotional, cooperative, gentle, self-sacrificing, self-effacing, and submissive. It was also appropriate to be spontaneous, artistic, creative, and expressive. She could not be aggressive, angry, ambitious, competitive, dominant, proud, independent, powerful, or authoritarian. She avoided highly "masculinized" pursuits and behavior such as weight lifting, truck driving, police work, military combat, fist fights, and race car driving. These expectations can be roughly condensed into five categories that reflect the roles, values, personality characteristics, behaviors, and communication and problem-solving styles of the traditional woman: (a) the beautiful sexpot (a woman's power is her beauty, which she uses to manipulate and control dominant males); (b) the madonna (women are expected to be mothers and are held responsible for the outcomes of their children); (c) the nurturer (a woman is expected to nurture others, putting their needs above her own); (d) the woman behind the successful man (a traditional woman is expected to find her fulfillment through her husband, taking a supportive role while staying out of the spotlight); and (e) the dependent child (a woman is expected to be dependent on a man for financial security and protection and is discouraged from learning activities that would make her self-sufficient).

The New Woman Ideology

The feminist movement has addressed the restrictive aspects of traditional feminine ideology by endorsing a woman's right to embrace the masculine principle, to reject such characteristics as being submissive, self-effacing, and self-sacrificing, and to engage in behaviors traditionally associated with men. She is now expected to be assertive, self-sufficient, ambitious, rational, and competitive. She is encouraged to be a leader, to achieve, to demand equal treatment, and to hold herself in high esteem. When the ideology of this "new woman" is transposed to that of the traditional woman, however, many of the old messages continue to bleed through. This results in the emergence of contradictory simultaneous injunctions, which are confusing and encumbering. The new woman is expected to be both rational and emotional, both cooperative and competitive, both independent and supportive, both powerful and empowering, both nurturant and aggressive, both a leader and a follower, both other-centered and self-centered. The *superwoman syndrome* has been coined to describe the woman who attempts to fulfill the dictates of both traditional and new woman roles. The superwoman, at best, is a fulfilled but exhausted individual. However, traditional and new woman ideologies are not attainable simultaneously by simply expanding the time spent trying to meet the requirements. The modern woman struggles with how and when to apply the contradictory messages. Although some women navigate the difficult choices skillfully, many self-sabotage, vacillate, or become immobilized. In this respect, the new woman and the new man face similar challenges.

Female Gender Role Strain

We now turn to a discussion of the ways in which women suffer from the three subtypes of gender role strain. Feminist theory and research over the last three decades has actually produced evidence to support the existence of gender role discrepancy strain, dysfunction strain, and trauma strain in women, without using Pleck's model as a guide. Although we discuss these issues as if they were discrete conditions, there is actually a great deal of overlap and interaction between them.

Gender Role Discrepancy Strain

Gender role discrepancy strain refers to the stress experienced by an individual who does not perceive herself to fit the mold of the "ideal woman." Although there is not a line of research that has focused directly on this question, it is clear from the available literature that many of the physical and emotional problems women struggle with today are a result of their attempt to meet unattainable standards of femininity, standards that are reflected in the norms of femininity ideology. Examples of this are the societal emphasis on beauty, marriage and motherhood for all women, and the introduction of the superwoman syndrome.

Beauty

The beauty standard requires a particular type of physical beauty, defined by fashion designers and the media, which can only be achieved through a combination of surgery, food deprivation, strenuous exercise, expensive cosmetics, and a very large clothing budget (Wolf, 1991). Even then, only women of a certain age and genetic background will succeed. Research indicates that most women suffer from body hatred; even the most beautiful and healthy of women find some defect on which to focus (Cash & Brown, 1987; Chernin, 1981; Freedman, 1986; Jackson, Sullivan, & Rostker, 1988; Stake & Lauer, 1987; Unger & Crawford, 1992; Ussher, 1989). Actresses and models have collagen lips, face lifts, tummy tucks, liposuction, and breast augmentation in order to continue working (Faludi, 1991). The average woman cannot afford the time and money required to acquire and maintain this standard of beauty; instead she obsesses over her appearance. Evidence of this obsession is found in most women's magazines on the rack, the majority of which focus on diet, exercise, makeup, clothing, hairstyles, and other requirements of a desirable feminine appearance (Basow, 1986; Lott, 1994).

Marriage and Motherhood

Discrepancy strain also occurs for women who do not choose to marry or have children. Despite the emphasis in the women's movement on achievements outside the family, advances in contraception that allow a woman to choose whether and when she will have children, and sex discrimination laws that make it more feasible for a woman to have a rewarding and successful career, many writers argue that most women continue to feel unfinished until they are in a relationship (Dowling, 1982; Kolbenschlag, 1981; Russianoff, 1981). As a result, many single women who appear on the surface to be living fulfilling lives are actually suffering from feelings of inadequacy because of what they perceive as a failure to achieve a woman's highest goal. Although marriage and family is often a desire for men as well, unmarried men do not carry the stigma that single women do (Faludi, 1991; Lott, 1994). On the other side of the coin, women who choose not to marry or have children are often the brunt of un-flattering labels regarding their deviance from the dictates of femininity ideology (Faludi, 1991). Society tends to look at such women as somehow defective, not truly feminine. Furthermore, women who attempt to combine career and family in an effort to have it all often face choices between what is best for husband and family and what is best for career. A choice for career over family leads to guilt feelings over the decision to be "selfish" and not devote their lives to serving others; the guilt is particularly strong if children have difficulties of any sort (Lott, 1994). Because society dictates that women take primary re-sponsibility for family, women who do not—whether by choice or inability—experience a discrepancy between their performance and that of the ideal woman.

The Superwoman Syndrome

A third area in which discrepancy strain occurs is a result of the additional requirements instituted for women since the feminist movement. No longer is it enough for a woman to be a wife, mother, homemaker, and beauty; now she must also have an interesting and financially successful career. The result of this additional demand is what Hochschild (1989) has called the *second shift* —that is, women work an average of 15 hours longer than men each week because of their taking major responsibility for housework and child care despite full-time employment outside the home. Women who find themselves exhausted and unable to meet the demands of the superwoman ideal also experience discrepancy strain. The new woman is supposed to be able to do it all.

Gender Role Dysfunction Strain

Gender role dysfunction strain, according to Pleck's model, is the result of successful gender socialization. In other words, when a woman has attained the socially reinforced personality characteristics, values, and roles appropriate for the ideal female, she will experience dysfunction because the standards themselves are associated with negative outcomes. Dysfunction strain can be seen in women in several areas: (a) depression; (b) eating disorders; (c) histrionic personality disorder; (d) dependency; (e) self-limiting behavior; (f) external locus of control; and (g) role overload.

Depression

Because women are socialized to believe that they are first and foremost wives and mothers who find their identity through husbands and children, their self-esteem tends to depend on the success of their relationships. They therefore make major sacrifices, emotionally and behaviorally, in order to make these relationships work. They tend to defer to the wishes of their families, hold in anger, not assert themselves, and take responsibility for the emotional health of all family members (Halas & Matteson, 1978; Hare Mustin, 1983, 1987; Kaschak, 1992). They tend not to have control over their own lives or over the relationships that define them. This may result in learned helplessness, passivity, and dependency. Little wonder that researchers (McGrath et al., 1990; Russo, 1985) report a depression rate for women that is twice that of men worldwide and an attempted suicide rate 2.3 times greater than that of men (Kushner, 1985).

Eating Disorders

As a result of cultural messages, women have come to equate power, success, and self-esteem with thinness (Root, 1990). They unfortunately do great damage to their bodies in an attempt to achieve this misguided goal. Traditional femininity ideology holds that a woman should be dangerously thin, an unrealistic goal for most women that results in various forms of eating disorders: compulsive eating, bulimia, and anorexia, as well as excessive exercise (Bloom et al., 1994, Gutwill, 1994).

Histrionic Personality Disorder

The criteria for the diagnosis of histrionic personality disorder in the *Diagnostic and Statistical Manual of Mental Disorders* (American Psychological Association, 1994) is an exaggeration of personality characteristics associated with traditional femininity—using physical appearance to draw attention, wanting to be the center of attention, engaging in sexually seductive behavior, speaking in dramatic ways with exaggerated emotion, considering every relationship with a man as potentially "the one," and being easily influenced by others, particularly a significant male other. It is clear that society expects a woman to engage in the very behaviors it deems pathological.

Dependency

Although young women from all socioeconomic groups now expect to work outside the home (Rand & Miller, 1972), they continue to make three fourths the salary of men doing the same work because of sex-based wage discrimination (Ferraro, 1984; U.S. Department of Labor, 1985 [as cited in Lott, 1994]) and are at a disadvantage politically and legally in spite of major strides in these areas, because the most powerful positions are still held by males (Center for the American Woman and Politics, 1984 [as cited in Lott, 1994]). Despite the positive messages of the women's movement that encourage women to be independent and autonomous, young women quickly recognize that the married woman has a socioeconomic advantage and the woman who pleases a powerful male is powerful by association. Therefore, many young women invest as much effort in finding a man to take care of them as they do in learning how to care for themselves. Even in the wake of the feminist movement, women still wait for a relationship with a man to give their lives direction (Dowling, 1982; Russianoff, 1981). In addition, despite working full time outside the home, women still take major responsibility for the family (Hochschild, 1989), which leaves little time to master those activities considered to be traditionally male both inside and outside the home. A lifetime of deferring to male expertise in these areas unfortunately leads to true dependency. Women do not learn the skills of self-sufficiency because they are discouraged from doing so. To make matters worse, because women who have been traditionally socialized to equate self-esteem with the success of their relationships, they will yield to their significant others in order to preserve the relationship. This distressing dependency results in women having less power to influence their relationships and to get their needs met.

Self-Limiting Behavior

Research shows that men tend to have more self-confidence and higher aspirations than women, despite equal intelligence or ability (Erkut, 1983; Gitelson,

Petersen, & Tobin-Richards, 1982; Gold, Brush, & Sprotzer, 1980; McMahan, 1982; Vollmer, 1984). This phenomenon may be caused by the fact that competition and achievement is stereotypically considered masculine in nature, while women are rewarded more for modesty (Basow, 1986). Women who underestimate their abilities limit their possibilities for success. Additionally, there is evidence that females attribute their successes to luck and their failures to personal inadequacy, while males do the opposite (Brown & Geis, 1984; Doherty & Baldwin, 1985; Gitelson et. al., 1982; Savage, Stearns, & Friedman, 1979). This external locus of control may be the result of actual obstacles to female achievement that exist in a patriarchal society. Nevertheless, believing that there is little relationship between one's efforts and abilities and one's level of success serves as a further disincentive for women to achieve. The traditionally endorsed ultimate goal of marriage for women also contributes to their ambivalence regarding academic and occupational achievement (Horner, 1978; Michelini, Eisen, & Snodgrass, 1981; Sadd, Lenauer, Shaver, & Dunivant, 1978).

Role Overload

"Superwomen" who combine career and family are exhausted and get physically ill more often than their husbands (Hochschild, 1989). But perhaps even more disturbing is the fact that there is no time for these women to pursue interests that are relaxing and lead to personal growth. Friedan (1981) saw this issue as one to be addressed on the "new feminist frontier"—the family. Once again, even modern gender messages require that women sacrifice their personhood to be successful at womanhood.

Gender Role Trauma Strain

In Pleck's model, gender role trauma strain occurs when a woman suffers trauma in the process of gender socialization. The most obvious traumas that women experience in the socialization process are devaluation, role restriction, sexual objectification and sexual abuse, and physical abuse.

Devaluation

In a patriarchal culture, masculinity is valued over femininity. This devaluation of females begins at birth and continues throughout life. Messages of devaluation can be subtle, because it is in language where the masculine pronoun is used to denote all people and always precedes the feminine when both are mentioned (Briere & Lanktree, 1983; Fisk, 1985; Hyde, 1984). They can also be more direct, as in the existence of the "glass ceiling," which prevents women from attaining powerful positions in industry or politics (Center for American

Women in Politics, 1984; Decade of the Woman, 1992; U.S. Department of Labor, 1985 [as cited in Lott, 1994]); or downright blatant, as seen in misogynistic rap music and pornography (Freudiger & Almquist, 1978). Although little girls absorb these messages very early in life, it is likely that the real trauma coincides with adolescence (Hetherington, 1995) when the pervasive emphasis on appearance, sexuality, marriage, and family has strong negative effects on educational, athletic, and occupational achievement (Basow, 1986; Belenky, Clinchy, Goldberger, & Tarule, 1986; Chafetz, 1978; Katz, 1979). Adolescent girls get a clear message that they are valued for their bodies, which exist to satisfy male sexual urges, and that their primary purpose in life is to serve the male in a large number of capacities. One of the most important ways in which girls and women serve men is by not challenging them competitively, whether in sports, academics, or work, thereby creating the illusion that men are superior, which contributes to masculine self-esteem at the expense of feminine self-esteem. The trauma of realization that all personal goals, needs, hopes, and dreams must become secondary to those of a significant male if one is to be considered truly feminine has a significant impact on girls' mental and physical health as well as achievement. Also traumatic is the burgeoning awareness that all values that girls have been socialized to adopt in order to be truly feminine (cooperation, nurturance, compassion, emotionality, affiliation, empowering others) are held in lower esteem by society than the traditional masculine values of control, competition, reason, aggression, power, and autonomy. Girls are placed in the double-bind position of being "feminine" and inferior or "unfeminine" and adequate. The result is either depression or rejection.

Role Restriction

It is at adolescence that girls become more acutely aware of the fact that, because society dictates that their primary role be that of wife and mother, other choices of life work are severely restricted. This mandate has major implications for athletic interests, career goals, and academic achievement. Girls who have previously done well in school lose interest in academics at adolescence because it is socially unpopular to be studious and smart; it does not contribute to physical appearance, which is a girls' primary asset; it discourages boys from dating them because boys "must feel superior"; and female role models demonstrate only moderate occupational achievement fraught with sacrifice and conflict (Dowling, 1982; Gilligan, 1982). Despite major strides in opening up new career opportunities for women in the last two decades (Decade of the Woman, 1992 [as cited in Lott, 1994]), young women still face the glass ceiling, the second shift, and lower pay relative to men in the same job. The evidence leads them to conclude that their energy is better spent on achieving an appearance and personality that will attract and retain male attention. Despite verbal messages to the contrary, girls soon discover that it is very difficult, if not impossible, to "have it all." This discovery is traumatic indeed.

Sexual Objectification and Sexual Abuse

Women and girls are even more severely traumatized by their sexual objectification. Through the media and other sources, women discover that men lust after their bodies for sexual gratification and that they are basically interchangeable (Lott, 1994). Identification as a mere sex object has many traumatic results, ranging from the development of poor self-esteem and eating disorders to their subjection to pornography, sexual harassment, and assault. Pornography is replete with themes of domination and exploitation of women (Cowan, Lee, Levy, & Snyder, 1988). Sexual harassment is widespread, occurring in home, social, work, school, and professional settings (Holroyd & Brodsky, 1977; Koss, 1990; Koss, Leonard, Beezley, & Oros, 1985; Lott, Reilly, & Howard, 1982; Muehlenhard & Linton, 1987; Simon, 1990). Research indicates that men and women perceive sexual harassment incidents differently—that is, men are more likely to see the behavior as harmless or invited than are women (Abbey & Melby, 1986; Lott, Reilly, & Howard, 1982). If one defines "sexual assault" to include fondling, molestation, and incest as well as rape, between 24 and 46% of women can expect to be sexually assaulted during their lifetime (Kohn, 1987; Koss et al., 1985; Russell & Howell, 1983). Date rape affects between 32 and 70% of women (Koss, et. al. 1985; Muehlenhard & Linton, 1987; Reilly, Lott, Caldwell, & DeLuca, 1992), and marital rape has until recently been deemed legal (Lott, 1994). The message to women is clearly one of vulnerability and intimidation. From infancy forward, women are aware that their sexuality places them in dire jeopardy.

Physical Abuse

Both men and women suffer physical abuse, but the research points to more severe abuse in greater numbers perpetrated against women by men (Barnett, Keyson, & Thelen, 1992; Dobash & Dobash, 1977/1978; Gelles & Straus, 1989; Jacobson, 1993). In about two thirds of the cases, women are attacked by their male significant others (Dobash & Dobash, 1977/1978). Some researchers (i.e. Behind Closed Doors, 1991) estimate that between 24 and 34% of American women will be assaulted by an intimate partner during their lifetime. Domestic violence is the single most common cause of injury to women in the United States from age 15 to 45, surpassing car accidents, muggings, and rapes combined (Rosenbaum, 1990 [as cited in Caralis, 1995]). The effects of this violence are staggering in terms of physical and mental health, leading to emergency room visits, hospitalizations, psychosomatic illness, alcohol and drug abuse, severe depression, poor self-esteem, loss of work, and engaging in violence against spouse or children (Gelles & Straus, 1989). Walker (1989) has labeled the cognitive and affective results of such abuse as *battered woman syndrome*. In spite of the fact that laws against domestic violence are being enforced with more consistency than was once the case, women are still traumatized by their vulnerability to violence perpetrated by male significant others in a patriarchal culture that tacitly endorses male dominance over women.

Implications of the Gender Role Strain Paradigm for Intervention and Intervention Research

This chapter first briefly reviewed the empirical literature on gender in family therapy research and presented an overview of the gender role strain paradigm. We then extended the paradigm to women, putting forth first a model for conceptualizing femininity ideology, and then reviewing evidence indicating that women do indeed suffer gender role strain of all three subtypes. Even though the available literature is supportive, we do need more and better data to solidify the empirical support for the effects of gender role strain for men and women, as well as for the major propositions of the strain paradigm. But with this caveat in mind, we can say that although the timing and pattern of discrepancy strain, dysfunction strain, and trauma strain and the specific behaviors involved may differ for men and women, both genders appear to be negatively affected by bifurcated gender role socialization processes.

Specifically, both women and men have learned to measure themselves using the yardstick of gender ideologies—beliefs about what they ought to be as women or men. These beliefs tend to be unattainable because they are idealized, restrictive, and do not fit individual personalities very well; as a result, many people may experience discrepancy strain. The available research indicates that discrepancy strain may result in lower self-esteem, anxiety, depression in both genders, appearance obsession in women, and increased risk for cardiovascular illness in men.

With regard to dysfunction strain, it has been found that some aspects of traditionally prescribed male and female role behavior may have negative consequences, which can be categorized under the headings of violence, sexual excess, socially irresponsible behaviors, and relationship dysfunctions for men (Brooks & Silverstein, 1995), and depression, eating disorders, histrionic personality disorder, dependency, self-limiting behavior, external locus of control, and role overload for women.

Finally, in regard to trauma strain, we have discussed how gender role socialization informed by traditional gender ideologies may be traumatic for both men and women. Traumatic consequences for men include limitations in emotional empathy (and the development of empathy along the lines of action), normative male alexithymia, the overdevelopment of aggression, the avoidance of emotional intimacy, and the development of a nonrelational orientation toward sexuality (Levant & Kopecky, 1995). The most obvious traumas that women experience in the socialization process are devaluation, role restriction, sexual objectification and sexual abuse, and physical abuse.

New Models of Intervention and Intervention Research

Before we can investigate the role of gender in the outcome and process of intervention we must redesign intervention based on an in-depth understanding of gender. The gender role strain paradigm literature clearly suggests a loosening of strict gender rules to prevent the negative effects of traditional gender socialization. However, people are so much a product of their socialization that they tend to impose gender rules on one another almost unconsciously. The first step in intervention, therefore, must be to make clients aware of the process and results of gender socialization. Through psychoeducational and experiential techniques, therapists can help their clients to understand not only the negative effects of gender socialization for both genders, but also the part they play in the process. Only then will they be motivated to change their own behavior in order to interrupt the perpetuation of negative gender messages across generations. In order to change their behaviors, men and women will often need skills that they have not acquired in the process of growing up with traditional ideology. Therefore, another important component of intervention models is *skills acquisition*. The following new models demonstrate how this might work in the areas of parenting as well as marital and family therapy.

Parent Education

We envision that the inclusion of components in parent education and family prevention programs that would provide parents with an awareness of the traumatic effects of gender role socialization, many of which already have some empirical foundation, might help reduce the incidence of trauma strain, discrepancy strain, and dysfunction strain for the next generation. This is already being done in some fatherhood education programs (Levant & Kelly, 1991). For example, Levant's fatherhood education program first discusses the changing role of fathers and how contemporary fathers were not prepared for the highly involved roles they are now being asked to take on with their children, thus giving fathers some perspective on the strains they experience in their roles. This program then helps to empower men to succeed as fathers by providing education in psychological skills that are important to parenting such as emotional empathy, emotional self-awareness, and conflict resolution. As is the case with most prevention programs, the ultimate outcome evaluation would require longitudinal studies of over 10 years in duration, which would be very difficult to accomplish; however, more formative evaluation designs could be devised.

Premarital Programs

Attempts to blend gender components have started to emerge in premarital and divorce prevention programs. Both Markman and Levant have developed gender-aware prevention programs for couples, but neither has been empirically evaluated (Levant, 1992; Markman & Kraft, 1989). Levant's program has three aims: (a) to remedy the psychological skill deficits that tend to result from gender role socialization through skills training; (b) to help participants learn about the other gender, in terms of the differences in gender role socialization and the resultant different skill profiles, frames of reference, and styles of communication; and (c) to help participants learn about themselves in order to put their own gender-based ways of knowing into a larger perspective. This latter aim is known by the Piagetian term *decentering*, which refers to the ability to remove one's self from the center of one's view of the world.

Family Therapy

Gender-sensitive family therapy approaches have been developed that take into consideration the results of gender socialization and the effects of gender role strain. The most important ingredient of these approaches is the knowledge base of the therapist, which should include an understanding of (a) the gender ecosystem, (b) the process of gender socialization, (c) androgyny, (d) empathic knowing, (e) gender co-evolution, and (f) the gender role journey. Also vital is the therapist's empathic attitude regarding the plight of both genders and a willingness to defy traditional gender messages in working toward solutions to the problems the family faces. An illustration of such a model can be found in Philpot, Brooks, Lusterman, and Nutt (1997). In the future, gender-aware marital and family interventions might be designed for the specific conditions that have been found to result from one of the three varieties of gender role strain (such as socially irresponsible behaviors or relationship dysfunctions for men, and eating disorders and role overload for women). Such programs might focus on changing gender ideology as a way to ameliorate the symptomatic behavior that has resulted from gender role strain. This is admittedly a bit of a long shot, because many of the conditions found to be associated with gender role strain probably have very complex etiologies.

Marital Therapy

Couple treatment seems to be a natural place for integrating gender-aware interventions, and in fact there already are some examples. Knudson-Martin

(1997), in a discussion of the politics of gender in family therapy, delineated three points on a hypothetical continuum of marital therapy practice with respect to gender: (a) the *cultural differences* approach (which can provide couples with a better understanding of how their differences are rooted in 3,000 years of gender role socialization), (b) the *power differences* approach (which is more explicitly political and change-oriented and aimed at creating gender equality), and (c) the *gender as process* approach (which integrates aspects of the other two approaches and for which the author provided a set of treatment recommendations).

With regard to couple treatment programs explicitly designed from a gender-aware perspective, we have been able to identify a handful of new approaches in which there is considerable overlap. These include:

1. *Philpot's "psychoeducational" approach.* The goal of therapy with a couple who has become entrenched in polarized positions over gender issues is depolarization through expansion of their cognitive maps. Most often, both spouses are locked into a repetitive, dysfunctional set in which each partner tries desperately to convince the spouse that his or her "way is the right way." They have become submerged in an either–or, right–wrong dichotomous manner of thinking, in which one perspective must defeat the other. To this end, they will attempt to triangulate the therapist as judge, each hoping to form a coalition with the expert in order to validate his or her position. It is at this point that the therapist can begin the depolarization process, which consists of four steps: (a) validation of both genders simultaneously, (b) psychoeducation regarding the results of gender socialization, (c) confrontation with the universality of the effects of socialization, and (d) brainstorming for solutions appropriate for the particular couple. The most important element of this approach is its nonblaming viewpoint, which unites the couple against a common enemy—gender socialization—in an effort to save their relationship (Philpot & Brooks, 1995; Philpot, Brooks, Lusterman, & Nutt, 1997).

2. *Brooks' "intergender translating and reframing" approach.* This is a six-stage treatment model: (a) the therapist becomes knowledgeable regarding the gender role pressures and socialization of each partner; (b) the therapist maintains therapeutic leverage by perpetuating homeostatic imbalance (i.e., resisting premature reconciliation); (c) the woman's empowerment is supported; (d) encouragement is given to the man for willingness to consider change; (e) consciousness-raising activities are provided to the man; and (f) the therapist monitors the situation regarding pos-

sible conjoint therapy for reconciliation (Philpot & Brooks, 1995; Philpot et al., 1997).

3. *Lusterman's "empathic interview" and "gender inquiry."* In order to really empathize and connect with another person, it is often necessary "to walk a mile in his or her shoes." Lusterman's empathic interview (basic communication skills) and gender inquiry (a list of questions regarding gender messages received at each developmental stage) make it possible for a couple to do just that. The purpose of the questions is threefold: they (a) teach, through personal example, that the gender ecosystem is at the core of many of the misunderstandings and dissatisfactions the spouses are experiencing and therefore depersonalize much of the conflict between spouses; (b) demonstrate how the sexes influence and mold one another within the family of origin and pass on similar destructive messages to future generations; and (c) expand cognitive maps and offer the possibility of change in the present to bring about change in future generations (Philpot et al, 1997).

4. *Silverstein and Levant's integration of the strain paradigm with the Bowen theory (Levant & Silverstein, 1997; Silverstein & Levant, 1996).* This approach has three phases: (a) learning to think gender, (b) learning to think systems, and (c) family of origin work.

Building on this emerging literature on couple therapy, we have identified a set of components that address gender role strain in men and women that could be integrated with any of the extant approaches to marital therapy. These components would begin with psychoeducation about gender, including information on the cultural differences resulting from bifurcated gender role socialization, the power differences resulting from a patriarchal society, the gender ideologies that translate the power differences into cultural differences, and the varieties of gender role strain. Skill training components could be included to help husbands to develop skills of emotional empathy and emotional self-awareness (Levant, 1994, 1997) and wives to develop skills of assertiveness and instrumental problem-solving. Couples could then engage in a discussion of their preferred gender ideologies, roles, and relationships in order to set their own agenda for change. A case study using this approach is presented in Levant and Silverstein (1997).

Case Example

To illustrate how this might work, we will briefly summarize a case treated with Silverstein and Levant's integrated gender role strain–Bowen family systems approach. The couple, Barbara and David, had a true postmodern marriage.

Both had high-powered careers and were committed to a role-sharing marriage. Then the normative developmental stress of a first child transformed this role-sharing couple into a traditional marriage, which led to severe conflict and marital impasse. Specific attention was paid, in 14 months of therapy, to resolving both gender role strain and emotional fusion as cofactors in this couple's marital impasse. With regard to gender role strain, David was able to use psychoeducation and skills training to improve his ability to be aware of and express his emotions (Levant, 1997); partly as a result of David's success, Barbara was able to let go to some extent the responsibilities for managing the emotional life of the couple. As David assumed more responsibility for his end, Barbara felt less emotionally flooded. With these gains under their belts and with the help of communication and negotiation skills training, they negotiated conditions for David to provide significant blocks of child care, thereby giving Barbara time to attend to her professional responsibilities and providing David with opportunities to get to know (and, to his surprise and great joy) fall in love with his son. The most consequential change occurred near the end of therapy, when David agreed to restructure his job so that he would travel less and spend more time with his son. With regard to resolving the emotional fusion, the first change was seen when David improved his ability to express his own emotions, thereby changing the overall emotional system of the couple and reducing the level of conflict. The next set of changes involved Barbara making some headway in being authentic with her mother, which helped her to be more proactively assertive with David, and with David confronting his fears of letting his colleagues down, enabling him to take the dramatic step near the end of therapy of drastically restructuring his job.

Intervention Research

We have described the handful of therapies designed to deal specifically with gender role strain. Because interventions based on treating the negative effects of gender socialization in families are so new, very little research has been done that assesses the efficacy of these fledgling treatment paradigms. Certainly this is a direction that family therapy research can take at this time. For example, outcome investigations of these new models of marital and family intervention should be conducted with a focus on gender strain. Research could incorporate the assessment of gender ideology and gender role strain pre- and postintervention and at follow-up to determine to what extent these variables change as a result of the focused intervention. Furthermore, studies could determine to what extent changes in gender ideology and gender role strain, if found, are associated with measures of outcome. Studies could also examine to what extent various patterns of gender ideology and gender role strain predict varying outcomes from different types of preventive and therapeutic approaches.

Conclusion

With the foregoing as a backdrop, it should be clear that marital and family intervention research ignores gender at great peril. Echoing the sentiments of Alexander et al. (1993), we believe that we have in fact reached the limit of our ability to help couples and families with therapy models based on our current understanding of marriage and the family, and we recommended enlarging the perspective by giving gender and other contextual considerations a more central place.

References

Abbey, A., & Melby, C. (1986). The effects of nonverbal cues on gender differences in perceptions of sexual intent. *Sex Roles, 15,* 183–198.

Alexander, J. F., Holtzworth-Munroe, A., & Jameson, P. (1993). The process and outcome of marital and family therapy. In A. E. Bergin & S. L. Garfield (Eds.), *Handbook of psychotherapy and behavior change* (4th ed., pp. 595–630). New York: Wiley.

American Psychiatric Association. (1994). *Diagnostic and statistical manual of mental disorders* (4th ed.). Washington, DC: Author.

Anastasi, A. (1958). *Differential psychology* (3rd ed.). New York: Macmillan.

Archer, J. (1996). Sex differences in social behavior: Are the social role and evolutionary explanations compatible? *American Psychologist, 51,* 909–917.

Avis, J. M. (1992). Where are all the family therapists? Abuse and violence within families and family therapy's response. *Journal of Marital and Family Therapy, 18,* 225–232.

Barnett, O., Keyson, M., & Thelen, R. (1992, August). *Women's violence as a response to male abuse.* Paper presented at the 100th Annual Convention of the American Psychological Association, Washington, DC.

Basow, S. (1986). *Gender stereotypes: Traditions and alternatives.* Monterey, CA: Brooks/ Cole.

Baucom, D. H., & Aiken, P. A. (1984). Sex role identity, marital satisfaction, and response to behavioral marital therapy. *Journal of Consulting and Clinical Psychology, 52,* 438–444.

Baucom, D. H., Notarius, C. I., Burnett, C. K., & Haefner, P. (1990). Gender differences and sex-role identity in marriage. In F. Fincham (Ed.), *The psychology of marriage* (pp. 150–171). New York: Guilford Press.

Beere, C. (1990). *Gender roles: A handbook of test and measures.* New York: Greenwood Press.

Beere, C. A., King, D. W., Beere, D. B., & King, L. A. (1984). The Sex-Role Egalitarianism

Scale: A measure of attitudes toward equality between the sexes. *Sex Roles, 10,* 563–576.

Behind closed doors: Family violence in the home. Hearing before the Subcommittee on Children, Family, Drugs and Alcoholism of the Committee on Labor and Human Resources, 102nd Cong., 1st Sess. (July 9, 1991) (testimony of Angela Browne).

Belenky, M., Clinchy, B., Goldberger, N., & Tarule, J. (1986). *Women's ways of knowing: The development of self, voice, and mind.* New York: Basic Books.

Bell, R. A., Daley, J. A., & Gonzalez, M. C. (1987). Affinity–maintenance in marriage and its relationship to women's marital satisfaction. *Journal of Marriage and the Family, 49,* 445–454.

Bem, S. L. (1974). The measurement of psychological androgyny. *Journal of Personality and Social Psychology, 42,* 155–162.

Bloom, C., Glitter, A., Gutwill, S., Kogel, L., & Zaphiropoulous, L. (Eds.). (1994). *Eating problems: A feminist psychoanalytic treatment model.* New York: Harper Collins.

Bograd, M. (1992). Values in conflict: Challenges to family therapists' thinking. *Journal of Marital and Family Therapy, 18,* 245–256.

Bradbury, T. N., Campbell, S. M., & Fincham, F. D. (1995). Longitudinal and behavioral analysis of masculinity and femininity in marriage. *Journal of Personality and Social Psychology, 68,* 328–341.

Briere, J., & Lanktree, C. (1983). Sex-role related effects of sex bias in language. *Sex Roles, 9,* 625–632.

Brooks, G. R., & Silverstein, L. B. (1995). Understanding the dark side of masculinity: An interactive systems model. In R. F. Levant & W. S. Pollack (Eds.), *A new psychology of men* (pp. 280–333). New York: Basic Books.

Brown, V., & Geis, F. L. (1984). Turning lead into gold: Evaluations of men and women leaders and the alchemy of social consensus. *Journal of Personality and Social Psychology, 46,* 811–824.

Caralis, P. V. (1995). *Opening pandora's box: Family violence, a physician's guide to identifying and treating victims of abuse.* Monograph published by University of Miami School of Medicine, Miami, FL.

Cash, T., & Brown, T. (1987). Body image in anorexia nervosa and bulimia nervosa: A review of the literature. *Behavior Modification, 11,* 487–521.

Center for the American Woman and Politics. (1984). *Women holding elective office.* New Brunswick, NJ: Eagleton Institute of Politics, Rutgers University.

Chafetz, J. (1978). *Masculine/feminine or human?* (2nd ed.). Itasca, IL: Peacock.

Chernin, K. (1981). *The obsession: reflections on the tyranny of slenderness.* New York: Harper & Row.

Chodorow, N. (1978). *The reproduction of mothering.* Berkeley, CA: University of California Press.

Christensen, A., & Heavey, C. (1990). Gender and social structure in the demand/

withdraw pattern of marital conflict. *Journal of Personality and Social Psychology, 59,* 73–81.

Christensen, A., & Shenk, J. L. (1991). Communication, conflict, and psychological distance in distressed, clinic, and divorcing couples. *Journal of Consulting and Clinical Psychology, 59,* 458–463.

Cowan, G., Lee, C., Levy, D., & Snyder, D. (1988). Dominance and inequality in X-rated videocassettes. *Psychology of Women Quarterly, 12,* 299–311.

Decade of the woman. (1992, December 31). *Providence Journal Bulletin,* p. A8.

Deaux, K. (1984). From individual differences to social categories: Analysis of a decade's research on gender. *American Psychologist, 39,* 105–116.

Dobash, R. E., & Dobash, R. P. (1977/1978). Wives: The "appropriate" victims of marital violence. *Victimology, 2,* 426–442.

Doherty, W., & Baldwin, C. (1985). Shift and stability in locus of control during the 1970's: Divergence of the sexes. *Journal of Personality and Social Psychology, 48,* 1048–1053.

Dowling, C. (1982). *The Cinderella complex.* New York: Pocketbooks.

Erkut, S. (1983). Exploring sex differences in expectancy, attribution, and academic achievement. *Sex Roles, 9,* 217–231.

Faludi, S. (1991). *Backlash: The undeclared war against American women.* New York: Crown.

Ferraro, G. A. (1984). Bridging the wage gap: Pay equity and job evaluations. *American Psychologist, 39,* 1166–1170.

Ferree, J. (1990). Beyond separate spheres: Feminism and family research. *Journal of Marriage and the Family, 52,* 866–884.

Fisk, W. (1985). Responses to "neutral" pronoun presentations and the development of sex-biased responding. *Developmental Psychology, 21,* 481–485.

Freedman, R. (1986). *Beauty bound.* Lexington, MA: Heath.

French, M. (1985). *Beyond power: On women, men and morals.* New York: Ballantine Books.

Freudiger, P., & Almquist, E. (1978). Male and female roles in the lyrics of three genres of contemporary music. *Sex Roles, 4,* 51–65.

Friedan, B. (1981). *The second stage.* New York: Summit.

Frieze, J. H., Parsons, J. E., Johnson, P. B., Ruble, D. N., & Zellman, G. L. (1978). *Women and sex roles.* New York: Norton.

Gelles, R. J., & Straus, M. R. (1989). *Intimate violence: The causes and consequences of abuse in the American family.* New York: Simon & Schuster.

Gilligan, C. (1982). *In a different voice.* Cambridge, MA: Harvard University Press.

Gilmore, D. (1990). *Manhood in the making: Cultural concepts of masculinity.* New Haven, CT: Yale University Press.

Gitelson, I., Petersen, A., & Tobin-Richards, M. (1982). Adolescents' expectancies of success, self-evaluations, and attributions about performance on spatial and verbal tasks. *Sex Roles, 8,* 411–419.

Gold, A. R., Brush, L. R., & Sprotzer, E. R. (1980). Developmental changes in self-perceptions of intelligence and self-confidence. *Psychology of Women Quarterly, 5,* 231–239.

Goldner, V. (1985). Feminism and family therapy. *Family Process, 24,* 31–47.

Gottman, J. M. (1991). Predicting the longitudinal course of marriages. *Journal of Marital and Family Therapy, 17,* 3–7.

Gutwill, S. (1994). Women's eating problems: Social context and the internalization of culture. In C. Bloom, A. Glitter, S. Gutwill, L. Kogel, & L. Zaphiropoulous (Eds.), *Eating problems: A feminist psychoanalytic treatment model* (pp. 1–27). New York: Harper Collins.

Halas, C., & Matteson, R. (1978). *Paradoxes: Key to women's distress. I've done so well—why do I feel so bad?* New York: Ballantine Books.

Hare-Mustin, R. (1983). An appraisal of the relationship between women and psychotherapy: 80 years after the case of Dora. *American Psychologist, 38,* 593–601.

Hare-Mustin, R. (1987). The problem of gender in family therapy theory. *Family Process, 26,* 15–33.

Hare-Mustin, R., & Marecek, J. (Eds.). (1990). *Making difference: Psychology and the construction of gender.* New Haven, CT: Yale University Press.

Hetherington, M. (1995, May). *Discussion of "the new psychology of men and family therapy research," paper presented by Ronald Levant.* First National Conference on Marital and Family Therapy Process and Outcome Research, Philadelphia, PA.

Hochschild, A. (1989). *The second shift: Working parents and the revolution at home.* New York: Viking Penguin.

Holroyd, J., & Brodsky, A. (1977). Psychologists' attitudes and practices regarding erotic and nonerotic physical contact with patients. *American Psychologist, 32,* 843–849.

Horner, M. (1972). Toward an understanding of achievement related conflicts in women. *Journal of Social Issues, 28,* 157–176.

Horner, M. (1978). The measurement and behavioral implications of fear of success in women. In J. W. Atkinson & J. O. Raynor (Eds.), *Personality, motivation, and achievement* (pp. 41–70). Washington, DC: Hemisphere.

Horney, K. (1973). *Feminine psychology.* New York: Norton.

Hyde, H. (1984). Children's understanding of sexist language. *Developmental Psychology, 20,* 697–706.

Jackson, L. A., Sullivan, L. A., & Rostker, R. (1988). Gender, gender role, and body image. *Sex Roles, 19,* 429–443.

Jacobson, N. S. (1983). Beyond empiricism: The politics of marital therapy. *American Journal of Family Therapy, 11,* 11–24.

Jacobson, N. S. (1993, October). *Domestic violence: What the couples look like.* Paper presented at Annual Convention of the American Association for Marriage and Family Therapy, Anaheim, CA.

Jacobson, N. S., Follette, W. C., & Pagel, M. (1986). Predicting who will benefit from behavioral marital therapy. *Journal of Consulting and Clinical Psychology, 54,* 518–522.

Kaschak, E. (1992). *Engendered lives: A new psychology of women's experience.* New York: Basic Books.

Katz, P. (1979). The development of female identity. *Sex Roles, 5,* 115–178.

Kaufman, G. (1992). The mysterious disappearance of battered women in family therapists offices: Male privilege colluding with male violence. *Journal of Marital and Family Therapy, 18,* 233–244.

King, I. A., King, D. W., Carter, D. B., & Surface, C. R. (1994). Validity of the Sex-Role Egalitarianism Scale: Two replication studies. *Sex Roles, 31,* 339–348.

Knudson-Martin, C. (1997). The politics of gender in family therapy. *Journal of Marital and Family Therapy, 23,* 421–437.

Kohn, A. (1987, February). Shattered innocence. *Psychology Today, 21*(2), 54, 56–58.

Kolbenschlag, M. (1981). *Kiss sleeping beauty goodbye.* Toronto: Bantam.

Komarovsky, M. (1982). Female freshmen view their future: Career salience and its correlates. *Sex Roles, 8*(3), 299–314.

Koss, M. (1990). The women's mental health research agenda: Violence against women. *American Psychologist, 45,* 374–380.

Koss, M., Leonard, K., Beezley, D., & Oros, C. (1985). Non-stranger sexual aggression: A discriminant analysis of the psychological characteristics of undetected offenders. *Sex Roles, 12,* 981–992.

Kushner, H. (1985). Women and suicide in historical perspective. *Signs, 10,* 537–552.

Levant, R. F. (1992). A gender-aware divorce prevention program. *Men's Studies Review, 9*(2), 15–20.

Levant, R. F. (1994, August). *Desperately seeking language: Methods for treating alexithymia.* Paper presented at the Annual Convention of the American Psychological Association, Los Angeles.

Levant, R. F. (1996). The new psychology of men. *Professional Psychology, 27,* 259–265.

Levant, R. F. (1997). *Men and emotions: A psychoeducational approach* [Video]. (Available from Newbridge Professional Programs, P.O. Box 949, Hicksville, NY 11801.)

Levant, R. F., & Kelly, J. (1991). *Between father and child.* New York: Penguin.

Levant, R. F., & Kopecky, G. (1995). *Masculinity reconstructed.* New York: Dutton/Plume.

Levant, R. F., & Pollack, W.S. (Eds.). (1995). *A new psychology of men.* New York: Basic Books.

Levant, R. F., & Silverstein, L. S. (1997). Integrating gender and family systems theories: the "both/and" approach to treating a postmodern couple. In S. H. McDaniel, D. D. Lusterman, & C. Philpot (Eds.), *A casebook for integrating family therapy.* Washington, DC: American Psychological Association.

Lott, B. (1994). *Women's lives: Themes and variations in gender learning.* Monterey, CA: Brooks/Cole.

Lott, B., Reilly, M., & Howard, D. (1982). Sexual assault and harassment: A campus community case study. *Signs, 8,* 296–319.

Markman, H. J., & Kraft, S. A. (1989). Men and women in marriage: Dealing with gender differences in marital therapy. *Behavior Therapist, 12,* 51–56.

Margolin, G., Talovic, S., Fernandez, V., & Onorato, R. (1983). Sex role considerations and behavioral marital therapy: Equal does not mean identical. *Journal of Marital and Family Therapy, 9,* 131–145.

McGoldrick, M., Anderson, C., & Walsh, F. (1989). *Women in families: A framework for family therapy.* New York: Norton.

McGrath, E., Keita, G., Strickland, B., & Russo, N. (1990). *Women and depression: Risk factors and treatment issues.* Washington, DC: American Psychological Association.

McMahan, I. (1982). Expectancy of success on sex-linked tasks. *Sex Roles, 8,* 949–958.

Michelini, R., Eisen, D., & Snodgrass, S. (1981). Success orientation and the attractiveness of competent males and females. *Sex Roles, 7,* 391–401.

Miller, J. B. (1986). *Toward a new psychology of women* (2nd ed.). Boston: Beacon Press.

Muehlenhard, C., & Linton, M. (1987). Date rape and sexual aggression in dating situations: Incidence and risk factors. *Journal of Counseling Psychology, 34,* 186–196.

Philpot, C. L., & Brooks, G. (1995). Intergender communication and gender-sensitive family therapy. In R. H. Mikesell, D-D. Lusterman, & S. McDaniel (Eds.), *Integrating family therapy: Handbook of family psychology and systems therapy* (pp. 303–325). Washington, DC: American Psychological Association.

Philpot, C. L., Brooks, G., Lusterman, D-D., & Nutt, R. (Eds.). (1997). *Bridging separate gender worlds.* Washington, DC: American Psychological Association.

Pleck, J. H. (1981). *The myth of masculinity.* Cambridge, MA: MIT Press.

Pleck, J. H. (1995). The gender role strain paradigm: An update. In R. F. Levant & W. S. Pollack (Eds.), *A new psychology of men* (pp. 1–32). New York: Basic Books.

Rampage, C. (1989). Revolution and resistance: A comment on Witkin. *Journal of Family Psychology, 2,* 447–450.

Rand, L. M., & Miller, A. L. (1972). A developmental cross-sectioning of women's career and marriage attitudes and life plans. *Journal of Counseling Psychology, 15,* 444–449.

Reilly, M., Lott, B., Caldwell, D., & DeLuca, L. (1992). Tolerance for sexual harassment related to self-reported sexual victimization. *Gender & Society, 6,* 122–138.

Root, M. (1990). Disordered eating in women of color. *Sex Roles, 22,* 526–536.

Russell, D., & Howell, N. (1983), The prevalence of rape in the United States revisited. *Signs, 8,* 688–695.

Russianoff, P. (1981). *Why do I think I am nothing without a man?* Toronto: Bantam.

Russo, N. (Ed.) (1985). *A woman's mental health agenda.* Washington, DC: American Psychological Association.

Sadd, S., Lenauer, M., Shaver, P., & Dunivant, N. (1978). Objective measurement of fear of success and fear of failure: A factor analytic approach. *Journal of Consulting and Clinical Psychology, 46,* 405–416.

Savage, J., Stearns, A., & Friedman, P. (1979). Relationship of internal–external locus of control, self-concept, and masculinity–femininity to fear of success in Black freshmen and senior college women. *Sex Roles, 5,* 373–383.

Silverstein, L. S., & Levant, R. F. (1996, August). *Bridging the gap from Mars to Venus: Treating couples impasses.* Paper presented at the Annual Convention of the American Psychological Association, Toronto.

Simon, K. (1990). *Etchings in an hourglass.* New York: Harper & Row.

Spence, J. T., & Helmreich, R. L. (1978). *Masculinity and femininity: Their psychological dimensions, correlates, and antecedents.* Austin, TX: University of Texas Press.

Stake, J., & Lauer, M. (1987). The consequences of being overweight: A controlled study of gender differences. *Sex Roles, 17,* 31–47.

Stapley, J. C., & Haviland, J. M. (1989). Beyond depression: Gender differences in normal adolescents' emotional experiences. *Sex Roles, 20*(5/6), 295–308.

Tavris, C. (1992). *The mismeasure of woman.* New York: Simon & Schuster.

Terman, L., & Miles, C. (1936). *Sex and personality,* New York: McGraw-Hill.

Thompson, E. H., & Pleck, J. H. (1995). Masculinity ideology: A review of research instrumentation on men and masculinities. In R. F. Levant & W. S. Pollack (Eds.), *A new psychology of men* (pp. 129–163). New York: Basic Books.

Thompson, L., & Walker, A. (1995). The place of feminism in family studies. *Journal of Marriage and the Family, 57,* 847–856.

Unger, R., & Crawford, M. (1992). *Women and gender.* New York: McGraw Hill.

U.S. Department of Labor, Bureau of Labor Statistics. (1985). *Employment and earnings, April 1985.* Washington, DC: U.S. Government Printing Office.

Ussher, J. (1989). *The psychology of the female body.* London: Routledge.

Vollmer, F. (1984). Sex differences in personality and expectancy. *Sex Roles, 11,* 1121–1139.

Walker, L. (1989). *The battered woman syndrome.* New York: Springer.

Walters, M., Carter, B., Papp, P., & Silverstein, O. (1988). *The invisible web: Gender patterns in family relationships.* New York: Guilford Press.

Whisman, M. A., & Jacobson, N. S. (1990) Power, marital satisfaction, and response to marital therapy. *Journal of Family Psychology, 4,* 202–212.

Witkin, S. L. (1989a). Scientific ideology and women: Implications for marital research and therapy. *Journal of Family Psychology, 2,* 430–446.

Witkin, S. L. (1989b). Responding to sexism in marital research and therapy. *Journal of Family Psychology, 3,* 82–85.

Wolf, N. (1991). *The beauty myth.* New York: Morrow.

CHAPTER 16

Integrating the Study of Ethnic Culture and Family Psychology Intervention Science

Daniel A. Santisteban

Joan A. Muir-Malcolm

Victoria B. Mitrani

José Szapocznik

Although strong research traditions have existed in both the family process and family therapy domain (Alexander, Holtzworth-Munroe, & Jameson, 1994) and in the culture and ethnicity domain (Guarnaccia, Canino, Rubio-Stepic, & Bravo, 1993; Marin & Marin, 1991), the promise of integrating the two with the goal of rigorously investigating how ethnicity-related dimensions influence core family and clinical processes has remained largely unrealized. Core processes in the family functioning and family therapy domains have been effectively articulated and made the targets of rigorous research (Liddle, 1995; Patterson, Reid, & Dishion, 1992; Schmidt, Liddle, & Dakof, 1996). Likewise, there is a substantial literature showing ethnicity-related differences in how symptoms develop, are expressed, are explained, and how and to whom people communicate their distress (Guarnaccia et al., 1993; McGoldrick, 1996; Rivera-Arzola & Ramos-Grenier, 1997; Szapocznik, Scopetta, & King, 1978). One of the important challenges for family intervention science is to integrate these two streams of research and rigorously investigate the intricate interplay between ethnicity, family functioning, and family intervention. As McGoldrick has stated, "there is burgeoning evidence that ethnic values and identifications are retained for many generations after immigration and play a significant role in family life throughout the life cycle. Second-, third-, and even fourth-generation Americans differ from the dominant [White European] culture in values, behavior, and life cycle patterns" (McGoldrick, 1989, p. 70). Inclusion of these culture and ethnicity-related variables can help the family intervention scientist to understand unique processes in families of diverse ethnic backgrounds and in predicting patient responses to some of our commonly used interventions. The push toward this integration is timely, given that ethnic minority groups now make up 27.2% of the U.S. population (U.S. Census Department, 1997) and given the interest in aptitude x treatment interactions (ATI) research (Shoham & Rohrbaugh, 1995), which examines the interplay between client characteristics and treatment interventions in an effort to improve the efficacy of our interventions.

The purpose of this chapter is to provide a framework that highlights the links between the study of ethnicity and the study of family processes and therapy. In this chapter we (a) define what we mean by ethnicity, race, and culture; (b) present the ethnicity-related dimensions that are most proximal to the understanding of family functioning and their links to family intervention science; (c) discuss how these dimensions change with acculturation and how the process of acculturation affects the family; and (d) articulate ethnic minority life experiences (i.e., immigration-related separations and racial discrimination) that are critical to understanding the attitudes and behavior patterns of families from diverse ethnic backgrounds. Throughout this chapter we will weave the literature available in this domain with the experiences of our 25-year program of clinical research with Hispanic, African American, and Haitian families. The chapter will end with recommendations on how the field can continue to develop knowledge in this critically important area.

Defining the Relationships Among Ethnicity, Race, and Culture

Culture, race, and ethnicity are often used interchangeably in the psychological literature, thus blurring the distinct though related meaning of each term (Carter, 1995). *Culture* can be described as knowledge, skills, attitudes, and behaviors that are shared by a group of people and transmitted from one generation to another (Carter, 1995). These elements of culture are expressed through "familial roles, communication patterns, affective styles and values regarding personal control, individualism, collectivism, spirituality and religiosity" (Betancourt & Lopez, 1993, p. 630). Because culture is learned, one of the primary tasks of the family is to socialize children into the family's identified culture.

The term *ethnicity* is derived from the Greek concept *ethnos,* which refers to people belonging to a nation or tribe, and *ethnikos,* which stands for "national" (Betancourt & Lopez, 1993). Members of an ethnic group share a common culture *and* common ancestry or country of origin, together giving the group a sense of shared history. Shared culture is an integral part of defining ethnicity in that members of an ethnic group share a cultural heritage that is transmitted from one generation to another (Betancourt & Lopez, 1993; Sue, 1991) and share similar customs, language, rituals, values, and attitudes that as a group distinguishes them from members of other groups (McAdoo, 1993).

The concept of ethnicity also contributes to the understanding of group differences through variables such as ethnic identification, language use, and perceived discrimination (Betancourt & Lopez, 1993). In this chapter we use the term *ethnic culture* to refer to the shared attitudes and behaviors attributable to belonging to the same ethnic group.

A critically important but often overlooked factor in understanding the complexity of ethnicity is the role of *race*. Race has a history in biological and anthropological classification systems, with each so-called race being defined as a geographically isolated population whose members were capable of breeding with members of other populations but generally did not (Zuckerman, 1990). In modern society, in which the isolation of the races has been greatly reduced, we tend to think of race as nested in ethnicity because race can be different for people of the same national origin. In countries in which different races are represented, one can identify intraethnic differences because of different ancestry. For example, a Chinese Jamaican and an African Jamaican share the same national identity and certain identified Jamaican cultural characteristics. These Jamaican characteristics, however, may be modified by their differences in ancestry—Chinese or African. The same is true within Cuban and Puerto Rican groups, depending on whether they see their ancestry as deriving primarily from Spain or from Africa. Although some scientists may choose to group along the lines of race rather than ethnicity, research has tended to reveal more within-group difference among racial groups than there are between-group differences, leading to the conclusion that race alone is inadequate for explaining variability in psychological phenomenon (Betancourt & Lopez, 1993; Segall, Lonner, & Berry, 1998). We use the term *ethnic cultures* but emphasize the profound importance of race in any complete conceptualization of ethnicity.

Value Dimensions Directly Relevant to Family Intervention Science

Efforts to investigate the interplay between ethnic culture and clinical processes require that we move beyond ethnic labels (Hispanic, Asian, African American) and consider the values, beliefs, and behaviors that are at the root of ethnic differences. Explaining the nature of these ethnic differences will allow us to take the field to the next level of inquiry. In this section we present some of the values, beliefs, and behaviors that have been shown to differ between ethnic cultures. However, this presentation differs from others that link values to ethnic groups (e.g., suggesting Hispanics are more family-oriented) by linking value orientations to the family process variables of interest to the family intervention scientist. We hope that this will help the family intervention scientist understand how ethnicity-related values or world views influence family processes in families.

We have found (Szapocznik, Scopetta, Aranalde, & Kurtines, 1978; Szapocznik, Scopetta, & King, 1978) that a useful model for organizing the information on values and beliefs is the values orientations work conducted by Kluckhohn and Strodtbeck (1961). Their model identifies a number of basic assumptions held by different ethnic cultures that are keys to understanding how different people view the world. Kluckhohn and Strodtbeck postulated five human problems—relational orientation, human nature, person–nature, activity orientation, and time orientation—that are common to all cultures. They posit that the solutions provided by each ethnic culture to these problems are indicative of world view or basic value orientation. In the remainder of this section we present Kluckhohn and Strodtbeck's five dimensions and show the profound influences that these differing values orientations can have on core constructs in family intervention science.

Relational Orientation

Relational orientation is the dimension that is most clearly linked to family theory and constructs. It represents the range of assumptions about the nature of interpersonal relationships, with a range of preferences including (a) hierarchical (vertical), (b) collateral (i.e., horizontal), and (c) individualistic (i.e., autonomy). Having a hierarchical as opposed to an individualistic orientation has been linked to being more family-oriented rather than individually or peer-oriented. Familialism has been often cited as a core construct among Hispanics and other ethnic minority cultures and has been shown to have three components: (a) perceived obligations toward helping family members, (b) reliance on support from family members, and (c) the use of family members as behavioral and attitudinal referents (Marin & Marin, 1991). When there is a high familialism, it is not uncommon to see individuals motivated to behave in more adaptive ways, for the potential benefit to the family and not merely for their own benefit. Those who view themselves primarily through their connection to family will be most in line with the assumptions of a family therapy model. Problems can be discussed in family terms, and it is expected that family will be involved. One of our first findings was that Hispanic parents were offended when individually oriented interventions meant that therapists would most often see the youth alone and the therapists informed parents that in order to ensure confidentiality, family participation would be minimal (Scopetta, 1972).

These issues of sensitivity or connectedness between and among persons in the family is usually described in family terms as *boundaries* or *resonance*. Boundaries can at one extreme be highly rigid or impermeable, leading to great emotional and psychological distance between people, and at the other extreme can be far too permeable, leading to a level of emotional and psychological closeness between people that is too great, and intolerable for some. White,

European–American culture tends to place a high value on individuality and autonomy, and boundaries between family members tend to be less permeable. A strength in these families is that members learn to be competent and independent; a weakness is that in difficult times family members may not be available to support one another or may not even be aware of each other's emotional needs. Family therapy often aims to promote interdependency in families and may, if taken to an extreme, run counter to the mode of those families who place a high value on self-sufficiency and individuality. The degree of closeness that is found in a Hispanic family is typically greater than that found in White European families (Marin & Marin, 1991). Extremely close or "enmeshed" families are very aware of each other's problems and needs and are often available for support. However, highly enmeshed families typically do not tolerate uniqueness, so that those who do not "fit in" can be ostracized and essentially ejected. In addition, highly enmeshed families may engender a level of dependency that can delay the emotional development of some family members. If a daughter or son in a Hispanic family is rebelling because she or he is not allowed to individuate, it may come into conflict with the tendency for greater emotional and psychological closeness in this particular family. This conflict needs to be addressed with the recognition that separation and individuation is culturally syntonic in the dominant culture, whereas closeness is culturally syntonic in the Hispanic culture. Therefore, therapists must always be attentive to personal and cultural values and be careful not to undermine either the need for self-sufficiency *or* the reliance on other family members in those individuals for whom this is important and adaptive.

The extent to which parents have a preference for markedly hierarchical family relations has powerful implications for a key family construct, namely conflict resolution. When parents view good family functioning as consisting of marked levels of authority (nonegalitarian), they can perceive any type of open disagreement between parents and adolescents as disrespectful and unacceptable. In fact, many Hispanic cultures seek to keep harmony in relationships and value *respeto* (respect), which may make frequent use of conflict diffusion. This view may clash with a mental health culture in which full conflict emergence with resolution is valued. Within this mental health culture, negativity tends to be more easily tolerated, and positive emotions are also more easily expressed. One of the critical implications of having a strongly hierarchical world view is that therapy interventions that openly encourage youngsters to speak their minds and tell parents what they really think may be seen as incompetent or misguided therapy. The intervention may be seen as making the problem worse than it was originally, by encouraging more of what is perceived to be the dysfunctional behavior (disrespectful challenging). In such families, an effective strategy may be for the therapist to ask the parents if the child or adolescent has permission to challenge or disagree with the parent.

When parents feel that the therapist acknowledges their position as leaders of the family, they are likely to give the child permission to challenge or disagree. The onus, however, may be on the therapist to provide a convincing therapeutic rationale for promoting this process of disagreement.

From an ATI perspective, one can see how certain ethnic culture characteristics of families can have a profound impact on the efficacy of some therapist–family interactions hypothesized to be therapeutic (e.g., direct negotiation and problem solving between adolescents and parents). The link between therapy process (negotiation) and outcome (improved family relations) seen among most families may not be found among families who are culturally influenced to be very highly hierarchical and respect-oriented. Some very interesting research provides evidence of the needs of matching relationship patterns to treatments. Findings suggest that partners in symmetrical and egalitarian relationships may benefit more from therapies emphasizing direct negotiation (Jacobson, Follette, & Pagel, 1986), while clients in complementary relationships (organized along traditional gender roles) may do better with less direct or overt interventions such as those promoted by the strategic interventions models (Goldman & Greenberg, 1992) or with interventions that promote acceptance (Christensen, Jacobson, & Babcock, 1995). Along similar lines, Gollan and Jacobson (chapter 6, this volume) report that couples whose affiliation and independence needs follow traditional gender roles (male as independent, female as affiliative) may show attenuated effects of behavioral marital therapy.

Another concept associated with the relational dimension is *allocentrism* (Hofstede, 1980), which refers to the orientation toward collectivism as opposed to individualism. Allocentrism refers to being connected with, interdependent with, and interested in the well-being of a particular ingroup and not just the self-interest of the individual (Marin & Triandis, 1985). Asian philosophy places importance of obligation to the group over the striving of the individual. The accomplishments of the individual are seen as the culmination of the efforts of many things and many people (Shon & Davis, 1982). In traditional Asian culture, for example, there is an emphasis on harmony in the family and society attained by adherence to well-prescribed rules for proper conduct. African Americans are also influenced by traditional African culture, which places emphasis on the well-being of the group over that of the individual. In traditional African culture, the importance of unity in the community supersedes even that of the family (Boyd-Franklin, 1989). African Americans have effectively used this value of collective unity to preserve their cultural institutions, which have been assailed by racism and discrimination. Within this ethnic culture, being in harmony with the ingroup is a powerful driving force and may promote relationships that are less confrontational than an individualistic orientation may generate. When a goal of an intervention is to make the individual more assertive regarding a member of the ingroup, this approach conflicts with the culture's orientation toward collectivism.

Along similar lines, Hofstede's (1980) concept of *power–distance* describes how some societies favor marked power differentials in which some persons or institutions (i.e., those highly intelligent or educated, of high social class, or of high moral status) must be looked up to and elicit intense respect, conformity, and deference. We have found that this orientation can have a very powerful impact in two key areas. First, families characterized by this orientation often favor hierarchical doctor–patient (expert–patient) relationships in which the doctor tells the patient what to do and the patient complies with little or no questioning. This is not uncommon among many of our Hispanic families but it is quite different from our experience with African Americans, who have a history of being wronged by so-called experts, are more skeptical, and consequently feel more comfortable in asking questions and challenging authority when necessary. Second, programs that include multisystemic interventions that attempt to help parents become active interventionists in the school or juvenile justice systems in which their children are involved will also be affected by this phenomenon. Hispanic parents often look on these institutions with such high respect and awe that it impedes them from seeking to have an impact on these systems. This is often compounded by the fact that language barriers further disempower Hispanic parents in relation to these important systems. In most poor immigrant families, children become fluent in English well before their parents and learn the language more quickly. It is not unusual for a child who is the subject of a disciplinary meeting between parents and school officials, for example, to serve as translator, thus compromising the executive power of parents in the eyes of the school and within the family. It is very easy to label the behaviors resulting from this level of respect and awe of large institutions as passivity, dependence, and lack of motivation. Research on treatment models that have as a change mechanism the modification of the interactions between ethnic parents and large institutions would do well to consider the influence of Hofstede's power–distance orientation in their work.

Human Nature

Human nature is the second problem postulated by Kluckhohn and Strodtbeck. It pertains to a culture's perception of innate human qualities as good or bad, with a range of (a) good, (b) neutral, or (c) bad. Many theories are based on the assumption that individuals are good, whereas learned behaviors are bad. In our clinical experience with families of diverse cultures, we have found that the tendency of parents of some cultures to see their misbehaving children as inherently bad or "influenced by evil" is qualitatively different from those who see behavior as bad but perceive the child as inherently good. Not surprisingly, the family members' position along the human nature dimension can contribute directly to a core construct in family therapy that is described as the rigidity of *identified patienthood* (Szapocznik & Kurtines, 1989; Szapocznik et al., 1991). Identified patienthood is defined as the extent to which all responsibility for a problem is attributed to one person while other contributions to the problem, including systemic contributions, are dismissed. The degree to which one individual is perceived as "the bad seed" may directly determine the extent to which family members are unwilling to accept the need to change family interactions to modify a problem manifested in the "bad seed" child. In some Haitian families, in whom we clearly confronted this phenomenon, not only was it difficult to expand the view of the problem to a familial and interactional one, it was also difficult to convince parents that "talking" to the adolescent could help with the problem (Gustafson, 1989). Our family therapy assumptions were limited when attempting to understand the Haitian family's perspective, and the interventions offered were not compatible with the perceived problem. It should not be surprising, for example, that many West Indian and African Caribbean families, who often attribute psychological symptoms to spiritual problems, will likely seek the counsel of a minister or an obeah practitioner who can enhance or exorcise the influence of good and evil spirits on events in peoples' lives (Gopaul-McNicol, 1994). The mismatch between a family's perception of what is needed and what a talking therapy has to offer is directly related to difficulties in engaging and retaining families in therapy (Santisteban & Szapocznik, 1994; Szapocznik et al., 1988). These examples demonstrate how an ethnic family's assumptions about human nature may interact with our well-established psychological constructs and determine a family's poor response to a therapy model that may be based on a different set of assumptions (i.e., that people are good and only the learned behaviors are bad). This example also demonstrates how a family intervention scientist studying success of engagement and retention in therapy or rigidity of identified patienthood among different ethnic groups may benefit from considering this important value dimension.

Person–Nature

Person–nature is the third human problem postulated by Kluckhohn and Strodtbeck and refers to the perceived relationship of people to natural phenomena, with a range of (a) subjugation to nature, (b) harmony with nature, and (c) mastery over nature. The epitome of Eurocentric values is the conquest of America by the Europeans and the conquest of the Wild West by "Americans." American "can-doism" and perseverance in the face of problems derives from a world view that supports mastery. We must therefore begin by acknowledging that most American models of therapy are founded on the value of mastery over nature (i.e., identifying and changing those characteristics that are problematic). However, many cultures see the role of individuals as accepting rather than conquering nature. The latter approach might show a preference toward creating a view of life that would allow graceful acceptance of life circumstances and fate. The endorsement of different world views regarding person–nature relations can lead to impasses that contribute to labels such as *resistance* and to low therapeutic alliance, which is partly dependent on agreement on the assumptions, goals, and strategies of treatment.

Activity Orientation

The fourth human problem postulated by Kluckhohn and Strodtbeck, activity orientation, refers to the nature of behaviors through which a person is judged or judges herself or himself, with a range of (a) doing (achievement-oriented), (b) being (who I am), and (c) being in becoming (a search for understanding about one's self). Although doing is an important value in some societies' cultures—that is, people define themselves through what they do (e.g., careers, education)—in Hispanic culture individuals often define themselves by what family or region of a country they come from (being). In our work with Hispanics we find that we use their emphasis on the inherent quality of being—of who you are—which gives the individual value that is not attached to what has been achieved. Highly achievement-oriented parents, like achievement-oriented societies, often describe and praise their children largely on what they achieve. Similarly, children learn to value their parents not for their inherent value but for what they achieve. Rigid adherence to an achievement orientation can be particularly destructive among poor families, in which children sometimes devalue their parents for their lack of material achievement. The concept of achievement orientation also has implications for working with individuals who need caregiving because of physical, emotional, or mental limitations. Families that emphasize being appear to accept more readily a family member who needs caregiving because of their greater acceptance of someone who is not producing, or at least not producing by material standards. Finally, it should be noted that models of therapy that have as their goal the promotion of personal growth (related to the value of being and becoming) and the achievement of a deeper level of understanding about the self may seem alien to persons who do not value this type of outcome.

Time Orientation

The fifth human problem postulated by Kluchkon and Strodtbeck, time orientation, refers to the emphasis placed on a particular time period, with a range of (a) past, (b) present, and (c) future orientation. An understanding of time orientation has considerable value for the planning and presenting of interventions. A therapist who implements a prevention intervention (which is by definition future-oriented) may be much more effective when working with a client who has a future orientation rather than with families that are present-oriented and focused on "today's" issues. A present-oriented family would work best when they can quickly see some rewards or benefits of the intervention. With the present-oriented client, the discussion might be more effective when it focuses on how the intervention will affect current circumstances or difficulties, such as important immediate precursors to the main problem to be prevented. For example, in drug prevention programs it may be more effective to emphasize the modification of current behavior problems rather than the prevention of future drug use by targeting risk factors. It should be noted that socioeconomic conditions or environment may have much to do with a present orientation, such as when a family must struggle to survive day to day or when a family lives in a dangerous neighborhood. The types of adaptations recommended in this section are consistent with the concepts proposed by Sue and Zane (1987), in which they recommend that interventions with minorities should be made clearly relevant to the clients' daily lives and that the credibility of the interventions and the therapist are crucial.

The links of past orientation to interventions and responses to interventions can also be considered. Some Far Eastern cultures place great value in the past, in the form of ancestry worship and reverence toward parents and other elders. In this instance, the future may be framed in terms of the past, such as in the statement, "Your child will grow to honor his ancestors." Native Americans call on their ancestors to help them cope with life. African Americans are formally embracing their African ancestry, as indicated by the growing number of families celebrating the holiday Kwanza. The principles of Kwanza are based on the African tradition and provide guidelines for healthy families and communities. The role of honoring ancestors or the aversion to dishonoring ancestors may be integrated into the intervention, as has been done in prevention projects for African American youths who are at risk for substance abuse (Cherry, Belgrave, Jones, Kofi Kennon, & Phillips, 1998).

Changes in Value Orientations Resulting From Acculturation Processes and Their Impact on the Family

Adding to the complexity of working with ethnic families is the fact that the ethnic culture of an individual does not remain static. Perhaps the greatest challenge to understanding an ethnic individual or family is understanding how these core values change as a result of contact with the culture of a new society that shares a different configuration of values (Santisteban, Coatsworth, Briones,

& Szapocznik, 2001; Szapocznik, Scopetta, Aranalde, & Kurtines, 1978). *Acculturation* has been defined as "the complex process whereby the behaviors and attitudes of an immigrant group change toward the dominant group as a result of exposure to a cultural system that is significantly different" (Rogler, Malgady, & Rodriguez, 1989).

As Berry (1980), Szapocznik, Kurtines, and Fernandez (1980), Szapocznik, Scopetta, Aranalde, and Kurtines (1978), and others have suggested, there are several types of behavioral and psychological responses that an individual might manifest while entering a society or context that does not have the same characteristics and values espoused by their culture of origin. *Alienation/marginalization* describes an individual who does not identify with any culture. Studies of Native Americans have shown this process to be very destructive, as young men and women have lost their native traditions and beliefs but are not an integral part of the nonnative American culture (LaFromboise, Trimble, & Mohatt, 1990). *Assimilation* refers to the process of becoming a part of the host society culture while rejecting the culture of origin. Full assimilation can often be found in youngsters who reject the values and beliefs of their original ethnic culture and parents in the process of fully accepting the culture of a new host society. *Withdrawal/separation* refers to the process by which the individual becomes totally embedded in her or his culture of origin and refuses to participate in the host society culture. Although some have suggested that being solidly entrenched in one's culture of origin can mean increased support systems and high self-esteem by being insulated from the negative stereotypes of the host society culture, most evidence suggests that the individual may be at risk because of the failure to learn the skills needed to survive in both the family's culture on the one hand and the host context on the other (Szapocznik & Kurtines, 1979; Szapocznik et al., 1980). *Integration/biculturalism* is the process by which an individual retains his or her ethnic culture while also learning the necessary skills to survive in the host society culture (Szapocznik & Kurtines, 1993; Szapocznik et al., 1986). Although not without its stresses (e.g., when the host society culture looks down on the culture of origin), this process appears to be the most adaptive of the possible solutions, with ample research evidence that indicates that becoming bicultural in a multicultural context can lead to better outcome and better adjustment on a number of indices (Szapoczniket al., 1980).

The differential impact of keeping or abandoning one's culture of origin became evident in our recent study of acculturation processes and parenting practices in relation to adolescent behavior problems (Santisteban et al., 2001). The data from our study showed that mother Hispanicism and familialism were strongly related to parenting practices and that these were strongly negatively related to adolescent externalizing problems. The analysis of parenting practices suggest that high levels of Hispanicism were associated with (a) higher parental involvement (as reported by both parents and adolescents); (b) parent reports of low withdrawal from disciplining behavior and higher effective parenting; and (c) adolescent reports of higher positive parenting, higher behavior control and monitoring, and more positive parenting. It is also important to note that familialism was highly correlated with the types of parenting practices that led to fewer behavior problems. These findings supported the hypothesis that there may be parenting practices associated with the original Hispanic culture and with high levels of familialism that can protect youths from behavior problems. It is important to note that these potentially successful parenting styles may be erroneously viewed as overly intrusive or as thwarting the youth's autonomy by professionals not familiar with the Hispanic culture. Realizing that what works or does not work for Hispanic parents and youths does not necessarily inform one regarding what works for a non-Hispanic family, these findings do suggest that, *for Hispanic parents,* the loss of a strong family orientation and parenting practices associated with their culture of origin may reflect a family process that does not serve its youths well.

A promising avenue for further research on acculturation and parenting is the investigation of culture-bound meaning that adolescents may attribute to specific types of parenting practices. As Mason, Walker-Barnes, Blaustein, and Martinez-Arrue (1998) have shown, youths from different ethnic and racial backgrounds give substantially different affective meaning (i.e., caring and loving versus controlling and manipulating) to their parent's parenting practices. We would expect that these affective meanings may help to explain how youths respond to specific parenting practices. For example, Mason et al. (1998) also found that Hispanic youths reported lower feelings of being controlled and manipulated by parents than did African American or White youths. It is possible, however, that with acculturation and the expectations of more autonomy and independence that these perceptions may change, so that Hispanic youths may begin to experience the same parenting as increasingly controlling and manipulative. Just as our findings suggest that parental acculturation variables may have an impact on specific parenting practices and lead to lower externalizing behavior, it may be that youth acculturation may have an impact on the youngsters' perceptions and attributions of specific parenting practices and therefore their responses to these practices. This line of research may shed light on such family therapy techniques as reframing, which are often used to modify the attributions made by youths regarding the intention and meaning behind certain parenting practices.

Another phenomenon that should be of particular interest to family intervention scientists occurs when family members show different acculturation responses, resulting in powerful intrafamilial stress. For example, the literature (Szapocznik, Scopetta, & King, 1978; Szapocznik, Scopetta, Aranalde, & Kurtines, 1978; Szapocznik & Kurtines, 1993; Zayas, 1992) describes how youngsters often reject their culture of origin and thus the culture of their parents (assimilation), whereas the parents show more of a pattern of withdrawal and separation, in which they become entrenched in their culture of origin and do not want to learn the ways of the host society culture. Intrafamilial differences in acculturation combined with developmental processes can result in severe family conflict. An example is when an adolescent's normal striving for independence is accelerated through assimilation into the mainstream culture of individualism and becomes incompatible with the parent's tendency to preserve family integrity by adhering to the traditional cultural value of parental control (hierarchical and lineal relations) and adolescent submission. Assimilated youngsters often have the more individually oriented idea that children will be "launched" from the home in late adolescence or early adulthood. This expectation, however, is usually incompatible with the traditional Hispanic parent's idea that children should remain in the parental home until they marry or are well into their 20s.

Youngsters' assimilation can cause them to reject other established family traditions as well. For example, one highly ethnic, culture-specific pattern found in some Asian American families has the husband's mother highly involved in giving her daughter-in-law direction for proper behavior, both with her husband as well as with the husband's family of origin. The expectation is that the husband's mother will help shape her daughter-in-law's behavior, given that the latter will become a member of her husband's family. It is clearly evident how a daughter-in-law's assimilation may lead to a strong rejection of this traditional pattern and may cause severe disruptions in the extended family. In these examples, the normal stresses expected during transition periods from one family life cycle stage to another are exacerbated because of clashing views on the nature, meaning, and timetable for these transitions. These and other intergenerational and intercultural family clashes have a direct impact on the level of bonding between nuclear family and extended family members.

Couple relationships can also be powerfully affected by acculturation. With acculturation can come an abrupt and accelerated reconfiguration of a couples' egalitarian versus complementary relations dimension toward more egalitarianism. When couples must reconfigure this very basic blueprint for their relationship in a short amount of time, it cannot help but disrupt family functioning and affect their ability to reach joint decisions and set clear and consistent rules and consequences. As we noted earlier, research has shown how egalitarian and complementary relationships may have different needs in terms of treatment and may respond differently to a given treatment package (Christensen et al., 1995; Jacobson et al., 1986). Also, as a child grows, the family dynamics become even more complex because the tensions already existing in the couple are exacerbated when the child or adolescent may side with one parent (usually the most acculturated) against another. For example, a traditional father who has a difficult time accepting his wife's need for more autonomy and independence may be ridiculed by an acculturated adolescent. Eventually, the adolescent ends up triangulated and in a very precarious and vulnerable position, risking deterioration of the father–child bond. These are concrete examples of how immigration- and acculturation-related changes in family processes directly influence constructs commonly studied by family intervention scientists, such as alliances, coalitions, and bonding.

In summary, acculturation processes are complex phenomena that provide a rich source of material for the family psychology intervention scientist. Different family members are likely to be at different levels of acculturation and biculturation, and the interactions between these different value profiles can result in powerful intrafamilial tensions that require family intervention and further family intervention research (e.g., Szapocznik et al., 1986; Szapocznik et al., 1989)

Major Life Experiences That Are Keys to Working With Ethnic Families

There are major life experiences other than acculturation that also result in powerful family trauma and should be targets of research. In this section we describe examples of life experiences that have a strong impact on the traditional family processes we target for change and investigation.

Effects of Immigration on Family Life

In working with families that are generationally close to the immigration experience (i.e., first- or second-generation immigrants), the first and most obvious consideration is the effects of the actual immigration on the family and the events that led them to emigrate (e.g., war, famine, persecution, upward mobility). For most immigrant families the immigration is a major life event because of the often perilous and traumatic paths that families must take to gain entry into the United States (Silove et al., 1997). For some, such as Mexican families, rather than a one-time event immigration may consist of an ongoing process that involves deportation and reentry. The fear of deportation and the deplorable circumstances associated with it bring their own set of stressors. In many instances, because of the enormous effort that it takes to establish the family in a new country, there may not have been an opportunity to process the painful family experiences that may have come with crossing the border. The failure to process these experiences means that they may continue to contribute heavily to the family's condition even when the presenting symptom appears at first glance to be unrelated.

In our work with immigrant families, another powerfully disruptive process has been that of immigration-related parent–child separations. When parents immigrate ahead of their children or must send their children ahead of them (Bemak & Greenberg, 1994), there is a breaking of ties with nuclear family members and resulting feelings of abandonment and loss. Our work in Miami parallels work conducted in other parts of the country (Foner, 1987) in working with mothers who came to the United States from Central America and the Caribbean to establish a home, send money back to the family, and later bring their children. Several years later, when the children are brought to the United States and problems emerge in the child's behavior, there are a number of powerful family dynamics that seem to operate beyond the radar of the family therapy clinician and researcher. These include (a) feelings of abandonment and resentment from the children toward the mother, as well as guilt for having those feelings; (b) dual loyalties on the part of the children toward their mother versus the family member who was the primary caretaker during the separation; (c) a cultural pattern dictating that the emergence of strong negative emotion around these issues is disrespectful; (d) for mothers who formed new relationships after emigrating, the mother's dual loyalty between the new relationships and the separated children; (e) very distant relationships between stepfathers and the separated child; (f) age-inappropriate behavior in the sense that the mother may treat her children as younger than their age, partly because she has not adjusted to the child's development that occurred during the separation; and (g) parental reluctance to set limits because of the guilt associated with the separation. Clearly, these immigration-related disruptions in the family can have profound influences on the family interactional patterns that family researchers and clinicians study and target for treatment. If these emigration and separation traumas remain unresolved, they may contribute to family interactions that are resistant to change.

Sociopolitical Status of the Ethnic Family

A second set of important processes in understanding an ethnic family is understanding the contextual and societal variables that contribute to the ease or difficulty of daily living. This important level of analysis is akin to what Snyder, Cozzi, and Mangrum (chapter 4, this volume) have called assessment of the interface between family and community, cultural, and societal levels. A critical factor at this level of analysis is how the particular ethnic group is perceived or judged by the host culture. Those who are looked down on because of race, class, or because they are perceived to be abusing welfare or taking jobs they do not deserve will have a much harder time in their everyday interactions with the dominant culture because of discrimination. For those whose skin color and linguistic characteristics make their group membership immediately evident, prejudice may be most acute. Among people who have been the targets of discrimination, such as people of color and those who do not speak English well, the experience of being people who are discriminated against may result in beliefs, values, and behaviors of distrust (Gamble, 1993). Distrust that is a response to prejudice in America should not be mistaken for characteristics of the original culture; these are instead natural reactions to overt or covert historical and current acts of prejudice. For example, family research that targets African American families and their relationships to extrafamilial systems such as schools or the courts must take into account cultural distrust resulting from their history of discrimination and neglect by many institutions. Historical precedents demonstrating the exploitation of African American research participants —as exemplified by the Tuskegee experiments, which ran from 1932 to 1972 (Gamble, 1993)—and of the misuse of findings as exemplified by the publication of the book *The Bell Curve* (Herrnstein & Murray, 1994) are still fresh in the minds of the African American community and fuel the distrust.

Another societal circumstance that impinges in a powerful way on family dynamics relates to the type of job opportunities available for males and females. It is well-established that job opportunities help to define the roles of male and female heads of households. The person in the family who gets the first or best job is more likely to have an enhanced position of power in the household (Foner, 1987). When women are more likely to get jobs, this may unbalance the power structure and cause strain in families whose culture has socialized them to expect male-dominated families. With immigrant families, when jobs mean increased contact with the host culture, it may mean that immigrant women may acculturate faster than their husbands, sometimes resulting in intrafamilial acculturation stress. As noted earlier, the natural tendency for the breadwinner to take more of a decision-making role in the family may also be thought of as a reconfiguration of the egalitarian versus complementary relations dimension toward more egalitarianism, with many of the same implications presented earlier. The research reported by Levant and Philpot (chapter 15, this volume) on male and female perceptions of gender roles and gender role strain can be greatly influenced by these types of relationship-defining processes. According to these authors, men and women making the transition from traditional to the newer gender ideology may find it difficult to reconcile contradictory ideas (e.g., cooperative versus competitive, other-centered versus self-centered, independent versus supportive). The inability to live up to the new "ideal" image can create gender role strain. The gender role strains and the unbalancing of power structures have a direct impact on weakening the parental subsystem and processes that are central to family theory.

Conclusion

In this chapter we have argued that the time has come for a more precise articulation of how ethnicity-related dimensions can be linked to family processes of interest to family intervention scientists. Throughout this chapter we have attempted to present dimensions on which people of different ethnic groups might differ and how the assessment of these dimensions can help the family intervention scientist to better understand ethnic family processes and differential efficacy resulting from commonly used family interventions. We have attempted to link specific values, beliefs, and world views to specific constructs that are at the core of family therapy and research. Clearly it is impossible and even undesirable for any one study to attempt to focus on all of these ethnicity-related dimensions. What is more reasonable to expect is that family intervention scientists working with ethnically diverse groups would consider in their research those values and beliefs that can be predicted to directly influence the study's target family interactions or constructs. This field of inquiry would appear to fall within the domain of ATI research (Shoham & Rohrbaugh, 1995), which suggests that treatment outcome depends on the match (or mismatch) between specific characteristics of clients and the treatment they receive. Only by reaching this level of specificity and match can clinical efficacy be improved for ethnically diverse patients who hold beliefs and values not represented by traditional models of intervention. The ultimate goal of this work is that we as family intervention scientists achieve a clearer understanding of specific interventions that may be more effective not with a person classified as belonging to this or that ethnic minority group but with a person who holds a specific set of measurable values and assumptions related to ethnicity.

References

Alexander, J. F., Holtzworth-Munroe, A., & Jameson, P. B. (1994). Research on the process and outcome of marriage and family therapy. In A. E. Bergin & S. L. Garfield (Eds.), *Handbook of psychotherapy and behavior change* (4th ed., pp. 595–630). New York: Wiley.

Bemak, F., & Greenberg, B. (1994). Southeast Asian refugee adolescents: Implications for counseling. *Journal of Multicultural Counseling and Development, 22*(2), 115–124.

Berry, J. W. (1980). Acculturation as varieties of adaptation. In A. Padilla (Ed.), *Acculturation: Theory, models and findings* (pp. 9–25). Boulder, CO: Westview.

Betancourt, H., & Lopez, S. R. (1993). The study of culture, ethnicity and race in American psychology. *American Psychologist, 48,* 629–637.

Boyd-Franklin, N. (1989). *Black families in therapy.* New York: Guilford Press.

Carter, R. (1995). *The influence of race and racial identity in psychotherapy.* New York: Wiley.

Cherry, V., Belgrave, F., Jones, W., Kofi Kennon, D., & Phillips, F. (1998). NTU: An Afrocentric approach to substance abuse prevention among African American youth. *Journal of Primary Prevention, 18,* 319–339.

Christensen, A., Jacobson, N. S. & Babcock, J. C. (1995). Integrative behavioral couple therapy. In N. S. Jacobson & A. S. Gurman (Eds.), *Clinical Handbook of Couples Therapy* (pp. 31–62). New York: Guilford Press.

Foner, N. (1987). *New immigrants in New York.* New York: Columbia University Press.

Gamble, V. (1993). A legacy of distrust: African Americans and medical research. *American Journal of Preventive Medicine, 9,* 35–38.

Goldman, A., & Greenberg, L. (1992). Comparison of integrated systemic and emotionally focused approaches to couple therapy. *Journal of Consulting and Clinical Psychology, 60,* 962–969.

Gopaul-McNicol, S. (1994). *Working with West Indian families.* New York: Guilford Press.

Guarnaccia, P. J., Canino, G., Rubio-Stipec, M., & Bravo, M. (1993). The prevalence of ataques de nervios in the Puerto Rico Disaster study: The role of culture in psychiatric epidemiology. *Journal of Nervous and Mental Disease, 181*(3), 157–165.

Gustafson, M. B. (1989). Western voodoo: Providing mental health care to Haitian refugees. *Journal of Psychosocial Nursing, 27,* 22–25.

Herrnstein, R., & Murray, C. (1994). *The bell curve.* New York: Simon & Schuster.

Hofstede, G. (1980). *Cultures consequences: International differences in work related values.* Beverly Hills, CA: Sage.

Jacobson, N. S., Follette, W. C., & Pagel, M. (1986). Predicting who will benefit from behavioral marital therapy. *Journal of Consulting and Clinical Psychology, 54,* 518–522.

Kluckhohn, F. R., & Strodtbeck, F. L. (1961). *Variations in value orientations.* Evanston, IL: Row, Peterson.

LaFromboise, T., Trimble, J., & Mohatt, G. (1990). Counseling intervention and American Indian tradition: An integrative approach. *Counseling Psychologist, 18*(4), 628–654.

Liddle, H. A. (1995). Conceptual and clinical dimensions of a multidimensional, multisystems engagement strategy in family-based adolescent treatment. *Psychotherapy, 32*(1), 39–57.

Marin, G., & Marin, B. V. (1991). *Research with Hispanic populations.* Newbury Park, CA: Sage.

Marin, G., & Triandis, H. C. (1985). Allocentrism as an important characteristic of the behavior of Latin American and Hispanics. In R. Diaz-Guerrero (Ed.), *Cross-cultural and national studies in social psychology* (pp. 85–104). Amsterdam: Elsevier.

Mason, C. A., Walker-Barnes, C., Blaustein, M., & Martinez-Arrue, R. (1998,). *Ethnic–cultural differences in the affective meaning of parenting behavior*. Poster presented at the meeting of the Society for Research on Adolescence, San Diego, CA.

McAdoo, H. P. (1993). Ethnic families: Strengths that are found in diversity. In H. P. McAdoo (Ed.), *Family ethnicity: Strength in diversity*. Newbury Park, CA: Sage.

McGoldrick, M. (1989). Ethnicity and the family life cycle. In B. Carter & M. McGoldrick (Eds.), *The changing family life cycle: A framework for family therapy* (2nd ed., pp. 70–90). Needham Heights, MA: Allyn & Bacon.

McGoldrick, M. (1996). Overview: Ethnicity and family therapy. In M. McGoldrick, J. Giordano, & J. Pearce (Eds.), *Ethnicity and family therapy*. New York: Guilford Press.

Patterson, G. R., Reid, J. B., & Dishion, T. J. (1992). *Antisocial boys*. Eugene, OR: Castalia.

Rivera-Arzola, M., & Ramos-Grenier, J. (1997). Anger, ataques de nervios, and la mujer puertorriquena: Sociocultural considerations and treatment implications. In J. Garcia & M. Zea (Eds.), *Psychological interventions and research with Latino populations*. Needham Heights, MA: Allyn & Bacon.

Rogler, L. H., Malgady, R. G., & Rodriguez, O. (1989). *Hispanics and mental health: A framework for research*. Malabar, FL: Krieger.

Santisteban, D. A., Coatsworth, J. D., Briones, E., & Szapocznik, J. (2001). *Investigating the role of acculturation, familialism and parenting practices in Hispanic youth behavior problems*. Manuscript in preparation.

Santisteban, D. A., & Szapocznik, J. (1994). Bridging theory research and practice to more successfully engage substance abusing youth and their families into therapy. *Journal of Child and Adolescent Substance Abuse, 32*(2), 9–24.

Schmidt, S. E., Liddle, H. A., & Dakof, G. A. (1996). Changes in parenting practices and adolescent drug abuse during multidimensional family therapy. *Journal of Family Psychology, 10*(1), 12–27.

Scopetta, M. A. (1972). A comparison of modeling approaches to the rehabilitation of institutionalized male adolescent offenders implemented by paraprofessionals. *Dissertation Abstracts International, 33*(6-B), 2822.

Segall, M. H., Lonner, W. J., & Berry, J. W. (1998). Cross-cultural psychology as a scholarly discipline: On the flowering of culture in behavioral research. *American Psychologist, 53*(10), 1101–1110.

Shoham, V., & Rohrbaugh, M. (1995). Aptitude x treatment interaction (ATI) research: Sharpening the focus, widening the lens. In M. Aveline & D. A. Shapiro (Eds.), *Research foundations for psychotherapy practice* (pp. 73–95). New York: Wiley.

Shon, S. P., & Davis, Y. J. (1982). Asian families. In M. McGoldrick, J. Giordano, & J. Pearce (Eds.), *Ethnicity and family therapy*. New York: Guilford Press.

Silove, D., Sinnerbrink, I., Field, A., & Manicavasagar, V. (1997). Anxiety, depression and PTSD in asylum-seekers: Associations with pre-migration trauma and post-migration stressors. *British Journal of Psychiatry, 170*(4), 351–357.

Sue, S. (1991). Ethnicity and culture in psychological research and practice. In J. Good-childs (Ed.), *Psychological perspectives on human diversity in America.* Washington DC: American Psychological Association.

Sue, S., & Zane, N. (1987). The role of culture and cultural techniques in psychotherapy: A critique and reformulation. *American Psychologist, 42,* 37–45.

Szapocznik, J., & Kurtines, W. (1979). Acculturation, biculturalism and adjustment among Cuban Americans, In A. Padilla (Ed.), *Psychological dimensions on the acculturation process: Theory, models, and some new findings.* Boulder, CO: Westview Press.

Szapocznik, J., & Kurtines, W. (1989). *Breakthroughs in family therapy with drug abusing problem youth.* New York: Springer.

Szapocznik, J., & Kurtines, W. M. (1993). Family psychology and cultural diversity: Opportunities for theory, research and application. *American Psychologist, 48*(4), 400–407.

Szapocznik, J., Kurtines, W. M., & Fernandez, T. (1980). Bicultural involvement and adjustment in Hispanic American youths. *International Journal of Intercultural Relations, 4,* 353–366.

Szapocznik, J., Perez-Vidal, A., Brickman, A., Foote, F. H., Santisteban, D. A., Hervis, O., & Kurtines, W. M. (1988). Engaging adolescent drug abusers and their families into treatment: A strategic structural systems approach. *Journal of Consulting and Clinical Psychology, 56*(4), 552–557.

Szapocznik, J., Rio, A. T., Hervis, O. E., Mitrani, V. B., Kurtines, W. M., & Faraci, A. M. (1991). Assessing change in family functioning as a result of treatment: The Structural Family Systems Rating Scale (SFSR). *Journal of Marital and Family Therapy, 17*(3), 295–310.

Szapocznik, J., Santisteban, D., Rio, A., Perez-Vidal, A., Kurtines, W. M., & Hervis, O. E. (1986). Bicultural effectiveness training (BET): An intervention modality for families experiencing intergenerational/intercultural conflict. *Hispanic Journal of Behavioral Sciences, 6*(4), 303–330.

Szapocznik, J., Santisteban, D., Rio, A., Perez-Vidal, A., Santisteban, D., & Kurtines, W. M. (1989). Family effectiveness training: An intervention to prevent drug abuse and problem behavior in Hispanic adolescents. *Hispanic Journal of Behavioral Sciences, 11*(1), 3–27.

Szapocznik, J., Scopetta, M. A., Aranalde, M. A., & Kurtines, W. M. (1978). Cuban value structure: Clinical implications. *Journal of Consulting and Clinical Psychology, 46*(5), 961–970.

Szapocznik, J., Scopetta, M. A., & King, O. E. (1978). Theory and practice in matching treatment to the special characteristics and problems of Cuban immigrants. *Journal of Community Psychology, 6,* 112–122.

U.S. Census Department. (1997). Populations projections of the United States by age, sex, race and Hispanic origin, 1995–2050. *Hispanic Yearbook.* Washington, DC: U.S. Bureau of the Census.

Zayas, L. H. (1992). Childbearing, social stress, and child abuse: Clinical considerations with Hispanic families. *Journal of Social Distress and the Homeless, 1*(3–4), 291–309.

Zuckerman, M. (1990). Some dubious premises in research and theory on racial differences: Scientific, social and ethical issues. *American Psychologist, 45*(12), 1297–1303.

Author Index

Numbers in italics refer to listings in reference sections.

Abbey, A., 315, 322
Abrams, D. B., 235
Acermean, T. A., 93, *101*
Adams, G., 96, *98*
Addis, M. E., 7, *14*, 76, *86*, 90, 95, *100*, 108, 116, *120*, *122*, 148, 151, 163, *172*, 230, *234*
Afifi, A. A., 198, *210*
Aiken, L. S., 204, *213*, 303
Aiken, P. A., 81, *84*, 110, *118*, 302, *322*
Ainsworth, M. D. S., 50, 56, *59*
Alexander, J. F., 3, 5, 8, *11*, 20, 23, 24, 25, 26, 29, 30, 31, *34*, *35*, 37, *38*, *39*, *40*, 51, 53, *63*, *64*, 180, 181, *192*, 263, 277, 302, 322, 322, 331, *347*
Allen, H., 289, *295*
Allen, J. P., 50, 58, *59*
Almquist, E., 314, *324*
Anastasi, A., 303, *322*
Anderson, C. M., 163, *170*, 301, *327*
Anderson, H., 20, *34*, 52, *61*
Anderson, P., 56, *59*
Anderson, S. A., *140*
Andrews, D. W., 241, 246, 248, 249, 250, *253*
Aranalde, M. A., 334, 340, 341, 342, *350*
Arbuthnot, J., 24, *36*
Archer, J., 303, *322*
Arias, I., 292, *295*
Arizmendi, T. G., 42, *59*
Armstrong, D., 82, *85*, 110, *119*
Arond, M., 136, *139*
Asarnow, J. R., *12*, *140*, 192, *210*, *253*
Asher, S., 147, *171*
Atilanao, R. B., 130, *145*
Autry, J. H., 4, *13*
Avery, A. W., 128, 129, 133, *139*, *144*, *145*
Avery-Leaf, S., 289, *294*
Avis, J. M., 302, *322*
Avner, R., 154, *174*, 229
Ayers, W. A., 199, *210*

Azar, B., 260, 277
Azrin, N. H., 152, *170*, 230, 232

Babcock, J. C., 111, *119*, 219, *233*, 336, *348*
Babor, T. F., 230, 232
Backer, T. E., 269, 277
Bader, E., 138, *139*
Baer, P. E., 11, *11*, 94, 96, *98*, 286
Bagarozzi, D. A., 130, 133, *140*, *145*
Bagarozzi, J. A., *140*
Bahr, S. J., 153, *171*
Bain, A. B., 129, *145*
Bakeman, R., 91, 92, *98*
Baker, M., 35
Baldwin, C., 307, 313, *324*
Ball, F. L. J., 159, *170*
Bank, L., 179, *195*, 204, *211*, 240, 245, 247, 250, 252, 256, 257
Bargiel, K., 92, *100*
Barker, R. G., 240, 252
Barling, J., 292, *295*
Barlow, D. H., 220, 232
Barnes, H., 87
Barnett, O., 315, 322
Barnett, R. C., 8, *15*, 96, *101*
Baron, R. M., 49, 59
Barrett, K., 37
Barton, C., 8, *11*, 24, 26, 28, 29, *34*, *35*
Basow, S., 310, 313, 314, *322*
Bass, D., 199, *210*, 259, *280*
Bateson, G., 20
Baucom, D. H., 54, *59*, 73, 75, 80, 81, 82, *84*, *85*, *86*, 87, 107, 108, 109, 110, *118*, *121*, 150, 168, *170*, 179, *192*, 218, 230, 232, 302, 303, *322*
Baumrind, D., 50, 54, *59*
Beach, S. R. H., 5, *15*, 56, *59*, 82, *85*, 105, 110, 112, *118*, 288, 290, 291, *294*, *295*
Beattie, M. C., 217, *234*
Beavers, W. R., 46, *59*, 93, *100*, 110, *120*
Beavin, J., 223, *237*

Becker, A., 127, *143*
Becker, D., 8, *14*
Becker, W. C., 284, *295*
Beckham, E. E., 217, *232*
Beere, C., 306, 307, *322*
Beere, D. B., 306, *322*
Beezley, D., 315, *326*
Begin, A. M., 228, *234*
Behrens, B. C., 82, *85*, 109, 110, *118*, 131, *140*, 248, *253*
Belenky, M., 314, *323*
Belgrave, F., 340, *348*
Bell, R. A., 302, *323*
Bellack, A. S., 219, *232*
Belsky, J., 135, *140*
Bem, S. L., 305, 306, 307, *323*
Bemak, F., 345, *347*
Benjamin, L. S., 58, *61*, 181, *192*
Bennett, L. A., 226, *236*
Bennett Johnson, S., 35
Bennum, I., 80, 82, *85*
Bentler, P. M., 153, *170*
Bepko, C., 117, *119*, 223, *232*
Berenson, D., *236*
Berg, I. K., 231, *232*
Berger, S., 188, *192*
Bernieri, F. J., 221, 225, *232*
Berry, J. W., 333, 341, *347*, *349*
Berscheid, E., 105, *119*
Betancourt, H., 332, 333, *347*
Beutler, L. E., 35, 42, *59*, 217, 220, 229, *232*, *233*
Bickman, L., 260, 261, *278*
Bierman, K. L., 183, *192*
Biglan, A., 246, *252*
Bijou, S. W., 240, *255*, 283, 286, *294*
Birnbauer, J. S., 283, *294*
Black, C., *252*
Blaske, D. M., 24, *35*, 48, *63*, 266, *278*
Blaustein, M., 342, *349*
Bleuer, J. C., 33, *39*
Block, J., 54, *59*, 153, *170*
Bloom, B., 147, *171*
Bloom, C., 306, *323*
Blumberg, S. L., 10, *15*, 125, 126, 130, 131, *143*, *145*
Bograd, M., 302, *323*
Bond, G. R., 265, *281*
Borduin, C. M., 3, *13*, 24, 26, *35*, 36,

37, 48, 50, 55, *62*, *63*, 234, 260, 263, 264, 265, 266, *278*, *279*, *281*
Borkovec, T. D., 8, *11*
Borman-Spurrell, E., 50, 58, *59*
Boscolo, L., 52, *59*
Boszormenyi-Nagy, I., 56, 57, *59*
Bowen, M., 20, *35*, 320
Bowlby, J., 56, *59*
Box, G., 133, *140*
Boyd-Franklin, N., 336, *348*
Bradbury, T. N., 50, 52, 54, *61*, 82, *85*, 105, *119*, 123, 124, 125, 127, *140*, 142, 303, *323*
Bravo, M., 331, *348*
Bray, J. H., 3, 5, 6, 7, 9, 11, *11*, *12*, 78, *85*, 89, 91, 93, 94, 95, 96, 97, 98, *98*, *99*, 109, *119*, 148, *171*, 188, *192*, 275
Breiner, J., 255
Brengelmann, J. C., 80, *85*
Brennan, R. T., 8, *15*, 96, *101*
Brent, D., 260, *280*
Breslow, L., 198, *210*
Brickman, A. L., *15*, *39*, *350*
Briere, J., 313, *323*
Bright, I., *15*, *39*, 41, *65*, *101*, 122, 195, 212
Bright, M. R., 148, *173*
Briones, E., 340, *349*
Brockman, A. L., *281*
Broderick, J. E., 82, *85*, 110, *118*, 287
Brodsky, A., 315, *325*
Brodsky, G., 240, *256*
Brondino, M. J., 265, 268, *279*
Bronfenbrenner, U., *12*, 263, *278*
Brooks, G., 318, 319, 320, *323*, *327*
Brown, B. S., 269, 270, 272, 274, *278*
Brown, C. H., 200, 201, 202, 203, 205, *210*, *212*
Brown, L. S., 117, *119*
Brown, P., 53, *65*
Brown, T., 309, *323*
Brown, V., 313, *323*
Bruce, M. L., 290, *297*
Brunk, M., 266, *278*
Brush, L. R., 312, *325*
Bryan, M., 130, *146*
Bryant, K. J., 4, *12*
Bryk, A. S., 8, *12*, 95, 96, 97, *99*
Buchanan, R. M., *62*
Buehlman, K., 154, 156, *171*

Bugental, D. B., 54, *59*
Bumpass, L. L., 126, *143*
Buring, J. E., 183, 185, *194*
Burke, L. E., *62*
Burland, A., 56, *63*
Burman, B., 106, *119*, 147, *171*
Burnett, C. K., 303, *322*
Burns, B. J., 262, *278*
Busby, D. M., *143*
Buston, B. G., 126, *146*
Byng-Hall, J., 57, *60*

Caldwell, C., 315, *327*
Calvo, G., *134*
Campbell, D. T., 94, *99*
Campbell, S. M., 303, *323*
Campbell, T. L., 207, *210*
Canino, G., 331, *348*
Cano, A., 290, *294*
Cantos, A. L., 292, *294*
Capaldi, D. M., 241, 243, 245, 252, *253*
Caplan, G., 198, 199, 201, *210*
Caralis, P. V., 315, *323*
Cargo, M., 42, *59*
Carlson, C. I., 75, *85*, 91, 93, *99*
Carlson, J. E., 93, *101*, 219, 229, *233*
Carnine, D., *252*
Carrere, S., 5, 154, *172*, 188
Carroll, K. M., 4, *12*
Carstensen, L. L., 161, *171*, *173*
Carter, B., 301, *328*
Carter, D. B., 306, *326*
Carter, R., 332, *348*
Cascardi, M., 292, *294*
Casey, R. L., 91, 92, *98*
Cash, T., 309, *323*
Catherall, D. R., 50, *64*
Cavell, T. A., 70, 71, *87*
Cecchin, G., 52, *59*
Cerreto, M., 152, *173*
Chafetz, J., 314, *323*
Chamberlain, P., 41, 49, 55, *64*, 179,
    180, *192*, *194*, 207, *210*, 243, 244,
    246, 248, 250, 251, 252, *256*, 275,
    281
Chambless, D. L., 4, *12*, 21, *35*
Chao, C. M., 117, *122*
Chase-Lansdale, P., 247, *253*
Chatters, L. M., 137, *146*
Chee, M., 105, *122*

Cherlin, A., 162, *171*, 247, *253*
Chernin, K., 309, *323*
Cherry, V., 340, *348*
Chodorow, N., 306, *323*
Choquette, K. A., 105, *122*, 220, *235*
Christensen, A., 74, *86*, 107, 111, *119*,
    120, 159, *171*, 219, 220, 223, 224,
    228, *233*, *234*, 302, *323*, *324*, 336,
    343, *348*
Christian-Herman, J., 289, *294*
Chung, S., 204, *212*
Clarke, G. N., 8, *12*, 117, *119*
Clarke, L. A., 288, *297*
Clements, M., 124, 125, 130, *140*, *143*,
    183, *194*
Clinchy, B., 314, *323*
Clingempeel, G., 247, *255*
Coan, J., 154, *172*
Coatsworth, J. D., 38, 340, *349*
Cohen, R. S., 159, *171*
Coie, J. D., 4, 10, *12*, 123, 124, 126,
    140, 184, 185, *192*, 198, 201, 203,
    205, 208, *210*, 246, *253*
Coiro, M. J., 247, *257*
Colarelli, S. M., 32, *35*
Cole, D. A., 7, *12*, 91, *99*
Colondier, G., 79, *86*
Combrinck-Graham, L., 206, 208, *210*
Compas, B., 50, *60*
Cone, L., *36*, *234*, 278, *279*
Conger, R. D., 124, *143*, 241, *253*
Conley, J. J., 81, *86*, 153, *173*
Constantine, J. A., 153, *171*
Constantine, L. L., 82, *87*
Conway, B., 138, *139*
Cook, J., 7, *12*, 97, *99*, 163, 164, 166,
    171
Cook, T. D., 94, *99*
Cook, W. L., 91, *99*
Cookerly, J. R., 110, *119*
Cooney, N. L., 217, *234*
Cooper, H. M., 24, *36*
Cordova, J. V., 107, 111, *119*, *120*
Cornelison, A., 20, *37*
Coulehan, R., 43, 53, 54, *60*
Cowan, C. P., 123, 135, *140*, 159, *170*
Cowan, G., 315, *324*
Cowan, P. A., 123, 135, *140*, 159, *170*
Cowen, E. L., 124, *144*, 197, 198, 202,
    208, *210*
Cox, F., 128, *140*

Cox, M., 123, *141*, 244, *255*
Cox, R., 244, *255*
Coyne, J. C., 5, *12*, 218, *233*, 288, *294*
Craighead, L. W., 289, *295*
Craighead, W. E., 289, *295*
Crane, D. R., 82, *85*, 110, *119*
Crawford, M., 307, 309, *328*
Crits-Christoph, P., *35*
Cronbach, L. J., 32, *35*, 215, 216, 229, *233*
Crosby, L., 241, *253*
Crowe, M. J., 110, *119*
Cummings, E. M., 56, *60*
Cunningham, P. B., 3, *13*, 260, *279*
Curran, P., 204, *211*
Cutter, H. S. G., 105, *122*, 218, 220, *235*

Dadds, M. N., 50, *60*
Dadds, M. R., 248, *253*
Daiuto, A., 107, *118*, 179, *192*, 218, 232
Dakof, G. A., 5, 6, *12*, *14*, 25, 37, 47, 51, 54, 55, 57, *60*, *63*, *65*, 206, 207, *210*, 230, *234*, 262, 264, 275, *280*, 331, *349*
Daldrup, R. J., 229, *233*
Daley, J. A., 302, *323*
Dance, K. A., 217, *233*
Darling, N., 50, *65*
David, S. L., 277
Davidson, K. C., 96, *99*
Davies, P. T., 56, *60*
Davis, D. I., *236*
Davis, Y. J., 336, *349*
Day, J., 20, *40*
Deaux, K., 303, *324*
DeBaryshe, B. E., 243, *253*
DeFrain, J., 123, 128, *144*
DeGarmo, D. S., 241, 243, 245, 246, 247, 248, 249, 250, *253*, *254*
DeKlyen, M., 50, *62*, 110, *120*, 151, *172*
Delaney, H. D., 94, *100*
DeLuca, L., 315, *327*
Dent, J., 129, *144*
Denton, W., 126, 133, 134, 137, 139, *140*, *145*
DeRosa, R., 289, *295*
DeRubeis, R. J., 49, *60*
Devine, V. T., 285, *296*

Diamond, G. M., 3, 8, *12*, *14*, 25, 48, 51, 53, 54, 56, *60*, *65*
Diamond, G. S., 5, *13*, 33, *35*, 41, 42, 43, 44, 45, 46, 47, 48, 52, 53, 56, 57, *60*, *63*, *65*
Diamond, L., 56, 57, 58, *61*
Dickey, M., 5, *13*, 41, 47, *60*, 65, 207, *212*
Dickson, F., 130, *146*
DiClemente, C. C., 48, *64*, 228, *235*
Dietzen, L., 265, *281*
Dimidjian, S., 163, *170*
Dishion, T. J., 200, 206, *211*, 241, 243, 246, 247, 248, 249, 250, *253*, *254*, 331, *349*
Doane, J. A., 56, 57, 58, *61*
Dobash, R. E., 315, *324*
Dobash, R. P., 315, *324*
Dobson, K., 5, *14*, 291, *295*
Doherty, W., 126, *140*, 307, 313, *324*
Donenberg, G. R., 259, *282*
Dornbusch, S. M. N., 50, *65*
Dornbush, M. P., 284, *295*
Dotson, D., 50, 51, *64*
Douglas, S., 261, *278*
Dowling, C., 306, 310, 312, 314, *324*
Drabman, R., 285
Drasgow, F., 93, *100*
Drotar, D., 5, *13*
Druckman, J. M., 125, 127, *144*, 183, *194*
Duemmler, S., 56, *63*
Dumas, J. E., 240, *254*
Duncan, S. F., 133, *140*
Duncan, T. E., 179, *195*, 250, *257*
Dunivant, N., 313, *328*
Dunn, N. J., 226, *233*
Dunn, R. L., 90, *99*, 108, 109, *119*
Durlak, J. A., 246, *254*

Eaton, W. E., 198, *211*
Eaves, L. J., 288, *295*
Eckert, V., 131, *141*
Eddy, J. M., 239, 246, *256*, *257*
Edwards, G., 230, *235*
Edwards, J., *279*
Edwards, P., 243, *257*
Efran, J. S., 21, 33, *35*, 36
Eidelson, R. J., 82, *85*, 128, *140*
Eisen, D., 313, *327*

Eldridge, K., 111, *120*
Elkin, I., 4, *13*, 42, 49, *61*
Elliot, R., 42, 43, 53, *61*, *63*
Elliot, R. K., 215, *236*
Elliott, D., 25, *35*, 205, *210*
Elliott, R., 22, *35*
Eltz, M. J., 50, *61*
Embretson, S. E., 93, *99*
Emery, R. E., 287, *295*, *296*
Endler, N. S., 287, *295*
Engl, J., 131, *141*, *146*
Engle, D., 229, *233*
Epstein, D., 52, *66*
Epstein, E. E., 218, 220, 223, *233*, *234*
Epstein, N., 73, 82, *84*, *85*, 107, *118*, 128, *140*, 181, *195*
Epston, D., 21, *40*
Erkut, S., 312, *324*
Erley, A. M., 5, 188
Estrada, A., 179, *193*
Estroff, S. E., 181, *192*
Esveldt-Dawson, K., 240, *255*
Evans, M. D., *60*
Eysenck, H. J., 21, *35*

Fairley, M., 56, *64*
Falicov, C. J., 73, *85*, 117, *119*
Faludi, S., 310, *324*
Farrington, D. P., 263, *281*
Fauber, R. L., 33, *35*
Fernandez, T., 341, *350*
Fernandez, V., 302, *327*
Ferraro, G. A., 312, *324*
Ferree, J., 301, *324*
Fetrow, R. A., 245, 246, 252, *257*
Field, A., *349*
Fincham, F. D., 50, 52, 54, *61*, 82, *85*, 112, 123, 125, *140*, *141*, 287, 290, *295*, 303, *323*
Finney, J. W., 217, *235*
Firth, J. M., 261, *278*
Fisch, R., 223, 231, *233*, *237*
Fisher, L., 17, *35*, 91, *99*, *100*
Fisk, W., 313, *324*
Fitzpatrick, M. A., 125, *141*, *144*
Fleck, S., 20, *37*
Fletcher, J. M., 96, *99*
Fletcher, R. H., 183, 184, 185, 186, *193*
Fletcher, S. W., 183, *193*
Florsheim, P., 58, *61*

Flowers, B., 183, *193*
Floyd, F. J., 123, 125, 130, *143*, 183, *194*, 218, *235*
Foerster, F. S., 43, *62*
Fogel, A., 31, *35*
Follette, V. M., *120*, *121*
Follette, W. C., 81, *86*, 94, *100*, 109, 110, 113, 114, *120*, *121*, 125, *142*, 148, *172*, 216, *234*, 302, *326*, 336, *348*
Foner, N., 345, 346, *348*
Foote, F. H., *15*, 39, *281*, *350*
Forehand, R., *255*
Forgatch, M. S., 3, *13*, 55, *64*, 179, *192*, 241, 243, 244, 245, 246, 247, 248, 249, 250, 251, *252*, *253*, *254*, *255*, *256*
Forthofer, M. S., 123, *141*
Fortune, A. E., 91, *100*
Foster, E. M., 261, *278*
Foster, S. W., 181, *192*
Foucault, M., 20, *36*
Fournier, D. G., 125, 127, 133, 136, *141*, *144*, 183, *194*
Fowers, B. J., 127, *141*, 153, *171*
Francis, D. J., 96, 97, *99*
Fraser, M. W., 265, *278*
Fredman, N., 91, *99*
Freedman, R., 309, *324*
French, M., 306, 307, *324*
French, N. H., 240, *255*
Freudiger, P., 314, *324*
Friedan, B., 313, *324*
Friedlander, M. L., 7, 10, *13*, 33, *36*, 41, 43, 47, 51, 53, 57, *60*, *61*, *62*, 179, 182, *193*
Friedman, L. C., 156, *174*
Friedman, P., 313, *328*
Friedman, R. M., 261, 276, *281*
Frieze, J. H., 306, *324*
Fruzzetti, A., 5, *14*, 291, *295*
Fucci, B. R., *36*, 234, *278*, *279*
Furey, W., *255*
Furstenberg, F. F., Jr., 244, *255*

Gamble, V., 346, *348*
Garcia, R., *37*
Garfield, S. L., 42, *61*, 217, *233*
Garvey, M. J., *60*
Ge, X., 241, *253*

Geis, F. L., 313, *323*
Geiss, S. K., 76, *85*
Gelles, R. J., 315, 316, *324*
Gergen, K., 21, 33, *36*
Gerrard, M., 93, *101*
Getter, H., 217, *234*
Getz, J. G., 94, 96, *98*
Giblin, P., 129, 132, *141*
Gilligan, C., 306, 314, *324*
Gilmore, D., 304, *324*
Gitelson, I., 312, 313, *325*
Glaser, R., 179, *195*
Glaser-Renita, R., 149, *173*
Glass, G. V., 21, *39*
Glenn, N. D., *141*
Glieck, E., 139, *141*
Glisson, C., 269, 273, *278*
Glitter, A., 306, *323*
Godley, M., 230, *232*
Gold, A. R., 312, *325*
Goldberger, N., 314, *323*
Goldklang, D. S., 246, *255*
Goldman, A., 107, *119*, 219, 224, *233*,
  336, *348*
Goldner, V., 301, *325*
Goldstein, M. J., 52, *61*, 74, *86*, 91, *99*,
  187, *193*, 207, *210*, 230, *233*
Goldstein, S., 284, *295*
Gollan, J. K., 107, *120*, 336
Gonso, J., 5, *13*
Gonzalez, M. C., 302, *323*
Goolishian, H. A., 20, *34*, 52, *61*
Gopaul-McNicol, S., 338, *348*
Gordis, L., 183, 185, *193*
Gordon, D. A., 24, 25, 26, 28, *36*
Gordon, D. E., 33, *36*
Gordon, K. C., 75, *85*
Gordon, R., 198, 199, 201, *210*
Gorman-Smith, D., 183, 188, *193*, 200,
  204, 205, 206, *212*
Gortner, E., 107, *120*
Gottman, J. M., 3, 5, 7, *12*, *13*, 49, *61*,
  82, *85*, 90, 92, 95, 97, *99*, 105,
  107, *120*, 124, 125, 131, *141*, 152,
  153, 154, 155, 159, 160, 161, 162,
  163, 164, 165, 167, *171*, *173*, 187,
  188, *193*, 220, 224, *233*, 302, *325*
Grady, F. A., 150, *173*
Grady-Fletcher, A., 107, *122*
Grant, M., 230, *232*
Gravatt, A. E., 128, *144*

Graves, K., 24, *36*
Gray, J., 134, *141*
Green, B. J., 8, *13*
Green, R. G., 91, *100*
Greenberg, B., 345, *347*
Greenberg, L. S., 4, *13*, 41, 42, 43, 48,
  57, *61*, 62, *64*, 107, 108, 109, *119*,
  120, *121*, 149, 172, 179, 182, 191,
  193, 195, 219, 224, 229, 233, 336,
  348
Greenwood, J., 56, *64*
Griest, D. L., 248, *255*
Griffin, B. L., 33, *39*
Grotevant, H. D., 75, *85*, 91, 93, *99*
Grove, W. M., *60*
Grych, J. H., 123, *141*, 287, *295*
Guarnaccia, P. J., 331, *348*
Guerney, B. G., Jr., 124, 125, 126, 129,
  132, 133, 138, *141*, *144*, 183, *193*
Guerra, N. G., 3, *15*, 205, 207, 208,
  212, 246, *257*
Gurman, A. S., 23, *36*, 105, 108, *122*,
  178, 180, *193*, *194*
Gustafson, K. E., *36*
Gustafson, M. B., 338, *348*
Guthrie, P. R., 261, *280*
Guttman, H., 181, *195*
Gutwill, S., 306, 311, *323*, *325*

Haas, S. D., 153, *173*
Hadley, W. W., 4, *13*
Haefner, P., 303, *322*
Haggerty, R. J., 199, *211*, 240, 246, *255*
Hahlweg, K., 5, 10, *14*, 49, *62*, 80, 82,
  85, 94, 95, *99*, 113, *120*, *121*, 124,
  125, 131, 132, 133, 138, *141*, *146*,
  148, 150, *172*, 181, *194*, 243, *255*
Halas, C., 311, *325*
Haley, J., 20, *35*, 263, *278*
Halford, K., 109, *118*, 131, *140*
Halford, W. K., 82, *85*, 105, *120*
Hall, J. A., *36*, *234*, *279*
Halliday-Boykins, C. A., 263, *278*
Halverson, C. F., 92, *101*
Hambright, A., 178, *195*, 247
Hammonds, T. M., 126, *146*
Hampson, R. B., 46, *59*, 93, *100*, 110,
  120
Han, S. S., 259, *282*
Hand, L. D., *279*

Hanish, L., 47, *65*, 199, 207, *210, 212*
Hanley, J., *37*, 265, 266, 268, *279*
Hannah, M. T., 154, *174*, 217, 229, *236*
Hanson, C. L., *37*, 266, *279*
Hansson, K., 24, 26, *36*
Hare-Mustin, R., 301, 306, 311, *325*
Hargrave, T. D., 75, *85*
Harmer, S. L., 127, *142*
Harold, G. T., 290, *295*
Harrell, J. E., 128, 129, 133, *144*
Harrison, R., 23, *39*
Harter, S., 50, *62*
Hauser, S. T., 50, 58, *59*
Haviland, J. M., *328*
Hawkins, D., *192*
Hawkins, J. D., *12, 140, 210, 253*
Hawkins, M. W., 158, *172*
Hawkins, R. P., 240, *255*
Hay, W. M., *235*
Hayes, R. L., 21, *36*
Hayman, R. E., 54, *65*
Haynes, S., *13*
Haynes-Clements, L. A., 128, 133, *144*
Hazan, C., 56, *62*
Hazelrigg, M. D., 24, *36*
Heath, A. C., 288, *295*
Heatherington, L., *36*, 41, 43, 47, 51,
    53, 57, *60, 61, 62*, 179, 182, 188,
    193
Heatherington, M., *194*
Heavey, C. L., 136, *142*, 159, *171*, 220,
    223, 224, *233, 234*, 302, *323*
Heffer, R. W., 70, 71, *87*
Heitland, W., 129, *142*
Helmreich, R. L., 305, 306, 307, *328*
Hemmelgarn, A., 269, 273, *278*
Henderson, J., *252*
Henggeler, S. W., 3, 6, 8, *13*, 24, 25, 26,
    27, 31, 33, *35, 36, 37*, 48, 50, 55,
    62, 63, 230, *234*, 260, 262, 263,
    264, 265, 266, 268, 269, 274, 275,
    278, 279, 280
Hennekens, C. H., 183, 185, *194*
Henry, D., 200, 204, *212*
Henry, W. P., 22, 29, *37*, 50, 58, *61, 62*
Herrnstein, R., 346, *348*
Hervis, O., *15, 39, 281, 350*
Hetherington, E. M., 5, 7, 9, *12, 13*, 33,
    98, *99*, 244, 247, *255*, 314
Hetherington, M., *325*

Heyman, R. E., 76, 77, 82, *86, 142*, 292,
    296
Hibbs, E., 260, *280*
Hiebert, W. J., 124, 126, 128, 133, 138,
    139, *145*
Hirsch, S. I., 20, *40*
Hoagwood, K., 260, 261, 262, 263, *278,
    280*
Hochschild, A., 306, 307, 310, 312, 313,
    325
Hof, L., 134, *142*
Hoffman, J. A., 168, *170*
Hoffman, L., 17, *37*, 52, *59*
Hofstede, G., 336, 337, *348*
Hogue, A., 8, 9, *12, 13, 14*, 48, 51, *60,
    62*
Hohman, A. A., 260, *280*
Hollingshead, A. B., 267, *280*
Hollinsworth, T., 207, *212*
Hollon, S. D., *60*
Holman, T. B., 124, 127, 133, *142*
Holmes, T. H., 147, *172*
Holroyd, J., 315, *325*
Holton, A., 243, *257*
Holtzworth-Munroe, A., 3, *11*, 50, *62*,
    82, *86*, 108, 109, 110, *120*, 125,
    131, *142*, 149, 151, *172*, 263, 277,
    302, 322, 331, *347*
Hooley, J. M., 187, *194*, 219, 234, 243,
    255
Horner, M., 307, 313, *325*
Horney, K., 306, *325*
Horowitz, H. A., 56, *65*
Horowitz, M. J., 42, *62*
Horvath, A. O., 50, *62*
Hoshmand, L. T., 21, *37*
Hosman, C., 131, *146*
Howard, D., 315, *327*
Howard, G. S., 21, *37*
Howard, K. I., 42, *64*
Howell, N., 315, *328*
Huesmann, L. R., 183, 188, *193*, 205,
    206, *212*
Hulbert, D., *142*
Hulgus, Y. F., 46, *59*, 93, *100*
Hulin, C. L., 93, *100*
Hummon, N., 226, *233*
Humphrey, D., *252*
Hunsley, J., 107, *121*
Hunt, M., 204, *212*
Huston, T. L., 79, *86*

Hyde, H., 313, *325*

Iverson, A., 82, *86*

Jackson, D., 20, *35*
Jackson, D. D., 152, *173*, 223, 237
Jackson, L. A., 309, *325*
Jacob, T., 5, *14*, 92, *100*, 218, 220, 221, 223, 226, *232*, *233*, *234*, *236*
Jacobson, N. S., 5, 7, *14*, 50, 62, 74, 76, 81, 82, *86*, 90, 94, 95, *100*, 105, 107, 108, 109, 110, 111, 113, 114, 115, 116, 117, *119*, *120*, *121*, 122, 125, *142*, 148, 149, 150, 163, *172*, 216, 219, 230, *233*, *234*, 291, 295, 302, 303, 315, *325*, *326*, 329, 336, 343, *348*
James, J. E., 248, *253*
James, L., *252*
Jameson, P. B., 3, *11*, 20, *37*, 263, 277, 302, 322, 331, *347*
Jensen, P. S., 260, 262, *280*
Jerremalm, A., 229, *235*
Johansson, J., 229, *235*
Johnson, B., *35*, 61, *62*
Johnson, P. B., 306, *324*
Johnson, S. M., 56, 57, *62*, 105, 107, 108, 109, 112, *120*, 149, *172*
Johnson, T., 117, *119*
Johnston, C., 54, *59*
Jones, A. C., 117, *122*
Jones, E. F., 139, *142*
Jones, R., 152, *170*
Jones, W., 340, *348*
Jordan, K., 50, 51, *64*
Jordan, P. L., 135, 136, *142*
Jorgensen, S. R., 129, 132, 137, 138, *145*
Jouriles, E., 9, *12*, 90, 95, *99*, 109, *119*, 148, *171*, 288, *294*
Joyce, A. S., 48, *62*
Jurd, A., 56, *64*
Jurich, A. P., 136, *145*
Jurwitz, S., *37*

Kadden, R. M., 217, *234*
Karney, B. R., 123, 124, 125, *142*

Kaschak, E., 311, *326*
Kashy, D. A., 70, 74, 77, *86*
Kaslow, N. J., 56, *59*
Kass, R., 285
Katt, J. L., *120*, *121*
Katz, L., 154, 156, *171*
Katz, P., 314, *326*
Kaufman, G., 302, *326*
Kaufman, K., 285
Kauneckis, D., 260, *282*
Kavanagh, K., 179, *192*, 247, 248, *254*
Kazak, A., 5, *14*
Kazdin, A. E., 5, 8, 10, *13*, *14*, 199, *210*, 240, 246, 248, 255, 259, 260, *280*
Keita, G., 307, *327*
Kellam, S. G., 151, *172*, 201, 203, 204, *210*
Kelly, E. L., 81, *86*, 153, *173*
Kelly, J., 317, *326*
Kendall, P. C., 3, *15*, 117, *122*, 203, 205, *211*, *212*
Kendler, K. S., 288, *295*
Kenny, D. A., 49, *59*, 91, *100*
Kent, R. N., 285, 287, *295*
Kessler, R. C., 123, *141*
Keyes, S., 54, *59*
Keyson, M., 315, *322*
Kidder, J. D., 283, *294*
Kiecolt-Glaser, J., 105, *122*
Kiernan, K. E., 247, *253*
Kiesler, D. J., 42, *63*
Kiesner, J., 247, *254*
Kilgore, K., 243, *257*
King, D. W., 306, *322*, *326*
King, L. A., 306, *322*, *326*
King, O. E., 331, 334, 342, *350*
Kitson, G. C., 123, *142*
Klein, D. M., *143*
Klein, N. C., 25, 27, *37*
Kliewer, W., 207, 208, *211*
Klinetob, N. A., 223, *234*
Kluckhohn, F. R., 334, 337, 338, 339, *348*
Kniskern, D. P., 23, *36*
Knudson-Martin, C., 319, *326*
Kobak, R., 50, 56, 58, *63*
Koerner, K., 116, *122*
Kofi Kennon, D., 340, *348*
Kogel, L., 306, *323*
Kohn, A., 315, *326*
Kokes, R. F., 91, *99*, *100*

Kolbenschlag, M., 306, 310, *326*
Kolevzon, M. S., 91, *100*
Kolpacoff, M., 207, *212*
Komarovsky, M., 307, *326*
Kopecky, G., 306, 317, *326*
Koss, M., 315, *326*
Kraft, S. A., 318, *327*
Krasner, B. R., 56, 57, *59*
Krasner, L., 283, 286, *297*
Krestan, J., 223, *232*
Krokoff, L. J., 131, *141*, 153, 163, *173*
Kumpfer, K. L., 206, *211*
Kurdek, L. A., 81, 82, *86*, 124, 125, 126, *142*
Kurtines, W. M., 8, *15*, 24, 25, *38*, *39*, *281*, 334, 338, 340, 341, 342, *350*
Kushner, H., 311, *326*

L'Abate, L., 79, *86*, 124, 126, *142*
LaFromboise, T., 341, *348*
Lambert, E. W., 261, *280*
Lamborn, S. D., 50, *65*
Laner, M. R., 128, *143*
Langhinrichsen, J., 292, *294*
Lanktree, C., 313, *323*
Lantz, J., 124, *142*
Lapann, K., *14*
LaPerriere, A., 8, *15*, *38*, *281*
Larson, A. S., 87, 127, *143*
Larson, B., 224, *233*
Larson, D., 123, *143*
Larson, J. H., 124, 127, 133, *142*, *143*
Larson, S. S., 123, *143*
Larus, J. M., 81, *87*
Larzelere, R. E., 245, *255*
Lashley, B. R., 91, *100*
Last, C. G., *232*
Lauer, M., 309, *328*
Layne, C., 223, *234*
Leber, D., 126, *142*, *146*, 159, *173*
Lebow, J., 20, *37*, 105, 107, 108, *121*, *122*, 178, *194*
Lederer, W. J., 152, *173*
Lee, C., 315, *324*
Leigh, G., 126, *140*
Lenauer, M., 313, *328*
Leonard, K., 218, 223, 226, *234*, 315, *326*
Leslie, L. A., 128, 129, *139*, *144*
Lester, G. W., 54, *59*, 109, *118*, 150, *170*

Lester, M. E., 126, *140*
Levant, R. F., 304, 306, 317, 318, 320, 321, *326*, *327*, *328*, 346
Levenson, R. W., 152, 153, 161, 162, 164, *171*, *172*, *173*, 187, *193*
Levinson, D. J., 77, *86*
Levy, D., 315, *324*
Lewis, E., 137, *146*
Lewis, H., 123, 207, *211*
Lewis, J. A., 219, *233*
Liddle, H. A., 3, 6, 8, 9, *12*, *13*, *14*, *15*, 24, 25, 27, 33, *35*, *37*, 41, 43, 44, 45, 46, 47, 48, 50, 51, 52, 54, 55, 56, 57, *60*, 62, *63*, *65*, 206, 207, *211*, 218, 230, *233*, *234*, 260, 262, 264, 275, 276, *280*, 331, *348*, *349*
Liddle, H. L., *63*
Lidz, T., 20, *37*
Liepman, M. R., 228, *234*
Linton, M., 315, *327*
Lipman, A. J., 117, *122*
Lipsey, M. W., 240, *255*, 263, 265, *280*
Litt, M. D., 217, *234*
Lobitz, W. C., 130, *146*
Loeber, R., 54, *63*, 200, *211*, 263, *281*
Long, B., *12*, *140*, 192, 210, 253
Longabaugh, R., 217, 219, *234*
Lonner, W. J., 333, *349*
Lopez, S. R., 332, 333, *347*
Lorber, M., 158, *173*
Lord, F. M., 93, 94, *100*
Lorion, R. P., 124, *144*, 198, 200, 201, 204, *211*, *212*
Lott, B., 310, 312, 313, 315, *327*
Luborsky, L., 42, *63*, 217, *234*
Lukens, M. D., 21, *35*
Lukens, R. J., 21, *35*
Lusterman, D-D., 318, 319, 320, *327*
Lyke, J., 6, 54, 57, *63*
Lykken, D. T., 244, *255*
Lyra, M., 31, *35*
Lyster, R. F., 137, 138, *145*

Maccoby, E. E., 54, *63*
MacDonald, M. G., 152, *173*
Mace, D., 126, 134, *143*
Mace, V., 126, 134, *143*
Mack, D., 128, *143*
Mahoney, M. J., 20, 21, *38*
Mahrer, A. R., 42, *63*

Maisto, S., 112, *122*
Malarkey, W., 105, *122*
Malgady, R. G., 341, *349*
Malone, J., 188, *194*, 293, *295*, *296*, 297
Maneker, J. S., 126, *143*
Mangrum, L. F., 70, 71, 81, 87, *122*, 150, 151, 345
Manicavasagar, V., *349*
Mann, B. J., *36*, 48, 55, *63*, 263, *278*, 279
Marecek, J., 301, 306, *325*
Margolin, G., 106, 107, *119*, *121*, 147, *171*, 302, *327*
Marin, B. V., 331, 334, 335, *348*
Marin, G., 331, 334, 335, *348*
Markey, B., 127, *143*
Markman, H. J., 5, 10, *13*, *14*, *15*, 82, *86*, 91, 92, 94, 95, *99*, *100*, 113, *120*, 123, 124, 125, 126, 130, 131, 132, 133, 134, 135, 138, *140*, *141*, *142*, *143*, *145*, *146*, 148, 172, 183, *192*, *194*, *210*, *253*, 318, *327*
Marlowe, J. H., 240, *252*
Marrs-Garcia, D., 203, *211*
Martin, J., 21, *37*
Martin, J. A., 54, *63*
Martin, N. G., 288, *295*
Martin, T. C., 126, *143*
Martinez, C. R., Jr., 241, 249, *253*, *255*
Martinez-Arrue, R., 342, *349*
Marvin, R. S., 50, 58, *63*
Mas, C. H., 29, *34*, *38*, 53, *63*
Mason, C. A., 342, *349*
Masterpasqua, F., 33, *38*
Matteson, R., 311, *325*
Matthews, L. S., 124, *143*
Maturana, H. R., 20, *38*
Maxson, P., 124, 126, 132, 133, *141*
Maxwell, S. E., 94, *100*
McAddo, H. P., 332, *349*
McCain, S., 130, *146*
McCrady, B. S., 218, 223, 228, *234*, *235*
McCubbin, H. I., 79, *86*, 87
McCunney, N., 128, 133, *144*
McCurry, S., 35
McDonald, D. W., 125, *142*
McGoldrick, M., 301, *327*, 331, *349*
McGrady, B. S., 220, *233*
McGrath, E., 307, 311, *327*
McGraw, K., 243, *257*

McGreen, P., *36*
McGrew, J. H., 265, *281*
McKay, J. R., 112, *122*
McKay, M. M., 47, *65*, 199, 205, 206, 207, 208, *212*
McMahan, I., 312, *327*
McMahon, R. J., 184, *194*, 240, *255*
McManus, M. J., 139, *143*
McPherson, A. E., 7, *12*, 91, *99*
Mehlman, S. K., 82, *85*
Melby, C., 315, *322*
Meleis, A. I., 135, *145*
Melton, G. B., *36*, *234*, 265, 266, 268, 279
Melton, G. M., 25, *37*
Messerly, L., 156, *174*
Meuser, K. T., 219, *232*
Meyers, R., 230, *232*
Micheletto, M., 127, *143*
Michelini, R., 313, *327*
Microys, G., 138, *139*
Miklowitz, D. J., 74, *86*, 187, *193*, 230, 233
Miles, C., 303, *328*
Milholland, T., *139*
Milkowitz, D. J., 207, *210*
Miller, A., 163, *170*
Miller, A. L., 312, *327*
Miller, J. B., 306, *327*
Miller, K. J., 220, *233*
Miller, S., 126, 130, 138, *144*
Miller, S. D., 231, *232*
Miller, S. L., *279*
Miller, T. I., 21, *39*
Miller, W., 134, *142*
Miller, W. R., 228, *235*
Minuchin, S., 20, 23, *38*, 44, 52, *63*, 263, *281*
Mitrani, V., 8, 33, *38*
Mohatt, G., 341, *348*
Montgomery, L. M., *15*, *39*, 41, *65*, *101*, *122*, 148, 149, *173*, 179, *195*, *212*
Moore, J. J., 92, *101*
Moos, B. S., 73, *86*
Moos, R. H., 73, *86*, 217, *235*
Moran, G., 54, *60*
Morgan, A. C., 129, *145*
Morgan, L. A., 123, *142*
Morris, J. E., 130, *145*
Morris, T. M., 93, *100*
Morrison, A., 153, *170*

Morrison, D. C., 240, *257*
Morrison, D. R., 247, *257*
Morrow-Bradley, C., 43, *63*
Moss, J. J., 137, *144*
Most, R. K., 133, 138, *144*
Mrazek, P. J., 199, *211*, 240, 246, *255*,
    262, *278*
Muehlenhard, C., 315, *327*
Mueser, K., 107, *118*, 179, *192*, 218, 232
Mulholland, T., 128
Munger, R. L., 262, *279*
Muran, J. C., 43, 48, *65*
Murray, C., 346, *348*
Murray, E. J., 8, *15*, *38*
Murray, J., *12*, *13*, *99*, 171
Murray, J. D., 97, *100*, 163
Murray, W. J., *281*
Murstein, B. L., 152, *173*
Muthen, B. O., 204, *211*
Muxen, M., *87*

Nachman, G., 5, *14*
Naster, B. J., 152, *170*
Nath, S. R., 203, *211*
Nathan, P. N., 288, *297*
Neeman, R., 154, *174*, 229
Neidig, P. H., *142*, 292, 293, *294*, *296*
Nelson, H. G., *235*
Nelson, K. E., 265, *278*
Nelson, M. L., 21, *38*
Neufeld, R. W. J., 217, *233*
New, M., 54, *59*
Newberry, A. M., 29, *38*
Newcomb, M. D., 153, *170*
Newell, R. M., *38*, 180, *192*
Newell, R. N., 51, *64*
Newfield, N., 82, *85*, 110, *119*
Newton, T., 105, *122*
Nirenberg, T. D., 228, *234*
Noel, N., 217, *234*, *235*
Noller, P., 125, *144*
Norcross, J. C., 48, *64*
Norris, M. P., 78, *87*
Notarius, C., 5, *13*, 91, 92, *100*, 303,
    322
Nuechterlein, K. H., 74, *86*
Nugent, J., 156, *174*
Nugent, M. D., 82, *87*
Nunnally, E. W., 126, 130, *144*
Nunnally, J. C., 93, *100*

Nutt, R., 318, 319, *327*

O'Brien, F. T., 220, *232*
O'Farrell, T. J., 105, 112, *122*, 218, 220,
    228, *235*
Oggins, J., 159, *173*
Okazaki, S., 93, *100*
Okuwambua, T., *15*, *39*, 41, *65*, *101*,
    122, 148, *195*, *212*
O'Leary, D., 76, *85*
O'Leary, K. D., 5, *15*, 81, 82, *85*, *87*,
    188, *194*, 284, 285, 286, 287, 288,
    290, 291, 292, 293, *294*, *295*, *296*,
    297
O'Leary, S. G., 285, 286, 287, *296*
Olmos-Gallo, P. A., *146*
Olson, D. H., 56, 75, *87*, 123, 125, 127,
    128, 133, 136, 139, *141*, *143*, *144*,
    153, *171*, 183, *193*, *194*, 219, *235*
Olson, T. D., 137, *144*
Oltmanns, T., 287
Onorato, R., 302, *327*
Oppenheim, R., 21, *36*
Orford, J., 230, *235*
Orlinsky, D. E., 42, *64*
Oros, C., 315, *326*
Osborne, L. N., 290, *295*
Ost, L., 229, *235*
Oswald, D. P., 261, *281*
Ouimette, P. C., 217, *235*
Ozechowski, T., 6, *15*

Pagel, M., 81, *86*, 110, *121*, 216, *234*,
    302, *326*, 336, *348*
Pan, H., 293
Papp, P., 301, *328*
Parke, R. D., 3, *15*
Parker, G., 56, *64*
Parker, K., *37*
Parloff, M. B., 4, *13*
Parsons, B. V., 5, *11*, 24, 25, 26, 29, *34*,
    37
Parsons, C. K., 93, *100*
Parsons, J. E., 306, *324*
Patel, H., 268, *281*
Patterson, C., 232
Patterson, G. R., 3, *13*, 41, 49, 54, 55,
    64, 179, 180, *192*, *194*, *195*, 200,
    204, 206, *211*, 240, 241, 243, 244,

Patterson, G. R. (*Continued*)
  245, 247, 248, 250, 251, *252, 253,
  254, 255, 256, 257,* 275, *281,* 331,
  349
Patterson, J., *210*
Patterson, J. M., 79, *86,* 207
Patterson, K. M., 220, *237*
Patterson, S. G., *254*
Pauker, S., 136, *139*
Paul, G., 21, *38*
Pelham, W. E., 286, *296*
Penn, P., 52, *59*
Perez-Vidal, A., *15, 38, 39, 281, 350*
Perlmutter, B. F., 91, *101*
Perna, P., 33, *38*
Petersen, A., 312, *325*
Peterson, D., *143*
Peterson, L., 243, *257*
Peterson, R. F., 240, *255, 257*
Petti, T., 260, *280*
Phillips, F., 340, *348*
Phillips, S. L., 91, *99, 100*
Philpot, C. L., 318, 319, 320, *327,* 346
Pickrel, S. G., 263, 268, *279, 280, 281*
Pinsof, W. M., 4, 5, 6, 7, 10, *13, 15,* 20,
  23, *36, 38,* 41, 42, 47, 48, 50, 51,
  62, 64, 90, 100, 114, *122,* 178, 179,
  180, 181, 184, *193, 194, 195,* 206,
  211, 230, *235,* 247
Piper, W. E., 48, *62*
Pleck, J. H., 304, 305, 306, 311, 313,
  327, 328
Pollack, W. S., 304, *326*
Pollane, L., *140*
Pope, K. S., *35*
Popenoe, D., 123, *144*
Porter, B., 287
Postner, R. S., 181, *195*
Poulin, K., 21, *38*
Poulos, R. W., 285
Prado, L. M., *146*
Price, G. H., 286
Price, R. H., 124, 133, *144,* 198, *211,*
  212
Prigogine, I., 32, *38*
Prince, C. C., 110, 111, *120*
Prince, S., *120*
Prochaska, J. O., 48, *64*
Pruitt, S. K., 284, *295*
Pugh, C., 25, *34*
Pugh, R. H., 93, *101*

Quinn, W. H., 50, 51, *64*

Racioppo, M., 221, *235*
Ragsdale, K., 149, *173,* 179, *195*
Rahe, R. H., 147, *172*
Rains, L., 248, *254*
Rakoff, V., 181, *195*
Ramey, S. L., *12, 140, 192,* 210, 253
Ramos-Grenier, J., 331, *349*
Ramos-McKay, J., 124, *144*
Rampage, C., 302, *327*
Rand, L. M., 312, *327*
Randall, J., *279*
Rankin, L. A., 107, *118*
Rankin, R. P., 126, *143*
Ransom, D. C., 17, *35,* 91, *99, 100*
Raudenbush, S. W., 8, *12, 15,* 95, 96,
  97, *99, 101*
Rauen, P. I., 133, *140*
Ray, J. A., 3, *13,* 244, *254*
Reckase, M. D., 93, *101*
Reid, J. B., 179, *192,* 205, 206, *211, 212,*
  239, 240, 246, 248, 250, *252, 256,*
  257, 331, *349*
Reiff, S., 284
Reilly, M., 315, *327*
Reis, B., 52, *60*
Reise, S. P., 93, *101*
Reiss, D., 56, *64,* 92, *101,* 226, *236*
Renick, M. J., 10, *15,* 130, 131, 132,
  143, 144, 183, *194*
Revenstorf, D., 80, *85,* 94, *100,* 113,
  114, *121,* 125, *141,* 148, 150, *172*
Rice, F., 128, *144*
Rice, J. L., 69, 70, 78, *87*
Rice, L. N., 41, 42, 43, *64,* 182, 191,
  195
Rice, T., 21, *38*
Richters, J., 187, *194*
Ridley, C. A., 128, 129, 132, 133, 137,
  138, *139, 144, 145*
Riggs, D. S., 293
Rio, A. T., 24, *39, 350*
Rivard, J. C., 265, *278*
Rivera-Arzola, M., 331, *349*
Robbins, M. S., 29, 33, *38,* 51, *64,* 180,
  192
Roberto, L. G., 181, *192*
Rodgers, A., 199, *210*
Rodick, J. D., *37,* 266, *279*

Rodriguez, O., 341, *349*
Roediger, H. L., 287, *295*
Rog, D. J., 260, *278*
Rogers, C., 50, *65*
Rogers, T., *255*
Rogler, L. H., 341, *349*
Rohrbaugh, M. J., 215, 220, 221, 222, 226, 228, 229, 231, 232, *235*, *236*, 237, 332, 347, *349*
Root, M., 306, 311, *327*
Rosen, L., 187, *194*
Rosenbaum, A., 286, 291, 292, *295*, *296*, 315
Rosenstein, D. S., 56, *65*
Rosenthal, R., 225, *232*, *236*
Rosicky, J. G., 207, *210*
Rostker, R., 309, *325*
Rounsaville, B. J., 4, *12*
Rovine, M., 135, *140*
Rowe, C., 3, 6, 9, *13*, *14*, 48, 54, 57, 62, 63
Rowland, M. D., 3, *13*, 260, 268, *279*, *281*
Rubio-Stipec, M., 331, *348*
Ruble, D. N., 306, *324*
Rudd, P., 91, *99*
Rushe, R., *99*, *171*
Rushe, R. H., *12*, 49, *61*, 90, 95, *99*
Rushton, J. P., 287, *295*
Russell, C., 56, *63*
Russell, C. S., 130, *145*
Russell, D., 315, *328*
Russell, J. N., 128, *143*
Russell, M., 137, 138, *145*
Russell, R. L., 50, *65*
Russianoff, P., 306, 310, 312, *328*
Russo, N., 307, 311, *327*, *328*
Rychtarik, R. G., 228, *235*
Ryckoff, I., 20, *40*

Sadd, S., 313, *328*
Safran, J. D., 43, 48, *65*
Salts, C. J., 126, 128, *145*
Salusky, S., 5, *14*, 291, *295*
Salyers, M., 265, *281*
Sandeen, E. E., 288, *294*
Sanders, M., *257*
Sanders, M. R., 82, *85*, 109, *118*, 248, *253*, 263, *281*
Sanderson, W. C., 35

Santisteban, D. A., 8, *15*, 24, 25, 27, *38*, *39*, 275, *281*, 338, 340, 341, *349*, *350*
Santos, A. B., *279*
Saperia, E. P., 182, *195*
Sarlin, N., 50, *61*
Sarwer, D. B., 76, *87*
Saunders, R. C., 261, *278*
Savage, J., 313, *328*
Sawyers, J. P., 123, *143*
Sayers, S. L., 73, 76, 82, *84*, *87*, 109, *118*
Sceery, A., 50, 56, *63*
Schapp, C., 131, *146*
Scherer, D. G., 265, *279*
Schiavo, R. S., 29, *34*
Schindler, D., 107, *121*
Schindler, L., 80, *85*, 125, *141*, 150, *172*
Schmaling, K., *172*
Schmaling, K. B., 5, *14*, 82, *86*, 109, *121*, 149, 291, *295*
Schmaling, K. D., 105, 106, *122*
Schmidt, S. E., 3, *14*, 47, 55, *65*, 331, *349*
Schoenwald, S. K., 3, *13*, 33, *37*, 260, 262, 263, 264, 266, 268, 272, 274, *279*, *280*, *281*
Schulman, S., 25, *39*
Schumacher, K. L., 135, *145*
Schumm, W. R., 126, 132, 133, 136, 137, 139, *145*
Schwartz, S., 248, *253*
Schwebel, A. I., 90, *99*, 108, 109, *119*
Schweid, E., 240, *255*
Scopetta, M. A., 331, 334, 340, 341, 342, *349*, *350*
Sears, R. R., 153, *173*
Sechrest, L., 216, 217, *236*
Segall, M. H., 333, *349*
Seilhamer, R. A., 92, *100*, 226, *233*
Seltzer, J. A., 244, *255*
Serrano, A. C., 5, *13*, 41, *60*
Sexton, T. L., 23, 25, 28, 30, 31, 33, *34*, *39*
Shadish, W., *195*
Shadish, W. J., 41, *65*, 95, *179*
Shadish, W. R., 5, 6, 10, *15*, 24, *39*, 94, *101*, 108, 114, *122*, 148, 149, *173*, 206, 207, 208, *212*
Shapiro, A. F., 157, *173*
Shapiro, D. A., 215, *236*

Sharon, T., 92, *100*
Shaver, P., 56, *62*, 313, *328*
Shaw, D. M., *62*
Sheehan, R., 129, *141*
Sheek, B. W., 128, *145*
Sheldrick, R. C., 203, *211*
Shenk, J. L., 302, *324*
Sher, T. G., 73, 81, 82, *84*, *87*, 105, 106, 109, *118*, *122*
Sherman, R., 91, *99*
Shirk, S. R., 50, *61*, *65*
Shoham, V., *118*, 179, *192*, 215, 218, 220, 221, 223, 225, 226, 229, 231, 232, *235*, *236*, *237*, 332, 347, *349*
Shoham-Salomon, V., 41, *65*, 107, 217, 229, *236*
Shon, S. P., 336, *349*
Shulman, L. S., 229, *236*
Shure, M. B., *12*, *140*, *192*, 210, 253
Siegel, T. C., 259, *280*
Sigal, J., 181, *195*
Silliman, B., 132, 133, 136, 137, *140*, *145*
Silove, D., 344, *349*
Silverman, M. M., 198, *212*
Silverstein, L. B., *323*
Silverstein, L. S., 320, *327*, *328*
Silverstein, O., 301, *328*
Silvester, J., 54, *59*
Simon, K., 315, *328*
Sinclair, C., 138, *139*
Singer, B., 217, *234*
Singh, N. N., 261, *281*
Sinnerbrink, I., *349*
Siqueland, L., 42, 44, 45, 53, 54, 56, 57, *60*, *65*
Sisson, R. W., 230, *232*
Skowron, E. A., 41, 57, *61*, 179, *193*
Sladezek, I. E., 138, *145*
Slough, N., 184, *194*
Sluzki, C. E., 52, *65*
Smalley, G., 134, *145*
Smith, B., 216, 217, *236*
Smith, B. H., 262, *280*
Smith, D. A., 82, *87*, 223, *234*
Smith, L. A., 25, *36*, *37*, *234*, 266, 268, *279*
Smith, M. L., 21, *39*
Smith, S. A. F., 5, *12*
Smutzler, N., *142*
Snodgrass, S., 313, *327*

Snow, R. E., 215, 216, *233*, *236*
Snyder, D., 315, *324*, 345
Snyder, D. K., 69, 70, 71, 74, 75, 77, 78, 81, 82, *85*, *86*, *87*, 107, 109, 110, 115, *122*, 150, 151, *173*
Snyder, J., 243, *257*
Snyder, J. J., 243, *257*
Sobell, L. C., 221, *236*
Sobell, M. B., 221, *236*
Sonis, W. A., 5, *13*, 41, *60*
Sosna, B. A., 48, *65*
Spanier, G. B., 95, *101*
Spence, J. T., 305, 306, 307, *328*
Sperry, L., 219, *233*
Spitalnik, R., 285
Splove, D., 56, *64*
Sprenkle, D. H., 56, *63*, 129, *141*
Sprotzer, E. R., 312, *325*
Spungen, C., 220, *235*
St. Peter, C., 243, *257*
St. Peters, M., 126, *146*
Stahmann, R. F., 124, 126, 128, 133, 138, 139, *142*, *143*, *145*
Stake, J., 309, *328*
Stanley, J. H., 52, *66*
Stanley, S., 123, *141*
Stanley, S. M., 123, 124, 125, 126, 130, 131, 132, 133, 135, 137, *140*, *143*, *145*, *146*, 183, *194*
Stanton, M. D, 5, *15*
Stapley, J. C., *328*
Stark, M. J., 228, *236*
Stearns, A., 313, *328*
Stein, R. J., 24, *35*, 266, *278*
Steinberg, J. A., 198, *212*
Steinberg, L. D., 50, 54, *65*, 93, *101*
Steinberg, M., 220, *233*
Steinglass, P., 220, 226, 227, *235*, *236*
Stengers, I., 32, *38*
Stets, J. E.., 292, *296*
Stickle, T. R., 107, *118*, 179, *192*, 218, 221, 225, 232, *235*, *236*
Stiles, W. B., 215, *236*
Stoolmiller, M., 179, *195*, 246, 250, 251, *257*
Storaasi, R. D., 125, *143*
Stout, R., 217, *234*, 235
Stouthamer-Loeber, M., 54, *63*
Straus, M. A., 91, *101*, 291, 292, *296*
Straus, M. R., 315, 316, *324*
Strickland, B., 307, *327*

Strodtbeck, F. L., 334, 337, 338, 339, 348
Stroul, B. A., 261, 276, 281
Strupp, H. H., 50, 62
Stuart, R. B., 152, 174
Stuebing, K. K., 96, 99
Sue, S., 35, 93, 100, 332, 340, 350
Sullivan, L. A., 309, 325
Summerfelt, W. T., 261, 278
Summers, K. J., 224, 237
Surface, C. R., 306, 326
Swanson, C., 13, 154, 172
Symonds, B. D., 50, 62
Szapocznik, J., 6, 8, 15, 24, 25, 27, 38, 39, 275, 281, 331, 334, 338, 340, 341, 342, 344, 349, 350

Talovic, S., 302, 327
Tarule, J., 314, 323
Tavris, C., 306, 328
Taylor, R. J., 137, 146
Tennenbaum, D., 92, 100
Terman, L., 303, 328
Terry, D., 20, 37
Terry, H. E., 17, 35
Thelen, R., 315, 322
Thissen, D., 93, 94, 101
Thompson, E. H., 305, 328
Thompson, K. C., 96, 99
Thompson, L., 301, 328
Thurmaier, F., 131, 141, 146
Tickle-Degnen, L., 225, 236
Tobin-Richards, M., 312, 325
Todd, M., 204, 213
Todd, T. C., 237
Tolan, P. H., 3, 15, 47, 49, 50, 65, 183, 188, 193, 195, 199, 200, 202, 203, 204, 205, 206, 207, 208, 210, 211, 212, 246, 257
Tonelli, L., 146
Torgerson, S., 288, 296
Touliatos, J., 91, 101
Trathen, D. W., 130, 132, 146
Triandis, H. C., 336, 348
Trimble, J., 341, 348
Trost, S., 226, 237
Truax, P., 108, 113, 121
Tuason, V. B., 60
Tucker, M. B., 137, 146
Turkewitz, H., 81, 87

Turner, C. W., 24, 29, 35, 38, 51, 53, 63, 64, 180, 192
Turner, R. M., 14
Tyree, A., 188, 194, 293, 295, 296
Tyson, R., 12, 99, 171

Ullmann, L. P., 283, 286, 297
Unger, R., 307, 309, 328
Unis, A. S., 240, 255
Urey, J. R., 37, 266, 279
Ussher, J., 309, 328

Valeri, S. M., 259, 282
van der Staak, C., 131, 146
Van Widenfelt, B., 131
VandenBos, G. R., 42, 65
Varda, S. S., 154, 174
Varela, F. J., 20, 38
Vega, W. A., 137, 146
Veroff, J., 159, 173
Vincent, J. P., 156, 174
Vivian, D., 82, 87, 292, 293, 294, 297
Vollmer, F., 312, 328
Vosler, N. R., 91, 100

Wackman, D. B., 126, 130, 144
Waehler, C. A., 21, 39
Wagner, E. H., 183, 193
Wahler, R. G., 204, 211, 240, 257
Wakefield, P., 220, 222, 228, 237
Waldron, H., 24, 28, 34, 35, 40
Walker, A., 301, 328
Walker, K., 157, 173
Walker, L., 316, 328
Walker-Barnes, C., 342, 349
Walsh, F., 301, 327
Walters, L. H., 92, 101
Walters, M., 301, 328
Waltz, J., 116, 122
Walz, G. R., 33, 39
Wampler, K. S., 92, 101, 129, 130, 146
Warburton, J. R., 24, 29, 35, 40
Ward, D. M., 268, 279, 281
Watson, S. M., 37, 266, 279
Watt, N., 192
Watt, N. F., 140, 210, 253
Watt, N. R. 12

Watzlawick, P., 223, 237
Weakland, J., 20, 35, 223, 237
Webster-Stratton, C., 184, 195, 207, 212
Weersing, V. R., 52, 66
Weinrott, M. R., 240, 252
Weinstein, S. E., 126, 142
Weiss, B., 259, 265, 282
Weiss, R. L., 54, 65, 82, 91, 100, 158,
    174, 224, 237
Weisz, J. R., 52, 66, 259, 262, 265, 280,
    282
Wells, A. M., 246, 254
Wells, K. C., 240, 255
West, S., 192
West, S. G., 4, 12, 140, 204, 210, 213,
    253
Whelan, J. P., 266, 278
Whisman, M. A., 50, 62, 110, 120, 151,
    172, 290, 297, 302, 329
Whiston, S. C., 33, 39
White, J., 12, 99, 171
White, M., 21, 40, 52, 66
White, S., 147, 171
Whitman, R., 252
Wickrama, K. A. S., 124, 143
Widaman, K. F., 93, 101
Wildman, J., 41, 61, 179, 193
Willett, E., 138, 139
Williams, C. A., 255
Williams, D. A., 35
Williams, R. A., 278
Williams, R. E., 220, 237
Williams-Keeler, L., 112, 121
Wills, R. M., 81, 87, 107, 115, 122, 150,
    151, 173
Wilson, D. B., 240, 255
Wilson, G. T., 115, 122, 287, 288, 297
Wilson, H., 244, 257
Wilson, M., 87, 195

Wilson, M. R., 15, 39, 101, 212
Wilson, P., 15, 39, 41, 65, 101, 122, 148,
    195, 212
Windle, M., 4, 12
Winkle, G. H., 240, 257
Wirtz, P. W., 217, 234
Witkin, S. L., 302, 329
Wittgenstein, L., 21, 40
Woehrer, C. E., 137, 146
Wolf, M. M., 283, 294
Wolf, N., 306, 309, 329
Wolfe, B. E., 231, 237, 286
Wolin, S. J., 226, 236
Wood, L. F., 121
Woody, S. R., 35
Worthington, E. L., 126, 146
Wynne, J. C., 20, 40, 41
Wynne, L., 5, 6, 10, 15, 32, 40, 56, 57,
    64, 66, 90, 100, 114, 122, 178, 184,
    195, 206, 211, 230, 235

Yasui, M., 252
Yoerger, K., 245, 256
Yost, E., 220, 232, 237
Youngstrom, E., 56, 63

Zane, N., 340, 350
Zaphiropoulous, L., 306, 323
Zarate, M., 38
Zayas, L. H., 342, 351
Zealberg, J., 279
Zelli, A., 183, 188, 193, 205, 206, 212
Zellman, G. L., 306, 324
Zill, N., 247, 257
Zuckerman, M., 333, 351
Zumtobel, D. C., 224, 233
Zweben, A., 228, 235

Subject Index

ABFT. *See* Attachment–based family therapy
Abuse
  sexual, 315, 317
  spousal, 289–290, 291–293, 315–316
Acceptance in relationships, 74–75
Accountability, 21, 22
Acculturation changing value orientations, 340–344, 346
Active listening, 149, 150
Adaptability, 77
ADHD (attention deficit hyperactivity disorder) and conduct disorders, 283–287
Adherence tools, 48
Admiration of partner, 154, 156–157
Affective and behavioral independence, 77
Affective domain, 73–75
African American families. *See also* Ethnic culture
  distrust of institutions, courts, and schools, 346
  family therapy in family psychology intervention science (FT-FPIS), sensitivity to, 25, 28
  functional family therapy, 28
  Kwanza celebration by, 340
  skeptical of and challenging to authority, 337
  well-being of group valued over that of individual, 336
Alcoholism, 215, 217–219, 220
  comparison of CBT and FST in couples with alcoholic male, 221–232
Alienation, 341
Alliance-building task, 45, 50–52
Allocentrism, 336
American Academy of Child and Adolescent Psychiatry, 4
American Psychiatric Association, 288, 291

Ancestry worship, 340
Anger
  as divorce factor, 154
  wife's perception of husband's, 158
Antabuse, 230
Asian American families. *See also* Ethnic culture
  acculturation and rejection of traditions, 343
  ancestry worship and reverence of elders, 340
  family therapy in family psychology intervention science (FT-FPIS), sensitivity to, 28
  functional family therapy, 28
  importance of group over that of individual, 336
Assessment of families and couples, 69–101
  affective domain, 73–75
  clinician rating methods, 92–93
  cognitive domain, 72–73
  communication and interpersonal domain, 75–76
  comparability in measurements, 93–94
  conceptual model for, 70–80
  confirmatory factor analysis (CFA), 93–94
  control, sanctions, and related behavioral domains, 79–80
  evaluating therapy outcomes with clinical significance, 94–95
  item response theory (IRT) methods, 93–94
  measurement issues, 90–95
  observational methods, 91–92
  preventive interventions, 127–128, 203–204, 206
  self-reports, 91
  shortcomings in, 69
  structural and developmental components, 77–79
  therapy process, 47–48

Assimilation into host society culture, 341

Association for Couples in Marriage Enrichment, 126

ATI. *See* Attribute x treatment interaction (ATI) research

Attachment-based family therapy (ABFT), 42, 50–58
alliance-building task, 45, 50–52
change mechanisms in, 45
evolution of single task, 44
parenting practices, 50, 54–56
process of, 44
reattachment task, 45, 50, 56–58
reattribution task, 45, 50, 52–54

Attention deficit hyperactivity disorder (ADHD) and conduct disorders, 4, 283–287

Attribute x treatment interaction (ATI) research, 215–238
comparison of CBT and FST in couples with alcoholic male, 221–232
couple affect, 224–225
defined, 216
demand-withdraw interaction, 223–224, 228–229
ethnic culture research needs and, 347
hypothetical applications of, 219, 220
interactional synchrony, 225–226
relational moderators, 220–227
symptom-system fit (SSF), 226–227
validity of, 217–218

Authority allocation in families, 79–80, 82

Autonomy
versus emotional security, 79
Hispanic culture's view of, 342

Awareness approaches to preventive interventions, 128

Battered women's syndrome, 316

BDI. *See* Beck Depression Inventory

Beauty and gender role discrepancy strain, 309–310

Beavers Timberlawn interactional instrument, 46

Beck Depression Inventory (BDI), 288, 289

Becoming a Family Project, 135–136

Behavior, defined, 178–179

Behavior exchange therapy, 149, 152

Behavior modification, 283

Behavior therapy, 283

Behavioral marital therapy (BMT), 107–108, 110, 148–149
alcoholics with marital problems, 220
clinically significant change due to, 114
comparison with insight-oriented couple therapy (IOCT), 115
comparison with integrative couple therapy (ICT), 111
no empirical research findings to support, 152
traditional gender roles and, 336
types of couples reporting benefit from, 216

Behavioral risk factors, 184

Behind Closed Doors, 315

The Bell Curve, 346

Bern Sex Role Inventory, 302, 303, 305, 306, 307

Beyond Power, 307

Biculturalism, 341

BMT. *See* Behavioral marital therapy

Body hatred, 309–310

Boundaries between persons in family, 334–337

Cannabis Youth Treatment Multisite Study, 4

Cascade model of dissolution, 153

Case-control designs for identifying risk and protective factors, 185

Case Studies in Behavior Modification, 283

CASSP (Child and Adolescent Service Systems Program), 261

CBMT (cognitive behavioral marital therapy), 107

CBT. *See* Cognitive behavioral therapy

CC. *See* Couple Communication

Center for the American Woman and Politics, 312

Center for American Women in Politics, 313–314

Center for Marriage and Family, 133, 137, 139

Center for Substance Abuse Treatment, 4
Center for Treatment Research with
    Adolescent Drug Abuse, 29
Centers for Disease Control and
    Prevention, 106
CFA (confirmatory factor analysis), 93–
    94
Change events, 43
    analysis of matrix of, 46
    stages of change for drug treatment,
    48
Change mechanisms. *See also* Process
    research; Task analysis
    in attachment-based family therapy
    (ABFT), 45, 49–50
    successful therapy outcomes and, 90
Child and Adolescent Service Systems
    Program (CASSP), 261
Childbirth education classes, 135
Children at risk. *See also* Preventive
    interventions for families
    marital problems, relationship
    between, 287
    multisystemic therapy applied to. *See*
    Multisystemic therapy (MST)
    psychoanalytical theory applied to,
    240
    sample programs from Oregon Social
    Learning Center, 248–250
Children's mental health services
    research, 260–262
Christian version of Prevention and
    Relationship Enhancement Program
    (PREP), 130
*Classroom Management: The Successful Use
    of Behavior Modification,* 285
Clinic versus research treatments in
    family therapy, 259–260
Clinical relevance, 177, 178–183
Clinical trials, 8, 32–33, 58
    couple therapy research, limitations of,
    114–115
    multisystemic therapy (MST), 266–
    269
Clinically significant change due to
    couple therapy, 113–114
Clinician rating methods, 92–93
Clinician's behaviors. *See* Therapist
    behaviors

Coalition for Marriage, Family and
    Couples Education, 139
Coding systems, 92
Coercive parenting, 243, 244, 249
Cognitive behavioral marital therapy
    (CBMT), 107
Cognitive behavioral therapy (CBT), 217,
    220–232
Cognitive domain, 72–73
Cohesion, 74
Cohort studies for identifying risk and
    protective factors, 186
Collectivism, 336
College classes for preventive
    interventions, 128, 132, 136–137
Commission on Chronic Illness, 124
Commitment to relationships, 74
Communication and interpersonal
    domain, 75–76
Communication and problem-solving
    training (CPT), 109, 149
Communication skills
    marital therapy and, 82
    therapy for, 5
Community
    development of community-based
    models of service delivery, 261–262
    multisystemic therapy, community-
    based, 266–274
    prevention programs in, 126, 139
    status of family with, 80
Competency-promoting task, 45
Conceptual model for assessment of
    families and couples, 70–80
Conduct disorders and attention deficit
    hyperactivity disorder (ADHD), 4,
    283–287
Confirmatory factor analysis (CFA), 93–
    94
Conflict resolution
    by couples, 159–161
    by parents with hierarchical family
    relations, 335
Conflict-avoiding type of marriages, 154
Consortium on Children, Families and
    the Law, 271, 277
Constructivist approach, 20–21, 33, 52
    attachment theory versus, 56
Contempt for partner, 153, 154, 157

Contextual factors
  in children's mental health services research, 260
  in family prevention therapy, 244–245
Contextualism, 111
Contingency contracting of couples, 152, 156
Continuum of care model in children's mental health services, 261
Costs
  of behavioral health care, 21
  of couple therapy, 117
  of family therapy, 178
  of health care, 23
  of integrated system of care, 261
  of multisystemic therapy, 268
Couple and Family Therapy Alliance scale, 51
Couple Communication (CC), 126, 129–130
Couple therapy, 105–174. See also Marital therapy
CPT. See Communication and problem-solving training
Criticism by spouse, 159
Cross-sectional studies
  designs for identifying risk and protective factors, 185–186
  family prevention therapy, 244–245
Cultural context. See Ethnic culture

Date rape, 315
Decade of the Woman, 313
Delinquency, 23
  multisystemic therapy (MST) and juvenile offenders, 269
  Office of Juvenile Justice and Delinquency Prevention (OJJDP), 274
  parental functioning linked to reductions in, 49, 209
  sample programs from Oregon Social Learning Center, 249
Delivery models
  development of community-based models of service delivery, 261–262
  multisystemic therapy (MST), 265–266
  preventive interventions for couples, 137–138

Demand-withdraw interaction, 223–224
Demand-withdraw pattern among couples, 159
Demographics and marital therapy prediction research, 80–81
Dependency
  of members in enmeshed family, 335
  of women, 312, 316
Deportation, 344
Depression
  couple therapy to treat, 112
  gender role dysfunction strain and, 311, 316
  marital problems linked with, 287–291
Devaluation of women, 313–314, 317
Developmental status of family therapy in family psychology intervention science (FT-FPIS), 17–31
  coherence in, 23
  continual evolution of, 32
  culture and, 22–23
  family-based, empirically supported treatments (FBESTs), 24–31
  meaning of developmental status, 17–18
  root elements of, 18–19
  science and scientific method, 21–22
  theory and practice, 20–21
Discipline by parents, 243, 249
Discovery-oriented process research, 42–43
  alliance-building task, 51
  reattachment process, 57
Discrimination, ethnic, 346
"Distance and isolation cascade," 153
Diversity. See Ethnic culture
Divorce, 109, 113
  depression resulting from, 289–290
  factors to predict likelihood of, 153–154, 162–163, 167
  harmful consequences of, 147
  Oregon Divorce Study, 249
  as outcome of couple therapy, how to view, 113
  preventive measures, 124, 131
  rates, 106, 109, 131, 163
  risk factors for, 124–126
  timing of, 156

Domestic violence, 289–290, 291–293, 315–316
Dyadic Adjustment Scale, 95
Dynamic systems theory, 31
Dynamic versus static risk factors, 125–126

Eating disorders, 311, 315, 316
EFT. *See* Emotionally focused therapy
Emotional bank account of marriage, 157
Emotional security versus autonomy, 79
Emotionally focused therapy (EFT), 107–108, 109
Emotions, 73–75
Empathy gains from skills training, 129
Employment opportunities and ethnic culture, 346
Enhancement programs
    Prevention and Relationship Enhancement Program (PREP), 10, 126, 130–132, 183
    Relationship Enhancement (RE), 126, 129, 132, 183
    sample programs from Oregon Social Learning Center, 248
Enmeshed families, 335
Enriching Relationship Issues, Communication, and Happiness (ENRICH), 128, 183
Entropy, 17–18, 77
Epidemiological research designs for identifying risk and protective factors, 185–186
Ethnic culture
    acculturation changing value orientations, 340–344, 346
    activity orientation in, 339
    alienation/marginalization in, 341
    assimilation, 341
    couple relationships and acculturation, 343–344
    cultural differences approach to marital therapy, 319
    cultural expectations, 73
    efficacy of couple therapy and, 117
    Eurocentric values and, 338–339
    family therapy in family psychology intervention science (FT-FPIS), sensitivity to, 22–25, 28

human nature in, 337–338
immigration's effects, 344–345
integrating family psychology intervention science with study of, 331–351
integration/biculturalism, 341
intrafamilial differences in acculturation patterns, 342–343
major life experiences with impact on, 344–346
measurement validity and, 93, 98
mismatch between therapy and culture, 338
past orientation, usefulness in interventions, 340
person-nature in, 338–339
power-distance concept in some societies, 337
preventive interventions for couples and, 137
relational orientation and assumptions about interpersonal relationships, 334–337
relationships among ethnicity, race, and culture, 332–333
sociopolitical status of family, 345–346
time orientation in, 339–340
values orientations work relevant to family intervention science, 333–339
withdrawal/separation from, 341
Eurocentric values and therapy, 338–339
Extended family systems, 75, 78, 80, 83
Extensionality in children's mental health services research, 260

Facilitating Open Couple Communication, Understanding and Study (FOCCUS), 127
Family hierarchy, 77–78, 335–336
Family psychology intervention science
    clinical research in, 4
    couple interventions and, 106
    current status, 24–28
    emerging area of, 3–15
    ethnic culture study integrated with, 331–351. *See also* Ethnic culture

Family psychology intervention science
(*Continued*)
  family therapy's developmental status
    in, 17–40. *See also* Developmental
    status of family therapy in family
    psychology intervention science
    (FT-FPIS)
  future trends, 9–11
  methodological issues and innovations
    in, 89–101. *See also* Methodological
    issues and innovations in family
    psychology intervention research
  process research, 41–66. *See also*
    Process research; Task analysis
  research infrastructure, 5–6
  research nature and quality, 6–9
  standards established for, 4
Family systems therapy (FST), 220–232
Family therapist coding system (FTCS),
  181–182
Family therapy
  attribute x treatment interaction (ATI)
    research, 215–237. *See also* Attribute
    x treatment interaction (ATI)
    research
  clinic versus research treatments, 259–
    260
  clinical relevance, 177, 178–183
  defined, 177
  development of, 17–40. *See also*
    Developmental status of family
    therapy in family psychology
    intervention science (FT-FPIS)
  family-focused prevention research,
    197–213. *See also* Preventive
    interventions for families
  gender issues, 301–330. *See also*
    Gender issues in marital and family
    therapy
  market relevance of, 178
  mental health services research and,
    259–282. *See also* Mental health
    services research perspective
  multisystemic therapy. *See*
    Multisystemic therapy (MST)
  preventive intervention model, 177–
    196. *See also* Preventive
    interventions for families
  protective factors, 184–185
  risk factors, 184–185
  therapist behavior, 181
Family types, research needs about, 9–10

Family-based, empirically supported
    treatments (FBESTs), 24–31
  integration of science, practice, and
    culture, 24, 31, 33
  as intervention science, 28–31
  success of, 24–28
  training manuals, 29–30
FBESTs, empirically supported
    treatments. *See* Family–based
Femininity. *See* Gender issues in marital
    and family therapy
Femininity Ideology Scale, 307
FFT. *See* Functional family therapy
FOCCUS (Facilitating Open Couple
    Communication, Understanding and
    Study), 127
Fondness for partner, 154, 156–157
FST (family systems therapy), 220–232
FTCS (family therapist coding system),
    181–182
Functional family therapy (FFT), 20, 24–
    30
  PhaseTask Analysis (PTA), 30

Gender issues in marital and family
    therapy, 22, 81, 301–330
  acculturation of immigrant family and,
    346
  behavioral marital theory and
    traditional gender roles, 336
  Brooks's "intergender translating and
    reframing" approach to marital
    therapy, 319–320
  case example using Silverstein and
    Levant's integrated strain-Bowen
    family systems approach, 320–321
  discrepancy strain, 305–306, 309–
    311, 316
  dysfunction strain, 305–306, 311–
    313, 316
  family therapy, 318
  female gender role strain, 309–316
  field of gender studies, 303
  gender ideology, 305
  gender role identity paradigm, 304–
    305
  gender role strain paradigm, 304–317,
    346
  literature review, 302–303

Lusterman's "empathetic interview" and "gender inquiry" approach to marital therapy, 320
marital therapy, 318–320
models of intervention and intervention research, 317–320
parent education, 317–318
Philpot's "psychoeducational" approach to marital therapy, 319
premarital programs, 318
Silverstein and Levant's "integration of the strain paradigm with the Bown theory" approach to marital therapy, 320–321
superwoman syndrome, 308–309, 310–311
traditional versus new woman ideology, 308–309
trauma strain, 305–306, 313–317
types of gender role strain, 305–306, 309
women, 306–316
Global coding systems, 92
Growth curve analysis, 95–96

Haitian culture, 338. *See also* Ethnic culture
Health problems
gender role strain paradigm and, 316
marriage satisfaction and, 106
Hierarchical family relations, effect of, 77–78, 335–336
Hierarchical linear modeling (HLM), 95–97
High school classes for preventive interventions, 128
Hispanic culture. *See also* Ethnic culture
emphasis on inherent quality of being, 339
family therapy in family psychology intervention science (FT-FPIS), sensitivity to, 25, 28
parenting practices, 341–342
Histrionic personality disorder of women, 312, 316
HLM (hierarchical linear modeling), 95–97
Human nature, 337–338

ICT. *See* Integrative couple therapy
Immigration's effects on family life, 344–345
Indicated prevention, 199–202, 209, 246
Infidelity, effect on other spouse, 289–290
Informative approaches to preventive interventions, 128
Insight-oriented couple therapy (IOCT), 115
Insight-oriented marital therapy (IOMT), 107, 109, 150–151
Institute of Medicine, 199
Integration into host society culture while maintaining identity of original culture, 341
Integrative couple therapy (ICT), 107, 111
Integrity of treatment in couple therapy, 115–116
Interaction research
attribute x treatment interaction (ATI) research, 215–237. *See also* Attribute x treatment interaction (ATI) research
Interactional risk factors, 184
Intervention research for marital and family therapy, 3–15
family-based, empirically supported treatments (FBESTs), 24–31
funding for research, 6
future study in, 9–11
gender issues, 317–321
model for clinically and prevention-relevant research, 186–191
research infrastructure, 5–6
research nature and quality, 6–9
scope of, 3–5
IOCT (insight-oriented couple therapy), 115
IOMT. *See* Insight–oriented marital therapy
Item response theory (IRT) methods, 93–94

Job opportunities and ethnic culture, 346
Journal of Marital and Family Therapy, 178

Juvenile justice systems' use of multisystemic therapy (MST), 274

Kwanza, 340

Life dreams, honoring in marriage, 161–162
Locke-Wallace Marital Adjustment Test, 289
Love maps, 156

MacDonald Sex Role Inventory, 306
Managed health care, 21, 23
    couple therapy, 117
    family therapy, 177, 178
Marginalization, 341
Marital Interact Coding System (MICS), 224–225
Marital rape, 315
Marital therapy, 105–174
    behavioral marital therapy. *See* Behavioral marital therapy (BMT)
    Brooks's "intergender translating and reframing" approach, 319–320
    characteristics of couples that show improvement, 151–152
    clinical significance, 113–114
    clinical trials, limitations of, 114–115
    cognitive behavioral marital therapy (CBMT), 107
    communication and problem-solving training (CPT), 109, 149
    conflict resolution, 159–161
    considerations for, 112–117
    current research, 107–112
    defining treatment response, 112–113
    demand–withdraw pattern, 159
    depression and marital problems, 287–291
    effectiveness of treatment, 116–117
    efficacy of couple treatments, 107–109
    emotionally focused therapy (EFT), 107–108, 109
    empirically based marital intervention, 167–169
    fondness and admiration, 156–157

gender issues, 81, 301–330. *See also* Gender issues in marital and family therapy
honoring life dreams, 161–162
insight-oriented marital therapy (IOMT), 107, 109, 150–151
integrative couple therapy (ICT), 107, 111
literature review, 148
long-term outcome, 109–110
love maps and knowing the partner, 156
Lusterman's "empathetic interview" and "gender inquiry" approach, 320
mathematical model of marital interaction, 163–167
meanings interview, 161
meta-emotion interview, 161
nonregulated couples, 153
opposite position intervention, 168
perpetual problems, 160, 162
Philpot's "psychoeducational" approach, 319
positive sentiment override (PSO), 158–159
power differences approach, 319
prediction research, 80–83, 110
preventive approaches, 123–146. *See also* Preventive interventions for couples
problem solving in, 159–161
for psychiatric disorders, 112
regulated couples, 153
relapse effect, 169
research needs, 169
shared symbolic meaning, 161–162
Silverstein and Levant's "integration of the strain paradigm with the Bown theory" approach, 320
sound marital house theory, 154–163
static versus dynamic risk factors, 125–126
strategic therapy, 107
strategies for prevention, 126–133. *See also* Preventive interventions for couples
treatment integrity, 115–116
turning toward versus turning away, 157
types of stable marriages, 154

usefulness in treatment of other disorders, 5
Market relevance of family therapy, 178
Marriage. *See also* Divorce
  childhood problems associated with marital problems, 287
  depression and marital problems, 287–291
  gender role discrepancy strain, 310
  mathematical model of marital interaction, 163–167
  research findings on, 152–154
  sound marital house theory, 154–163
  therapy. *See* Marital therapy
Marriage enrichment, 126
  informational and awareness approaches, 128
  selecting target groups for, 134
Marriage Guidance Centers, 134
Masculinity. *See* Gender issues in marital and family therapy
Mathematical model of marital interaction, 97, 163–167
Meanings interview, 161
Measurement. *See* Assessment of families and couples
Medically ill children and family-focused prevention, 207–208
Mental health services research perspective, 259–282
  children's mental health services research, 260–262
  contextuality, 260
  continuum of care model, 261
  extensionality, 260
  multisystemic therapy, 262–276. *See also* Multisystemic therapy (MST)
  service systems research, 261
  systems of care, 261–262
Mentoring, 293
Meta-analyses
  criticisms of, 115
  of family therapy, 24, 179
  of marital therapy, 148, 151
  of preventive interventions, 129
Meta-emotion interview, 161
Methodological issues and innovations in family psychology intervention research, 89–101
  clinician rating methods, 92–93

comparability in measurements, 93–94
  measurement issues, 90–95
  modeling and statistical methods, 95–97
  observational methods, 91–92
  research need for standards, 97–98
  self-reports, 91
Metropolitan Area Child Study family intervention, 207
Metropolitan Area Child Study Group, 203
MICS (Marital Interact Coding System), 224–225
Military
  spousal abuse study, 293
  use of Prevention and Relationship Enhancement Program (PREP), 132
Minnesota Couple Communication Program. *See* Couple Communication (CC)
Minority culture. *See* Ethnic culture
Modeling, 95–97
Monitoring by parents, 243, 245, 249
Motherhood and gender role discrepancy strain, 310
MST. *See* Multisystemic therapy
MTA Cooperative Group, 286
Multicultural applications. *See* Ethnic culture
Multidimensional family therapy, 24–28
  process of, 44
Multisystemic therapy (MST), 24–28, 262–269
  clinical trials, 266–269
  community and economic factors, 273–274
  dissemination to service delivery community, 269–274
  effectiveness of, 55
  factors relating to successful implementation, 270–272
  implications for family intervention science, 275–276
  model of service delivery, 265–266
  provider organization factors, 273
  therapist factors, 272
  training organization-provider organization interface, 274
  treatment principles, 264–265
  treatment theory, 263–264

The Myth of Masculinity, 304

National Institute of Mental Health
   multisystemic therapy (MST), support
      provided by, 272, 274
   Prevention Intervention Research
      Center (PIRC), 239–240
   Prevention Steering Committee, 246
   supported research on PREP, 131
   universal versus selective prevention,
      adoption of terms, 198–199
National Institute on Drug Abuse, 4, 29
Native American families. *See also* Ethnic
      culture
   alienation/marginalization of youth,
      341
   family therapy in family psychology
      intervention science (FT-FPIS),
      sensitivity to, 28
   functional family therapy, 28
Negative affect reciprocity, 158
Negative reinforcement, 244, 249
Negentropy, 77

Observational methods, 91–92
Office of Juvenile Justice and
      Delinquency Prevention (OJJDP),
      274, 277
Opposite position intervention, 168
Oregon Divorce Study, 249
Oregon Social Learning Center (OSLC),
      55, 240–244, 248–252
Outcomes
   change mechanisms and, 90
   clinical relevance and, 178–183
   couple therapy and long-term
      outcomes, 109–110
   evaluating therapy outcomes with
      clinical significance, 94–95
   family therapy in family psychology
      intervention science (FT-FPIS), 29
   linking process to outcome, 48–49,
      179–180
   measuring task outcome and
      components, 47–48
   preventive interventions for couples
      and long-term outcomes, 132–133

Parent pursuing-child distancing process,
      57
Parent training, 248
   gender role, 317–318
Parenthood, transition to
   drop in marital satisfaction at, 156
   preventive interventions at, 135–136
Parenting style and practices, 50, 54–56,
      79, 206–207, 241–244, 341–342.
      See also Preventive interventions for
      families
Perpetual problems, 160, 162
Personal Attributes Questionnaire, 305,
      306, 307
Person–nature and ethnic culture, 338–
      339
Pills or Skills for Hyperactive Children, 286
Positive affect in marriage
   conflict resolution and, 160–162
   importance of, 155–156
Positive connotation, 53
Positive involvement of families, 243,
      249
Positive sentiment override (PSO), 158–
      159
Positivism, 32
Postmarriage enrichment as prevention,
      134
Power differences approach to marital
      therapy, 319
Predictions
   of couple's response to therapy, 110
   of marital dissolution, 153–154, 162
   in marital therapy research, 80–83
Premarital counseling and programs,
      126, 132
   assessment approaches, 127
   gender role, 318
   goals of, 184
   Prevention and Relationship
      Enhancement Program (PREP), use
      in, 130
   selecting target groups for preventive
      interventions, 134–135
Premarital Personal and Relationship
      Evaluation (PREPARE), 127, 183
PREP. *See* Prevention and Relationship
      Enhancement Program
Preparation for Marriage (PREP-M), 127
PREPARE/ENRICH, 128, 183

Prescriptive treatment, 21
Prevention and Relationship
    Enhancement Program (PREP), 10,
    126, 130–132, 183
    modified version for parenthood
    interventions, 136
Preventive interventions for couples,
    123–146
    assessment approaches, 127–128
    Couple Communication (CC), 126,
    129–130
    criteria for efficacy, 133
    delivery of programs, 137–138
    follow-up, 138
    informative and awareness approaches,
    128
    long-term outcome tracking needed,
    132–133
    parenthood, transition to, 135–136
    practical issues for couples, 133–138
    Prevention and Relationship
    Enhancement Program (PREP), 10,
    126, 130–132
    primary prevention, 124
    recruitment and screening of couples,
    136–137
    Relationship Enhancement (RE), 126,
    129
    research needs, 10, 132–133
    risk and protective factors, 124–126
    secondary prevention, 124
    selecting target groups, 134–136
    skills training approaches, 128–132
    strategies for prevention, 126–133
Preventive interventions for families,
    177–196
    clinical relevance, 177, 178–183
    contextual factors, 244–245
    criteria for efficacy, 203
    differences from treatment research
    and programming, 202–205, 245–
    247
    examples of family-focused prevention,
    206–208
    family-focused prevention research,
    197–213
    indicated prevention, 199–202, 209,
    246
    linking basic and applied research for,
    239–258

measurement aspects, 203–204, 206
medically ill children, 207–208
model for clinically and prevention-
    relevant research, 186–191
parent training, 248
prevention relevance, 177
primary prevention, 183
processes of intervention, 250–251
program design, 204
proximal effects and distal status,
    204–205, 209
resistant behavior, 250–251
risk and protective factors, 184–185,
    209
sample programs from Oregon Social
    Learning Center, 248–250
school-based prevention for children at
    risk, 206, 249–250
secondary prevention, 183
selective prevention, 199–202, 209,
    246
social interactional dimension,
    recognition of, 241–243
tertiary prevention, 183, 184
underemphasis on families when
    dealing with children at risk, 205–
    206
universal prevention, 198–202, 209,
    246
Primary prevention
    interventions for couples, 124
    interventions for families, 183
Problem solving
    communication and problem-solving
    training (CPT), 109, 149
    by couples, 159–161
    by families, 243, 249–250
Process research, 41–66. See also Task
    analysis
    clinical relevance as goal of, 178–183
    discovery-oriented, 42–43
    historical context, 42, 180
    specific descriptive tradition in, 180–
    182
    task analytic tradition in, 182–183
    treatment development informed by,
    55
Project MATCH, 215, 217, 228
Project MATCH Research Group, 215,
    217

Protective factors
  couple therapy and, 124–126
  epidemiological research designs for
    identifying, 185–186
  family therapy and model for clinically
    and prevention-relevant process and
    outcome research, 184–191
PSO (positive sentiment override), 158–
  159
Psychotherapy research, 262

Q-sorts, 92
Quid pro quo arrangements, 152

Racial culture. *See* Ethnic culture
Rape, 315
Rapid Couples Interaction Scoring
  System (RCISS), 153, 154, 189
RE. *See* Relationship Enhancement
Reattachment task, 45, 50, 56–58
Reattribution task, 45, 50, 52–54
Reciprocity in families, 243, 249
Reframing process, 44, 45, 50, 52–54
Reinforcement of behavior
  negative reinforcement, 244, 249
  token reinforcement, 284
  versus use of Ritalin, 286
Relapse effect after therapy, 169, 294
Relationship Enhancement (RE), 126,
  129, 132, 183
Religious organizations
  Prevention and Relationship
    Enhancement Program (PREP), use
    of, 130, 132
  prevention programs, generally, 137
Repair efforts and positive sentiment
  override, 158
Reprimands, 285
Research needs
  change methodologies that produce
    successful therapy outcomes, 90
  couple interventions, 105, 117
  diversity and measurement validity, 98
  ethnic culture within ATI research,
    347
  gender issues, 321
  interventions for marital and family
    problems, 9–11

  marital therapy, 169
  measurement standards, 97–98
  parenting practices, effectiveness of
    improving, 56, 207
  predictive utility for marital therapy,
    82
  preventive couple interventions, 132–
    133
  reattachment processes, 58
  task analysis, 54
Research treatments, 259
Resistant behavior to preventive
  interventions for families, 250–251
Risk factors
  couple therapy and, 124–126
  epidemiological research designs for
    identifying, 185–186
  family therapy and model for clinically
    and prevention-relevant process and
    outcome research, 184–191, 209
Ritalin, 286
Role overload of women, 313, 316
Role restriction of women, 314–315, 317

Same-sex couples, 117
SASB (structural analysis of social
  behavior), 181–182
Scale of Stressful Life Events, 147
School-based classes for preventive
  interventions, 128, 132, 136–137
School-based prevention for children at
  risk, 206, 249–250
Secondary prevention
  interventions for couples, 124
  interventions for families, 183
Selective prevention, 199–202, 209, 246
Self-blaming, 293
Self-control, 79
Self-esteem, 314, 315, 316
Self-limiting behavior of women, 312–
  313, 316
Self-reports, 91, 182
Sex differences. *See* Gender issues in
  marital and family therapy
Sex-Role Egalitarianism Scale, 306
Sexual abuse of women, 315, 317
Sexual objectification of women, 315,
  317

Single parents
  family therapy in family psychology
    intervention science (FT-FPIS),
    sensitivity to, 28
  sample programs from Oregon Social
    Learning Center, 249
Single women and gender role
    discrepancy strain, 310
Skill encouragement, 243, 249
Skills training approaches to preventive
    interventions, 128–132
Social context
  developmental status of family therapy
    in family psychology intervention
    science (FT-FPIS), 22–23
  gender role strain paradigm, 304
Social Interactional Learning Model, 245
Sociopolitical status of ethnic family,
    345–346
Sound marital house theory, 154–162
  potential contributions of, 162–163
Specific Affect Coding System (SPAFF),
    154
Specific descriptive tradition in process
    research, 180–182
Spousal abuse, 289–290, 291–293, 315–
    316
Standards and assumptions, 73, 83
State University of New York at Stony
    Brook, 285
Static versus dynamic risk factors, 125–
    126
Stonewalling by spouse, 159
Strategic structural family therapy, 24–28
Strategic therapy, 107
Structural analysis of social behavior
    (SASB), 181–182
Structural and developmental
    components, assessment of, 77–79
Substance abuse, 4
  couple therapy to treat, 112
  family therapy to treat teen substance
    abuse, 248, 262
Superwoman syndrome, 308–309, 310–
    311, 313
Symbolic meaning, sharing in marriage,
    161–162
Synchrony analysis in attribute x
    treatment interaction (ATI) research,
    225–226
Systems-based family therapy, 20

Tailoring Treatment for Alcoholics Is Not
    the Answer, 215
Tangible Reinforcers: Bonuses or Bribes, 285
Task analysis, 43, 182–183
  evolution of single task, 43–44, 182
  linking process to outcome, 48–49,
    179–180
  measuring task outcome and
    components, 47–48
  as research step in examining change
    processes, 46
  treatments as multiple tasks, 44–46
Tertiary prevention interventions for
    families, 183, 184
Therapist adherence, 116, 274
Therapist Behavior Coding System, 48
Therapist behaviors
  associated with decreased risk factors
    and increased protective factors,
    190–191
  family therapy, 181
  inducing resistance, 250–251
  multisystemic therapy (MST), factors
    in success of, 270, 272
Time orientation and ethnic culture,
    339–340
Token reinforcement, used in behavior
    modification of children, 284
Training
  communication and problem-solving
    training (CPT), 109, 149
  multisystemic therapy (MST), provider
    organization training, 274
  parent training, 248
  skills training approaches to preventive
    interventions, 128–132
Trauma-related conditions, couple
    therapy to treat, 112
Treatment competence, 116
Treatment manuals, 4, 24, 31, 115–116,
    180, 265
Treatment research versus prevention
    research, 202–205
Turning toward versus turning away, 157
Tuskegee experiments, 346

U. S. Census Department, 332
U. S. Department of Labor, 312, 313
U. S. Surgeon General, 259

Universal prevention, 198–202, 209, 246
University of California, Santa Barbara, 221
University of Denver, 131
University of Miami School of Medicine, 29
University of Utah Department of Psychology, 29
University-based clinical trials of multisystemic therapy (MST), 266–268

Validating-type marriages, 154
Values, 73, 83
Violence by spouse, 289–290, 291–293, 315–316
Volatile-type marriages, 154

Washington State Community Juvenile Accountability Act Conference, 23
Withdrawal into culture of origin, 341
Women. *See* Gender issues in marital and family therapy

About the Editors

Howard A. Liddle, EdD, Northern Illinois University, is director of the Center for Treatment Research on Adolescent Drug Abuse and professor of epidemiology and public health at the University of Miami. His program of clinical research has included serving as principal investigator on two National Institute on Drug Abuse (NIDA) center grants, several large-scale controlled trials, treatment development, and process studies. His research addresses the development, testing, and refinement of a family-based treatment for adolescent substance abuse. This treatment model has been recognized as an "exemplary" or "best practice" model by the Center for Substance Abuse Prevention, Office of Juvenile Justice and Delinquency Prevention "Strengthening Families" initiative and as an empirically supported treatment in the NIDA publication, *Principles of Effective Drug Treatment*, and the Center for Substance Abuse Treatment, Treatment Improvement Protocol Series volume, *Adolescent Substance Abuse*. His research on the efficacy of multidimensional family therapy has been recognized with career achievement awards from the American Association for Marriage and Family Therapy, the American Family Therapy Academy, and the Division of Family Psychology (Family Psychologist of the Year Award). He is active in the research grant review process, serving on NIDA's treatment research study section. He is also actively involved in expert panels and scientific committees that address adolescent substance abuse in NIDA, the National Institute on Alcohol Abuse and Addiction, the Center for Substance Abuse Treatment, and the Center for Substance Abuse Prevention. He was the founding editor of the *Journal of Family Psychology* in 1987, and he is also known for his work in the family therapy training and supervision area. His 1988 book, *Handbook of Family Therapy Training and Supervision*, remains a classic textbook in that specialty.

Daniel A. Santisteban, BA, Rutgers University, PhD, University of Miami, has led efforts in both the clinical and research arenas in his role as research associate professor of psychiatry and behavioral sciences at the University of Miami Center for Family Studies. He has been the principal investigator on two National Institute on Drug Abuse-funded treatment development studies designed to develop new variants of family therapy to address the special needs of adolescents with borderline personality diagnoses and clinically referred Hispanic youth and families. He has also served as co-principal investigator and project director on several large-scale clinical trials for testing the effectiveness of family interventions. He is a family therapy trainer within the Center for Family Studies Training Institute and has focused on developing new culturally appropriate family treatment interventions for specialized populations. He has also published in the area of family therapy efficacy, engagement of reluctant family members into treatment, and on the important role that cultural factors play in treatment and research.

Ronald F. Levant, EdD, Harvard University, is a clinician in independent practice, clinical supervisor in hospital settings, clinical and academic administrator, and academic faculty member. He has served on the faculties of Boston, Rutgers, and Harvard Universities. He is currently dean and professor, Center for Psychological Studies, NOVA Southeastern University. He has authored, coauthored, edited, or coedited more than 150 publications, including 12 books and 80 refereed journal articles and book chapters in family and gender psychology and in advancing professional psychology. He has also served as president of the Massachusetts Psychological Association, president of APA Division 43 (Family Psychology), cofounder and first president of APA Division 51 (Society for the Psychological Study of Men and Masculinity), two-term member and two-term chair of the APA Committee for the Advancement of Professional Practice, two-term member of the APA Council of Representatives, and Member-At-Large of the APA Board of Directors. As a member of the Board of Directors he chaired the task force that resolved the longstanding issue of representation of small state psychological associations and divisions on the APA Council of Representatives through the creation of the "wildcard plan," which brought an expanded Council into being in January 1999. He is currently serving as recording secretary of the APA.

James H. Bray, PhD, is director of family psychology programs and associate professor in the Department of Family and Community Medicine at Baylor College of Medicine in Houston, Texas. He has received numerous awards, including election into the National Academies of Practice for Psychology, the Karl F. Heiser APA Presidential Award for Advocacy on Behalf of Professional Psychology, and the 1992 Federal Advocacy Award from the APA Practice Directorate. He has published and presented numerous works in the areas of divorce, remarriage, adolescent substance use, intergenerational family relationships, and collaboration between physicians and psychologists. He was principal investigator of the federally funded longitudinal study Developmental Issues in StepFamilies Research Project and is principal investigator of a federally funded project on alcohol and other drug abuse in families with adolescents. He is a member of the APA Council of Representatives for the Division of Family Psychology. As a family and clinical psychologist he conducts research and teaches resident physicians, medical students, and psychology students. In addition to his research, he maintains an active clinical practice focusing on children and families.